ORSON WELLES

The Rise and Fall of an American Genius

By Charles Higham and published by New English Library:

AUDREY: A Biography of Audrey Hepburn
BETTE: A Biography of Bette Davis
MERLE: A Biography of Merle Oberon (with Roy Moseley)
OLIVIA AND JOAN: A Biography of Olivia de Havilland and
Joan Fontaine
ORSON WELLES: The Rise and Fall of an American Genius

ORSON WELLES

THE RISE AND FALL OF

AN AMERICAN GENIUS

CHARLES HIGHAM

New English Library

Copyright © 1985 by Charles Higham
Discography copyright © 1985 by Miles Kreuger

First published in the United States of America by
St Martin's Press in 1985

First published in Great Britain in 1986 by
New English Library, Mill Road, Dunton Green, Sevenoaks, Kent.
Editorial office: 47 Bedford Square, London WC1B 3DP.

Design by Joe Marc Freedman

Printed in Great Britain by
St Edmundsbury Press, Bury St Edmunds, Suffolk

British Library Cataloguing in Publication Data

Higham, Charles, *1931–*
    Orson Welles: the rise and fall of an
    American genius.
    1. Welles, Orson   2. Moving-picture
    producers and directors – United States
    – Biography
    I. Title
    791.43'0233'0924   PN1998.A3.W4/

ISBN 0 450 39284 8

For Gerald Turbow,
Victoria Shellin,
and Tamar Cooper,
good friends and true

CONTENTS

ACKNOWLEDGMENTS

My first debt is to the devoted genealogists and historians who helped me along the difficult path of exploring Orson Welles's hitherto unknown family origins. Mrs. Eleanor Campbell in Illinois and Mrs. Lois Stein in Wisconsin were my chief helpers, unraveling complicated details in the most expert manner. I am also grateful to Ann Kosicki in Wilkes-Barre, Pennsylvania, Rhoda Ladd in Wellesboro, Pennsylvania; Dixie Painter in St. Joseph, Missouri; Casey O'Connor in Wilmington, Delaware; Gail Graham in Emporia, Kansas; Jim Edgar, secretary of state for Illinois, in Springfield; Carl Landrum of Quincy, Illinois; Dr. Richard Keehn of Kenosha, Wisconsin (who was indispensable on the commercial history of the Heads and the Wellses); John Morley and Helen Ionta of Skaneateles, New York; and Clare M. Ward and Florence Christoph in New York. The staffs of the Mormon libraries in Salt Lake City and Los Angeles assisted me considerably. Without the help of these people, and that of Mr. Richard Coe of the Sons of the American Revolution in Glendale, California, who drew the family trees from my source notes, I could not have completed the first chapters of this book.

I was assisted in many parts of the world. Juan Montez in Madrid, Donatella Ortona in Rome, Olivier Eyquem in Paris, and Roy Moseley in London gave much help. In New York, Darcel Dillard conducted interviews, as did Anthony Slide in Los Angeles; Slide and Howard Davis did the research of published materials; in Washington, D.C., Carl Sferazza was extremely helpful in doing research into the National Archives and Records Service and the Library of Congress. The staff of the U.S. Tobacco Museum in Greenwich, Connecticut, was most cooperative in the matter of Welles's father's smoking habits. The Paul Green Foundation of Chapel Hill, North Carolina, gave great assistance by allowing me access to Paul Green's letters and diaries, and Rhoda Wynn and Brenda Kolb were towers of strength in supplying and checking accurate information. At the Lilly Library of Indiana University, Becky Gibson was extremely kind in making available to me the Orson Welles/Mercury Theater Collection, and Michael Romary did fine work assisting me to read through and annotate more than 5,000 documents in just over a week, working from nine in the morning until ten at night. At Purdue University, several members of the staff helped to piece together the story of George Ade and Orson Collins Wells; similarly, the librarians at Princeton were of great assistance in establishing information on Booth Tarkington.

Robert Gitt and David Bradley showed me the Welles films again; Marcie Copertino interviewed Lea Padovani for me in Miami, at the recommendation of Jane Chesis. Welles's childhood years in Grand Detour and Chicago, Illinois, were illuminated for me by the generous loan of a scrapbook owned by Mrs. Eleanor Grant and kept by her late sister, Sigrid Jacobsen, Orson Welles's nursemaid; this Rosebud of documents included photographs of Welles as a child; lovingly kept clippings of his achievements from the earliest days, including the columns of Ashton Stevens, his supporter and a friend of the family; and postcards and letters from the child Orson that revealed much of his character and established the dates of his earliest travels.

Others who assisted in piecing together his childhood years included Ethel Welker; Mary Michaels; Lester C. Wickline; Chuck Moser; Duane Paulsen; Mary Mull; Rebecca Belmont; Mary Page; Claire Head; Elvina Skinkel; Ashley Foxley; Claudia Cassidy; Terence Tobin; Mrs. Mischa Elman; Robert Yule; Mary Respess; Mary Sheffield; Nora Hoff; Myrtle Young; Roger Hill, who was especially helpful on Welles's work in the theater at the Todd School; and the staff of the Green Ridge Cemetery of Kenosha, Wisconsin.

In Ireland, Thomas Kenny of Kenny's Book Shop, Galway, and John Gilmartin, superintendent of police for Galway, assisted me (along with several members of the faculty of Dublin University) to establish the facts of Welles's period in Ireland. Michael Conroy confirmed details of himself and his late brother Isaac, details directly in contradiction of those supplied in Welles's interviews. The Gate Theater Collection housed at Northwestern University, Illinois, provided particulars of Welles's work at the Gate, along with rehearsal books, reviews, related clippings, in-house memoranda, and dozens of letters to and from Welles up to 1961. The memoirs of Micheal MacLiammoir filled out the picture. I drew from my interviews with MacLiammoir conducted when, following my recommendation, he was cast in Curtis Harrington's film *What's the Matter with Helen?* in 1971.

For an account of the Katharine Cornell theater seasons in New York and on tour, I have drawn from Miss Cornell's memoirs; I have also drawn from a talk given by John Hoyt at Studio One in Hollywood in 1975, in which he gave a detailed account of the tour. I drew from interviews with the late Jo Mielziner I conducted in New York in 1976, when I was writing a life of Katharine Hepburn. John Houseman's trilogy of memoirs was, of course, a very good source on his association with Welles in the theater, and his papers at the University of California at Los Angeles gave further details supplemented by him in person. I am most grateful to him for giving me access to this closed collection.

Arlene Francis and Martin Gabel, Virgil Thomson, Aaron Copland, the late Archibald MacLeish, the late Agnes Moorehead, Norman Lloyd, and Mary Wickes supplied information, much of it recorded before this book was planned. The memoirs of Howard Koch, Jean Rosenthal, and Hallie Flanagan were excellent sources. Paul Stewart gave several useful interviews over the years. On the *War of the Worlds* broadcast, I drew from Howard Koch's book on the subject and from Professor Hadley Cantril's sociologist's account of the panic. The late Bernard Herrmann, quite the most difficult and hostile of subjects, gave me some interviews, most of which were laced with gratuitously insulting remarks about Orson Welles and his films, to which he contributed his best work as a composer. At one stage Mr. Herrmann blackmailed me into giving him my score of his fake opera in *Citizen Kane* in return for the source of its libretto, and then he deceived me in the matter of that source.

On the early years in Hollywood, I obtained a number of taped interviews for an earlier critical work written when I was Regents Professor at the University of California at Santa Cruz. I have drawn from those interviews more extensively than I was able to do at the time. Among the good and generous people who assisted a young and then unknown writer with warmth, considerateness, and concern were Richard Wilson, Welles's devoted right-hand man through all the troubled years of the Mercury Theater and the Mercury film production unit; Lucille Ball; the late Dolores Del Rio; Joseph Cotten; William Alland; Patricia Medina Cotten; Perry Lieber; the late Don Prince; the late Dorothy Comingore; Vernon Harbin; Maurice Seiderman; Robert Wise; James G. Stewart; Stanley Cortez; the late Mrs. Walter (Fieldsie) Lang; John Fante; David Stuart; the late Norman Foster; the late Louis Armstrong; Frank Capra; the late Dolores Costello; the late William Castle; Anne Baxter; the late Hazel Scott; Joseph Biroc; Elizabeth Wilson; Shifra Haran; the late Bosley Crowther; Robert Stevenson; the late Russell Metty; the late Brainard Duffield; Elsa Lanchester; and the late Glenn Anders.

In later years I was granted interviews with a number of other significant figures who could fill in the middle and later periods. These included Viola Lawrence; Milton and Gitta Lubowiski; Bill Harmon; Herbert Lightman; Arthur Knight; and (again) Richard Wilson. Rebecca Welles was kind enough to talk to me about her father. The late Henry Hathaway had much to say about working with Welles, so did Alexandre Trauner; Lea Padovani; the late Kenneth Tynan; Herbert Wilcox; Charlton Heston; Martin Ritt; Maurizio Lucidi; Audrey Stainton; Jeanne Moreau; Mickey Knox; Willy Kurant; Francesco Lavagnino; Cecile Aubry; Edmond Richard; Alessandro Tasca; Sidney Hayers; Stéphane Audran; and Gary Graver.

A special note of thanks goes to the people at St. Martin's Press, particularly Toni Lopopolo, Andrew Charron, and Carol E. W. Edwards, for their courteous warmth and consideration, to Victoria Shellin, who typed a very difficult manuscript, and to Robert Carringer, who read and checked the accuracy of the book.

WELL(ES) LINE

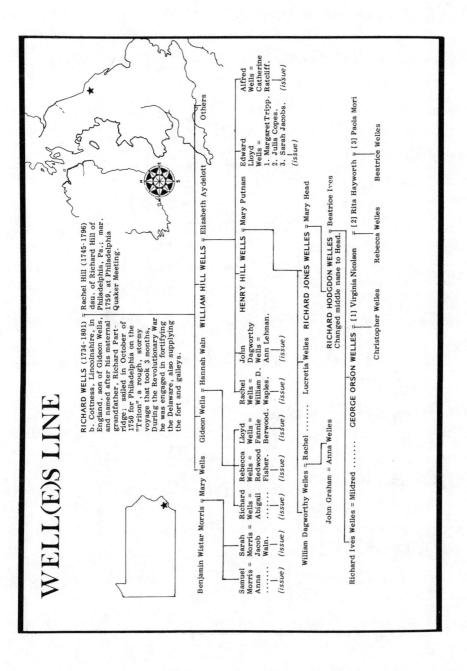

RICHARD WELLS (1734-1801) b. Cottness, Lincolnshire, in England, son of Gideon Wells, and named after his maternal grandfather, Richard Partridge; sailed in October of 1750 for Philadelphia on the "Triton", a rough, stormy voyage that took 3 months, During the Revolutionary War he was engaged in fortifying the Delaware, also supplying the fort and galleys. ⊤ Rachel Hill (1745-1796) dau. of Richard Hill of Philadelphia, Pa.; mar. 1759, at Philadelphia Quaker Meeting.

Benjamin Wistar Morris ⊤ Mary Wells   Gideon Wells = Hannah Waln   WILLIAM HILL WELLS = Elizabeth Aydelott   Others

Samuel Morris = Anna ...... (issue)

Sarah Morris = Jacob Waln. (issue)

Richard Wells = Abigail ...... (issue)

Rebecca Wells = Redwood Fisher. (issue)

Lloyd Wells = Fannie Berwood. (issue)

Rachel Wells = William D. Waples. (issue)

John Dagworthy Wells = Ann Lehman. (issue)

HENRY HILL WELLS ⊤ Mary Putnam

Edward Lloyd Wells = 1. Margaret Tripp. 2. Julia Copes. 3. Sarah Jacobs. (issue)

Alfred Wells = Catherine Ratcliff. (issue)

William Dagworthy Welles ⊤ Rachel ......

John Graham = Anna Welles

Lucretia Welles   RICHARD JONES WELLES ⊤ Mary Head

RICHARD HODGDON WELLES ⊤ Beatrice Ives
Changed middle name to Head.

Richard Ives Welles = Mildred ......

GEORGE ORSON WELLES ⊤ [1] Virginia Nicolson   [2] Rita Hayworth ⊤ [3] Paola Mori

Christopher Welles   Rebecca Welles   Beatrice Welles

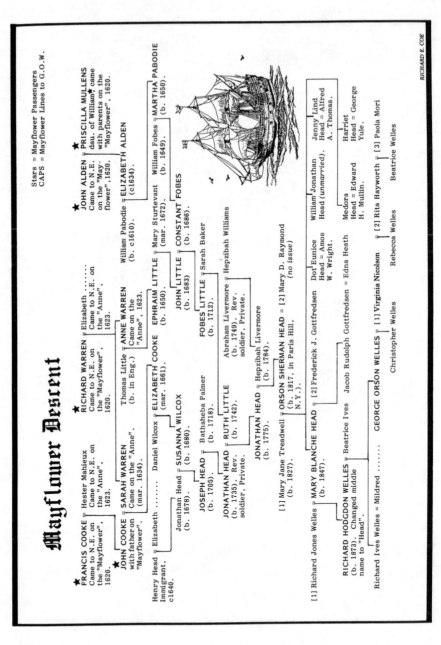

Mayflower Descent

Stars = Mayflower Passengers
CAPS = Mayflower Lines to G.O.W.

★ FRANCIS COOKE = Hester Mahieux
Came to N.E. on Came to N.E. on
the "Mayflower", the "Anne",
1620. 1623.

★ JOHN COOKE = SARAH WARREN
with father on Came on the "Anne".
"Mayflower". (mar. 1634).

Henry Head = Elizabeth .... Daniel Wilcox = ELIZABETH COOKE
Immigrant, (mar. 1661).
c1640.

Jonathan Head = SUSANNA WILCOX
(b. 1678). (b. 1680).

JOSEPH HEAD = Bathsheba Palmer
(b. 1705). (b. 1718).

JONATHAN HEAD = RUTH LITTLE
(b. 1735). Rev. (b. 1742).
soldier, Private.

JONATHAN HEAD = Hepzibah Livermore
(b. 1775).

[1] Mary Jane Treadwell = ORSON SHERMAN HEAD = [2] Mary D. Raymond
(b. 1817, in Paris Hill,
N.Y.).

[1] Richard Jones Welles = MARY BLANCHE HEAD = [2] Frederick J. Gottfredsen
(b. 1847).

RICHARD HODGDON WELLES = Beatrice Ives
(b. 1873). Changed middle
name to "Head".

Richard Ives Welles = Mildred .... GEORGE ORSON WELLES = [1] Virginia Nicolson

Christopher Welles

★ RICHARD WARREN = Elizabeth ....
Came to N.E. on Came to N.E. on
the "Mayflower", the "Anne",
1620. 1623.

Thomas Little = ANNE WARREN
(b. in Eng.) Came on the
"Anne", 1623.

William Pabodie = ELIZABETH ALDEN
(b. c1610). (c1634).

EPHRAIM LITTLE = Mary Sturtevant William Fobes = MARTHA PABODIE
(b. 1650). (mar. 1672). (b. 1649). (b. 1650).

JOHN LITTLE = CONSTANT FOBES
(b. 1683). (b. 1686).

FOBES LITTLE = Sarah Baker
(b. 1712).

Abraham Livermore = Hepzibah Williams
(b. 1749). Rev.
soldier, Private.

(no issue)

Dot Eunice
Head = Amos
W. Wright.

Jacob Rudolph Gottfredsen = Edna Heath

[2] Rita Hayworth = [3] Paola Mori

Rebecca Welles Beatrice Welles

★ JOHN ALDEN = PRISCILLA MULLENS
Came to N.E. dau. of William,★ came
on the "May- with parents on the
flower", 1620. "Mayflower", 1620.

William Jonathan Jenny Lind
Head (unmarried). Head = Alfred
A. Thomas.

Medora Harriet
Head = Edward Head = George
H. Mullin. Yule.

RICHARD E. COE

INTRODUCTION

When Orson Welles died on October 10, 1985, at the age of 70, he was as famous as he had ever been. His Paul Masson wine commercials, glowing with good cheer, had recently reestablished him as a public figure with a whole new generation that could barely have known his name. His massive bulk, red face, and atmosphere of genial expansiveness proved very attractive to the young. And this was only appropriate, since he was always young at heart: a maverick romantic, a liberal, a radical, an opponent of dictatorships and the acquisitive society, a critic and enemy of the sources of power. Even at a time when we in America are seeing in the Reagan era a resurgence of the up-and-at-'em values of the Eisenhower society, which he hated, even though the quests for money and power and beauty are again the obsessive concerns of millions, Welles still has a special place in American hearts. In a sense, he represented the rebel as Establishment figure, enshrined in the pantheon, puffing away at giant cigars, relishing the wine of life. It was no accident that his favorite part was that of Falstaff.

Welles was many things to many people. He was a magician, a costume designer, a magazine editor, an actor, a producer, a director, an editor, a novelist, a graphic artist, a political columnist, and a painter and illustrator. And that is to name only a few of his talents and preoccupations. Once, early in the 1940s, he stood before an audience in the Middle West whose ranks had been thinned by the advent of a thunderstorm. Summarizing all the professional commitments in which he was involved, he said, in his characteristically thunderous voice, "What a pity there are so many of me—and so few of you." The genial laughter that greeted this statement indicates the affection Welles immediately engendered through his delightfully false modesty and his air of not taking himself too seriously. Some forty years later he excited a similar response in a prodigiously vaster crowd at an antinuclear demonstration in Central Park, during which he joined thousands of people to argue with impassioned excellence for the abolition of death-dealing weaponry around the world.

Like many who appear in the visual arts of film and television, Welles delighted in confusing and unsettling admirers and interviewers by creating a largely fictitious picture of his past that even the most determined scholars accept out of uncritical admiration. His impish sense of humor suggested that inside his vast bulk some elf was jumping up and down with glee as tape recorders turned and notes were solemnly taken, while all the time that elf was thinking unprintable thoughts about the absurdity of human credulousness. Only once (apart from his aborted book with Peter Bogdanovich, *This Is Orson Welles*, and a brief piece in the British *Fortnightly* magazine) did he commit an autobiographical statement to paper. The reminiscence appeared in a characteristically odd place: Paris *Vogue*, whose Christmas issue of 1982 he edited, filling it with his own agreeable sketches and designing the bold and impressive layout along with that magazine's art department. The autobiographical fragment, allegedly drawn from a memoir in progress, was titled "My Father Wore Black Spats." Aside from that arguably accurate statement, little in the piece is correct.

Welles wrote that his father "lived to be a great age before setting himself on fire." This sentence is so charged with apparent meaning that it can only attract, even rivet, attention. Yet there is not a word of truth in it. His father died at the early age of fifty-eight, and the fire to which Welles refers was in fact caused by the servants in his father's hotel, who were testing a new flue by wafting the flames up it with newspapers. Welles describes the hotel as small; in fact it was very large. He says that the fire took place after "we'd just returned from China, and there was a nice Christmasy fall of snow on the ground the night of the fire. . . . The few old cronies my father had invited were yet to arrive, and most of the hotel staff had been given the night off to go to Dixon, six miles away, for the movie show." In fact the fire took place in the late spring of 1928, almost exactly two years before Welles went to China and Japan with his father, and it was already unseasonably hot in that part of Illinois. His father did not have, as Welles asserts, houses in Jamaica and Peking, nor was the hotel "America's most exclusive." There was no such thing as a "Dick Welles" cigar named for a horse that won the Kentucky Derby; a complete list of the winners of the Derby shows that none of them was called Dick or Richard Welles, and the U.S. Tobacco Museum in Greenwich, Connecticut, discloses that the Dick Welles tobacco was made especially for his father and was neither cheap nor available to anyone else.

The deliberate confusions go on and on. Richard Welles did not break the bank at Monte Carlo,* invent an airplane, or invent the World War I army picnic or mess kit, which was used by the Union forces in the Civil War.

Welles proved equally deceptive to interviewers. The best known of them was Kenneth Tynan, who wrote of him in *Show* magazine and in *Playboy* without checking a single fact. Welles told Tynan that he was from unmixed English colonial stock, when in fact his family had both Welsh and French elements; that his father was born in Virginia and moved to Wisconsin because he owned two factories there, when in fact he was the son of an obscure Missouri railroad clerk who had gone to the Badger State because he had fallen in love with and married the tempestuous daughter of the Kenosha district attorney.

Welles told Tynan that he owed his name to a Chicago businessman, when in fact he owed it to his district attorney great-grandfather, Orson Sherman Head. He inaccurately claimed to be related to Under Secretary of State Sumner Welles and to Adlai Stevenson (as a child, he had claimed kinship with Gideon Welles, Lincoln's secretary of the navy). He told Tynan he had met Ravel and Stravinsky through his mother, when in fact he had not, and that he had been a spy in World War II, posing as a ballbearings magnate in Lisbon: a fantasy.

In interviews with his friend the critic Maurice Bessy, head of the Cannes Film Festival, who wrote a book-length essay in French on Welles's life and philosophy, he incorrectly told Bessy that he had a relative who had fallen drunk and drowned in the sea, he claimed that his father had designed a collapsible picnic kit and he said that his father owned most of the village in which he lived (Grand Detour) and forbade the use of gas and electricity there. Welles's father was supposed to have lived on the outskirts of that village in an enormous house, "baptized a hotel," where the staff were retired circus artists and music hall performers and were maintained freely as clientele: all sheer nonsense. For years Welles had made the claim that he had nine eccentric great-aunts, one of whom bathed in ginger ale and another of whom vanished from a rickshaw in China; to this effrontery he now added for Bessy the new myth that several of these great-aunts had lived to be over a hundred years old. He claimed that his brother Richard had joined a monastery and that at seven, he, Orson, could perform *King Lear* in the attic of his home while still unable to subtract, when in truth, as his grades show, he was good at mathematics. Page after page of this entertaining nonsense vitiates any interest Bessy's book could have as a work of amateur

---

* A Charles Wells did.

psychology, rendering worthless all of the author's critical interpretations based on Welles's childhood.

This had been Welles's amusing intention; after all, he was a magician, one who had written in French a preface to a book on magic, and it is the magician's chief art to deceive. The biographer who wishes to tackle the facts of Welles's life is handicapped by having to work his way through a maze of absurdities repeated in book after book, article after article, talk show after talk show, television special after television special, until the task seems almost too daunting. The only solution seemed to be to sweep the whole mass of misinformation aside and start entirely from scratch.

I began, as Alice in Wonderland was advised to do, at the beginning. The accuracy of Welles's birth date was confirmed by obtaining the birth certificate from Kenosha, Wisconsin. The local historian, Mrs. Lois Stein, working out of a building that once was the home of Welles's uncle by marriage, the automobile manufacturer George A. Yule, told me in our first conversations that Welles not only had ignored his birthplace completely but had annoyed most of Kenosha's inhabitants by fabricating one element after another of his past. She told me of many names that have never occurred in a single interview with Welles or in articles about him. She talked of his antecedents in the Head family, powerful lawyers and businessmen, among them the aforementioned Orson S. Head, the terrifying district attorney of Kenosha, whose aggressive demeanor and massive bulk found their reflection in the character and appearance of his celebrated real-life great-grandson. She told me of the Gottfredsens, the brewing dynasty of that area, whose gross and bullying demeanor set the tone for many figures Welles pilloried in his pictures. With Mrs. Stein's aid and that of members of the Head and Gottfredsen families, I was able to piece together the story of Welles's grandmother, the formidable, redheaded Mary Head Wells Gottfredsen, who left home at the age of fourteen and a half to marry beneath her station, then radically defied everyone and was abandoned with a young child by Welles's grandfather. She then boldly married a Gottfredsen, flaunting her marriage in the face of her disapproving family by setting a motif of beer bottles into the facade of her home and designing the African mahogany overhangs with reliefs of hops and hop leaves, the sources of her husband's fortune.

Working at the Mormon temple in Los Angeles, with its store of censuses going back over a hundred years, poring over faded and badly inscribed lettering microfilmed from ancient records, and working with historians, city directories, and land sales firms in St. Joseph, Missouri; Skaneateles, New York; Wilmington, Delaware; Madison, Wisconsin; Chicago; Detroit; and six other locations, I assembled piece by piece the puzzle, the details of which Mrs. Stein could only indicate. I was surprised to discover that Orson Welles, who was not noted for his modesty, had completely hidden the distinction of his liberal forebears on both sides of his family. It was startling to find that his finest American ancestor on his father's side was a Quaker, Richard Wells, from Cottness near Sheffield, Yorkshire, whose own father, Dr. Gideon Wells, had been the personal physician to many aristocratic figures. A leading personage of the Quaker community of Philadelphia and the author of important books, Richard Wells was the father of, among others, the accomplished William Hill Wells, twice senator from Delaware, helper of the slaves, outstanding Federalist, who stood next to Benjamin Franklin at the signing of the Declaration of Independence. William Hill Wells's son Henry Hill Wells, another distinguished figure of politics and the bar, was a leader of the Underground Railroad, the operation that helped slaves escaping from the South; he was a fine contrast with Orson Head, who, despite direct descent from John Alden of *Mayflower* fame, lacked principles, ill-treated blacks, and, according to common rumor, forced his sexual attentions on some of them.

The Wells line of the family ran on through Orson Welles's grandfather Richard and thus into muddy waters. Welles's father, Richard Hodgdon (later Head) Wells, was born in the humble station house of a tiny depot north of St. Joseph, Missouri, to parents whose honeymoon had been disrupted by an earlier hotel fire. Welles's father grew up in an atmosphere of family tension, bickering, and anguish nor far removed from that to be found in Welles's masterpiece *The Magnificent Ambersons*. The mansion Rudolphsheim, designed by Mary Wells Gottfredsen with the beer bottles in the facade, was similar to the Amberson house; it was a residence in which every footfall echoed vibrantly to the high ceilings and in which material opulence and vulgarity dwarfed Richard Welles's tiny figure as he made his way up the grand mahogany staircase.

With a background liberal on one side and grossly materialist on the other, with quarrels and clashes the very order of the day, it is not surprising that Orson Welles grew up with the obsessions that preoccupied him; nor is it entirely surprising that he should have invented a past in order to conceal the painful divisions that plagued his own. Death is a persistent theme in all his work, and it is important to know that his first memories were of the agony of death. When he was born, and until he was almost two years old, he and his parents shared their home with his mother's mother, Lucy Ives, who was dying of cancer of the stomach, and whose screams of pain when the morphine no longer worked filled the wooden house in Kenosha. As soon as he was conscious, Welles was aware of the pain suffered by his older brother, Richard, whose agonized stammer, awkwardness, and lack of interest in anything signaled the encroaching disturbance that was soon to engulf him and divide him from the world in an institution for the insane for a full ten years of his life. His father's disdain of Richard Jr. and his virtual cutting him out of his will were increased burdens on the young Orson.

Nor is it surprising to discover that at an early age Welles was confronted still more directly by death. His mother, Beatrice, a talented pianist and monologuist, died when he was just past his ninth birthday; the anguish of her loss at the age of forty from hepatitis haunted him for years and gave a poignant edge to the scene of the death of Isabel Amberson, which he directed with extraordinary artistry almost twenty years later. Welles turned to a remarkable man, Dr. Maurice Bernstein, for consolation and support—yet he knew little of Dr. Bernstein's true character until much later. An able orthopedic surgeon who provided Welles's nursemaid Sigrid Jacobsen with a surgical boot, who attended Lucy Ives in her final illness and was involved emotionally with Beatrice Welles, Dr. Bernstein proved to be a more powerful influence even than Welles's father during those early years. Behind the excellence of his medical work, behind his easy charm and warmth of manner, Dr. Bernstein was greedy and unscrupulous; he used, married, and discarded Mina Elman, sister of the violin virtuoso Mischa Elman, and later equally misused the Chicago opera star Edith Mason, drawing her into a ménage à trois with her former husband. Later Dr. Bernstein tried to milk Welles of every possible cent when Welles achieved fame. As part of his legend-building, Welles reinvented Dr. Bernstein as a noble and selfless humanitarian single-mindedly bent on the young Orson's welfare.

With his brother in an asylum and his father dead of a heart attack, Welles still managed to summon up extraordinary reserves of strength of will and courage to set out in life on his own. Gifted with the liberal intelligence of his paternal forebears the Wellses, and the heavy and imposing physical appearance, temperament, and elemental force of the Head family, he went off to Ireland and made his first splash at the Gate Theater in Dublin, playing men considerably older than he with all the dynamic assurance that his great-grandfather Orson had brought to the demolition of a witness or the overpowering of a judge's objections. Although he was never athletic, the boy had the sheer bulk of the Head family to assist him in his headlong course through life. His chubby features, slanting, flashing eyes, and big hands and feet impressed everyone who met him. He had the eloquence of William Hill Wells and the maverick, willful, runaway determination of his grandmother Mary.

In his stage career in New York, first with the Katharine Cornell company and later with his own, he established himself as a force of nature in the theater. His productions, whether of Shakespeare or other authors, became vehicles for his passionate convictions, which were allied to those of the American left: that power corrupted, that the lust for riches and prosperity contained the essence of evil, and that despots and dictators must be brought down. An early opponent of Hitler and Mussolini, he provoked charges of communism, charges that delighted him not only because of their absurdity but because they offered him the chance for argument and controversy. With his more pragmatic and sensible collaborator John Houseman, he transformed the American stage overnight. By disposing of the intermission and cutting his productions to a mere ninety or one hundred minutes, he took theater to the edge of cinema. He broke free of the proscenium arch, extended the apron stage into the heart of the audience, and invented patterns of light and darkness that matched those to be found in German expressionist movies and, paradoxically, those that figured in the Hitler mass rallies he despised. He went beyond Gordon Craig, beyond even Meyerhold and the Moscow Art Theater in creating effects that enveloped the audience and made it a part of the theatrical experience. By revolutionizing and freeing the stage, he was able to use it as a vehicle for the liberal sentiments that animated him. At the same time, driving his foodless and sleepless cast through long nights of rehearsal and re-rehearsal, he was able to convey the essence of his dreams and nightmares, visions that left him sleepless. A poet of the macabre not unlike Poe, he was a haunted man, driven by terrifying ancestral memories of his belligerent and demented family, fearful always that madness would strike him as it had seemingly struck his brother, afraid of death as only one who had witnessed it at close quarters and in such agonizing circumstances could be afraid.

It was this quality of visionary dreams and nocturnal terrors that gave a devastating force to his creations of *Macbeth*, *Julius Caesar*, and *Danton's Death*, in which blood, fire, and brutality dominated the theater for an evening and left the audience exhausted and exhilarated all at once. It was his ambition, an ambition in which he succeeded, to take the actors with him through the dark tunnel of his imagination, milking them of emotion, making them the slaves of his dreamings. None who worked with him would ever forget the experience, and none would ever quite match it again. Those who abandoned him out of commercial ambition or fear could never quite forgive themselves. And yet, as they may have foreseen, from the first day that Welles swept like a fire through the American theater, not only his career as a theatrical artist but the very theater to which he committed his strength and energy were equally doomed.

By the time he entered it, theater in the grand sense of the word was already beginning to seem an anachronism. As a serious vehicle for ideas, theater was doomed by the collapse of the liberal intellectual movement in World War II and during the McCarthy era. As a purveyor of seriousness, or of high artistic purpose, Broadway was soon to be the victim of the rise of popular culture and the vulgarization and the enslavement of the elite. There would be no hope in the so-called new world of the GI Bill and the spread of mass education for more than token examples of intelligence in those grubby streets off Times Square. Musicals would soon dominate because World War II audiences demanded escape from the pain and pressure of the everyday. Thus it was—or seemed to be—fortunate that just when World War II approached Welles was offered an opportunity in the movies, one for which he had in truth been reaching all along.

He was given the unthinkable: a contract with a Hollywood studio, RKO Radio Pictures, that allowed him complete artistic control of his own work. Not since D. W. Griffith and the equally ill-fated Erich von Stroheim, both destroyed by Hollywood, had a creative person been given anything approaching such a chance. Most directors were laborers in the vineyard, their work cast and prepared by producers and the editing placed in other hands following the completion of principal photography. Welles was to be allowed not only the freedom to direct a work of his own choosing but the right to edit it and to approve the final cut before it was released. He was thus in the position of a novelist, poet, or critic who was able to resist editorial interference.

And so he went to California, taking with him Houseman and several actors from the Mercury Theater. He embarked on one of his most beloved projects, a film version of a work he had already adapted for radio, a medium he had revolutionized through his inspired use of sound. That work was *Heart of Darkness*, from the novel by Joseph Conrad; it was the story of a quest for a mysterious despot who lords it over a tribe in the deepest recesses of the jungle. In this novel Welles saw a parable of power, and of power's misuses, that was in line with his work in the theater. In writing the script, perhaps his greatest, he wanted to revolutionize movies; he planned to shoot the picture with the camera as the eyes of the narrator, thereby extending the first-person approach he had used on radio. Yet the inventive and stylized approach of his writing proved to be the project's downfall.

Casting problems were given as excuses for the abandonment of the project, excuses that have seen their way into articles and critical books on Welles; in fact the real reason *Heart of Darkness* was abandoned was the disappearance of the European market following the start of World War II. This calamity meant that only Americans would see the movie, and Americans were not thought to have the cultural and intellectual background that would enable them to absorb the film's complexities, shadowings, and subtleties. Moreover, the film industry at the time was under siege by isolationist forces in Congress that were determined to stop anti-Nazi propaganda on the screen. Those same forces (despite disclaimers by the studio then and later) also destroyed Welles's two other anti-Nazi projects, *The Smiler with a Knife*, about a fascist takeover of America, and *Mexican Melodrama*, about a similar coup d'etat in Mexico. Both scripts stemmed from Welles's (and the liberal left's) knowledge, revealed in such newsletters as George Seldes's *In Fact* and Albert E. Kahn's *The Hour*, that powerful forces were at work in the Americas to overthrow democracy, forces most clearly expressed in the notorious Christian Front movement of New York.

Welles had to settle for second best, and by a miracle his next project became a masterpiece. *Citizen Kane* summarized his liberal critiques of wealth and the acquisitive society in a work that was essentially satirical and yet conjoined its racy journalistic attack with the poetic, deeply personal observation of a born romantic. In it, he portrayed a witty, gifted, charming man who destroyed himself through a lust for money and property. The co-writer, Herman J. Mankiewicz, with his long experience in the newspaper world and in writing movie comedies, and the script editor, John Houseman, with his own acumen and expertise, provided the blueprint for the picture in the early drafts of the screenplay, but it was Welles who tore through those scripts, removed their heavy, deliberate, fustian elements, added the crucial opera scenes that reflected the experiences of his own youth, and electrified, galvanized, and revivified the format and structure to create an entirely individual work of his own.

With the great cameraman Gregg Toland, who worked in tune with him, sharing his youth, energy, and inspiration and providing him with a correct photographic style, he at one stroke revolutionized the cinema as he had revolutionized the stage. *Citizen Kane* was as deliberately artificial, as totally "created" in-house, as any film in the heyday of German cinema; with the skill of a magician, Welles provided a chiaroscuro of American power, a captivating and dazzling visual structure that evoked not only elements of his own childhood, character, and upbringing (like Kane, who was separated from his mother at the age of eight, and Welles's mother died when he was that exact age, Welles inherited his fortune, albeit a much smaller one, at the age of twenty-five) but disclosed a range of characters drawn from his own immediate circle, with elements from the life of the newspaper tycoon William Randolph Hearst. From other tycoons, from other events, people, places, landscapes, whether of reality or of dreams, he drew together the elements that created the greatest of all American films, a work that from its first brooding views of an iron fence and a castle floating in the mist has all the insolence, inventiveness, wit, and dynamism of a superb work of art.

Welles moved ahead to *The Magnificent Ambersons*. There is no need to stress the parallels in this film with his memories of Rudolphsheim or with his grandmother's testy, scratchy behavior in the character of Aunt Fanny, that frustrated spinster whose thwarted love for an automobile manufacturer (and ill-fated investment in automobile lamps) dominates the film in a way that it never dominates the novel. Nor is there a need to belabor the fact that the picture parallels the vanishing of the pre-automobile age through which Welles's father lived, and in which, as an inventor of similar headlamps, he played a minor but not insignificant part. The movie was conceived on a level of romantic morbidity: it is a story of vanishings, of deaths, of doors closing with black wreaths, a recollection of mortal frailty that can only have been inspired by Welles's earliest experiences. And by a disagreeable paradox, it spelled the death of Welles's career as a popular American artist of the screen. For he made the fatal mistake of forgetting that he was making a picture for the American public. Although his sudden disappearance in 1942 (he went to South America to film the doomed epic *It's All True*) disrupted post-production of *Ambersons*, the fact is that even if he had completed the picture to his satisfaction, it would never have been a commercial success. It was too grim, too truthful, too harsh; it was not alleviated by the sanctimonious or uplifting elements that rescued a similarly morbid work, *Kings Row*, from commercial oblivion. The preview in Pomona was a disaster, even when a happy ending was tacked on to try to save it and Norman Rockwell was commissioned to design the advertisements; no one was deceived. Bosley Crowther in *The New York Times* was unkind. The audience, already in the grip of war and looking for escape, had no patience with the picture, and word of mouth killed the film.

Moreover, like *Citizen Kane* and Welles's thriller *Journey into Fear*, *Ambersons* ran much over budget, a cardinal sin in Hollywood. The memory of this sullied Welles's name; only the commercial success that eluded him could have extinguished it.

Welles stayed on in South America for months, his efforts to finish *It's All True* futile. The common view, supported by Welles's inventions, is that the new regime at RKO Radio Pictures effectively destroyed his career by canceling *It's All True*; in fact George Schaefer, head of RKO, who had brought Welles to Hollywood, complained of Welles's extravagance and misbehavior in South America—extravagance and misbehavior that resulted unfairly in Schaefer's dismissal by that new regime and in the summary removal of the Mercury Theater people from RKO.

Welles returned to North America with his career as an artist endangered. His marriage to Rita Hayworth backfired: instead of earning him a further career, it reduced him to being merely her actor husband. When he made *The Stranger* in 1946, he was again concerned with the theme of fascism, prophetically reaching forward to that era in which Nazis would be sheltered in the United States, but the film was conventional in mode and devoid of revolutionary techniques. In *The Lady from Shanghai* Welles played the part of an Irish liberal who had fought for the loyalists in the Spanish Civil War; yet in portraying this man as a hero and his enemies as evil and corrupt lawyers (sinister reflections of Orson Head and his kin), Welles did not go beyond the baroque. The movie, watchable and exciting though it is, does not have the intellectual or moral cogency of its predecessors; it is merely a grotesquely pleasing artifact.

In making his trilogy of Shakespeare, *Macbeth*, *Othello*, and *Chimes at Midnight*, which again dealt with the corruption of power, Welles again staked a claim to the prominence in motion pictures that he had enjoyed in the theater. He daringly followed Verdi in his progression, thus risking a dangerous comparison. His achievement was considerable: *Othello* and *Chimes at Midnight* are among the best films he gave us, and both are clear reflections of his liberal vision, dealing with the themes of betrayal by power, the defeat of love, and in *Chimes at Midnight* the disappearance of the age of chivalry. *Othello* was informed by personal anguish: the loss of the woman Welles loved more than any other, the Italian actress Lea Padovani.

Welles became a kind of public sport, wandering about Europe, telling tall tales, and unwittingly reminding even his admirers that he had been denied by the fairy godmothers at his cradle the one gift without which all other gifts are finally useless: discipline. Prone to blaming Hollywood for his failure to work there (except intermittently, as in the television pilot *The Fountain of Youth* and the thriller *Touch of Evil*), Welles overlooked the fact that his methods of work were unacceptable in Hollywood. He demanded unlimited time, the capacity to improvise, the trick, common to all artists, of weaving in and out of a theme according to his own instincts. Such an approach was unacceptable in an industry guided only by the principle that time means money. Producers, many of them admiring of Welles, feared that he might ignore budgetary considerations, stretch a shooting schedule to unheard-of lengths, and spend without thought. They worried that if he were to be independently financed, his love of luxury would make his living expenses during production prohibitive. When *The Fountain of Youth*, supposed to be shot within ten days, took a month to make and was followed by an expensive party charged to Desilu Productions, the seal was set on Welles's doom as a potential television craftsman. Although his defenders sought to assert that he was essentially economical, pointing to the tight budgets on which *Citizen Kane, The Stranger*, and *Touch of Evil* were made, their efforts proved fruitless. Stories kept filtering back from Europe of broken deals, disrupted meetings, abandoned appointments, of pictures begun and abandoned, of schedules changed again and again. Welles was making his films as a novelist makes a novel or a poet makes a poem, but he was using the most expensive surrogate for canvas or paper: celluloid. No one interested in filmic art could fail to admire the touching grandeur of his approach to a somewhat intractable medium; no one with a commercial mind could fail to fear it.

The solution was clear: Welles had to flatter, wheedle, cajole, entertain, suborn, and seduce any financier inspired or crazy enough to back this artist in the manner in which Middle European princes supported composers in the eighteenth century. Many patrons were found, among them Louis Dolivet, who had been a leading figure of the Free French and a friend of Welles in the 1940s, and Alexander and Michael Salkind, egregious figures on the international film scene. Mysterious Spanish financiers would turn up to present large checks over elaborate Madrid luncheons, and sometimes people who had not formerly been involved in movies would assist the genius in his headlong work. Money was grist to his mill; it would disappear, engulfed by his talent. He would take months, sometimes years, to pay his players or his craftsmen associates, suddenly presenting an embittered colleague with a bundle of cash at the moment it was least expected.

Welles would combine in equal parts parsimony with extravagance, miserliness and meanness with extreme generosity, sudden bursts of inspiration with months of boredom and exhaustion. The erratic elements in his nature emerged more and more strongly, yet he still could secure the devotion of almost anyone who swam into his orbit. He overpowered people with bear hugs, kisses, and passionate affection, or he awed them with explosions of volcanic rage, impatience, and frustration. As he grew more and more immense, swelling to a giant 350 pounds, his face stamped with sadness while his laughter became more Jovian, he retained his center as a poet. Whatever else he might have been, he never let go of that.

Above all, he was flawed with a fear of completion. Not only was he nervous about the comparisons that might be made between work of recent vintage and *Citizen Kane* or *The Magnificent Ambersons*, but was seized by a painful unease about putting the finishing touches to his films. *The Deep, Don Quixote*, and *The Other Side of the Wind* are still gathering dust on shelves; he once said that the pleasure of making pictures is largely in the experience, the invention, the experiment, rather than in seeing a finished result. He often turned from the screen when early works of his were projected on television. Clearly, he feared that not only would a completion have the finality of death, but it would present him as well with an inescapable vision of all that he had lost.

At the time of his death, Welles was planning to make a new version of *King Lear*. It had originally been intended to make the film under the auspices of Jack Lang, Minister of Culture for France, a project which had been dogged by many problems; when the French interest waned, Welles hoped to proceed on locations in the California desert, raising money from disparate sources.

Another project which had collapsed after much preparation was *The Cradle Will Rock*, rewritten by Welles himself from an original screenplay by a fellow liberal, Ring Lardner, Jr. This was the story of the 1937 Welles fashioning of Marc Blitzstein's opera of a steel town. Rupert Everett had agreed to play Welles, and Amy Irving to play Welles's first wife, Virginia. However, a series of disagreements between interested parties resulted in the disintegration of this project; even Steven Spielberg, whose live-in girlfriend was Amy Irving herself, failed to yield to any pressure to finance this project.

It is certainly sad to reflect that before he died Welles was dogged by the misfortunes that had marred most of his career; but it is good to know that he was active until the end, shooting a one-man show with his friend and cameraman Gary Graver, some of it devoted to his magic act; pages of instructions and stage directions were found in his typewriter on the morning of his death. The critical assessments in the press were glowing; forty years of muddle and disorganization were happily forgotten; and the consensus was that, whatever may have happened since, *Citizen Kane* and *The Magnificent Ambersons* remained sufficient monuments to their creator's genius, and were still to be considered the finest of all American films.

PROLOGUE

The Dynasty

On an October day in 1750, Richard Wells, a handsome Quaker lad of sixteen summers, set sail from the port of London aboard Captain James Shirley's mail packet *Triton*, bound for the colonial port of Philadelphia. He was undertaking the journey at the behest of Richard Partridge, his maternal grandfather, the shipping and general agent for the provinces of Pennsylvania, New Jersey, Rhode Island, and Connecticut, in order to learn the basic elements of the provincial trade.

His ancestry was distinguished to a degree. Richard Wells's father, Dr. Gideon Wells, was both poet and physician and attended the health of many ruling families of England, including the parents of George Gordon, Lord Bryon. The Lords De Welles, from whom he was descended, the family name having been shortened in the course of history, came from the town of Welle in Lincolnshire, near the Yorkshire town of Aulford on the river Ouse; members of the family married into the British royal house of Plantagenet; Lord Anthony Welles was a friend of William Shakespeare. The manor of Aulford, known as Cottness, was the family seat: a magnificent estate, at one time having a moat and drawbridge, it was surrounded by beautiful gardens and flowered walks and bowers.

Young Richard's crossing on the *Triton* in the fall of 1750 was a considerable ordeal. Because of severe weather, the voyage from London to Philadelphia took almost three months, and, as Captain Shirley had not taken on enough provender, the food had to be rationed to one biscuit, a portion of beef, and a ladle of water a day. Moreover, the mountainous Atlantic sea was, as Richard wrote to his brother Anthony in England, "enough to jumble your guts out." It was with exhausted relief that the starved youth at last saw land at Rhode Island.

In December the *Triton* inched her way up the icy Delaware River toward her destination. Through his telescope Richard could see the frozen cedar swamps and winter-stripped forests of the basin, until at last, when the town was least expected, Philadelphia emerged. In 1750 the Quaker capital was populated with some 13,000 souls and riddled by small creeks where the yellow fever virus bred. Its monotonous flatness of contour, its grid street design and squares wearying to a European eye, were relieved by red brick colonial buildings with white towers or gleaming spires, surrounded by whitewashed cedar fences, well-swept wood block sidewalks, and beautifully planted flower gardens. Dominating the scene was the imposing State House, the focus of Philadelphia lawmaking and a magnet for every lawyer in town.

Richard began work with diligence in John Smith's struggling firm, which imported dry goods and watches from London. Reports on his progress were good, and his parents and grandfather were well pleased. He took to skating on the Delaware River, shot game, and found a young woman to love. The beautiful Rachel Hill, descended from Meredydd, an ancient king of Wales, was the daughter of a physician and trader who had been seriously affected by privateer attacks on his vessels and had gone to live on the tropical island of Madeira, where he made a living as a wine merchant. Richard Wells was of impetuous disposition, wayward in his affections, and Rachel, attracted at first, became disturbed by his erratic behavior. He seemed to have an eye for other young women, while she was unwilling to share even his mind with other girls. Her father felt strongly that he needed to have his daughter happily married, and for all his problems, this thought was paramount.

Hill's fortunes improved, and he returned to Philadelphia to settle his debts. In the meantime, he used all his powers of persuasion on his daughter, writing to her impassioned letters that urged her to overlook Richard's faults and foibles and to make him hers, which she did; they were wed in 1759. Simultaneously, he urged Richard not to be uncertain about becoming an American; he asked him repeatedly to go back to Britain and to sell the great manor of Cottness.

Richard was uneasy about selling his ancestral property, rich as it was in legend and family glory, but his family suffered financially upon his father's death in 1760, and his mother had to sell some of her jewelry. Although the laws of England permitted no legacy or result of probated property sales to go to a younger brother, Richard sold Cottness in 1760 and shared the payment with his youngest sibling, Gideon. (His brother Anthony had died of smallpox four years earlier.) Another portion of the proceeds was accorded through a trust to his mother.

Richard returned to the New World with substantial funds of his own.

Joined in the Quaker faith, he and his bride obtained a house of brick and cedar eighteen miles upriver at Burlington, New Jersey. The dry goods business that he had started did not succeed, and he temporarily retired from commerce to devote himself to his family. But in 1773 the demands of his children and their upbringing caused him to return to Philadelphia, where he became principal officer of the Bank of North America.

The couple had twelve children in all, five of whom, named Richard, died in infancy. Of those who survived, the most important was William Hill Wells, who was destined for a major career in politics and the law.

The family grew up with all the joy and security that the Quaker faith bestowed upon its members. The Wellses were law-abiding and peace-loving; as pacifists, they took no part in the many conflicts of their era. The war against the French passed them by. They kept to themselves, and under Richard's expert guidance the Bank of North America flourished; Richard also made a name as an author of books on British-American diplomatic associations.

William Hill Wells enjoyed a classical education, emerging as a person of wit, style, intelligence, charm, and decency of character. A contemporary portrait by the celebrated cameo artist Charles Fevret De Saint-Memin shows a pale complexion, a chiseled profile, and an impression of delicate firmness and aristocratic demeanor. William was his father's son in every way. Behind the impeccable facade—the elegant clothes, the powdered wig, the black or blue silver-buttoned coats and breeches, the exquisitely polished buckle shoes—the young man had an impassioned and wayward temperament. He lived by his own rules. His decisions were final and seldom conventional. His intellect soared wide and free. Influenced by his father's writings on the colonies (two examples of William's speeches survive in the Library of Congress), he believed in a peaceable but firm separation from the old country, the establishment of an American Federalism that would not be belligerent or harsh toward the ancestral nation yet would strike free of the Hanover kings of England and their questionable influence. Although the term would not be entirely appropriate, he was at heart a Whig, at times almost a radical, and a man who deeply loved his adopted country, the low-lying hills, lakes, cedars and cypresses, swamps, and green fields of Pennsylvania and New Jersey.

William was also a devoted Quaker, and when his father died, he continued in the faith. He traveled to England and Europe and kept a vivid diary; he was admitted to the bar in Burlington, New Jersey, having graduated at a remarkably early age. With his future laid before him, possessed of family wealth and a position comparable to that of the Morrises in Philadelphia society, he fell in love with a young woman of striking beauty and presence named Elizabeth Aydelott.

Just turned sixteen in 1789, Elizabeth, on the face of it, enjoyed an ideal pedigree that would make their union acceptable to the Hills, the Morrises, and the Wellses. She was alleged to be the daughter of the late John Dagworthy, a gifted military commander who had had a brilliant career as one of Washington's British generals. Though somewhat rebellious and snobbish by nature, in many ways despising the provincials whom he served, Dagworthy had proved to be an effective commander in the war against the French by playing a leading part in the seizure of Fort Duquesne in 1758. He had been rewarded with twenty thousand acres of Maryland, later recharted as Delaware, that became known as Dagworthy's Conquest. The largest single property in the state, it consisted half of swampland filled with marketable cedars (the standard wood used for fences and facings in those days) and half of cedar forest. Dagworthy had built the grand colonial mansion of Dagsboro, where he raised his family, and he had favored Elizabeth Aydelott as his daughter and passed her off as such. But, as the Wellses, the Hills, and the Morrises discovered to their shock and confusion, Elizabeth was illegitimate, and indeed no one knew whether she was an illegitimate daughter or an illegitimate niece of the general.

The only certainty was that she was not of the proper stock; to marry her would not be appropriate for a person in William's position. Moreover, she was not a Quaker, and to marry her in the Episcopalian faith would mean expulsion from the Quaker meeting halls. To the outrage of the Quakers, William went ahead with the marriage in 1790—and was dismissed from the Quaker faith ("read out of meeting"). The couple moved from New Jersey to Dagworthy's Conquest.

A keen Federalist, one of the founders of that early American political party, and a friend of Benjamin Franklin, William rapidly emerged as a liberal in the Delaware legislature. He formulated and supported a bill that called for license fees on businesses in order to provide funds for the education of the needy. He took a strong interest in abolitionism and opposed the repression of the poor. As a result he was greatly beloved by the struggling farmers of Delaware, and Dagsboro became a focus of many decent-thinking people.

Shortly before 1800, William's older brother Gideon and his wife, Rachel, had moved to northern Pennsylvania, and there they had gotten into severe financial difficulties. Through the influence of William and Gideon's sister Mary and her husband, Benjamin Morris of Philadelphia, they had plunged all their savings into sixty-five thousand acres of trackless wilderness haunted by bears, leopards, and wolves; during the winter, when the temperature often fell to twenty degrees below zero, the land was covered with snow two feet deep. This disastrous investment threatened to bankrupt Gideon and his brother-in-law, who was already heavily in debt. With three other partners, they tried to attract land purchasers and settlers to what they called the Pine Creek Company, but almost nobody came.

In desperation, Benjamin Morris built a primitive road running north and south, giving access to the property, but still no one was interested. Benjamin and Gideon then turned to William in the hope that his distinction and prestige would draw people to this desolate, wind-swept purgatory. Meanwhile, William had been elected to the U.S. Senate in January 1799, taking the seat of the late Senator Joshua Clayton. For him to abandon his position in government would certainly be a serious move, but he hated Thomas Jefferson, who had become president in 1801, and, as a Federalist, he was aggravated at having to serve with Jefferson in office. In 1805 he resigned his seat and set out from Dagworthy's Conquest on horseback for the wastes of Pennsylvania, accompanied by his courageous wife, Elizabeth, their five children, and six black slaves.

The living conditions there were even worse than they could have imagined. They had to build two cabins, one for themselves and their family, about sixteen feet square, made of logs and bark, too small for an adult to be able to stand up straight in, and another, slightly larger, for the slaves, who under the state laws of Pennsylvania had been freed by the fact of their leaving Delaware. The fire had to be kept going all night in order to provide a modicum of heat; the water froze at the pump in the yard, and it was almost impossible to bathe. When the family members could take ablutions, they had to share a big iron tub all together. They built an outside privy of brick over a hole in the ground. In order to have meat, they had to bring in large quantities of salt pork at great difficulty by sled, or William and his brother had to shoot deer or even bear. In order to practice law at offices at Williamsport, William had to ride horseback each morning on the primitive north-south road, often through blizzards, his steed often stumbling over tree stumps, sometimes with snow up to its belly. His clothes would be frozen stiff, and at times he had to chop through ice with an axe to cross a creek. It was an unlikely life for an elegant senator and squire with a classical education, and it was barely endurable for Elizabeth, who had been raised in wealth and luxury.

In 1805 Benjamin Morris and his wife, Mary, arrived with their two children to try to improve the property. In October of that year, William and two partners were appointed trustees by the governor of Pennsylvania to accept proposals for the site of a county town. Through the passage of legislation, the Pine Creek Company was allowed to establish Wellsboro, named for the Wells family. But when resentful Western Reserve landowners fired on them at night, claiming they owned the territory, William and Elizabeth had had enough. They returned to Delaware to raise their young family.

Making up for lost time, the Wellses entertained glamorously at Dagsboro. William became more and more prominent in politics, enjoying the benefits of his cedar sales. But his adherence to Pine Creek served him ill, and the War of 1812 against the British further affected his fortunes. Six banks of Philadelphia failed, and he had investments in all of them. The British seizure of Washington in 1814 damaged his investments in that city. Opposed to the war, since he still felt loyalty to his native land, William devoted much of his second Senate session between 1813 and 1817 to voting against fiscal war meaures that included a high tariff. Yet he could not escape the financial consequences of the conflict.

Under President James Monroe, William had further problems. He began signing notes indiscriminately, invested too heavily in leather, and tried futilely to sell off his properties in England. He lost his estate in Pennsylvania by handing it over to his own slaves to live on, a generous and impractical gesture that proved futile because the slaves were driven from the land in short order by the local populace.

In 1818 the deteriorating state of the economy reached a nadir. An industrial and commercial storm broke, brought on by expansion, speculation, and extravagance, and William was seriously affected. His chief consolation in those years was the emergence of his son Henry Hill Wells as a lawyer. Henry was attractive and well dispositioned, possessed of his father's well-made figure and handsome features. Although Henry lacked William's brilliance, he was of similar moral character, and in 1821 he became secretary of state of Delaware under Governor Joseph Haslet. When Haslet died two years later, Henry continued as secretary of state under Governor Charles Thomas, his proud father and two associates having bonded him with $2,000.

As his health declined along with his fortunes in the 1820s, William accorded the management of Dagsboro and its slaves to his daughter Rachel and her husband, the able and accomplished Colonel W. D. Waples, while continuing to live in the house with his wife. Shortly

before he died on March 11, 1829, William performed a typically eccentric act. He drew up a will of unique oddity, witnessed by three
people, correctly made out under all the conditions laid down by law,
beautifully inscribed and embellished—but with a blank sheet where
the legacies should have been listed. It was not merely a question of
dying intestate; it was a question of providing no inheritance for anyone. Even though his fortune had been reduced from scores of thousands to a little more than $2,000, even though he had given away his
estates in Tioga County to his servants and abandoned his claims to the
innumerable debts that filled his office files, he still had as husband and
master Dagworthy's Conquest, the manor of Dagsboro, and the cedar
concessions that were supplying almost every fence in Delaware and
Pennsylvania. Yet for reasons unknown he had decided to leave nothing to anyone; they all had to fend for themselves. Interestingly, when
Rachel, his mother, died in 1841, she left no money to any of her children. Perhaps it was a tradition among these people that their offspring
would make their way in life without help.

Henry Hill Wells found himself a bride in Mary Putnam; her clan
had money, but Henry seems to have been as impractical as his father;
despite his legal knowledge and his position as secretary of state of Delaware, he did not accumulate a substantial fortune. He followed in his
father's footsteps in opposing slavery, and indeed it is accepted by Delaware historians that he took an interest in the Underground Railroad,
the network that helped the slaves escaping from the South to reach
Canada, starting in 1833. His removal with his wife and daughter to
Wilkes-Barre, Pennsylvania, in August 1835 was significant: Wilkes-
Barre was a crucial point on the Underground Railroad, standing as it
did on the Susquehanna River, a main artery of the network.

Henry, Mary, and two-year-old Lucretia found a pleasant home in
Wilkes-Barre, and the young man was readily admitted to the Wilkes-
Barre bar on August 4, 1835. He set up a law practice in the town,
which soon grew into an industrial center far removed from the stately
and parklike atmosphere surrounding Dagsboro. Wilkes-Barre was
rough and tough, a mining community, and Henry Hill invested as
much as he could in it, though not with much skill. Three more children were born of the marriage: William Henry, who lived only one
year, William Dagworthy, born in 1837, and Richard Jones, Orson
Welles's grandfather, born in 1842.

The Wellses fared reasonably in Wilkes-Barre; the boys grew up
with the typical small-boned, delicate, but strong frame of the family.
They enjoyed a modest education that was not comparable in quality
with that of William Hill or Richard, and indeed they lacked the sheer

excellence of their immediate forebears. In truth, they were not much above mediocrity.

In the early 1850s Henry Hill and his family made a move. They suddenly took off to the obscure village of Skaneateles on the Finger Lakes in northern New York State, reaching that town by traveling up the Susquehanna Valley by riverboat and then by stagecoach, a spectacular journey through the mountains. It might well be asked why a prominent lawyer of Wilkes-Barre would abruptly depart for Skaneateles; in fact Skaneateles was the nerve center of the Underground Railroad and the headquarters of James Channing Fuller, a close associate and supporter of the Underground Railroad leader Gerrit Smith. And just ten miles away, in Auburn, lived the famous Harriet Tubman, the heroic black woman who became famous for assisting the slaves. (One of her favorite escape routes lay across the property of Dagsboro itself, through the cedar swamp that occupied some ten thousand acres of Dagworthy's Conquest.)

The Wells family moved in next door to James Channing Fuller. Fuller had recently returned from Kentucky, where he had acquired a large family of slaves and then helped them to freedom. A cousin of the Wellses, the Reverend Thaddeus, aided the Underground Railroad through his ministry in a local church. Unhappily, Henry Hill Wells did not live to aid the Railroad for long; he died in 1856, after only two years in Skaneateles, and was buried in St. Stephen's graveyard.

His daughter Lucretia stayed on in Skaneateles, but his sons William Dagworthy and Richard Jones Wells drifted away. Or not exactly drifted; they made their way, one after the other, to another crucial focus of the Underground Railroad: Quincy, Illinois. There the two boys, the sons of a well-to-do lawyer, turned up as, respectively, a freight clerk and cashier on the Chicago, Burlington and Quincy Railroad and a messenger for American Express (which their father's namesake, Henry Wells, had recently visioned as part of the Wells Fargo commercial development when he was freight agent at Auburn, near Skaneateles). Why did the two boys undertake these jobs? The most likely explanation is that they wanted to help the Underground Railroad by working in the overground railroad.

When William D. Wells arrived in Quincy in 1859, there was no depot there, only a platform of wood blocks used for the steam trains of the CB&Q of Chicago. Quincy was a brawling frontier town, a gateway to the still undeveloped West, and just about as far as a man could travel before he had to switch to a stagecoach. Quincy's location on the Mississippi River made it an important military point; it was to be headquarters for much of the Union army forces during the Civil War, and from Quincy the troops would cross the river to conquer and pillage the divided and compromised state of Missouri.

William was present among the local population when the announcement of the surrender of Fort Sumter was read out on April 13, 1861. As railroad freight agent and cashier during the war years that followed, William handled shipments of guns, ammunition, swords, bandages, medications—all the paraphernalia of war. He disbursed money to officers who commandeered many of the trains. One train after another steamed in filled with the wounded from the front; he saw to the problems of shifting the sick and dying into the field hospitals. Each day the streets resounded with the rattle of the recruiting drums as men and boys were enlisted for service. William was responsible for the funds for a special train that would pick up Colonel Ulysses S. Grant's 21st Illinois Volunteers Regiment at Naples and take the men to a steamboat for St. Louis following their march from Springfield. He made the arrangements for a special train that came from Palmyra and Hannibal with eight hundred rejoicing Union troops to reunite with the Quincy celebrators following the surrender of Vicksburg.

In 1864, with the war still raging, William was involved in the requisitions that resulted in the building of a new railroad depot that would help link Quincy with the West. And it was then, in April, following the death of their mother, that Richard Jones Wells arrived from Skaneateles as an American Express messenger. Richard joined William in a room at the Quincy House, a fashionable hostelry that they can have afforded only by using their patrimony.

In June 1864 the CB&Q shipped a locomotive to Missouri, on loan to the Hannibal and St. Joseph Railroad; caught in a powerful river current, the pontoon capsized and the engine sank to the bottom of the river in full sight of the depot.

The boys sought a transfer to St. Joseph, Missouri, the last whistle-stop before the West. Stories came from there every day of the thrilling events on the CB&Q-owned Hannibal and St. Joseph Railroad, as Quantrill's Raiders and other guerrillas attacked the line, seizing mail and holding up the passengers. The boys longed for more adventure, yet there was a tremendous amount to do in Quincy; Richard was carrying messages for the Union troops at considerable danger to himself, while the transshipment of the wounded and other logistical problems kept William busy day and night.

On October 31, 1864, William married Rachel Austin, who came from the well-to-do Austin family of Kansas City. With Austin money they built a handsome house on Main Street, not far from the Quincy House, but they never lived in it. Instead, in 1867, William, as he had wanted, was transferred to St. Joseph. Richard left American Express and joined him as freight agent.

William, Rachel, their baby daughter Anna, and Richard stayed in simple lodgings in St. Joseph. Apparently they had run through their money; Richard was even forced to inhabit a humble boardinghouse, Beno's, in the worst part of town. He was at Beno's when a twist of fate brought to town a very young girl who was to affect the future of the Welleses.

Her name was Mary Blanche Head. She came from Kenosha, Wisconsin, on the pleasant shore of Lake Michigan, about sixty miles northwest of Chicago; whether she had run away from home or was visiting relatives in St. Joseph with a chaperone is not known. She was fourteen and a half, with dark auburn hair, a heavy, sullen face, smoky blue eyes, and a stocky figure for a girl. She had a fierce and ambitious disposition, was rebellious and uncontrollable, and became ill-tempered and harsh when crossed. Young as she was, Mary Blanche knew what she wanted and pursued her objectives without self-questioning or quarter.

She was the eldest child of Orson Sherman Head, the harsh and terrifying former Wisconsin state senator and district attorney for Kenosha, who was born in Paris Hill, Onondaga County, New York, on October 9, 1817. Head was descended directly from the cooper John Alden (see chart), the best known of the Pilgrim fathers who crossed the Atlantic on the *Mayflower;* Alden had married Priscilla Mullins, daughter of the well-known merchant William Mullins, and had lived to the advanced age of eighty-eight, dying in Duxbury, Massachusetts, on September 22, 1687. John and Priscilla's daughter Elizabeth married William Pabodie. Their daughter married William Fobes, whose daughter Constant married John Little. Their son Fobes Little had a daughter Ruth, who married Jonathan Head, grandfather of Orson Head. Another of Alden's descendants was the poet Henry Wadsworth Longfellow, whose poem *The Courtship of Miles Standish* gave a somewhat romanticized version of the events in which Alden and his wife were involved.

Orson Head and his brothers Daniel, George, Henry, Oren, and Lysander had worked the farmland with their hands under the harsh discipline of the patriarch Jonathan Head, thereby building the powerful physiques and robust health that made them look so formidable in later life. Orson Head's square shoulders, broad chest, and sturdy limbs impressed everyone who met him. His blazing red hair and red beard had an unnerving quality, combined with a fierce blue-eyed gaze that looked right through everyone.

Trained in the law in New York City, he had followed the call of the West and in 1841 had settled in Southport, which nine years later became Kenosha. Admitted to the bar, three times elected district attorney, he became known as a dangerous and deadly prosecutor of whom it was said that "there was no more chance for falsehood to survive one of his examinations than for a kernel of wheat to pass unbroken between the upper and nether millstones." He was known to display a hint of sentiment only over his horses, stabled at the back of his house, or when he recited to his family the text of Lincoln's speech at the dedication of the Gettysburg cemetery.

Married to Mary Jane Tradewell in 1846, Orson Head had seven children, the oldest of whom, Mary Maria, born in 1847, died in infancy. Unwilling to accept the fact of the baby's death, and following a custom current at the time, Orson and Mary Jane accorded not only the first name but the birthdate of this lost infant to their second child, Mary Blanche, born in 1853. Thus, Mary Blanche acquired the birthdate of 1847. But she often proved forgetful of the date, and this led to confusion for everyone from census takers to historians and from maintainers of birth records to graveyard keepers. Her sisters, of whom there were four, Dot Eunice, Jenny Lind, Harriet, and Medora, also became confused about the year in which each was born.[*]

Mary fully lived up to her father's personality. Her face, looking at us from portraits, with its sullen features, heavy brow, and thick lips, had an appearance of power and forcefulness. Certainly, whether her visit to St. Joseph was legitimate or the act of a runaway, she behaved with extraordinary boldness once she got there. Since Richard was working with his brother in the freight department of the Hannibal and St. Joseph depot when she arrived by train, it takes little imagination to see how they met. He would have taken care of her luggage, and she would have taken note of his Wellsian good looks, his wavy brown hair, brown eyes, and slender figure in his brass-buttoned blue uniform. For someone of her station, the daughter of a former state senator and district attorney whose home was worth $20,000 (about $2 million today), to show the slightest interest in a freight clerk was shocking by the standard of the time. Yet Mary, at fourteen and a half,

---

[*] A brother, William, was born between Dot Eunice and Jenny.

entered immediately into an affair with the young cashier and soon after, with great daring, decided that they would get married.

How Mary found the nerve to confront her father and stepmother* with her decision (Richard's parents were dead) is difficult to imagine, granted even her great strength of will, yet confront them she did, and she even insisted that the marriage take place in Kenosha! Orson Head's rage can have known no bounds.

In those days, railway clerks and agents had no vacations, so Richard would have had to obtain special dispensation to make the long journey to Wisconsin. There is no telling what grim welcome awaited their arrival at the Head mansion. The grandiose residence in the colonial style must have resounded with Orson Head's screams—screams famous in the county but normally reserved for lying witnesses in the courtroom. Yet Mary proceeded with the marriage arrangements, and just before Halloween, on October 29, 1868, abruptly announced in the local papers and unaccompanied by a party or a reception, the shameful nuptials took place.

No doubt Richard, himself a rebel, and Mary, relishing her new womanhood, greatly enjoyed this bucking of the Kenosha establishment. But their fierce temperaments did not make for a harmonious relationship. And soon after they returned on the limited five-day leave granted by the railroad to St. Joseph, they were greeted by a horrifying mishap.

With a dowry of $60,000 Mary was able to install herself and her new husband in the popular Pacific House, one of the finest hotels in St. Joseph. Owned by the genial James H. Bagwell and located at Third and Francis streets, the hostelry, with its square structure and portico front, an American flag fluttering from the roof, was a familiar sight in St. Joseph. The Wellses took a suite of rooms.

On December 15, 1868, the hotel was overflowing with visitors for the Christmas season. Many of them were in transit, preparing to make the journey west by stagecoach in the hope of new gold strikes or bonanzas at the end of the rainbow. Others were still hoping to cash in on the business boom that had followed the Civil War. At 1:30 A.M., while Richard and Mary were asleep, an arsonist, never identified, crept up the hotel's back stairs into the attic lumber room and set the logs afire. In a few moments the building, poorly secured against such a calamity,

---

* Mary Jane Head had died in 1863; Orson Head had married Mary S. Raymond in 1866, one year before young Mary Head left home, possibly in objection to her new parent.

was ablaze in the winter snow. When the alarm jangled Richard and Mary awake, they rushed to the window of the third floor, and ropes and ladders were thrown up to extricate them. Fire and smoke behind them, they made a perilous descent to the street. They had lost everything; not a single possession of anyone in the building other than the merchant tailor and barber who occupied shops on the ground floor was saved. James Bagwell was insured to only half the value of the building.

The fire made front-page news in the St. Joseph newspapers. Undaunted, the couple found an expensive house to rent on North Frederick and Eleventh streets; a tall wooden structure, it had an attic and a root cellar. They remained at that address for a year, joined by a Canadian servant named Matilda, then shifted to a similar house on Eleventh and Felix streets. Felix was one of the better addresses in the city—although the dirt street, the wooden paving blocks that made up the sidewalks, and the squat, ugly buildings of the district ultimately weighed down the spirit.

The couple had tired of St. Joseph by 1871. When Richard was demoted as freight agent to the depressing little town of Saxton, it was the last straw. Because of the lack of local accommodations, they were housed in rooms in the depot freight building. They had run through Mary's dowry, and Orson Head would advance them no more money.

They put what little they had on thirty-eight acres of land south of St. Joseph in the hope of farming there, but their extravagance was such that Richard was unable to keep up the payments. When the land was to be sold on the steps of the courthouse, Mary summoned up the nerve to ask her father to step in and save the property, and a furious Orson Head bought the land from them.

In the depressing station house quarters at Saxton, on November 12, 1872, Mary gave birth to a son, Richard Hodgdon Wells.* There was an announcement in the Local Notes of *The St. Joseph Morning Herald* next day: "Mr. R. J. Wells, cashier at the Hannibal depot, was made happy on Tuesday night. The cause of his happiness weighs ten pounds." Their joy was short-lived; within a month Richard had been fired.

The couple returned with their infant son to Kenosha, where Orson Head had become ill. He made his last will and testament, never referring to Richard by name. Mary, he wrote, would inherit one-

---

* Later, by common consent, his middle name was changed to Head in honor of Mary's father.

seventh of his estate, but she would not receive one cent of her patrimony during her (unnamed) husband's lifetime. Indeed, until Richard died, she would be paid nothing save a small income that would meet any out-of-pocket expenses for herself and her child. Orson also snubbed Richard by specifying that Daniel and Franklin Head, Mary's uncle and cousin, would be guardians of Mary and her son in place of her still anonymous husband. Even the land Richard and Mary had bought and lost was deliberately precluded from her legacy.

For two years the couple had to endure the ordeal of living with the dying Orson Head and his second wife in the house on the commons. The massive mahogany stairway, the large, echoing rooms, and the gloomy portico were the equivalent of a tomb for their ambitions and hopes.

At last Orson was stricken with pneumonia, and even his powerful constitution gave out under the onslaught of the virus in the severe winter of 1875. After his death, Richard and Mary lived on with her stepmother, brother, and sisters; it was not a happy atmosphere, for every glance and whisper in town pointed out the social differences between Mary and her husband. Unable to obtain work with the railroad, Richard had to take a cashier's job with a manufacturer of harness trimmings, probably George A. Yule, superintendent of the Bain Wagon Works, which owned much of the transportation business in that part of Wisconsin.

It was not a good marriage. The couple, having survived fire, parental wrath, and loss of land, could not survive each other's temperament. Richard was irresponsible toward his son, and in 1881, no doubt maddened by his wife's temper and by the slights he received in Kenosha, he abandoned her and fled the Head mansion for the urban delights of Chicago. He became an inventor of harness and bridle pieces for Charles C. Champlin of Champlin and Spencer, Harness Makers, and for Dwight Brothers, Saddlers, both in that city. Mary's lawyer uncle Daniel and Daniel's son Franklin engaged the police to search Kenosha; finding no trace of Richard there, they tracked him down through Ward A. Dwight in Chicago, and Franklin Head served him personally with the divorce papers. By July 1881 the uncontested divorce was concluded. The marriage had lasted less than thirteen years.

What was Richard to do now? Should he go back to his brother William in St. Joseph? Should he return to friends in Wilkes-Barre or Skaneateles? Whatever he may have thought of those possibilities, he pursued neither of them. Instead he moved to Athens, near Wellsboro, Pennsylvania, where his father had served briefly in the judiciary, and continued designing harness pieces. Richard never tried to have access to his son or contact with his wife. Mary declared him dead in 1885, when she met and married Frederick Gottfredsen, prosperous son of one of the best-known brewers in Kenosha, in order to collect her inheritance. But he was not dead. After disappearing for fourteen years, he turned up in New York City, making and patenting furniture at Theodore Roosevelt's birthplace, 28 East 20th Street, in the basement that had once served as a kitchen. By 1901, he had left the state, his whereabouts unknown. Mary continued to enjoy her illegal patrimony.

Once again, in a hasty affair and a lightning marriage, Mary acted in rash defiance of her family and her community. The Gottfredsens were not even true-blue British-Americans but were part Danish, and in those days brewers were almost as far down on the social ladder as freight agents. The wrath of the Head uncles at this new example of filial intransigence can scarcely be imagined. A Gottfredsen in the Head mansion—unthinkable! Mary had to move out.

She took yet another bold step. With her husband's beer money she built a house that was even more opulent and grandiose than the Head mansion; typically, she built this splendid Italianate folly in the height of contemporary architectural style only a few steps away from the Head house on the exclusive commons itself. Now her uncles, looking from their windows at the spreading elms of what was soon to be known as Library Park, must also take in the obtrusively ornate facade that Mary had selected. She even allowed herself the supremely vulgar touch of setting multicolored beer bottles into the front of her house to remind everyone that she had married a brewer. And within the great mansion she commissioned the architect to deisgn elaborate motifs of hops and hop leaves in the woodwork, the heavy African mahogany sconces, imported at vast expense, that frowned over the handsome folding doors that led from the living room to the library.

Her eccentricities increased. With a rich husband and a baby on the way (Jacob Rudolph, for whom she named her house Rudolphsheim), Mary would now have to act the role of great lady. She must entertain: she must give society balls. But everyone in Kenosha would be made to suffer as they attended these obligatory occasions. Many great houses of that time had a vestibule on the third floor through which guests would pass on their way to the ballroom, leaving their coats and furs at a kiosk of substantial size and presenting their compliments to the hostess. Not for the first time in her life, Mary broke with convention. She saw to it that all her guests entered the ballroom by a tiny, narrow back stairway no wider than the servants' staircase and twice as dark. So low was the overhang of the ceiling that the partygoers had to bend almost double to make their way upstairs. Moreover, she charged each person for entry! Each guest had to pay a fee to undertake this disagreeable journey. And they had to present their tickets to a clerk seated in a tiny cramped office with a cubbyhole before they were allowed in, as though they were attending a charity function.

Not surprisingly, attendance dwindled with time, and according to the survivors of the Head family the Gottfredsens finally lived in isolation. Frederick attended to a general store that he owned and to the business of the brewery and the malt works; because of mismanagement the business fell on hard times, and by the 1890s the Gottfredsens were reduced to being franchised agents for the Pabst Brewery of Germany and were no longer in charge of their own formulas.

Mary spent her lonely days accompanied by only a housekeeper and the two boys, Richard and his half brother Jacob Rudolph, known as Rudy. She seldom saw her sisters, about whom Richard, who was prone to daydream, wove elaborate fantasies that he later handed on to his sons. And later still his son Orson claimed that Medora, then married to a Millburn, New Jersey, businessman, had been wooed by the magician Herman the Great (when in fact Herman the Great had a lifelong devotion to his wife and was never known to have looked at another woman). Jenny Lind, named for the famous Swedish soprano and married to Dr. Alfred Thomas of Dayton, Ohio, survived the Dayton flood but was not, as the young Orson always claimed, having a party as the *Johnstown* flood reached the second story of her home. Orson even changed the account to make her a victim of the Johnstown flood because it was a more famous calamity.

Dot Eunice was now Mrs. Tom Brown of Chicago; Orson pretended she had fallen out of a rickshaw in China and disappeared, but this was untrue and her visit to China had been simply part of a package tour. The only aunt who could be described as eccentric at all was Harriet, Mrs. George A. Yule, whose husband was superintendent of Bain Wagon. Richard claimed that she wore a riding habit at all times, that she had a red wig she waved at friends, and that she had her chauffeur drive to the outskirts of Kenosha in her automobile, dragging her by a rope while she worked off poundage. She was also supposed to be fond of bathing in ginger ale. In fact, the only oddities in her behavior were that she went out running behind her auto in the mornings and she enjoyed an electric Turkish bath chamber in her house (today the headquarters of the Kenosha Historical Society).

The turn of the century saw Mary, in her late forties, still more isolated. Richard had been only a moderately good student at public school, but he did have a flair for inventing various contraptions, and he was outstanding in mathematics; the family decided that while his half brother would go into the brewing business, Richard would go into the Bain Wagon Works, run by Aunt Harriet Yule and her husband, after Edward Bain died in 1898.

Yule proved to be a stern but efficient executive. This important company, which covered four blocks and consisted of twelve buildings from one to four stories in height, was of modern mill construction, equipped with an up-to-date sprinkler system and an enormous warehouse. The plant alone had a capacity of 18,000 wheeled vehicles annually and employed some 450 men, many of them of foreign, particularly German, birth. Indeed, Kenosha itself was a microcosm of industrial America at the beginning of the automobile age; it swarmed with immigrants who worked in the sweltering or freezing Bain factory with little or no annual leave, strained to the limit and living in mere shacks or run-down ancient stone houses in the near slums yet grateful for a chance to prove themselves in the New World, to form the bases for their children's future and prove that muscle and sinew could be turned to profit for the America that had given them freedom from drudgery in the Old World.

Unlike the Gottfredsens and the Heads, who were tough business people bent only on earning profits, George A. Yule was a benign despot. Richard, still resident at Rudolphsheim, joined a recently formed subsidiary of Bain Wagon, the Badger Brass Company, upon its incorporation in 1897. The twenty-five-year-old greatly benefited by his aunt and uncle's industrial power and his mother's certain influence; he went straight into the partnership of the company, not only as general treasurer and secretary but as co-founder and partner along with the local industrial leader Charles N. Frost and Uncle George Yule. Badger Brass, in essence, was set up to buy and sell all kinds of lamps, lamp stands, novelties, implements, and utensils made of brass, copper, zinc, tin, or any other commodity or material, and to manufacture and sell tools, machinery, and appliances for the manufacture of the lamps and their attachments. Richard's job as secretary-treasurer was to countersign all deeds, leases, and conveyances executed by the corporation, to affix the seal of the corporation thereto, to keep records of the proceedings of the board of directors and the stockholders, and to keep all books, papers, records, and documents belonging to the corporation. He was to disburse all monies for investments or for the employees. His was a position of great trust and importance that, in addition to his role as director, kept him busy around the clock, to the great pride and joy of his mother and the pleasure of his gratified aunt and uncle.

Although he tended to daydream in private and to enjoy the bottle a little too much, Richard in his youth was much admired in the community. Gifted with the fine good looks of the Wells family, with reddish brown hair and dark brown eyes, he had a pleasant, charming disposition and was devoted to his work. And of course the advent of the automobile age, combined with the bicycle craze, kept him busy supervising lamp production; he rejoiced in his own inventions, and in fact began devising fixtures that he would patent in the next few years.

1

Richard Wells—or Welles as he now spelled his name—lived at Rudolphsheim until 1901, when he was twenty-nine, then moved from 180 Deming Street to number 210 just down the street. However, he continued to give his address as 180. In 1903 his first invention was patented: an acetylene gas heater, complicated but useful, that was to find its first lodging at Rudolphsheim. Later he created a series of lamps, with reflectors, burners, and special sockets, that replaced the existing lamps made by Badger. Some of these products became popular and were manufactured by Badger for the celebrated Solar Lamp Company of Chicago. An advertisement, reproduced in Floyd Clymer's *Treasury of Early American Automobiles* (page 68), shows a selection of Richard's lamps with the slogan, "High candle power they light the way—as bright as day—it is the Badger way." (The name Badger derived from Wisconsin's being known as the Badger State, after the early miners who lived like badgers in the hillsides.)

Richard devised a complicated catalog chart, providing a guide to every minute part of an automobile. This Heath Robinson drawing, accompanied by a long and infinitely complex paragraph of description that contains no periods, can be examined today in the patent books. Richard also took an interest in early airplane flight and presented young fliers at the first air show in northern Wisconsin in 1903, shortly before Orville and Wilbur Wright made their successful pioneer flight at Kitty Hawk, North Carolina, on December 17.

Richard would often go to brawling, nearby Chicago to enjoy the fleshpots. Like many young men of his time, he became a stage-door Johnny, hanging around the theaters and paying court to the buxom actresses who were sensual, skittish, but often available. He would wine and dine them in expensive restaurants, fully living up to the Wells tradition of extravagance and love of the good life. Already he was growing rich from the profits of his patents, which he assigned one by one to Badger Brass and Bain, those companies flourishing in the wake of the new and exciting automobile craze. He met in Chicago a woman who was temporarily to settle the thirty-one-year-old Richard down. Her name was Beatrice Ives.

Just twenty-one in 1903, Beatrice was intelligent and talented. Today, after two-thirds of a century, those who met her, even those who were only children at the time, still speak of her in awestruck tones. She made the profoundest impression; her dreamy white forehead, dark eyes, and pale features were combined with a spirit of great nobility and decency. Her faults were severity, puritanism, and sternness.

Beatrice's background was no less fascinating than that of Richard Wells. Her grandfather, John G. Ives of Springfield, Illinois, had been secretary of the Illinois Board of Trade; prominent in the grain business, he had been a near neighbor of Abraham Lincoln, who walked past his offices on Market Square every morning on the way to his own offices, doffing his stovepipe hat to his friend John. Ives had flourished, erecting the Aetna Mill and, with his wife, Abigail, raising a family. Their son Benjamin, Beatrice's father, became general manager and partner of Ives and Postelthwaite, coal merchants, of Chicago, and later of the Phoenix Fuel Company in that city. Moving restlessly all over the city, from Lake Park to Dearborn Street, to Oakwood and Prairie and Buckingham Place, the family suffered severe financial losses in the coal industry slump of the 1890s and had to borrow on insurance policies. Lucy Ives was a sweet woman of warm and tender temperament who loved music, a passion that her daughter inherited. She and Beatrice gave music lessons to support the impoverished father.

Richard Welles, whose taste in music ran not to the classics but to jazz, was nevertheless fascinated by the beautiful Beatrice, and she with him. The match of an inventor-treasurer of a brass fixtures company and a musical young woman with a talent for the piano was slightly unlikely, yet the romantic excitement of the good-looking couple overrode all objections. The marriage took place in Chicago on November 21, 1903, before the Reverend J. H. Edwards, rector of the Church of Our Saviour, and in the presence of Richard's mother, his half brother, and Beatrice's parents. The wedding was the talk of Kenosha. The couple moved into Richard's house, just around the corner from Rudolphsheim, and one year later, at that address, Beatrice gave birth to a son, Richard Ives.

Richard Ives Welles was out of place in the erratic but brilliant Wells and Ives families; he lacked the sheer intelligence that was evident on both sides of the family. He was backward, shy, insecure, and handicapped by so severe a stammer that he became the laughingstock of the local children, and this drove him even further into himself. Although he inherited the Wells good looks, strongly resembling William Hill Wells, and was equipped with the physique of the Head side of the family, his absentmindedness and awkwardness of demeanor made him a disappointment to his parents and especially to his grandmother Mary, who never forgot that the fruit of her loins had produced a pathetic imitation of the Wellses. She had some consolation in the fact that her brother-in-law William, from whom she seldom heard since he retired from the railroad and moved to Emporia, Kansas, had sired a daughter, Anna Welles, who had considerable gifts as a graphic artist. And she could always tell people the true story that while that child was at school in 1883, she had sat beside Jesse James's children, and that the entire Welles family had heard the shots that killed the famous bandit just next door to their house.

In the first years of the twentieth century, Kenosha grew rapidly from small town to city as a rich admixture of Germans, Slavs, Poles, and Russians poured into town, helping to enrich Badger Brass and Bain Wagon and the Gottfredsen breweries with their labors. Beatrice was active in helping immigrants to get settled and encouraging them to set up house. She was a prominent figure of the Kenosha Women's Club, where she sponsored lectures on philosophy, religion, and history. While her husband promoted trotting races and automobile shows, Beatrice gave piano recitals and ran Choral Society concerts. She was a leader in women's suffrage, and her speeches called for better treatment of women and urged women to enter politics. It says much for her charm that she was able to sweep with irresistible force through the stone ranks of official manhood that opposed her in the growing town.

Richard loved movies, but Beatrice did not go to them frequently; instead, she was busy fighting the growth of the red-light district and the dissolute behavior of some barkeepers. It was all the more ironic that Richard would drink more and more heavily, until by 1912 he was a hopeless alcoholic.

Beatrice became the first woman in northern Wisconsin to be elected to office in an official organization when she became head of the Kenosha Board of Education. Some male members of the board were upset by her appointment, fearing a female takeover of school administration in the area. Beatrice joined forces with the educationist Mary Bradford, and at the first meeting of the board, Beatrice faked a fierce attack on Mary's report, thereby creating the impression that the two women had their differences and would not present a common front. Lulled into false security by the thought that they might drive the women apart, the male board members soon found they were mistaken. Learning that they had been deceived, they became fierce in their efforts to dislodge Beatrice and Mary Bradford, but the two women carried all opposition before them.

While Richard continued to be a movie buff, Beatrice headed the local censorship board and called for the banning of allegedly immoral films. She was at the forefront of those who attacked Theda Bara's sensational vehicle *A Fool There Was* in 1914, and she violently opposed the sight of women with bare shoulders, men without their shirts, and other signs of moral decay. She forbade all children under twenty-one, including her own son, to see *A Fool There Was* or any other movie of that caliber.

Richard introduced an autobus car to Kenosha in 1911; through a deal with the Motor Transportation Company of Chicago, he secured vehicles that were built for twenty passengers and could carry thirty at a pinch. His were among the first buses in America that traveled without British-style conductors to collect the fares; the passenger entered the bus and paid the driver, who then deposited the money in a machine beside him. The bus route Richard introduced ran from the Chicago and Northwestern Depot by way of Kemper Hall and the country club to Sixty-eighth Street, beginning at 6:00 A.M. and running two or three times an hour until midnight. The able Mark Hansen managed the line for Wells.

Richard, Beatrice, and their son, called Dickie, lived at 210 Deming Street until 1906, then moved into Rudolphsheim for a period of two years, apparently suffering financial problems. As a partner and treasurer of Badger Brass, and with a substantial income from his inventions, Richard should have continued to be wealthy; yet local research shows that in fact he had had financial setbacks. Why? Once again, it seems that the familiar pattern of the Wellses—quick prosperity followed by financial decline—was repeating itself. The answer can be found in Richard Welles's addiction to drink, and one can only assume that he made unfortunate investments outside Badger that left him bereft. Indeed, after the couple moved out of Rudolphsheim, they took up residence in 1910 at a very modest address, 433 Pleasant Street, just down the road from the factory, and then—humiliation of humiliations—they had to take in boarders. By 1913 they were at 463½ Park Avenue, letting their lower rooms to traveling salesmen; the house, though nice enough and only a stone's throw from Rudolphsheim, was certainly not of the standard of the mansions occupied by Richard's partners, Frost and Yule.

It was part of the curse of the Welleses that this should be so. In

1911 the beloved Benjamin Ives died of cancer of the gonads, and his wife came to live in the already cramped upstairs portion of the Park Avenue residence. Lucy was suffering from stomach cancer and by 1915 it had begun to spread through her body.

In that year Beatrice, rejoicing in her second pregnancy after a ten-year interval and many useless attempts, looked forward to having another son. She and her husband never contemplated the idea of a daughter; they had long wanted their backward, pathetic Richard to have a brother with whom he could play when the Kenosha boys shunned him and he was left to ride on the rubber tire swings or to play in the icehouse with the neighborhood girls.

When Beatrice was well along with child, she and her husband decided to take a cruise of the Caribbean. Beatrice was not in the strongest of health, and it was thought that a voyage would improve that health and make the childbirth easier. So the couple went to New York and set out on a fourteen-day voyage of the islands. On board, they were seated at a table in the dining saloon with two old acquaintances, both bachelors, who traveled everywhere together. Their names were George Ade and Orson Collins Wells.

George Ade was then at the height of his fame as one of the most brilliant satirical humorists and comic authors of the day. He had had a string of successes and secured an enormous audience nationwide—his books sold in the scores of thousands—and he possessed a charming public personality that earned him many adherents. Orson ("Ort") Collins Wells, who was not related to the Wellses but was a friend of theirs, was immensely rich from inspired investments in stocks in the 1890s in Chicago. He was a hugely fat man, weighing 300 pounds, with a bald head that shone like a billiard ball when it caught the light. He had a loud voice and a cordial, imposing manner. He strode, shoulders swinging, shaking everyone's hand with a bone-cracking grip. A passionate traveler, he was known popularly as "Circumnavigation Wells." He had something in common with Richard Welles: the racehorse owner J. B. Respess had named two stallion racers Ort Wells and Dick Welles after these men.* In 1910 he had undertaken a journey to India

---

* Dick Welles was holder of the world's records for a mile and for three-quarters of a mile and was the best-known member of the string owned by the millionaire J. B. Respess in Woodlawn, Ohio. Born of King Eric by Hanover, in 1900, the bay horse was the sibling of Ort Wells. It won races at Harlem, Washington Park, Chicago, Morris Park, Hawthorne Park, and Latonia in the first years of the century, until it was lamed while frisking in its stall and was thus prevented from entering the World's Fair Handicap at St. Louis. The horse remains legendary to this day.

and the Dutch East Indies that George Ade commemorated in a vividly effective essay. His letters to Ade, written from the Chicago Athletic Club, still make entertaining reading. The bachelor pair proved amusing at the dinner table during the Wellses' tour of the islands.

As the cruise ended, Beatrice told her delighted table companions that if, as she expected, she had a boy, she would name him George Orson in honor of the two men. This was a charming but empty compliment, for the formidable Mary Head Wells Gottfredsen had already laid it down that, since Richard Ives had been named after the Wellses and the Iveses, a second son must be named after her own father and uncle, Orson and George Head.

Soon after their return to Park Avenue in Kenosha, Beatrice gave birth, on May 6, 1915, to a boy of a whopping ten pounds whom she named George Orson. The following day the SS *Lusitania* was sunk by German torpedoes off the coast of Ireland, with twelve hundred travelers losing their lives.

Mortality would become a central theme of Orson's work, and an agonizing, protracted death was the first thing of which he was aware as a baby. Lucy Ives, living in the guest room of the cramped house on Park Avenue, was suffering from cancer of the stomach, the pain of which morphine could not fully ease. She had constant attacks of vomiting or hemorrhaging, her screams of agony filled the residence day and night, and there was a constant movement of nurses while Beatrice, sensitive and delicate by nature like all the Iveses, struggled against the inevitability of her mother's death.*

The most frequent visitor to Park Avenue in the first months of Orson Welles's life was Dr. Maurice Bernstein, who attended Mrs. Ives. He was a twenty-nine-year-old, Russian-born physician with a high forehead, a hawk nose, and penetrating dark eyes. His slender, tightly knit figure exuded energy, determination, and manic zeal, and his insistent, high-pressured voice made a strong impression.

The son of Jacob and Tuba Bernstein, immigrants to Chicago in the 1880s, he was educated at Northwestern University Medical School, began practicing in Chicago in 1908, and three years later moved to Kenosha,† where he set up practice at his residence on Main Street. Working locally in concert with Chicago's Michael Reese Hospital, Dr. Bernstein developed considerable research in the fields of bone, joint,

---

* *Citizen Kane* begins with a death—Kane's own; his wife and son were killed in an auto crash. *Ambersons* is full of deaths.

† He was exiled from Chicago because of a scandalous episode in which he was charged with attacking, beating, and leaving injured a clinic supervisor.

and deformity surgery and hemophilia. A specialist in hormone ther-
apy, he helped raise $400,000 to give Chicago its first foot hospital. He
worked on the discovery of mucin as a treatment for stomach ulcers,
vitamin D deficiency as a cause of decayed teeth in children, methods of
discovering a child's sex before it was born, and the infantile paralysis
virus. He combined surgical reforms with a greedy, acquisitive nature.

On a visit to New York in 1915, Maurice Bernstein met Mina, a
would-be singer and oldest sister of the Russian virtuoso violinist Mischa Elman, who had just begun his dazzling career in America (after a
brief residence in England) and had settled in Manhattan with his three
sisters. According to Mischa Elman's widow, Dr. Bernstein fastened
relentlessly on Mina, knowing that Mischa was building a fortune as a
musician. He flattered and wooed her until she fell hopelessly in love
with him. Mischa Elman despised him, seeing that he was a fortune
hunter, and was horrified when Mina said that Bernstein required, in
the old Russian tradition, a $15,000 dowry (a quarter of a million in
today's money) before he would marry her. Mina was so besotted with
the physician that she was compelled to ask her brother for the favor.

Mischa Elman had no alternative to seeing his sister's heart broken,
and he signed the check. The marriage took place in Buffalo in 1917;
the couple went with the family to Niagara Falls for their honeymoon.
When they returned to Kenosha to live, Dr. Bernstein grew cold and
whatever love he may have pretended disappeared. Gradually, Mrs.
Elman says, Mina learned Dr. Bernstein's true purpose in marrying
her, and they were divorced only four months later when Orson Welles
was two. Devastated, she never married again.

Dr. Bernstein entered into an affair with Beatrice Welles. Apparently he thought she had money, an idea that was to be dashed
when her intestate estate showed a balance of only $1,400 in her ac-
counts. He attended Lucy Ives as a cover; Beatrice was suffering from
an alcoholic husband, which often means sexual deprivation for a
woman; and she and Maurice were young and passionate.

The matter was soon resolved. In 1918 Lucy died and, freed of their
responsibilities toward her, the Welleses decided to move to Chicago.
Dr. Bernstein, now their closest friend, wanted to advance his medical
career, and Richard was tired of brass lamp manufacturing and disliked
the idea of having to change, along with the rest of the country, from
solar lamps to electric lamps in cars. At the age of forty-six he took an
early retirement. He could have gone on to considerable riches in the
automobile age; instead, he sold out of the company, which was dissolved. Richard left Badger far more comfortably off than he had ever
been, taking with him over $100,000, a substantial sum in those days

(the equivalent of close to two million today), and only his incapacity at investment kept that sum from growing. Richard, Beatrice, and their children took up residence in the Windy City, then, for a variety of reasons, rapidly split apart.

Richard's drinking greatly offended Beatrice, along with the extravagance and humorous eccentricities that began to emerge in his middle years, inherited from the clan. Moreover, Beatrice was ambitious: in harness with Dr. Bernstein rather than with her husband (which gave rise to further tales of a cuckolding association), she decided to crash musical society. True, she was gifted as a pianist; true, her Kenosha recitals had earned her a local reputation. But Chicago was the focus, the very citadel, of musical life in the Middle West. Its opera company was superb, its orchestra among the finest in the country. The greatest stars on both sides of the Atlantic would come to the city and perform for enthusiastic audiences. The empress of the musical scene was Mrs. Edith Rockefeller McCormick, who melded two fortunes through a famous marriage. The daughter of John D. Rockefeller, who at the time was arguably the richest man in America, she had married in 1895 the wealthy Harold F. McCormick, heir to Cyrus Hall McCormick, inventor of the McCormick reaper, which was to be found on farms from one end of the country to the other.* In 1918, when the Welleses arrived in Chicago, Mrs. McCormick was temporarily absent, a pupil of the philosopher and psychologist Carl Jung in Switzerland, but her presence still dominated the city and its musical life as few had ever done.

How would it be possible to enter the charmed circle of Mrs. McCormick and her friends of the North Shore, the crème de la crème of Chicago society? Dr. Bernstein supplied the solution; all doors opened through his influence, and Beatrice, who had abandoned her husband and moved into a handsome North Shore apartment at 150 East Superior Street, could at last achieve her vaulting ambitions.

She began to give recitals, and she presided over the Lake Side Musical Society, the name given to the special circle of musical enthusiasts who helped organize the soirees at her home, to which she invited Maurice and Mischa Elman and other prominent figures. And her son Orson, unlike his elder brother, exhibited musical feeling and knowledge as a child.

Dr. Bernstein became Orson's unofficial guardian, known to him as "Dadda." The doctor called Orson "Pookles." Dr. Bernstein bought

---

* Harold McCormick died in October 1941, a few months after the premier of *Citizen Kane,* which was based in part on his life.

Orson a magician's box of tricks, oil paints and canvas, watercolors and an easel, and the boy showed considerable prowess with a paintbrush and even dreamed of being a professional artist like his cousin Anna, whom he never met. Dr. Bernstein gave Orson a puppet theater that he played with and allegedly even wrote for at the age of five.

On weekends Richard Welles, Sr., and his older son (in one car) and Dr. Bernstein, Beatrice, and Orson (in another) would travel to the tiny colonial village of Grand Detour, Illinois, about a hundred miles west of Chicago, where the atmosphere had scarcely changed in more than a hundred years. There was a strong flavor of early American history in Grand Detour, a quality seldom to be found in a rapidly industrializing America. There was the barn in which John Deere had fashioned an early plow, and here was a wooden bench upon which Abraham Lincoln supposedly had sat. Dominating the hamlet was the grand old Sheffield House Hotel, run by the genial Charles Sheffield and his wife. The wooden hostelry was a focus for weekenders from the Windy City, offering excellent food, a fine cellar (in the period before prohibition), an icehouse, a smokehouse, and beautiful grounds near the celebrated art colony that made Grand Detour an attraction for Sunday painters.

In December 1920 a sensation rocked Chicago and Kenosha—indeed, most of musical America—that would influence Orson when he was to make *Citizen Kane.* Harold F. McCormick's mistress, the temperamental singer Ganna Walska, was due to appear in the title role of *Zaza,* an opera by Leoncavallo, at the Chicago Opera House, which McCormick and the tycoon industrialist Samuel Insull together ran and financed. The promised appearance of this celebrated Polish mistress of one of the city's most prominent business leaders ensured a sellout of the house weeks before the premiere. Not a soul would have dreamed of missing the spectacle of the high-strung diva boldly and deliberately insulting her lover's wife by making an American debut in her lover's own theatrical establishment. Then the night before the performance was to take place, apparently warned by her Italian coach and orchestra leader that she was not quite ready for her appearance, and terrified of the consequences a failure would have, Mlle. Walska fled the city and at the last minute, with twenty-six trunks, made her way up the gangplank of a ship bound for Europe. This incident must have been the constant talk of the Welles and Bernstein households at the time, and it must have made the deepest impression on Orson, even though he could not have understood its full implications. Mrs. McCormick, her rival shamed and exiled, returned in triumph to her mansion at 1000 Lake Shore Drive. She divorced

McCormick almost exactly a year after the *Zaza* debacle, and she reopened her great salon, where Mischa Elman spectacularly appeared.
Chicago historians agree that Beatrice must have been present at Mrs.
McCormick's soirees from that moment as frequently as Mrs. McCormick was present at Beatrice Welles's entertainments.

A brochure announcing Beatrice's tours of 1919–1920 indicates
that she introduced a new form of piano recital, "Interpreted Music."
The program consisted of a number of "cantillations and various
charming Spanish dance rhythms." She would accompany her recital
with a discussion of the vagaries of Spanish music in relation to barbaric and oriental countries. *The Kenosha Evening News* said, "From
the time Mrs. Welles struck her first chord, in her opening number, her
audience was held entranced by the forceful current of beauty which
underlay her selections." Other reviews, by *The Illinois State Journal* of
Springfield and *The Racine Journal News*, were equally enthusiastic. A
critic for the Racine paper wrote, "Mrs. Welles combines with the
spoken word an interpretive piano setting, and thus out of a union of
poesy and music evolves an intriguing combination through the medium of a musical voice and an affectionate intimacy with the piano."

Mrs. Welles quickly captured all hearts in Grand Detour, and for
the summers of 1920 and 1921, when Orson was five and six years old,
she took a pleasant colonial house on Route 3, the third oldest in Grand
Detour, with flower bushes and trees fronting it, a proper porch, and
elegant curved windows. (The house still stands and has been carefully
restored by its present owners.) While Beatrice stayed with Orson at
the summer home, Richard Jr. remained with his father at the Sheffield
House. Whenever possible, Orson would visit his father at the hotel.
There a man of all work, Olie Emery, who took care of the furnaces
and the upkeep of the hotel, fascinated Orson, who has recalled that
this man was handicapped by a wooden leg—though everyone else in
Grand Detour insists that he was whole. Orson has remembered Emery
as being a former figure of chautauquas or medicine shows, but those
who knew Emery intimately say that this is untrue and that he worked
for the Sheffield family from childhood.

Everyone surviving from that period in Grand Detour (eleven indi-
viduals were available recently for interview) concurs in a picture of
Orson and his elder brother. Where Richard Jr. was below average,
dull, and endlessly stammering, Orson, though disinterested in physical
activity, was prankish, full of humor, and overtly contemptuous of
what he called the "hayseeds" with whom he was confined. He looked
down on everyone in town and walked around as snootily as George

Minafer, the high-toned anti-hero of *The Magnificent Ambersons.*
Children would mock Orson and his chubby figure with the savage
song, "Georgie, Porgie, pudding and pie." But while the boys despised
him for his disinterest in football, baseball, or any other form of athletics (the young Ronald Reagan, then living in nearby Dixon, was of
course the exact opposite), the girls fancied Orson because he entertained them with impromptu shows in a tent of his own making, playing every part in Shakespeare, both Romeo *and* Juliet, Antony and
Cleopatra, hilariously changing from male to female clothes borrowed
from anyone who would lend them. In playing such famous "moments" as the balcony scene and wooing himself with expertise, he reduced the children to delighted fits of giggles.

Mrs. Nora Hoff (née Jones) and her many brothers and sisters were
fascinated by Orson. Nora remembers that he built a contraption that
was supposed to enable the viewer to see the stars; when boys were
foolish enough to pay him a penny to gaze into the complicated set of
pipes he had rigged up, he would kick them in the rear end and thus,
Nora recalls, make them "see the stars another way." Bruno Catalina,
who today runs a local bar, was among his victims: "I said, 'I don't see
no stars up there,' and the SOB hauled out and kicked me in the butt,
and both me and the contraption went over. I chased him into his
hotel, but he was too cowardly to come out. Finally I got my revenge. I
stole one of his toy trains."

For all his antics, Orson suffered from hay fever, sinus headaches
and other sinus problems, and a mild form of asthma, so until well into
his childhood he had a private nurse, what the British call a nanny. Her
name was Sigrid Jacobsen. Beatrice had engaged her to do the sewing,
and she continued to look after the boy when his mother grew increasingly unwell. Sigrid, who died in 1982, wore a surgical boot supplied
by Dr. Bernstein (she was born without toes on one foot) but performed
her duties expertly; according to her sister Elizabeth, who is still alive
and remembers Orson well, Sigrid was devoted to the boy.

In September 1922 Orson was in Oshkosh with his mother, who
wrote to Sigrid Jacobsen, "We are so cold we are filling the hot-water
bag, and wish we had more woollen things to wear. It is beautiful here
but Orson says not so lovely as Grand Detour." It was during this trip
that Beatrice became extremely frail because of the cold.

Sigrid Jacobsen remembered that Welles often presented puppet
shows and plays, insisting that everyone from the neighborhood children to the maids attend. Sigrid helped him in the preparation of his
puppets, with which he was very particular, making "bad" puppets
with black thread and "good" puppets with colored threads and candy

hearts. Sometimes Welles would have fits of temper. Once he cut the belt of Sigrid's sewing machine; on another occasion he cut the front of her dress to pieces.

Ethel Waneberger, later Ethel Welker, lived next door to the Welleses and vividly remembers how her sister Nellie used to cook for the Welleses and act as housekeeper; the family would take evening meals at the hotel. Mrs. Welker and Chuck Moser recall that Orson graduated from his tent to a small wooden playhouse that he set up outside the steps of the Sheffield General Store, regaling the customers with his theatrics. "We all thought he was goofy," Chuck Moser says, "but I guess we were the goofy ones. He got to Hollywood, and we didn't." According to Moser, Orson frequently visited with Burt Flick, a neighbor who kept a winepress, which fascinated the boy. He says that Orson would also go into the attic of the hotel to look for old clothes; and Edith Portner, another survivor of that era, says Orson found fancy hats and coats too large for him in the old steamer trunks and wore them whenever he could.

According to Mrs. Myrtle Young, Beatrice taught Orson a smattering of several languages. Sometimes he addressed people in these languages, instead of in English, and no one understood a word. She remembers that Richard was constantly being crucified by the boys of the town, and on one occasion they dared him to jump from a bank into a gravel pit—and he broke both legs. The brothers both resented the fact that their mother wanted them to wear velvet knee pants and neckties when they wanted to wear more boyish clothing. Mrs. Young's sister, Nellie Winebrenner, would be doing the dusting in the hotel and Orson would drive her nearly mad by reciting to her incessantly. Orson loved lemonade, strawberry shortcake, and apple pie; he stuffed himself with everything sweet until he grew round as a balloon.

Sometimes the boys' behavior was extremely erratic. Frances Wakenight, cook at the hotel, told how Orson terrified the local children with ghost stories. Everyone remembered that Orson complained so bitterly about having nothing to do during the long, hot summers that once when he was seven his father, in despair as to how to please him, went to Chicago and bought him a houseful of toys, then created a toy house to put them in. Among the toys was a train; Orson loved it and played with it incessantly, watching the tiny engine and carriages, operating by clockwork, hurtle around the track and make their way through mysterious green tunnels and across painted fields. Today Ashley Foxley, aged eighty-six, Richard Sr.'s closest friend, lives in the toy house.

Ashley Foxley has never forgotten his beloved friend. Richard, he says, was the most brilliant man he ever knew; together they went to the movies, especially the William S. Hart westerns and the Buster Keaton comedies. Foxley was fascinated by Richard's chain-smoking, for he used one Virginia straight-cut cigarette to light another.*

Photographs in Sigrid Jacobsen's scrapbook show Orson happily lost in a haystack, playing with his dog Caesar, marching with a stick held up, seated astride a donkey, posing in a sailor suit on a large, smiling crescent moon with a face on it, gazing intently in an artist's smock and beret, standing in a cute aviator's suit, and climbing a pole in the yard of Sigrid and Elizabeth Jacobsen's country home outside Chicago.

Orson constantly wrote to Sigrid from Grand Detour, and on one occasion he sent her a pin ("May it always remind you of me"). His letters to her still exist.

In 1924, when Orson was eight, his mother was attacked by a dread disease. In those days antibiotics were unknown, and virus ailments struck with deadly force at those who were run down or constitutionally weak. Hepatitis, then known as yellow jaundice, was especially feared because it was highly contagious and often proved to be fatal. A mere forty years old, with her whole life in front of her, Beatrice was stricken with that unpleasant-smelling sickness. The liver is the first line of defense in the human body, and, dangerously weakened by the illness, Beatrice began to slip away more and more rapidly at the time of Orson's ninth birthday. Once again as during the agonizing death of Lucy Ives, the precocious Orson was made aware of mortality. In the large and handsome apartment at 150 East Superior Street, Beatrice spoke to him of her approaching end, quoting Shakespeare, her shining eyes appearing dark by the light of the candles on his birthday cake. Eyes that had been green were now almost black with suffering; her flesh was yellow and flabby with sickness. She told Orson to blow out all the candles on the cake, and as he did so, for there was no other light in the room, it became utterly dark. In this charged and symbolic way, she told him what death was, and he may never have recovered from that terrifying moment.

Within a week the beautiful Beatrice Welles was dead. Richard Sr. had moved to 150 East Superior Street to join Dr. Bernstein in taking care of her. The funeral was crowded with mourners, many of whom

---

* Ashley Foxley did not recall Richard's smoking cigars, although according to the U.S. Tobacco Museum in Greenwich, as early as 1903 Richard had had his cigars made especially for him by the Stelle-Wedeless Company of Chicago, and his name was used for his own exclusive brand. The blend, which was not commercially manufactured, was also used for cheroots and chaws.

regarded her with intense love and admiration. Orson was utterly stricken by her death; he was deeply admiring of his mother and had been agonizingly close to her suffering. Because of the suddenness of her illness, she died intestate, leaving only $1,400 and some jewelry. Thus Orson received no formal legacy from her.

For a short period Orson was sent to Hillside Farm at Syosset, New York, with the wife and children of the art teacher Dudley Crafts Watson, his mother's cousin, to recover from his grief. In the meantime, Dr. Bernstein moved from his home at 65 East Chicago Avenue to share a house with Richard Welles, Sr., at 3167 Cambridge. In July 1924 Bernstein and Welles were together in Spain, France, Italy, and Austria. Some eighteen months later, Richard Sr. decided to buy the Sheffield House, the popular owner of which, Charles Sheffield, was retiring. Contrary to statements made by his younger son, he spent over $10,000 on improvements to the hotel, which included building a new wing. And contrary to other statements by Orson, he was a genial host who welcomed visitors from all over. He ran the hotel with Frances Wakenight as housekeeper.

Meanwhile, Richard's addiction to alcohol became more serious. He is still remembered by many in Grand Detour as the town drunk, a person seldom sober from morning to night. He defied prohibition by importing grapes from California, and he and a neighbor secretly pressed the grapes in the cellar. Moreover, one of the waitresses of the hotel, Ethel Moser, would go to Chicago and bring back substantial supplies of bootleg liquor. Richard owned a blue 1923 Chevrolet four-door sedan, which he drove with great incompetence until finally he piled it up on a bridge, injuring both himself and his passenger, Ethel Moser. After that, threatened with the suspension of his license, he relied on Ethel's brother, Chuck Moser, to drive him. Chuck was an excellent driver, and he often chauffeured Orson as well his father. Moser remembers that even at that early age, Orson never stopped talking for an instant, keeping up a rat-a-tat-tat line of blarney and reciting favorite verse to the stupefaction of his less educated and quite underpaid driver.

When he was not at Grand Detour, Orson spent much of his time at Dr. Bernstein's Chicago house or at Highland Park, a Chicago suburb dominated by the Ravinia Musical Festival, where Dr. Bernstein and his friend the music critic Edward C. Moore shared a home, and where Dudley Crafts Watson's Trillium Dell was a haven for artists. Highland Park was an enlightened community of souls who enjoyed a civilized life in that heyday of culture in the Middle West. The homes of the Welleses' nearest and dearest friends were open to every distinguished musician who appeared at Highland Park. The amusement park there had a bandstand, a merry-go-round, and a small theater. In the summer, Frederick Stock would conduct the Chicago Symphony, or Walter Damrosch would bring his New York Symphony, or Ruth St. Denis and Ted Shawn would appear in a program of dances in the wood pavilion that dominated the park. On a raised terrace edged with shrubbery at the left of the pavilion was the stage, and Orson often claimed that he appeared as the baby of *Madame Butterfly* in a performance there; in fact, the only performances of the opera at that time were concert duets without supporting cast. Whether or not Orson appeared as Peter Rabbit in a Marshall Field Christmas pageant cannot be established with complete certainty. However, his ardent love of the theater is certainly agreed upon by all eyewitnesses and friends who have survived.

On one visit to Grand Detour in 1926, Orson indulged himself in a rare and elaborate adventure. Dudley Crafts Watson, who often stayed at the Sheffield House, was in Europe that summer with his wife, and his daughter Marjorie and her nurse were in residence at the hotel. Orson took a fancy to Marjorie, and together they decided to take off from the dreary little town and go from door to door, raising money that they could use to embark on careers as child actors. Like Orson's grandfather, they disappeared, and for a while all efforts to trace them proved futile. They made their way through the woods, sleeping on pine needles and logs, until at last they were located on the other side of the state, traveling now as two boys, with Marjorie dressed in Orson's spare clothes. They were found performing on a street corner for a penny a show, and the police sent them home with a warning.

Occasionally Orson traveled with his father to Kenosha to see his grandmother Mary, who was now in her seventies. Frederick, her second husband, had died in 1911, and she was living alone, save for a housekeeper, in the great house of Rudolphsheim, keeping a lamp burning the year round next to Frederick's favorite armchair. She was growing increasingly eccentric and strange. Although she embraced Christian Science and followed the precepts of Mary Baker Eddy in believing that all illness was a fantasy and that high spiritual values must be maintained, she also—or so Orson alleged—practiced a form of witchcraft. In later years he spoke of her practice of sacrificing pigeons before an altar set up on an elaborate indoor miniature golf course of green paper on the third floor, where once the ballroom had been. He said that she was a practicing witch, a black magician influenced by the evil works of the diabolist Aleister Crowley and by the confused precepts of the occultist Madame Blavatsky. A later owner of the house, Mrs. Mary Page, who now lives in Texas, remembers that she found, many years ago, in Mary's private and frequently locked walk-in closet, some evidence to support this picture: the remnants of a wooden altar, with a strange, multicolored stained-glass window in the Tiffany mode set above it, overlooking a small internal corridor. The altar was accompanied by Latin inscriptions that Mrs. Page did not understand and by a gold star that she thought was the basic symbol of Judaism but was quite clearly a pentagram, a symbol of both black and white magic frequently used as a protection from (or invocation to) the powers of darkness. Mary Page nervously covered it with several coats of paint.

Whether she was a black magician or not, Orson was terrified by the formidable old woman, and she held him in contempt because he was artistic, unathletic, and showed no indication that he could follow in the Head tradition of business or the law. He overcame his fear of her to some degree by trying to terrorize her, plunging a rubber dagger into his breast and falling, seemingly senseless, at her feet. She told him not to be such a silly fool, to behave himself like a little man instead of an idiot; he should be an automobile man, like his father. This response, joined with Mary's hatred of anything theatrical or affected, caused a fierce and bitter opposition between these two great egotists that continued for years and later had a deep influence on the scenes between George Minafer and his Aunt Fanny in *The Magnificent Ambersons.*

In 1926 it became obvious even to Orson's eccentric father and Dr. Bernstein that, in spite of their careful tuition, Orson had to experience the rough-and-tumble and academic training of a school. Prodigious though he was in drawing, reading, and music, he needed to be more of an all-rounder if he was to make his way in the world. Thus he was sent to Madison, Wisconsin, where a friend of Dr. Bernstein's, the psychologist and lecturer Dr. Frederick G. Mueller, was a well-established presence at Madison State University. Mueller and his wife, Minnie, who saw Orson as a child genius, took him under their wing, and invited him to stay with them at Camp Indianola on State Street. Under Mueller's guidance, Orson attended Madison Public School, where Dorothy E. Chapman was principal. In 1926, Orson studied arithmetic, in which he was weak, language (very strong), geography and history (almost equally strong), and reading, spelling, writing, drawing, and music, in all of which he excelled. He was rapidly elevated from grade 4B to grade 5B and by May his arithmetic had improved so greatly that he was awarded 80 points. He also starred in and directed plays.

The Madison Journal for February 19, 1926, described Orson's activities in an article, "Cartoonist, Actor, Poet and Only Ten." The article stated incorrectly that Orson was descended from "Gideon Welles, who was a member of President Lincoln's cabinet." It told how Orson, reading a story and becoming interested in one of the characters, would suddenly decide to paint that person in oils, which he would then do with great enthusiasm. He edited *The Indianola Trail,* the camp paper, and illustrated it with cartoons in pen and ink of the other boys. During the long evenings at the camp, he gave performances and readings that lasted three or four hours. He dictated to Frederick Mueller a poem, "The Passing of a Lord," about an aristocrat who sat upon a satin chair, "his trousers ironed without a singe," his wig powdered, with silver buckles at his knees; he seems to be very composed, but, the youthful poet adds with precocious cynicism, "The Lord sat still and was unaware, A moment before there had been a shot, The aim was true but the Lord knew not; The next day they found him in a pool of his blood."

Orson's father moved to Madison to be with him, staying with Orson and Dr. Mueller at Camp Indianola that summer. Then he and Dr. Mueller decided that Orson was too brilliant for the Madison School, and he sent him to the famous Todd School at Woodstock, Illinois, from which the unfortunate Richard Jr. had been expelled for misbehavior ten years earlier (Richard, a drifter at twenty-one, was now working in the government fisheries at Bozeman, Montana).

The Todd School was a smart choice. Established in 1848, the campus at Woodstock consisted of fourteen acres on the edge of the town, some fifty miles northwest of Chicago. There were an additional 260 acres of bridle paths, woods, and athletic fields as well as an airport and a farm. With their elegant white porticoes and pillars, their white-painted brick facings and handsome green or red shutters, the buildings had an early colonial look, and many of them had been built in the height of high style in the mid-nineteenth century. Enrollment was restricted to boys of potential good attainment; each boy would be encouraged to follow his bent, no matter what that might be, along the lines of Clayesmore School in Dorset, England. A boy who was not athletic would not be humiliated or forced into athletic activity; a boy who showed athletic prowess would be encouraged to develop it.

The dominating force of Todd was its slender, genial headmaster, Roger Hill, who inherited the school from his father shortly after Welles became a pupil there. Orson soon plunged into designing stage sets, setting up play productions, and in every way indulging his tastes. He was happy in his new environment—and he was able to gratify his flair for eccentricity. On the night he arrived he terrified some of the younger boys in the dormitory by telling them ghost stories. He startled his history teacher by appearing in class with a garish white face and a scarf tied around his neck to resemble a hangman's noose. He informed Dr. Hill solemnly that, while the stage machinery in the school playhouse was excellent, the lighting equipment was not. When some small effort was made to have him exercise in the gym, he forged a letter from Dr. Bernstein saying that Orson was "delicate and could not be expected to take part in any athletics whatsoever." He put on a Halloween magic show, he donned drag as Mary, Mother of Jesus, in the 1926 Christmas Nativity play, and he acted in *Dust of the Road* as Judas and *The Servant in the House* as Christ. He also directed and performed in *Richard III, Julius Caesar,* and *Androcles and the Lion.*

When one boy attacked Orson with his fists, Orson disappeared into the bathroom and covered his face with red paint, then emerged looking so badly bloodied that no one attempted to assault him again. He gave magic displays, insisting he had learned the craft from no less than Harry Houdini; he sang and danced in a musical revue, he painted excellently (his chief ambition was to be a painter), and he sketched and caricatured with great style.

Orson appeared at Todd in the musical show *It Won't Be Long Now,* with music by Carl Hendrickson and "foolishment" by Roger Hill. Among the scenes of the play were the interior of the Night Hawks Club, New York City; a beach where a moving picture company (!) was shooting a Hawaiian scene; the "Palace of the Shriek" in India (a program note read, "If you don't believe this, choose your own country. We won't argue with you"); and a courtyard in Bullencia, Spain ("The management is not responsible for any Bull thrown in this scene"). The inclusion of film and Spanish bullfight scenes could scarcely have been more prophetic of Orson's future. Orson appeared as Jim Bailey, a "pal with troubles of his own" of Bob Warfield (played by Donald Topliff), said to be "in search of his dream girl." The production contained another note of prophecy: Orson joined in a song at the end of Act One, "Around the World We'll Go," which was clearly remembered when he staged his famous production of *Around the World* in 1947.

A later show at Todd was *Finesse the Queen,* book and lyrics by Roger Hill, score by Carl Hendrickson. Another precursor of *Around the World,* this musical production was set in "The Little Gondolivia" café in New York, a replica of the Gondolivia palace ballroom, aboard a ship on the Atlantic, and in the palace ballroom itself. Welles appeared as William J. Spurns, after the famous detective William J. Burns, "who has a clew." He joined in finale numbers composed by

Hendrickson, including "We're Back Again," "Gondolivia," "Wedding Bells," and "Waltz of the Rose."

In 1927 Richard Ives Welles, aged twenty-three, was declared insane, suffering from symptoms of advanced schizophrenia and dementia simplex. According to a psychiatrist, dementia simplex is a form of schizophrenia in which the patient does not like to go out, limits his activities to a minimum, tends to sleep all day, and generally feels detached from the world. It is a form of catatonia that in some cases involves panic before experience, great agitation, and paranoid delusions accompanied by bizarre behavior. Richard's father, who thought him ungrateful and rebellious and was annoyed by his many advances of money from the estate, had him committed to a guardian, Irene M. Lefkow, and then to the state for institutionalization.* Richard was incarcerated in Kankakee State Institution for the insane, which housed almost four thousand inmates; he was to remain there for ten years.

In contrast, for Orson the years at Todd were in every way the best of his life. Even though he was overweight and unathletic, he had so strong a personality, so great a charm, that many of the boys cottoned to him and laughed uproariously at his jokes. He liked the informality of the school, the fact that boys dressed as they pleased, and most of the time he wore sloppy cardigans, shirts open to the third button in a style twenty years ahead of its time, and baggy, badly pressed trousers. His hair was a mess, and he affected makeup in the daytime when he felt like it. He attracted stares on a visit to Cuba with Dr. Bernstein during the 1927 summer vacation.

Orson grew enormously tall very fast. At the age of thirteen in 1928 he was already over six feet tall and weighed more than 180 pounds, a precocious flat-footed giant built like Orson Head. His almond-shaped eyes, with their oddly Chinese look, flashed humorously or defiantly at everyone.

He had a gift for the blarney from the first. He repeated and embellished the stories about his aunts that his father had originally told, always extending their number from four to nine, and he maintained these fantasies years later, when he regaled the writers Peter Noble, Kenneth Tynan, and Maurice Bessy with them. Frequently he assumed other people's identities. On one occasion he posed as the son of Edward C. Moore; on another he pretended to be Roger Hill's son, a pretense that collapsed abruptly when a clerk observed the initials O.W.

---

* Richard Sr.'s chauffeur, Le Roy Wallin, signed the commitment papers with Richard Sr. The fine hand of Dr. Bernstein, whose partners also signed the commitment papers, can be seen in this unfortunate matter.

in his hat; and he was especially prankish during a student tour of Germany in 1929.

Orson's visits to Grand Detour were infrequent during this period. As a largely absentee host, Richard Sr. maintained the hotel as best he could, making as many improvements to the old property as possible while battling his drinking problem. On the morning of Monday, May 14, 1928, he was sleeping late, heavily hung over after a night of drinking bootleg liquor, when members of his staff, led by his new housekeeper, Mrs. Admont, began burning papers in the kitchen range to ascertain that the updraft through the new stovepipe was satisfactory. The fire went up the flue and entered an upstairs lumber room—an echo of the fire at the Pacific House in St. Joseph that had threatened Richard Welles's father and mother in 1886. The blaze was not discovered until 9:30 A.M., when it had already ignited the roof of the two-story frame structure. Mrs. Admont called the Dixon Fire Department and alerted the guests; as flames engulfed the building, two waitresses helped the indisposed Dick Welles down the stairs. Half overcome by the effects of smoke and drink and unable to rescue any of his personal possessions, he watched helplessly from the lawn as his property was consumed. Crowds poured in to watch the fire, but by 10:00 A.M. the inn was a mass of smoldering ruins. Orson was at school at the time.

On October 6, 1929, Maurice Bernstein, having married and disposed of an unsuccessful singer, now married a brilliantly successful one: Edith Mason, a star of the Chicago Opera Company.* She had been married in 1919 to her favorite Italian conductor and former coach, Giorgio Polacco, and divorced him to wed Dr. Bernstein. But Polacco had laid down some interesting conditions for surrendering his wife to the ambitious physician and surgeon: Miss Mason must give up eating pie and agree in writing to abandon her addiction to it; Dr. Bernstein must force her to give up smoking; and he and she must pay Polacco one hundred thousand dollars for the loss of her sexual favors.

Dr. Bernstein agreed to the first two conditions only. Consequently, after the marriage Polacco moved in with the Bernsteins and shared Edith with Maurice at her house on Lake Shore Drive.† Orson was a frequent guest of the bizarre ménage à trois. Two years later Edith divorced Dr. Bernstein and remarried Polacco.

---

* On the wedding night, Orson wrote in an undated letter to Sigrid Jacobsen, the couple motored to Kenosha with Orson and put flowers on Beatrice Welles's grave.

† When the Italian complained that the Bernstein auto was drafty, they returned it to the dealer.

Orson was in Munich on a boys' walking tour on August 24, 1929, and he wrote Sigrid, "How you'd love it here . . . the beer. Oh! Baby! Well, it won't be long now till I see you and then I can tell you all about it." The next year, just before his fifteenth birthday in May, he took off with his father for a trip to the Orient. Orson would greatly exaggerate in the years to come the events of the voyage and their visits to Chinese cities, but the trip—as Richard Welles told his friend Ashley Foxley—was nothing more than a cruise to celebrate a birthday. Richard Sr. did not maintain an elaborate residence in Shanghai, nor did father and son spend any length of time there.

Dr. Bernstein added his own fantasies to the boy's life of travel. In 1941 he wrote Herbert Drake, Orson's *Citizen Kane* publicist, that Orson had been caught smuggling jewels from Canada in his shoes and that he had made a tour of Europe on a bicycle (when he could not even ride one). Dr. Bernstein said that the young Orson was a roisterer and a wastrel, "reminiscent of an ancestor who had been fished out of the mud flats of the Mississippi." Such tales added to the growing mythology that countless interviewers and friends would be fooled by over the years.

The trip to the Orient took place as Richard Sr.'s health declined in consequence of his drinking habit. While Orson returned to Todd in the fall of 1930, his father moved into the Bismarck Hotel in downtown Chicago, hiding in his room and seeing almost no one. The determined Dr. Bernstein obtained a firmer hold over the estate; in the meantime, Richard Sr. and Richard Jr. had come in conflict. Richard Sr.'s will, made out on October 20, 1927, when he was fifty-four and his son was in Kankakee, bitterly attacked his older boy. The unhappy father wrote, inter alia:

> Because of the extraordinary advances heretofore made for and on behalf of my said son Richard I. Welles, which were not made for George Orson Welles, and because of the apparent irresponsibility and ingratitude of said Richard I. Welles, I direct my said trustee to turn over and pay to the said Richard I. Welles one seventh of the net income of my said estate, for his support, maintenance and education until he shall have attained the age of 35 years; and the remaining six-sevenths thereof, or so much thereof as may be necessary, shall be applied to the support, maintenance and education of my said son George Orson Welles until he shall have reached the age of 25 years.

Thus Richard Sr. left a mere one-seventh of his estate, or about $6,500, to Richard and about $37,000 to Orson. However, Richard never received a penny of his patrimony due to his "insanity"; Dr. Bernstein retained it. The proviso that this inheritance was to be held in trust until Orson's twenty-fifth birthday was echoed, even to the age, in the discussion of the legacy of Charles Foster Kane in *Citizen Kane.* Mysteriously, the amount of the legacy was altered in later documents signed by officers of the First Union Trust and Savings Bank in Chicago, which stated that only $20,000 had been left.

Three days after Christmas 1930, Richard Welles died. According to John Houseman, the well-known associate and former close friend of Orson Welles, Orson's father perished by his own hand in his room in the Bismarck Hotel. According to the death certificate signed by Dr. Bernstein, the causes of death were chronic myocarditis, a disease of the heart, and chronic nephritis, a disease of the kidneys, followed by cardiac failure. Interestingly, the death certificate shows that Dr. Bernstein, allegedly Richard Head Welles's closest friend, knew nothing whatever about Richard's father or mother; birthplace, names, and all other details were marked "Don't know" by Richard's half brother Rudolph Gottfredsen, and Dr. Bernstein was co-signator. And this is yet another mystery: since Richard and Rudolph had the same mother, why did Rudolph write "Don't know" when asked for her name and birthplace? The eccentricity of all concerned can only be marveled at.

Rudolph took charge of the body and carried it by train to Kenosha on December 29, after depositing a grip, or leather bag, containing personal effects, including Beatrice Welles's jewelry (a necklace, bracelet, earrings, and brooches), with the First Union Trust and Savings. The funeral was held at 2:00 P.M. on December 30 in Mary Head Wells Gottfredsen's mansion, Rudolphsheim. Orson later claimed that the old woman he hated introduced into the Lutheran service elements of a highly questionable character: portions of the infamous writings of Aleister Crowley and Madame Blavatsky. However, the service was not conducted by a Lutheran minister; Mary, a Christian Scientist, always wanted her son to be buried in the Episcopal faith, and thus the Reverend Kenneth Martin, highly respected in the area, delivered a perfectly normal Episcopal burial service, local church authorities confirm, and the body was placed in Green Ridge Cemetery, alongside Beatrice and not too far from the hated Orson Head.

Dr. Bernstein was appointed Orson's guardian on New Year's Day 1931 (Orson had been living with him for several years). Dr. Bernstein continually nibbled at the estate, seeking recompense for every cent he laid out on Orson's education at Todd and giving Richard nothing, not even clothing. He itemized school and miscellaneous supplies, medical supplies, laundry, transportation to and from Chicago, clothing bills he had not paid, and numerous other expenses, many of which he had not met. Years later, when Orson was established in Hollywood, Dr. Bernstein nagged and niggled for the very funds that he claimed he had not been repaid; the same spirit that drove him to marry Mina Elman and Edith Mason for their money animated him now.

In June 1931 Orson graduated from the Todd School with honors. Dr. Bernstein, who with Orson's approval was applying for full guardianship, wanted him to go to Cornell University while Orson wanted to enroll in a drama school in Chicago. However, Dr. Bernstein (who later claimed credit for Orson's theatrical career) was quite opposed to any such ambition, and indeed his wife Edith Mason, who was then planning to divorce him and remarry the Italian conductor, was equally opposed and entered into a rare agreement with her husband in the matter.

The house in Highland Park and Edith Mason's residence on Lake Shore Drive trembled with violent arguments over the fate of the young prodigy. In the end, the sixteen-year-old managed to talk everyone into the ground and secured an agreement that he be allowed to travel to Ireland on a painting expedition; presumably relieved by the decision and glad that the arguments would temporarily be at an end, the quarrelsome Bernsteins conceded to the plan. Dr. Bernstein grudgingly made Orson a loan of $500, then exaggerated the sum when he tried to squeeze the estate of more money, and fought the bank trustees to do so.

The stingy Dr. Bernstein produced sufficient money for a second-class fare on the Cunard White Star Line vessel the *Baltic*, in August 1931. Without much clearer an idea than that he wanted to be a painter, if he could not be an actor, Orson set out on what was to be a momentous journey.

2

Still vibrating from the arguments over his future, the boy left in a restless temper for Ireland. His plan was that, once he had painted and walked around the Emerald Isle, he would head for London and find a place in the theater. He disembarked at Galway with a backpack containing paints and brushes, an open-necked shirt, and baggy shorts. He found himself inspired by a book he had picked up. Its title was *Field and Fair: Travels with a Donkey in Ireland,* translated from the Gaelic of Padraic O Conaire (Patrick Conroy) by Cormack Dreathnach, published by the Talbot Press in 1928

Padraic O Conaire was a distinguished minor writer who enjoyed a reputation as a reflective, sometimes pessimistic author with a lyrical bent who wrote in the native Irish language. Born in 1881 in Galway and taught first at a convent, he had gone to London to join the civil service and had fallen in with vagabond poets and literary gypsies of every description. He hated intellectuals and preferred men of the soil who drew their poetry, their song and story, from the Irish earth. From the beginning of World War I, frequently arrested for vagrancy or for suspected political activities against the British, he had made his bed in the woodlands, fields, and jails of his native country. *Field and Fair* told the story of his journey, with a little black ass he loved, by cart along the highways and byways of Ireland, a journey he described in a style fastidious, gentle, and informed with a strong poetic sense.

The young Orson Welles was fascinated by the book, and for a time it was his bible. Similarly, he decided to follow the local custom of the day of traveling with an ass and a cart. Among those who helped him were a brother and cousin of Padraic O Conaire, whom he found at Galway: Michael Conroy and Isaac Conroy, both ironmongers' assistants. They were impressed with the young visitor from America who filled their ears with blarney about his literary and theatrical attainments and no doubt told them of his admiration for their relative's work.* However, having obtained the donkey and cart, Welles completely failed to follow the prescription laid down in *Field and Fair.* He got only as far as Clifden in Connemara before tiring of the gypsy life and selling the donkey and cart to a tradesman, P. K. Joyce, who dined out on the story for years afterward. Welles then took a boat to the Aran Islands off the Irish west coast, where he was greeted with rain and a plague of flies.

In Aran, Welles sketched some of the men and women he met, capturing the weatherbeaten faces that Robert Flaherty would soon immortalize on film in *Man of Aran.* But the drawings remained in his portfolio, and he ran short of money and wrote Dr. Bernstein for assistance. (It was typical of Dr. Bernstein that the help did not come.) Welles lingered on in the islands, enjoying the simplicity of the life, and when the weather cleared, he responded to the warm, soft curves of the ancient land.

With what little cash he had left, he reluctantly returned to the mainland, then took train and barge across the heart of Ireland to the elegant Georgian city of Dublin. He failed to pay his rent at the boardinghouse he found, and when his landlady cut off the electricity in his room, he, feeling sad, wrote in his diary of his anguish and loneliness, his fear and uncertainty of what would become of him in the big city and "quite at his wits' end."

Then suddenly the boy was seized by an inspiration. Padraic O Conaire had influence, and some of his stories had been illustrated by the gifted actor Micheal MacLiammoir, who was then running, with his lover Hilton Edwards, the newly established and already highly regarded Gate Theater. In September 1928 Edwards and MacLiammoir, with two others, had announced the opening of the Gate Theater studio, "for the production of modern and progressive plays, unfettered by theatrical convention." It was an imitation of Peter Godfrey's Gate Theater in London; the intention was to launch seldom performed or newly written dramas and comedies along with the classics. With its opening, and a fine introductory performance of *Peer Gynt,* the Gate Theater quickly established its reputation.

Hilton Edwards was British; he had been with the Old Vic in London before touring in Ireland with Anew McMaster's company in 1926. There he had met MacLiammoir, who was playing in the company, and they had begun their lifelong partnership in a production of

---

* Later, Welles erroneously stated they were in the judiciary, Micheal as lawyer and Isaac as chief of police.

MacLiammoir's Gaelic version of the play *Diarmuid and Grainne* in Galway.

Micheal MacLiammoir was a fin de siècle throwback, a late-nine-teenth-century dandy whose writing and drawing evoked a more or-nate and extravagant era. His personality, on and off stage, was theatrical in the best sense: flamboyant yet disciplined, jeweled, lush, enjoyably overripe. Edwards was in many ways in conflict with him, but their mutual affection and the beautiful Harcourt Terrace house they shared in Dublin earned them the love of theatrical figures the world over.

When Welles decided to approach the two men for a job as an actor, the sixteen-year-old showed a startling boldness. But he had the courage of poverty and near starvation, for Dr. Bernstein had not sent him so much as a nickel. Without writing or calling, Welles went to the stage door of the Gate and asked to see its distinguished managers. Hilton Edwards, who was usually delegated the task of disposing of im-portunate young actors in search of work, came to the door and looked Welles up and down, barely able to disguise his astonishment. Dressed in bohemian clothing, with a loose, open-necked shirt and baggy pants, his black hair brushed straight back, his slanting eyes flashing fire, and his mouth curled in a supercilious smile, Orson Welles appeared daunting indeed. He was drawn up to his full height, and despite his fleshy look his huge chest and the big bones of his arms and legs gave him the appearance of preternatural strength. And then the ambitious boy began to talk, and the instant the golden, rolling basso voice rever-berated in Edwards's ears, the skeptical manager was fascinated in spite of himself.

Before Edwards could say anything, Welles began an elaborate and largely fictitious account of his achievements that included a season with the Theater Guild in New York and with the only slightly less dis-tinguished Goodman Theater in Chicago. He said he had written plays, and he poured out vastly exaggerated details of his travels until Ed-wards, flushing with a combination of embarrassment and excitement, asked him to wait a moment. Edwards went to his partner and told him, "Something strange has arrived from America. Come and see what you think of it."

Reluctantly, MacLiammoir obliged. Once again the impatient youth gave a résumé of his imaginary life, adding considerably more color this time around. And he was lucky; the two actor-managers were looking for somebody to play Duke Karl Alexander, the brutally anti-Semitic, bullying nobleman who dominated the play *Jew Süss*, adapted by Ashley Dukes from the novel by Lion Feuchtwanger. In this travesty of the best-selling book, Dukes reduced Karl Alexander from a military commander and prince to a trifling buffoon and popinjay, with the result that the author of the novel, who had not authorized the stage version, disowned it outright.

On an impulse, MacLiammoir and Edwards gave Welles a copy of the play to read for them. Extremely nervous and feeling quite unsuited to the part, which called for a man in his forties, he was nevertheless fortunate in having the aristocratic lineage that bestowed on him the precisely correct demeanor. The ancestry he knew little of served him well; despite his youth and unease, he read with splendid diction, a demonic intensity driven by hunger, and an astonishing range of wickedness, drunkenness, and tyrannical force. Pure ham his acting may have been, yet the partners looked at one another and knew they had made a discovery. They did not believe for an instant that he had been with the Theater Guild—they smelled an amateur at first sniff—but they knew that he had the raw talent that would rivet audiences, that with their guidance he could only succeed. Above all, he had the outrageous physical assurance without which no performer can triumph. He was worth taking a chance on; and the chance was taken, as Welles wrote in great excitement to Roger Hill the next day.

He was paid very little, though it was slightly more than the streetcar fare he had asked for. He doubled as assistant press agent and scene painter during rehearsals; obviously, his new employers wanted to be sure he would be useful in case he fell on his face on the first night. He proved to be a good mixer, blending in well with the other actors and subduing the American in his accent with considerable ease. He kept everybody in the company afloat on a tide of imaginary reminiscence—extravagant stories that changed color, style, and content with every repetition. At late-night suppers in depressing, cheap cafés in Dublin, where everybody went Dutch to pay the bills, he was invariably uproarious; he regularly spent what little he had and was constantly being threatened with eviction by his landlady. It scarcely helped that he came from a Protestant family. As he went on and on about bicycling or walking along the great wall of China, acting in Greece in the classical tongue, and indulging in Turkish baths in Turkey—all these accounts punctuated with the stories of his nine incredible aunts—he was the toast and the joy of everyone.

As an actor, Welles was a bold adventurer, and quite irresponsible. He did not really care whether he was a hit in *Jew Süss*. The first-night audience was uneasy about him, an unknown American. He was saved by the fact that his role called for an unpleasant person whom the audience could heartily dislike at once. When he appeared on stage there were catcalls from the gallery, and for a moment he felt paralyzed, but from his first line he riveted everyone. Indeed, he enjoyed an ovation at the final curtain; the audience barely restrained itself from leaping to its feet. J. J. Hayes, Irish correspondent of *The New York Times,* was present at the performance and wrote from Dublin on October 21, "There are a naturalness and ease about [Welles's] acting, which at once caught the packed house on his first appearance." The local reviews were equally enthusiastic; *The Irish Independent* said:

> His is a notable performance. There are few more unpleasant characters in dramatic literature than Karl Alexander, Duke of Württemberg, but there was a touch of humanity and simplicity in his swinishness which in less expert hands might have been lost. It is this quality that makes him tolerable. Orson Welles captured [that quality] magnificently, for he played the part with supreme naturalness.

While playing in *Jew Süss,* Welles rehearsed for his second part, as Ralph Bentley, a Montana millionaire, in *The Dead Ride Fast,* a play by David Sears. Sears's first drama, *Juggernaut,* had been staged by the Gate with great success, and Sears was seen as one of the most promising dramatists in Ireland.

The setting of the play was a mansion on the west coast of Ireland, formerly owned by the mysterious Fintan O'Driscoll, who was rumored to have had dealings with the devil. When a young man, Larry Kavanagh, buys the house from the descendants of the alleged diabolist, he is told that on no account must the painting called *The Dead Ride Fast,* which hangs in facsimile in several rooms of the house, be removed, or the consequences will be dire. Kavanagh becomes convinced that the rumors about O'Driscoll are correct, and the plot develops into a powerful melodrama as Welles's Ralph Bentley and his daughter Joyce, lost in a snowstorm, take shelter in the house. Occultism, madness, necromancy: the play's themes echo the young Welles's experiences at Rudophsheim, and he must have thought of his remarkable grandmother as the bizarre story unfolded. J. J. Hayes, writing from Dublin on November 21, said in *The New York Times,* "I have never seen on any stage a more true-to-life portrait than that of the wealthy self-made American millionaire, who, away from his field of activity, gives himself up with complete abandon to the enjoyment of the hour. Played by Orson Wells [sic], the young American actor, Ralph Bentley came to life in most convincing fashion." If ever there was a dry run for Charles Foster Kane, this was it.

A third role was now added to Welles's repertoire in what was proving to be a challenging season. With great skill he had twice already converted himself into middle-aged men, first as a belligerent duke, then as an obstreperous American millionaire. Now he appeared in Percy Robinson's *The Archdupe* as both Marshal François Bazaine of France and the Republican Mexican colonel who charged and executed the final punishment of the Emperor Maximilian of Mexico, whose story formed the matter of the play. Percy Robinson, an Irishman from Cork, had been fascinated by the story of the ill-fated emperor from childhood and was inspired to write the play by the death in Belgium in 1927 of the insane Empress Carlotta, who was psychologically destroyed when her husband, a victim of circumstances, fell afoul of Mexican revolutionaries and was shot to death. The play moved skillfully from Maximilian's assumption of the Mexican throne to his ultimate betrayal by traitors to France. On December 8, J. J. Hayes again wrote with enthusiasm, citing "brilliancy" in the writing.

> The production has raised the Gate Theater to a new pinnacle of achievement and Hilton Edwards has accomplished unusual things in the staging. At the premiere Orson Welles, the young American actor, scored heavily. . . . As the French general he succeeded in maintaining that balance which left it in doubt whether Bazaine was a traitor or merely indolent and procrastinating.

The season continued into the new year. On December 29 Welles opened in *Mogu of the Desert*, by the distinguished Irish writer Padraic Colum. Unfortunately, the play represented the author at the nadir of his talent. It was an absurd concoction of ingredients drawn from the Arabian Nights and was scarcely worthy of the Gate's attentions; designed basically as a Christmas attraction, an equivalent of the pantomime in England, its story lacked coherence and sense. Nevertheless, the actors flung themselves into the absurdities with enthusiasm. Hilton Edwards, padded out with an artificial stomach, played with luscious campiness as Ali the beggar, and Welles had a field day camping it up even more extravagantly as King Chosroes of Persia, wearing one of the first of his many artificial noses, a massive white turban with a jeweled pin, flowing purple and silver robes, and fingernails made of blue and silver metal that were three inches long. Audiences were indifferent to this quasi-oriental charade, and they were certainly not stimulated by the fact that both Edwards and Welles abandoned their usual eloquence and mumbled into their artificial beards. Few people bothered to see the play.

It seemed that only a successful production of *Hamlet* could rescue the Gate from the sudden loss of prestige, and indeed *Hamlet*, starring Micheal MacLiammoir, was given with considerable style, in a triumphant battle with the Gate's notorious acoustics. Welles made a terrifying ghost of Hamlet's father, and Hilton Edwards was admirable as Claudius; the intrigues, alarums, and excursions of the Danish court were conveyed with zest and vigor, and critics commented favorably upon Welles's makeup. He also played Fortinbras. Simultaneously, in repertory, he appeared with success as Baron Lamberto, owner of the mysterious house in Italy in which the Grim Reaper appears in the guise of a shadowy, handsome artistocrat who attempts to seduce the heroine into the Shadowy Kingdom in *Death Takes a Holiday*, adapted by Walter Ferris from the play by Alberto Cassella. Once again Welles's performance was extremely well received; but his restless spirit would not allow him to stay in Dublin.

Welles's success had gone to his head. The megalomania that would soon consume him had seen its birth, and the encouragement and affection heaped on him by his bosses convinced him that he was a peerless actor who must now conquer Broadway. He was oblivious, as were others who were dazzled by his personality, to his failings as a performer: the reliance on grandiose effects, the use of the voice to overcome flaws in technique, and the tendency to play all out in scenes that called for a more subdued treatment. Yet his virtues were considerable: the domineering and forceful presence, the capacity to imitate men of different ages with the appropriate posture, walk, and physical inflexibility—astonishing in someone who was only sixteen—and above all the electricity and demonic intensity he inherited from the ferocious Orson S. Head along with the strength of will to pulverize anyone who stood in his way. Welles has never acknowledged his great-grandfather as the source of his power; he has never even mentioned him, so deep was his loathing of his grandmother.

In addition to performing, Welles was busy designing and superintending the construction and painting of scenery at the Gate, and he was helping out in other ways at the Peacock, a theater normally used as a studio by the famous Abbey Theater (then on an extensive tour of the United States) but at that time being run by the Gate. Welles said he would stay on in Dublin if Edwards and MacLiammoir cast him as Othello, but they felt that the part of the Moor was beyond his range, and after a violent argument, Welles decided to return to America. He proceeded first to England, but he was unable to work there because of a Ministry of Labour rule against foreign employment at a time when many British actors were out of work. Later he claimed that he had met George Bernard Shaw at Shaw's house at Ayot St. Lawrence and that Shaw, simple and unpretentious, chatted happily with him about early theatrical experiences in Dublin.

In New York, Welles took his clippings and applied to the Shubert management for a part in *The Silent House*. He was brutally rejected, and no agent would handle him; he simply did not have the introductions that were essential in the city, and his success at the Gate apparently meant nothing.

He moved on to Chicago, where he stayed with Dr. Bernstein. But Chicago was filled with unhappy memories: his mother's death at 150 East Superior, his father's death at the Bismarck Hotel, his brother's mental illness (Richard was still languishing in the institution in Kankakee); and perhaps with relief he moved on to Woodstock, to stay with Roger Hill. To fill the time, the two men began work on school acting editions of Shakespeare, and Hill, sensing Welles's disappointment, decided to give him a chance. He had edited *Twelfth Night* for presentation by the Todd Troupers at the forthcoming Chicago Drama Festival competition; he asked Orson to help design the play, to co-direct it, and to appear in it as Malvolio. Adapting an idea originally used by Kenneth MacGowan, Welles with Hill designed an intriguing set consisting of a twelve-foot-high book whose pages turned with the scenes of the play. During the festival, Welles made his first venture in the cinema when he filmed and narrated a portion of the production. The reviews of the performance were encouraging; at least Chicago acknowledged Welles's talent. But there were no offers from theatrical managements of consequence and again Welles, feeling depressed, saw no firm future for himself.

Once more Hill proved to be a deeply sympathetic friend. The two took off for the Chippewa Indian Reservation at Lac du Flambeau in the Wisconsin north woods, and together they wrote a play, *Marching Song*, about John Brown and the freeing of the slaves. The play fascinates as a series of echoes of Welles's slave-aiding ancestors, and it contains significant references to the Underground Railroad. The manuscript begins with a boldly illustrated Welles title page, including an illustration of the drop curtain, and the play moves in a halting, episodic measure that closely resembles a D. W. Griffith film in its stately, pageantlike presentation. The protagonist is the Kansas-based rationalist liberal atheist John Henry Kagi, who attends a meeting to hear

John Brown.* John Brown's son is an echo of Richard Ives Welles at
Kankakee; he is portrayed as crazed, deeply disturbed, an idiot "with a
loose, wet mouth and saucer eyes." There are references to William
Hill Wells's idol, George Washington; a character named Hazlett is
clearly based on Governor Joseph Haslet. Confused and episodic, the
play is a corkscrew journey through Orson's ancestral memories. The
New York producer George C. Tyler liked the play but could not find a
backer; the Gate Theater was not interested.

Returned to Chicago, Welles worked with Hill on the acting editions of *Twelfth Night, Julius Caesar,* and *The Merchant of Venice.*
Welles's introductions gave a biography of Shakespeare and discussed
the correct way to present the plays, emphasizing the humanism of the
author and the necessity of avoiding elaborate stage directions that
Shakespeare had not intended and Welles intensely disliked: the utmost freedom must be found in presenting the plays. These editions
were published in 1934 by the Todd Press and in 1939, in the same
form, by Harper.

With little prospect of work and wondering whether he would ever
appear in a play again, Orson dragged out of Dr. Bernstein a further
advance on his legacy and headed for Europe and North Africa. He
drew scenes for the illustrated acting version of *The Merchant of Venice* in Morocco, turned out stories for pulp magazines, and polished
Marching Song, which was again rejected by everyone to whom it was
submitted. Welles toyed with the idea of writing a comedy about apha-
sia, then abandoned it; in Spain he dabbled in bullfighting, not only as
an aficionado but, according to him (and one doubts it), as a picador.
Years later he showed what he claimed were his scars to an admirer,
the theater critic Kenneth Tynan. Inevitably he ran out of money, and
he returned to the United States in frustration and misery, having destroyed most of the sketches and writings he had done on the trip.

In the fall of 1933, at a party given by a friend of the Hills, Mrs.
Hazel Buchbinder, one of whose sons was at Todd, Welles met the novelist and playwright Thornton Wilder. To Welles's amazement, Wilder
knew all about his career at the Gate. While everyone else seemed to
have ignored or forgotten it, Wilder recollected not only the excellent
reviews in *The New York Times* but also the fact that a friend, the earl
of Longford, patron of the Gate, had written to him admiringly of

---

* William Dagworthy Wells, Orson's great-uncle, was still living in Emporia,
Kansas at the time.

Welles's talent. Wilder whisked Welles away from the party on a round of late-night speakeasies,, and as dawn broke, Wilder scribbled out notes of introduction to friends in New York, all of whom were influential in the theater. One of those friends was the witty columnist and broadcaster Alexander Woollcott, who responded immediately.

Welles went to New York to meet Woollcott. The king of the airwaves was a surprising presence, fat, with a high-pitched voice, and alleged to be impotent. (Asked for a definition of nothing, the actress Margaret Sullavan, noted for her bitchy wit, is said to have replied, "A night with Alexander Woollcott.") Woollcott introduced Welles to another elegant theater figure, Guthrie McClintic, the producer-director husband of Katharine Cornell. The McClintics' marriage was similar to that of Alfred Lunt and Lynn Fontanne, the most imposing husband-and-wife acting team on Broadway at the time; their marriage was not a sexual union but a wedding of like minds and brilliant talents dedicated utterly to the theater. They adroitly combined classics with modern plays, running each production for only a limited time, in repertory with others. These productions, of which Miss Cornell was the distinguished star, were noted for their fastidious elegance, conventional beauty, formal excellence, and severely composed style; they lacked daring, experimentalism, and openness of approach and were by no means avant-garde. The McClintics brought fine works to a large public, achieving through the repertory approach a harmonious balance of the classical and the commercial. As an actress, Katharine Cornell drew her inspiration from the depths of her own character. She would think her way into a part and then play it with fervent commitment in a manner that was not so much theatrical as a frank expression of her own disciplined yet impassioned personality. Dark, attractive, and compelling, she was yet unable to adjust to the more crude demands of the Hollywood screen, and therefore, aside from a tiny moment in *Stage Door Canteen*, she was never seen in movies; thus all visual record of her talent is lost forever.

To be a member of the McClintic-Cornell company was a distinction for an actor. Woollcott was convinced that the bright youth with whom he lunched and dined would fascinate McClintic, and he called Miss Cornell to say, "Undisciplined and inexperienced he may be, but yours is the talent which can mold him."

The McClintics met with Welles at their home on Beekman Place at the end of August 1933. At the time, the McClintics were preparing a national tour of *Romeo and Juliet*, their first venture into Shakespeare; *Candida*, by George Bernard Shaw, one of Miss Cornell's triumphs, to open in Seattle; and *The Barretts of Wimpole Street*,

Rudolph Besier's successful play about the poet Robert Browning and his delicate lover, later his wife, the poet Elizabeth Barrett. Looking at the fiery young man, listening to him read, the McClintics were fascinated and decided almost on the spot to cast him as Mercutio in *Romeo and Juliet*. They also decided to cast him as Octavius, the stuttering brother of Elizabeth Barrett—an oddity in that Orson's brother Richard had always been hampered by a severe stammer. He was also chosen to play Marchbanks, the eager youth who falls in love with Candida, and this was a serious mistake. At eighteen he quite lacked the physical beauty and slender, delicate fragility of Marchbanks, a part that would have been ideal for Leslie Howard or Douglass Montgomery. Welles's lumbering, heavy, flat-footed presence, for all its power in performance, was totally unsuited to that role.

In rehearsal in New York, Welles proved to be persuasive as Mercutio. Mercutio, kinsman of the prince of Verona and friend of Romeo (played by the coldly precise Basil Rathbone), was noted for a tough and bawdy wit, a hot temper, and skepticism at his friend's protestations of romantic love. Welles brought an especially hard edge to his playing, conveying in the Queen Mab speech a remarkable sense of corruption and antiromanticism that suggested a combination of, to quote one critic, "fairy delicacy and sexual disease." The McClintics were delighted with him in the part, and his essential virility and masculinity overcame the lack of physical athleticism that was normally the feature of actors in the role. Despite certain handicaps, through sheer will and desperation he mastered the dueling scenes with his enemy, Tybalt. In the street brawl between the rival clans, and in his death from Tybalt's sword, played with eyes frozen open by some effort of will, Welles performed with a ferocious energy and intensity that no mere athlete could have matched.

He joined the company for the lengthy tour in high spirits, convinced that his chance had come. The tour opened with *Romeo and Juliet* in Buffalo, Cornell's birthplace, on the evening of November 29, 1933. Unfortunately, despite Cornell's glowing and ardent performance as Juliet and McClintic's glossy, handsome production with its sumptuous costumes and sets, the audience response was lukewarm, and the tour was handicapped by public indifference toward the play. By contrast, both *Candida* and *The Barretts* were well received, and the troupe, generally in a good temper, proceeded west on a journey that was to take several months.

Two Pullman cars were hired for the tour and connected to one train after another as they circled the nation. In the company were forty actors, two stage managers, and a crew of carpenters, prop men, stagehands, and electricians; the wives of several of the actors, led by the irrepressible Ouida Rathbone, accompanied them. The baggage included more than a hundred costumes as well as elaborate scenery and stage furniture. The company went first to Los Angeles (Welles's initial visit there), then to Oakland, Sacramento, Salt Lake City (where he was described by one paper as a sea calf, and by another as a moon calf), Cheyenne, San Antonio, Houston, New Orleans, and Savannah. Seventy-five stops were scheduled, of which thirty-eight were one-nighters. It was a tremendous operation, for trucks had to be standing by to carry everything to and from the theater at each stop.

The morale of the company was high. Welles, who shared hotel rooms and a berth on the train with the actor John Hoystradt (later John Hoyt), was in antic spirits for most of the journey. Hoyt remembers that Welles had a tendency to misbehave: he was often late, and once he missed a train and plunged a cash advance from his father's estate into the cost of a private plane to fly to the next stand. This absurdity infuriated Katharine Cornell, who was a stickler for punctuality and hated the slightest sign of obstreperousness or informality in her actors. On one occasion, Welles exasperated Cornell beyond endurance. At the Mark Hopkins Hotel in San Francisco he and another actor dressed up in capes and mustaches and approached the McClintics at their dining room table, heckling them loudly, to the irritation of the other diners. Coldly, Miss Cornell told them to return the clothes to wardrobe and call it a night; the next day, she berated them in her dressing room. After a similar escapade in Indianapolis, Welles sent her a note of abject apology.

> Somebody slaps me in the face, and after the stars have cleared away and I've stopped blubbering, I am made aware of discomforting realities. I see that my boots are rough-shod and that I have been galloping in them over people's sensibilities. I see that I have been assertive and brutal and irreverent, and that the sins of deliberate omission are as nothing to these. This of course is good for me . . . just as the discipline of this tour is good for me. . . .

In Los Angeles he was consistently awkward as Octavius Barrett, and this may explain why he was reluctant to play the part after a certain time. His gaucheries generally began to grate on McClintic, who undoubtedly made up his mind that Welles would be largely dropped from the New York season, which was to take place at the end of the tour. In Cheyenne, Welles learned to his annoyance that *Romeo and*

Juliet, which was doing badly, would be shelved in Cincinnati; when this took place and he could no longer be Mercutio, his interest in the tour drained away.

An incident took place during the seemingly interminable trip around the country. On Christmas Eve 1933 the McClintics threw an elaborate Christmas party for the company, with drinks to celebrate the end of prohibition. They were due in Seattle at 8:00 A.M. the next day, but during the festivities in the parlor car, they were told that the tracks had been washed out. However, Cornell insisted they proceed. As the crews worked to make repairs, the train snailed over a trestle bridge in rain, amid thunder and lightning. Welles and the others, already high on alcohol, stared out into the darkness and watched anxiously as the workmen used acetylene torches on the bridge supports. They wondered every minute whether the structure would give way under the weight of the train.

At last the performers, feeling exhausted, heard the announcement of their arrival in Seattle at forty-five minutes before midnight. To their surprise, they were told that an audience of twelve hundred people was still waiting in the theater for them to appear. Rushed through the storm to the playhouse, they began dressing immediately. Cornell suggested that the audience, as a reward for its loyalty to her, should be accorded the privilege of seeing the stage set of *The Barretts of Wimpole Street* being assembled. Thus the curtain was raised, and while the stagehands placed chairs and tables in position, Guthrie McClintic entertained the crowd with amusing stories. The cast gave its finest performance, and there was a standing ovation when the play came to an end at 4:00 A.M.

Sometimes the players had to act in odd locations: a rodeo arena, a converted church, a theater next door to a basketball court with the referee's whistle interrupting the dialogue, a sandstorm in Amarillo. The noise on the train at night was so severe that sleep was virtually impossible. At the end of the tour Welles received a body blow: he was told that when the repertory opened in New York, he would be dropped from both *Candida* and *The Barretts* and would appear in *Romeo and Juliet* not as Mercutio but as Tybalt. It was a nasty stab of McClintic's; not only was Tybalt the lesser role, he was a villain, a savage enemy of Mercutio.

During the hiatus before the New York opening, Welles decided to embark on an elaborate scheme: a Woodstock repertory season featuring the Todd Players and starring Micheal MacLiammoir and Hilton Edwards, who would be brought from Ireland. It was a typically bold idea of Welles to import the leaders of one of the most distinguished theaters in Ireland to an obscure provincial town. But he was determined to take the gamble that his former employers would enjoy working with him as an equal now that he had made an impression on the Cornell tour. He cabled the two men, asking them to join him for the summer season at the campus in Woodstock, Illinois.

> Three plays running a fortnight each stop Hamlet for Micheal, Tsar Paul for Hilton, something for me so far undecided stop I am trying my hand at production stop Lovely school to live in and small Victorian theater can pay your expenses of course and whatever is going stop now do say yes it will be a kind of holiday and lots of fun stop Love Orson.

MacLiammoir and Edwards had thought of going to America, not to appear in the theater but to tour New Mexico and see the Painted Desert. They had been encouraged by a friend and supporter, Vivian Butler-Burke, who had made financial contributions to their theater. An American of considerable means, born of an Irish-American family and educated in France, Germany, and Italy, Butler-Burke was quite willing to finance MacLiammoir and Edwards in their trip to the United States.

Edwards was somewhat reluctant to embark on the trip to Woodstock, but MacLiammoir thought it would be an exciting adventure. Edwards feared that the trip would mean playing to a lot of stagestruck students in a hick town; he would rather go to Seville and relax. Butler-Burke made up their minds for them. She wanted them to go to New York, and this would be a way of achieving her ambition.

Following their acceptance of his invitation, Welles began to prepare for the season. Roger Hill financed much of it himself and exerted his influence on the Woodstock Chamber of Commerce to assist the venture further. Local press members promised to help. It was decided to add *Trilby* to the season so that Welles could play Svengali, the singer Trilby's impassioned mentor. An echo of the play, along with echoes of Maurice Bernstein's two singer wives, can be found in the scenes in *Citizen Kane* in which the Italian music teacher drives Susan Kane through preparations for her part in grand opera.

On a hot summer morning in 1934, MacLiammoir and Edwards arrived in New York harbor. They were met by Vivian Butler-Burke and Welles, and soon a knot of reporters and photographers had gathered to interview the famous Irish pair. Welles had worked expertly with Butler-Burke to ensure the maximum publicity; there would be a long series of women's club luncheons, Irish society shindigs, radio talks, interviews, and press conferences. Often, to the great delight of Irish-Americans, the two arrivals would talk in Gaelic. Their amusing eccentricities, MacLiammoir's fin-de-siècle charm poised against Edwards's more down-to-earth, twentieth-century pragmatism, created ripples of amusement in everyone who met them. Many who would be offended by the idea of homosexuality were greatly taken with Mac-Liammoir's deliciously extravagant theatrical effeminacy. The whirl of activity was exciting and exhausting, and among the many who welcomed them was the Chicago actor Whitford Kane, who of course gave his name to Orson Welles's later classic.

The Todd School, with its white colonial houses and pillared porticoes, gave a warm welcome to the new arrivals. The heat was so severe that the Irish couple slept on the porch of their cottage, causing ribald comment around the campus. Welles staggered his guests by devouring massive pies and ice cream and, in rehearsal, playing Svengali with a fierce, barbaric humorlessness that they felt was contrary to the wit and style called for by the role. They were more pleased with his Claudius in *Hamlet* and his Count Pahlen in *Tsar Paul* (*Pavel I*), the first part of a trilogy by the neglected, Paris-based White Russian playwright Dmitry Merezhkovsky, who had fled the Soviet Union in 1920.

The season was successful largely because of the influence of John Clayton, a distinguished theatrical figure who advised Welles and Hill to launch the season with a big society party and send invitations to all the leading figures. The result was spectacular coverage in the newspaper columns, and it became the thing to go to Woodstock that summer. Hill kept up the social activities: he gave dinners and even succeeded in luring the influential Claudia Cassidy, a leading Chicago critic whose word was law. She recalls to this day that she was immensely taken with both Welles and his Irish friends and the beauty of the setting at Woodstock, which was so far from her usual haunts. Lloyd Lewis of *The Chicago Daily News* wrote of the season, "Mr. Welles shows remarkable vigor of imagination and dramatic instinct, and with regimentation of his industry he will, I think, go far on the stage" (July 14, 1934). MacLiammoir's *Hamlet* was much admired. Even Welles's Svengali had its adherents.

During the season, Welles slipped away to Kenosha in response to an invitation to a tea party in his honor. Among the guests was his grandmother, the dreaded Mary Head Wells Gottfredsen. It can be imagined what tension existed between them; it cannot have been a very comfortable occasion, for Welles had never desisted from telling people about her black magic practices.

At this time Welles wrote a play, *Bright Lucifer*, set in the north woods of Wisconsin. The characters were W. B. Flynn, editor of the *National Weekly*, known as Bill; his younger brother, Morgan, a tall, dark movie star addressed as Jack; and Bill's ward, Eldred, a boy suffering from hay fever (as Orson Welles did). Bill and Jack are roughing it in the woods, catching fish and enjoying the fresh air. They speak of Eldred's rudeness; Jack hates the boy, regarding him with the contempt that most people in *The Magnificent Ambersons* had for George Minafer. Jack Flynn is also unhappy with his lot as a star of monster films and dreams of returning to Broadway in legitimate theater. There is an Indian reservation nearby—just as there was when Roger Hill and Welles wrote *Marching Song*—and drums sound from the Indian camp, precursors of the drum effects that Welles was to use in his "voodoo" *Macbeth*. (That they are referred to as Devil Drums in the dialogue is another foreshadowing of the later production.)

Eldred emerges; he is a miniature Welles, believing only in himself and his five senses. References to spiritualism and black magic remind us of Welles's grandmother. Jack Flynn resembles John Barrymore; Jack is said to have had a vision of painting his yacht black, which Barrymore did, imitated later by Errol Flynn (years later Flynn was to rent his craft to Welles for *The Lady from Shanghai*). Jack conceives the idea of putting on his horror-movie makeup and terrorizing the Indian camp. Meanwhile, Eldred talks to Bill just as Orson must have talked to Dr. Bernstein. ("You've tried to be just like a father to me, haven't you? . . . I have my mother's eyes, haven't I? I used to wear bangs and we went on little walks together and you taught me the alphabet.") Jack, made up "dark and hairy, the head like a great, crazy, cracking egg, punctured with two blind eyes," and with a mouth full of red, dripping teeth—the ghoul of his Hollywood career—steals the corpse of a squaw from the camp. In the complicated narrative, this has more than a suggestion of necrophilia about it. In an argument with his brother, Jack lies wickedly that Eldred is homosexual. ("There isn't a generation ready for busy little bitch boys!")

As the play wears on, the necrophiliac and homosexual themes emerge more strongly. Jack says, "I was out in the marshes with a dead, naked Indian squaw!—All night—my arms!" Later he echoes Welles's own nightmares as he describes the scene: "The moon out there on the marshes—like a staring eye. A big blind eye in the silence. Silence, my breath screamed in it. My footsteps . . . My own breath—panting—coming up on me like a locomotive. One of those nightmare locomotives that never run you down."

Jack taunts Eldred viciously as a "little bitch." Eldred, with his obsession with hell, darkness, evil, charms, chants, bells, books, and candles, vampires and werewolves, and screaming demons ("These things exist! They are!") seems more and more like Welles himself. In the second half of the play his speeches achieve great forcefulness, unleashing the tormented imagination to which John Houseman has referred and which for Welles made sleep an ordeal—one in which dreams would come, as they did to Macbeth, to trouble sleep. The play becomes paroxysmal in its final pages, perhaps more purely reflecting Welles's disordered subconscious than anything he ever wrote or would have dared to stage. Eldred even makes a toast "to haunt Hitler, Mussolini," thereby unleashing Welles's obsession against fascism. When Jack shoots Eldred in the final scene, the action seems to be the release of a suppressed passion. Clumsy and poorly constructed though it is, this work is indispensable for an understanding of the author's mind.

Welles was pleasantly distracted during the summer season by the presence at Woodstock of the beautiful Virginia Nicolson, daughter of the well-to-do Mr. and Mrs. Leo Nicolson of Wheaton, Illinois, who was understudying Constance Heron in Todd plays. On August 23, 1934, she took over the part of Elizabeth in *Tsar Paul*.

Welles was attracted to her instantly. So far as is known, he had not had a romantic interest in a woman before; his preoccupation with his career and his extreme egomania had rendered him more or less oblivious to women as serious sexual objects or even as human beings. But there was something about Virginia that fascinated him. She had great presence; she had the style that came from a wealthy upbringing. Moreover, she was extremely intelligent and well informed, and she had a fine gift of conversation. He could scarcely fail to be captivated by her. Of course, he was just turned nineteen and she was only eighteen, so their feelings for each other had the fiery intensity of youth. It is probable that their affair began at Woodstock in that late summer of 1934.*

Welles cast Virginia in his next film, *Hearts of Age*, which was shot at Woodstock in the midst of the festival. It was intended to be a spoof of such films as Jean Cocteau's *Blood of a Poet*, and it showed the influence of horror movies, which were then enjoying a vogue: Todd Browning's *Dracula* and James Whale's *Frankenstein* were big hits,

---

* Welles never wrote or spoke about Virginia in public, but in his script for an autobiographical *film à clef*, *The Cradle Will Rock*, he showed her as eager to escape her family, anxious for stage success, using him as "the first train out of town," and possessed of a zealous, tough nature—a most unflattering portrait of his first wife, and one utterly in contradiction to that supplied by all his contemporaries.

providing fantastic horrors that gave people an escape from the actual horrors of the Depression. At the same time, German movies of the silent era, with their emphasis on grotesque makeup, elaborate lighting effects, and somber, moody nighttime confrontations, were popular with intellectuals and college students. *Hearts of Age* was put together on a shoestring; a kind of Halloween frolic, it was never intended to be taken seriously. The film began with a globe spinning in close-up, an old lady (based on Mary Gottfredsen?) in bonnet and shawl sitting on a bell that is being rung by a black man with a blond wig. A ghostly hand beckons from a tomb, and a strange, Caligariesque man takes his top hat off to the old lady, who looks at him with intense anger. The old lady continues to rock in her chair in a parody of Lillian Gish in the film *Intolerance*, and the sinister man shuffles through the tombstones.

This satire on surrealism in the movies, based on German expressionism, may be taken simply as a jeu d'esprit or as an unconscious reflection of the Gothic childhood Welles enjoyed in Kenosha. It also reflects an obsession with death that recurs in all his work, a morbid interest in skulls, graves, and grave inscriptions. The bell is clearly a death knell, and the resemblance to Mary Gottfredsen of the strange old lady who symbolizes age and personal oblivion may not have been intended, but it certainly cannot have been accidental.

With great sadness, coupled with deep appreciation, Welles saw MacLiammoir and Edwards off from New York at the end of the Todd season. Whatever differences they may have had in Ireland were long forgotten. For the rest of their lives—except for a twelve-year hiatus— the two men would be utterly devoted to Welles, even, as it was to turn out, to their own disadvantage. They loved him, were fascinated by him, were sometimes appalled by him, but if need be they would have followed him into hell itself. And so would Virginia Nicolson, who announced to her astonished parents that she was to marry her large and clumsy lover come Christmas, when he would already be launched upon the New York production of the McClintic-Cornell *Romeo and Juliet*.

3

In the new out-of-town season of the Cornell company, and in New York, Welles—to his intense annoyance—was replaced in the role of Mercutio by Brian Aherne, a tall, silky British actor with little more than matinee idol charm and a modicum of acting ability whom Cornell had desperately wanted to play Robert Browning in *The Barretts of Wimpole Street*. As part of the bargain, Aherne had insisted on playing Mercutio as well, and Welles had to take the lesser role of Tybalt. In his memoirs, *A Proper Job*, Aherne writes that he was convinced Orson's savagery in the dueling scene sprang from the intense personal hostility Welles really felt.

Romeo and Juliet opened at the Martin Beck Theater in New York City on December 20, 1934. More sumptuous than ever in the settings of Jo Mielziner, the production delighted the society audience, and next day Brooks Atkinson, supreme arbiter of theater at *The New York Times*, wrote:

> Miss Cornell has hung another jewel on the cheek of the theater's nights. . . . *Romeo and Juliet* . . . is on the high plane of modern magnificence. Probably no one expected anything less radiant from her resourceful workshops, where she and Guthrie McClintic prepared the dramas for her repertory. But the result is no less exalting to those who sit before the footlights, listen to the lines of Shakespeare's verse on the lips of modern actors and reflect the glow of Jo Mielziner's costumes and settings.

Welles could take pleasure in Atkinson's reservations over Brian Aherne. ("He carries his exuberance to the point of scattering the character, and he speaks the Queen Mab lines in a casual style that loses the fancy of Shakespeare's verse.") By contrast, Atkinson cited Welles's Tybalt as an instance of a minor part played with something better than minor authority. Even his misspelling of Orson as Orsen could not detract from the pleasure of the review. The company celebrated happily, and Welles's misbehavior on the tour was quickly forgotten.

His joy was increased; he and Virginia Nicolson were married in a candlelit afternoon ceremony on December 23, 1934, at the home of her godparents, Mr. and Mrs. Herbert S. Gay, in Llewellyn Park, near East Orange, New Jersey. Dr. Bernstein was the best man, and the bridesmaid was Virginia's sister Carryl. The minister, Reverend Burns, was the co-author of *I Am a Fugitive from a Chain Gang*. The couple stayed in a modest home in Bronxville and commuted into New York.

John Houseman told me the couple were very much in love, and the inscription on their joint Christmas cards of the time confirm this—but Welles seeks to give a very different impression in his script of *The Cradle Will Rock*.

Among those who came to admire Welles's performance as Tybalt was a plump, sober, and accomplished director named John Houseman. Born in Romania in 1902, of a Jewish-Alsatian father and a British mother of Welsh-Irish descent, he had had an erratic education that included a period in England as a day boy at Clifton Preparatory School. Shortly after the month of Orson Welles's birth he made his first trip to the United States, where his father was serving as head of a French purchasing commission. His international background and cosmopolitan education served him well; he emerged in his young manhood as a person of great intelligence, taste, and learning, and he hated the world of trade into which he had been born as much as Welles did. Trapped in the depressing offices of the Continental Grain Corporation at 1 Broadway, he tried unsuccessfully to write at night. Interestingly, when he was in Chicago in the mid-1920s, Welles was there; in his memoir *Run-Through*, Houseman wrote of his fascination with the homes of Lake Shore Drive, where Mrs. Edith Rockefeller McCormick was then giving the musical soirees that the young Orson attended.

For two and a half years Houseman traveled across the continent on behalf of his company, succeeding in the grain export business and making deals with remarkable expertise. He also fell in love with the actress Zita Johann, who appeared with a very young Clark Gable in the play *Nachinal*. Houseman married Johann in 1929, and through her he made his first major theatrical contacts and began writing or collaborating on plays; meanwhile, Johann appeared in the fading D. W. Griffith's last film, the unsuccessful *The Struggle*. The couple went to Hollywood, where Johann appeared in *Tiger Shark* with Richard Arlen and Edward G. Robinson. Houseman embarked on a brilliant career with his admirable production of *Four Saints in Three Acts*, the opera by Gertrude Stein and Virgil Thomson (who was to be a lifelong friend).

When Houseman saw *Romeo and Juliet* on its opening night, one actor in the cast made a real impression on him. His infallible gift for recognizing major talent, a gift that would serve him well throughout his life, had him riveted by the appearance of the furious Tybalt. In *Run-Through* Houseman describes Welles's presence.

Death, in scarlet and black, in the form of a monstrous boy— flat-footed and graceless, yet swift and agile; soft as jelly one moment and uncoiled, the next, in a spring of such furious en- ergy that, once released, it could be checked by no human in- tervention. What made this figure so obscene and terrible was the pale, shiny child's face under the unnatural growth of dark beard, from which there issued a voice of such clarity and power that it tore like a high wind through the genteel, modu- lated voice of the well-trained professionals around him.

This extraordinary reaction, quite untypical of Houseman, was sim- ilar to that of many other people on first seeing Welles in performance. Like so many of his contemporaries, Houseman felt that night a mix- ture of fear and excitement that comes only from encountering the force and character of genius. It was not a vision of smoothness or pol- ished professionalism that Houseman saw, but a vision of a talent in the rough, dangerous, with a cutting edge and emitting an unnerving fire. For him Welles was a frightening gust of wind in the stately halls of the Cornell production. Houseman had a compulsion, equivalent to a de- sire for a woman, to work with this man.

He soon found his opportunity. The poet, playwright, and editor Archibald MacLeish, who had won the 1933 Pulitzer Prize for poetry, had written a play that reflected his concern with the economic situa- tion that had helped precipitate the Wall Street crash. *Panic*, an ex- perimental play composed in a spare free verse, shows how destiny destroys the bold and optimistic banker McGafferty. At the outset McGafferty is certain of finding a solution to the economic problems that plague the nation; then a group of jobless men burst into his of- fices, and a blind prophet in their midst condemns him to a nameless terror. He is destroyed by this onset of the mob and its symbolic leader. The poet believed that the fall of American industry was due to super- natural forces beyond the control of any commercial tycoon, and with great passion and intensity he conveyed his fantasy in the mode of sprung rhythm, the lines muscular, taut, and powerful to a degree.

The play was very short and uncommercial; to many it seemed pretentious, forced, and unconvincing in its thesis of the workings of fate. Oddly, although Houseman had not envisaged producing the play, he found an item in the Sunday theater section of *The New York Times* stating that MacLeish had given the play to Nathan Zatkin (Houseman's partner) and himself for their new Phoenix Theater. MacLeish was annoyed by this premature announcement; however, unable to find interest on the part of the Theater Guild, Jed Harris, or the Theater Union among others, MacLeish decided to make *The New York Times*'s fantasy a reality. He took Houseman to lunch and handed him the script. Houseman was fascinated by the challenge of presenting a play that no one else seemed to be able to get off the ground.

Houseman and Zatkin raised $500, had a telephone installed in their shabby office, and set up as the Phoenix Theater, a pretentious name for a tiny operation. Now the question was who could play McGafferty? It was a tremendous part for an actor. Edward G. Robinson and John Barrymore were committed to Hollywood contracts; Paul Muni was offered the part, but his wife, who ruled him with an iron hand, did not like the play and turned it down. Luckily, Houseman remembered that Welles had played an American millionaire at the Gate in *The Dead Ride Fast*. Bribing the doorman at the Martin Beck Theater to take him to Orson's dressing room, he found Welles stripped to the waist and seated, stomach protruding even at that age, before his mirror, surrounded by scattered sheets of paper containing scrawled notes and drawings for a play about the Devil. He agreed to meet Houseman in a bar across the street. Later they walked to Grand Central Station, where Welles left for Bronxville with the play under his arm.

He and Virginia read *Panic* that night and liked it immensely. Welles's political sympathies, already emerging clearly, were far removed from the Republican leanings of Dr. Bernstein, with whom he was still constantly in touch. Welles was a liberal, greatly influenced by such journalists as George Seldes and I. F. Stone; he believed that the rich were corrupt, evil, and destructive; his views were of the sort that the right wing would have dubbed Communist. Yet he believed in free enterprise, he was purposefully opposed to tyranny, and he was strongly critical not only of the Rockefellers and Morgans but of the rising figures of Mussolini and Hitler in Italy and Germany, whose appeasement by the free world infuriated and maddened him. Thus *Panic*, written from the left of center, was a play that appealed to him on a deep personal level, and of course McGafferty was first cousin to the millionaire in *The Dead Ride Fast*. He asked to act the part and said he would break with the Cornell company if he could play it.

The following day he and Virginia visited Houseman's dismal office. At first MacLeish was unimpressed with him, hardly able to believe that this huge, nineteen-year-old bumpkin could play his fifty-five-year-old tycoon protagonist. But Houseman had no doubts. He asked Welles to read McGafferty's final speech of desperation and terror, and the youth delivered it superbly. Then Welles read the play through, taking every part, before he rushed off with Virginia to make the Wednesday matinee of *Romeo and Juliet*.

Welles did indeed leave *Romeo* for the starring part in *Panic*, even though—and this says much for his boldness—it could play for only three nights because of its uncommercial nature. With equal audacity, Houseman hired Jo Mielziner to design the play's set, an environment far removed from the opulence of the *Romeo and Juliet* mise-en-scène. The *Panic* set was not much more than a platform and a pit running upstage, with beams of light shooting out from the air (an idea borrowed ironically from Hitler's midnight rallies), all executed with flair by Mielziner. The great Martha Graham came in to direct the choruses, and Virgil Thomson provided the sound effects of a telegraph key and a metronome. Divorced now from Houseman, Zita Johann joined the cast, which also included Russell Collins, later to be a member of Welles's stock company.

James Light directed the intimate scenes, Martha Graham the mass street scenes, and Houseman produced and promoted the production. Welles threw himself with his customary intensity into the show. Where he had been uneasy about playing Octavius Barrett, known he was unsuitable as Marchbanks, and doubted the perfect casting of himself as Mercutio, Welles seized upon the part of McGafferty with hammy relish. The role provided yet another basis for *Citizen Kane*, and much of Welles's interpretation carried over to the later performance. Perhaps because he was newly married, perhaps because he was grateful to Houseman for making him a star, he behaved with a discipline, a punctuality, and a considerateness during the preparations for *Panic* that he had seldom shown before and would almost never show again.

Since *Panic* was designed for specialized audiences and would be performed for three nights only, there was no necessity for compromise in presenting it. Its topical significance did not escape the attention of the critics who reviewed it—favorably. There had been word of Hitler's rise to power, and already it was clear that the Western world was going to hand the German leader whatever he wanted. Moreover, in the depths of the Depression, the Ford factories saw riot squads armed with hoses suppressing union outbreaks, and company unions, labor organizations that had sold out to capital, were frequent. Malcontents were joining the German-American Bund and the Communist party, seeking some form of identity through manifestations of quasi militarism. Welles's decision to appear in the play thus sprang from a very real sense of its importance and was a full expression of his political position.

The first night of *Panic* was held for subscribers to the Phoenix Theater, which was formed for both tax and financing purposes as a kind of club. The second performance, on March 15, 1935, was open to the public, which was charged the extraordinary sum for those days of $5.50 a seat. It was largely a society audience, one that—as might have been predicted—hated the show, not only because an intrinsic philistinism reacted against the free verse, but because the audience itself was being pilloried by the work. In fact there were murmurs of "communism" and "agitprop" as people left the theater, and many booed and hissed the play at the final curtain.

Among those in the audience who resented this expected harsh response (which can only have delighted the iconoclastic Orson Welles) was Brooks Atkinson, who praised the play for its "terse beauty" and admired Welles's performance under the "crisp and forceful" direction of James Light. However, he pointed to one failing in the play: that it was fate, not an intrinsic blind greed and extravagance, that brought about the collapse of industry. He put his finger on the fact (without quite saying so) that Archibald MacLeish had weakened just when he should have struck home in protest against oppression.

The third night was booked by *New Times*, a magazine with Communist leanings devoted to the struggle against fascism. Every seat was sold, and the audience of left-wingers was thrilled by the frankness of the play. The presence of a sympathetic audience seemed to galvanize Welles and the others to a fury of dedicated playing. After the performance there was a lengthy debate and discussion featuring the playwright and screenwriter John Howard Lawson, an intellectual of wayward gifts, Stanley Burnshaw, and V. J. Jerome. Although MacLeish was not a Communist but, like Welles, a liberal of true American stamp, it was clear that these leaders of the Communist ranks wanted to enlist the poet and playwright permanently in the service of Moscow. Finally, after lengthy speeches by these combative figures, followed by loud applause and cheering, MacLeish appeared on stage, quietly and with agreeable seriousness thanking his collaborators. The evening ended in a glow of exhausted mutual admiration; it had been one of the great occasions of the American theater, an event unthinkable in the present-day political emasculation of Broadway and so daring even for its own time that it lost $3,500.

In the wake of the three glorious nights of experiment and adventure, Welles and Virginia, still in the first flush of their marriage, moved from Bronxville into Manhattan with their dog Budget, first to a room on Riverside Drive and later to West Fourteenth Street. So cramped were their quarters on Riverside Drive that the huge Victorian bath, equipped with claw feet and a dribble of rust under the taps, was housed in the living room and had to be turned into a bed at night, for the landlord had not supplied even the modest comfort of a Murphy bed. Grown heavier, with his odd, preadolescent face bubbling with eunuchoid baby fat, Welles at twenty already showed folds of flesh around his middle and on his arms and legs. He would spend hours soaking in a hot tub, making notes on sheets of paper that were scattered around his wooden bath rest with its traditional 1930s equipment of soap and loofah. With John Houseman during that spring of 1935, often using a suite on Forty-fourth Street that had housed the Mendelssohn Society of America, he began laying plans. The two men thought of doing Christopher Marlowe's *The Tragical History of Doctor Faustus* but finally decided upon John Ford's *'Tis Pity She's a Whore*, a bawdy and erotic melodrama with comic aspects that intrigued and amused both men.

Seated in his bathtub while Virginia fetched numerous cups of coffee, Welles, with his usual impatient brilliance, drew sketches for the production; actors were being roped in at the Forty-fourth Street offices, where they went when everybody else had turned them down. To fill the time and to lay down the basis of the production, the out-of-work performers began to rehearse a project for which no funds had been raised or were in prospect. Welles cast the popular Hiram ("Chubby") Sherman in the important part of Poggio, a clownish victim of a stabbing.[*]

The producer and director located a theater, the Bijou on Forty-fifth Street, which was available for a song because it had been dark for many seasons. An eccentric old lady was found as an "angel" for the production, but it turned out that she was more interested in restoring the theater than in supporting the play, and the project collapsed. For a time that summer Welles was idle, filled with dreams that had little

---

[*] Welles had known Sherman in Chicago, where Sherman became the intimate friend and colleague of Welles's acquaintance, the actor-producer Whitford Kane.

chance of realization and certainly not beseiged by offers of work. One event relieved the almost uniform flatness of 1935: Welles hired as secretary, and later business manager, a remarkable woman named Augusta Weissberger. Her brother was a dandyish, skillful, agile, mentally quick, and polished gentleman attorney, Arnold Weissberger, who then worked for a Wall Street law firm. Welles was trying to obtain the release of the last portion of his estate, which had been drained by Dr. Bernstein, and from which Richard Welles, who was stuggling to free himself from Kankakee through successive writs of habeas corpus, was drawing small sums to pay for cheap clothing. Welles told Augusta he would be grateful if she mentioned him to her brother. She did, and in the following year Welles became Weissberger's client.

While Welles trod water professionally, events were taking place that would lead him to a major career as a theatrical director and actor. President Franklin D. Roosevelt's Works Progress Administration head, Harry Hopkins, who was dedicated to finding employment for the talented during the Depression, wanted to set up a Federal Theater Project that would engage the services of out-of-work actors. Hopkins approached the determined and feisty little Hallie Flanagan, who had been head of Vassar's Experimental Theater since 1925, and asked her to take on the project.

She sought advice from Frank Gillmore, president of Actors' Equity; Dr. Henry Moskowitz, president of the League of New York Theaters; Theresa Helburn of the Theater Guild; Cheryl Crawford of the Group Theater; and the playwright Elmer Rice. Only Rice responded.

Armed with Rice's support, and given more or less carte blanche by Hopkins, Flanagan plunged into her work with great energy and drive. She secured Washington-sponsored theatrical presentations that not only would give employment to performers but would bring theater to people in regions that might otherwise never be aware of it. By the late summer of 1935, following the National Theater Conference at the University of Iowa, she was hard at work carrying out government orders, preparing estimates, figuring a budget, and fielding the many problems presented by the WPA. She wanted to have rotating companies in the New York boroughs as well as an experimental theater, and she sponsored plays through many provincial cities. It was an audacious scheme, unprecedented in American history, and her boldest stroke was to defy national racism and set up the Negro Theater Project of the WPA, drawing from the vast reservoir of black talent, centering its activities in the heart of Harlem, and openly defying those who would deny even minimal employment to what were then called colored people.

With Harry Hopkins's blessing, Hallie Flanagan declared that there would be jobs for several hundred performers and theater personnel, thus ensuring substantial employment for blacks who would normally be relegated to manual labor. (Her plan ran into violent opposition, which she discusses vividly in her memoir, *Arena*.) Encouraged by Edith Isaacs and Rosamond Gilder, editors of the distinguished magazine *Theater Arts Monthly*, John Houseman came in, and, with the actress Rose MacLendon, became joint head of the Negro Theater Project. Embarking on the task of putting the program together, he enlisted the support of Augusta Weissberger and her brother. In October the Negro Theater Project moved into the Lafayette Theater on Seventh Avenue in Harlem, a long-abandoned playhouse overrun with cockroaches and rats. Thrilled with the chance to be doing something challenging, the powerful and dauntless black stage crews worked around the clock to modernize and enhance the theater, while hundreds of others began dance practice or musical preparations with energy and dedication. Houseman ran the operation like a Napoleonic general, lacking only a tricorne to complete the image. Everything Welles heard about the project excited him, and he longed to be part of it. When Houseman reopened the Lafayette with his striking production of Frank Wilson's *Walk Together Chillun!* on February 5, 1936, Welles's desire to work in the black theater consumed him.

He had long been mesmerized by Shakespeare's *Macbeth*, in part because the play was so complete an expression of the dangers of power and the ruinous effects of corruption and evil; these themes, visible in the Head family, obsessed him and filled his nightmares. Once again his having been raised in a family devoted to the acquisition of wealth, power, and importance, while exposed to his mother's interest in art and literature, inspired him in his projects. Virginia was seized with the idea of making a voodoo version of *Macbeth*, based on the character and career of Henri Christophe, king of Haiti, who had set up his court of Sans Souci in the mountains of the tropical island. With Budget barking and jumping on them, the couple enthusiastically unraveled their approach to the classic drama.

The court of Henri Christophe was conducted with wild extravagance in a grotesque parody of the court of Louis XVI. The courtiers and their ladies, dubbed with such titles as the Duke of Marmalade or the Duchess of Raspberry Jam, dressed in multicolored finery—huge, toppling wigs and jewel-encrusted hoopskirts and bodices or cutaway coats and breeches. By 1935 Sans Souci and the Citadel that towered above it on the tallest mountain of Haiti were ruins, later to be immortalized in Rose Macaulay's book *The Pleasure of Ruins.* Vines thick as a man's arm burst through cracks in the marble floor of Sans Souci, embracing the mirrors with their green tendrils; bats flitted through the shattered roof, and not even an echo of a ghostly waltz remained to suggest the elaborate parties that had once been held in the deserted marble halls. And the Citadel was haunted by a single powerful poetic image: there was a legend that when Henri Christophe was killed and thrown into a lime pit, his black hand stuck out of the lime and pointed accusingly at his killers, resisting all efforts to force it under. Given Welles's love of the exotic, his fascination with black magic, and perhaps his memory of his grandmother's practices, it is not surprising that Welles expanded on Virginia's idea to visualize a setting transferred from blasted heath to fetid jungle, ready to explode with the diabolical fury of a voodoo ritual.

Preparations began at the start of 1936. Virgil Thomson, commissioned to compose the music, set about creating a symphonic background that would effectively incorporate voodoo drums; he studied the thudding heartbeat of the drums, which created their own language, conveying across miles of jungle or tropical forest messages in bush telegraph that were subtle, intricate, and powerful. The intent from the outset was to make *Macbeth* an experience of Total Theater, incorporating every conceivable form of black music and drama into its structure. Asadata Dafora Horton, the choreographer and coordinator, assembled a troupe of actors, dancers, and drummers from Africa, led by a witch doctor named Abdul. They fascinated Welles and enthusiastically played up to him, filling his ears with an exciting babel of voices. Hating the Uncle Remus and mammy images of screen and theater, Welles was delighted to be giving these striking performers an opportunity to work. The irony of the fact that they were portraying evil—in essence, exploiting the most destructive elements in their culture—for the benefit of white audiences seems not to have occurred to anyone connected with the production.

Welles insisted on calling Abdul "Jazbo." When Abdul asked for twelve live goats, he had visions of the animals' being sacrificed on stage and was relieved when Abdul explained that he needed goatskins to fashion new drums. The Federal Theater Project had to contend with a great deal of red tape before the goats could be supplied, killed, and turned into musical instruments.

The *Macbeth* company and stage crew numbered almost 150 people. Welles, involved in his most ambitious venture yet and grounded always by the sober intelligence of Houseman, whipped the disparate group into shape through sheer insane energy, dreaming visions that his often maddened but more frequently captivated army of blacks did their utmost to fulfill. The leader of the company was the amazing Jack Carter, a superbly built mulatto almost six feet, five inches tall and two hundred pounds of brawn and muscle. Violent, fierce, and unbridled, a part-time gangster, he could take on anybody with his fists, and he was said to be able, when sober, to shoot a hole through a dime at thirty paces.

Welles knew that if anybody was to be crossed it was not Jack Carter; he must flatter him, cajole him, control him with seeming invisibility, making Carter's megalomaniac decisions always seem to be the actor's own. Because Welles himself feasted on flattery, because his own ego was already colossal in the wake of his success in *Panic,* he understood exactly what was needed to feed the fires of genius. He knew that a dangerous insecurity underlay the personality of his actor-criminal and drove him to drink excessively, brawl exhaustingly, and make love to a variety of steamy and available women with untrammeled fury. Carter had the personality, the presence, the dynamic energy needed to play Macbeth; stripped to the waist, he looked like a Greek god cast in black marble; dressed in Napoleonic uniform, he was a surrogate Henri Christophe. And if his command of the verse erred into roughness, if musicality was lacking, he more than compensated for these faults by the elemental force with which he delivered Shakespeare's lines. Whenever the company quailed before the all-night schedules, whenever an almost voiceless Welles, collapsing from lack of sleep, wanted the company to continue when it was not prepared to do so, Jack Carter would scream and break up the furniture until everyone fell into line. His devotion to Welles was extraordinary; indeed, much to Virginia's dismay, Carter and Welles would disappear from the theater well after midnight, on mysterious journeys that gossip concurred led them into brothels and bars of a highly suspicious character, where they supposedly drank and whored until dawn.

By the time the opening date of *Macbeth* was announced—April 14, 1936—the black community of Harlem was in a frenzy of excitement. Never mind that a black was being shown as a murderer and his wife an inciter to deadly crime; no matter that the show falsely emphasized certain mythic undercurrents of African and Caribbean culture; no matter that actual witch doctors and voodoo drummers would appear on stage. The fact was that blacks would be seen in Shakespeare for the first time, that blacks were working with two of the more prestigious new figures of the American theater, and it would be demonstrated that blacks could rise to the heights of cultural achievement. With his genius for publicity, Welles made sure that Harlem was splashed with garish posters announcing *Macbeth*. As the first night approached, he began a series of violent last-minute corrections, improvements, cuts, and transpositions that effectively changed the structure of the work and galvanized and transformed those performers who were showing weakness or verbal obscurity. Dashed off at white heat, his rehearsal notes betray a thunderous force at work, complaining, haranguing, almost screaming with untrammeled energy: "What, for Christ's sake, has happened to Ross? Tommy, take the emotion out of your voice . . . Jack should be further back on ramp . . . Cripples should have entered after he starts downstairs . . . Choir stinks."

Advance bookings were so heavy that virtually every seat for the first night was sold, and ticket scalpers roamed Harlem offering house seats at exorbitant figures. Welles and his publicity assistants coordinated the opening with an already planned mass demonstration against Italy's invasion of the kingdom of Ethiopia in Africa, an inspired gimmick that paid off. An entire black Elks band, dressed in vivid, garish uniforms of scarlet, blue, and gold, was hired to march through the streets as night fell, carrying flags announcing the play. The eighty-five performers, blaring away at their trumpets and banging away at their drums, were almost mobbed by about ten thousand people who crammed the streets as the police fought to rope off four city blocks. The audience, dressed in white tie and tails and silk gowns and ermine wraps and led by many fashionable figures who were making their first journey into Harlem, had to struggle through hundreds of fanatical people to reach their seats (the top price of which was fifty-five cents).

The hubbub in the theater before the curtain rose was indescribable. Backstage the players were beside themselves with excitement and could hardly wait to perform. Even the critics, led by Brooks Atkinson, felt the tension of suspense as Virgil Thomson's glowering, sinister music, combining voodoo rhythms with waltzes, burst from the orchestra assembled in the pit below the stage. Orson Welles's notes for the lighting and staging of *Macbeth* still exist. The stage was dark and the house lights turned off as the play began, then out of the darkness came a low roll of thunder drums, followed by a rain drum, then silence as the act drop was raised. A voodoo chant began; lights sneaked up on the jungle scene; the voodoo chant faded, and a vocal solo was the cue for a cellophane rain effect.

In the opening scene Macbeth and Banquo made their way through a tropical forest to be greeted, not by long-haired witches stirring a pot, but by an array of warlocks and voodoo acolytes whirling around the composite figure of Hecate, seen here as a voodoo priest. A tower, a bridge, a gateway all evoked the atmosphere of the Citadel, and the thunder and lightning suggested a storm in the Haitian mountains. In the many telescopings and truncatings of the Shakespeare text, Macbeth was seen to be driven by fate, haunted by images of black magic; Hecate was in effect a demon, cursing Macbeth to his doom. Again and again the director emphasized the corruptions of power; the atmosphere of thunder, lightning, jungle, mountain, and witchcraft evoked a world in which everything was saturated with evil. Nat Karson's angular and abstracted sets at times suggested Gordon Craig, at times Erwin Piscator; due to Welles's efforts, the lighting by the hard-driven Abe Feder evoked a range of textures, moods, and colors from dawn to darkest night.

The performances were riveting: Jack Carter, Edna Thomas as Lady Macbeth, Eric Burroughs as Hecate, and the ex-boxer Canada Lee as a cigar-puffing Banquo. Canada Lee in particular was a find, the ghost scene among the most powerful in the production. Welles's screaming and yelling, the clangor and conflict of the rehearsals, all paid off on that night of nights. And so did Thomson's score, with its fanfares and drums blending with the sound of thunder and driving wind.

The reviews were generally strong. Brooks Atkinson wrote that the first witches' scene was "logical and stunning and a triumph of the theater art"; though he had reservations about the tone and tenor of the approach to verse drama, he responded vibrantly to the excitement of the evening. A dissenting voice was that of Percy Hammond in *The New York Herald Tribune*, who wrote of "the inability of so noble a race to sing the music of Shakespeare." In an odd and inexplicable lapse from his normally refined seriousness, John Houseman in his memoir seems whimsically to attribute the death of Hammond from viral pneumonia that season to a voodoo curse put upon him by Asadata, Abdul, and the other members of the African players. (Hammond was ailing before the production began.)

Macbeth had a successful run of ten weeks at the Lafayette, then moved to the Adelphi on Fifty-fourth Street. Following the move to Broadway Jack Carter began to fall apart; he drank more and more heavily and suddenly, without warning, left the Adelphi and the play permanently during an intermission. The stage manager, Tommy Anderson, took over the part of Macbeth to complete the performance, and the audience responded gallantly. At later performances Welles and Houseman made drastically improvised explanations to the audience. Welles himself played Macbeth in blackface in Indianapolis when the actor who had taken over the role fell ill.

The huge success of the "voodoo" *Macbeth* unequivocally launched

Welles as a major figure of the theater. The production dazzled, shocked, and excited New York as few productions had done. Where most Broadway plays were stylish, handsome, and elegant, this *Macbeth* was crude, raw, bold, and fearless in its attack. As Welles celebrated his twenty-first birthday with Virginia on May 15, 1936, he could scarcely have been blamed if his ego was colossally inflated. He was on fire now with his own talent; he was ablaze with peerless ambition.

Welles and Houseman decided to give up the black theater and start a so-called Classical Theater, using the grand old Maxine Elliott Theater that had once housed Jeanne Eagels's astonishing performance in *Rain* by Somerset Maugham. The office was set up in a converted powder room in the basement, and with the reliable Augusta Weissberger in attendance, Welles and Houseman operated on a round-the-clock schedule. Welles took the studio dressing room.

In addition to basking in the glory of *Macbeth*'s success, Welles was making his first mark in radio in the series *The March of Time.* He would soon emerge as Lamont Cranston, the mysterious hero of *The Shadow*, a popular drama series produced by Irving Reis; Cranston, gifted with the power to make himself invisible (easy enough to suggest in an aural medium), defeated all manner of sinister villainy on land, on sea, and in the air, accompanying his victories with unnervingly hollow laughter and booming, overtly campy comment. The rest of the cast was encouraged to compete with him in sheer, unadulterated hamminess, acting all out with crude and vigorous emphasis. Welles's love of vaudeville, of burlesque, served him well in *The Shadow*'s absurd situations, and this cheerful hackwork constantly fed, with money, his more elevated projects.

The new classical producing unit at the Maxine Elliott Theater became known as Project 891, embodying the same principles as the experimental theater units of the Federal Theater Project. Fifty-five cents would again be top of the scale in ticket prices, and young people could once more experience living theater for the first time. Experiment would be the order of the day; there would be no restriction on the daring and inventiveness with which the two main partners would plunge into their ventures. To the already vigorous group that included Abe Feder and Nat Karson, Houseman now added a manic child, the tiny, quiveringly intense Jean Rosenthal, a lighting expert who at twenty-one matched not only Welles's age but his talent for using light like a painter and making it an intrinsic part of the production, as Stanislavsky or Craig had done. The partners' first choice for production was *The Italian Straw Hat*, which had been filmed at the end of the silent film era by one of Welles's favorite directors, the Parisian wit René Clair. Written purely to amuse, the play had been put together by the popular dramatist Eugène Marin Labiche in 1851, when it enjoyed a lengthy run and a successful tour of France. W. S. Gilbert, of Gilbert and Sullivan, adapted it into English in 1873 with equally great success and later rewrote it as an operetta with music by George Grossmith. Since then, except for the film version, the play had lain in limbo; when Welles and Houseman rediscovered it after forty years, the farce was long overdue for revival.

The story concerns a youth who rides horseback on his wedding morning; the horse takes a fancy to an Italian straw hat and eats it. The owner of the hat is upset, her lover demands that the youth replace the ornament, and at the wedding party everybody chases the horse. When it is discovered that an exact copy of the hat exists, wedding guests, bride, and groom begin another chase, and the complications are endless until finally a third hat is discovered. The plot made no sense at all; it is clear that Welles and Houseman, looking for a change of pace, saw the work as a surrealist farce. They engaged the playwright Edwin Denby to help adapt it, and Virgil Thomson was asked to arrange the music to be composed by Paul Bowles. Welles would direct and play the part of the bride's father. He worked out the decor and costumes in antic colors and styles, deciding that a frantic pace like that of the Keystone Kops silent film comedies would be ideal. Labiche's text vanished in a mass of effects and situations; the music was extremely elaborate and called for a thirty-three-piece orchestra, a piano in the stage boxes, a pianola player, a gypsy orchestra, and a lady who tootled on a trumpet. Virginia Welles was the bride, Joseph Cotten the frenzied bridegroom, and Arlene Francis the milliner Tillie; the players were encouraged to act in the manner of the flickering images of early movie comedies. Unfortunately, the emphasis on constant action, movement, and excitement backfired.

Meanwhile, John Houseman, always valuable as a mooring rope for Welles's ballooning talent, was distracted by preparations for a production of *Hamlet* with Leslie Howard, and he went to California to discuss the production while Howard was shooting *Romeo and Juliet* with Norma Shearer. He also had to go to Canada in order to be readmitted to the United States under a special quota. Held up unconscionably in Toronto, he wondered whether he had a future; the Federal Theater Project people, working energetically to secure his immigration, maintained in their persistent applications that they were giving him unusual privileges in terms of his elevation to a special salary and an executive role in the project. At the beginning of September he was finally able to return to New York as a resident alien, and by then Welles was completely out of control. The production had become increasingly complicated, meaningless, and extreme; the playwright sportingly took to playing one-half of the horse, spending rehearsals (and later, performances) grubbing along uncomfortably on his knees.

Evidently *Horse Eats Hat*, which opened on September 26, 1936, was unworthy of the talents of those connected with it and was as irritating as it was amusing. The frenzied pace wearied cast and audience alike, though there were those who believed in the production; just enough people enjoyed it—some of them returned again and again—to keep the play running until December 5. Brooks Atkinson summed up the evening: "It was as though Gertrude Stein had dreamed a dream after a late supper of pickles and ice cream, the ensuing revelations being crisply acted by giants and midgets, caricatures, lunatics and a prop nag." Not much more needed to be said, and it was years before the play was revived again.

Horse Eats Hat offered its tireless producer, director, and co-adaptor a number of major problems. In the midst of it he somehow managed to segue over to the St. James Theater to appear in a short-lived production of Sidney Kingsley's *Ten Million Ghosts* as an airman who protested the international arms traffic and directed his fury at a figure not dissimilar to Sir Basil Zaharoff, who would later be the subject of Welles's film *Mr. Arkadin*. It was a play very much after Orson's heart, for it illustrated his obsessive concern with the brutal and thoughtless exploitation of the masses by the armaments manufacturers. That he should have wished to embody the opinion of the left liberals on this particular form of exploitation was again characteristic of him; so was his reckless decision to leave his own production and the major role he was playing in it in order to embark upon this ambitious and extravagant venture. He even subsumed his own ego by allowing another actor to take his part in *Horse Eats Hat*, and he fielded the complaints of Houseman in the matter. Houseman himself broke the sacred bonds of the alliance by taking off to direct Leslie Howard at last in a production of *Hamlet*.

Ten Million Ghosts was a catastrophe. The scenery, built elsewhere, could not be fitted into the St. James Theater, and the September opening was delayed; the premiere finally took place on October 23, 1936, following a radical series of adjustments in settings and the staging. The presentation involved a device that Welles used later in *Citizen Kane*: at the end of the second act the armaments dealers were seen in a private theater, watching newsreels showing the butchery of American and British youth on the battlefronts of World War I. At the moment of the greatest horror, Welles, playing the airman André Pequot, suddenly stood up and, silhouetted against the flickering images on the screen, denounced the munitions men. They in turn stood and cried, "This is our business!"

The production suffered the fate of most revisionist history on the American stage. Despite respectful reviews by Brooks Atkinson and other critics, there was no advance sale and the play closed after one night. Welles promptly returned to *Horse Eats Hat*.

Welles's marriage, not quite two years old, was running into difficulties. It was impossible for Welles to sustain a relationship with anyone; even though he had given her a small part in *Horse Eats Hat*, Virginia felt threatened day and night by the innumerable demands on his attention. She saw little of him while he was involved with *Ten Million Ghosts* and distracted by the endless pressure of broadcasts and discussions on other productions. At one stage he was going to Chicago once a week to do a broadcast. Incredibly, his energy and health more or less held up—after all, he was only twenty-one—and his ego, fiery and uncontrollable, devoured everything in his path.

The Spanish Civil War was a dominant element in Welles's life at the time, as it was for all liberals of his era; he was to reflect an interest in it in the character of Michael, the sailor in *The Lady from Shanghai* who had fought for the liberal cause, and he constantly pleaded with Washington to give arms to the Stalin-supported Loyalists and not to the Hitler-backed Francoists.

Dogged by bad reviews and unpopular with the Federal Theater Project executives because it lacked serious content, *Horse Eats Hat* closed on December 5, 1936. Welles and Houseman (who had returned from the tour of *Hamlet*) saw that only a classical drama in the grand tradition could satisfy their backers and bring them the prestige that Welles's *folie de grandeur* with *Horse Eats Hat* had denied them. After some consideration they settled on *The Tragical History of Doctor Faustus* by Christopher Marlowe, first produced in 1588 and based on the old German legend that in a later century gave rise to Goethe's *Faust*. This impassioned play, the work of a young dramatist at the height of his powers, was an extraordinary parable of human greed and lust for power. Mephistopheles,* the hellish demon who tempts Faustus with the temporal pleasures of the flesh and worldly success, was not conceived by Marlowe in ambiguous terms. The ending of the play left the audience in no doubt of the eternal sufferings with which

---

* This was spelled Mephistophilis in the play.

Faustus would be tormented. Its effect was powerful to a degree, and its picture of damnation struck deep into the Christian soul.

As Welles's introductions to the Todd Theater editions of Shakespeare disclosed, it was his deep concern to bring to modern audiences the naturalism and openness of the Elizabethan theater. He sought meaning rather than music in the verse, and he extended the apron stage deep into the audience to secure total involvement. He also decided upon a raw visual and dramatic style for the play. He again cast a black as a villain (and thereby oddly earned the approval of the black community): Jack Carter, who had left *Macbeth* so abruptly, was brought back from whatever gutter to play Mephistopheles with ferocious intensity. In addition to acting Faustus, Welles drew on his ability as a stage magician, using black velvet and startling perspectives of light and scenery to create an illusionist's abstract vision of the struggle between good and evil. In one sequence, the reception of Faustus by the Pope in Rome, there was a striking moment in which a pig, a side of beef, two chickens, and a pudding flew up from their dishes at a feast and performed pagan whirls before disappearing into the black velvet drapes. The effect was achieved largely by having members of the cast dressed in black; at the same time, puppets representing the Seven Deadly Sins were made to accompany the action, spinning in and out of it and even settling obscenely in a stage box.

Welles's genius was unleashed in one daring device after another, almost shockingly bold and direct, moving to the very edge of melodrama but achieving high tragedy at every turn. Spectators had the impression that the action was swelling out of a black cave, beyond it a kind of sinister and shapeless mound over which the actors moved; badgered and bullied to do his best, the lighting expert and designer Abe Feder achieved startling results, a kind of cosmic chiaroscuro, as the drama critic Stark Young commented. Sudden columns of light divided the dark—a device that would also find its way into *Citizen Kane*. There were a total of seventy-six lighting cues and sound effects; so many lights were used that at one time the grid sustaining them broke and fell onto the stage, causing momentary panic and the temporary closure of the Maxine Elliott Theater.

In addition to the exhausting preparation, entailing the radical revision of contemporary theatrical modes. Welles managed to cram in other activities. He would go to CBS for a radio broadcast between 8:00 P.M. and 8:30 P.M., wearing his makeup for *Doctor Faustus.* A taxi would be waiting at approximately 8:45 P.M. to take him to the theater, where he would throw on his costume while the chorus was appearing on stage. The pressure seemed to stimulate him even more than usual, and when he appeared before the audience in his startling makeup and clothing, he acted with a savagery that was unsettling and disturbing to many. Because of the complexity of the show, there was a new problem every night, and many theatergoers, irritated by the fact that the play ran only about an hour and twenty minutes, thought they were not getting their money's worth.

Doctor Faustus, which opened on January 8, 1937, was a great success nonetheless. Word of mouth and encouraging reviews conjoined to create enthusiasm, and soon there was standing room only. By May 1937, *The New York Times* reported, 80,000 people had seen the show; it was the talk of New York. However, there were dissenting voices among the critics. Welles's early supporter Edith Isaacs, writing in *Theater Arts Monthly,* said that Welles, "in spite of his keen intelligence, has not the presence, nor the power of projection, to carry such a role." But Brooks Atkinson was respectful, talking of Welles's "robust" performance as "mobile and commanding." This more than assuaged Welles's unease about some of the other critical comments; with Atkinson behind him, he had little to worry about.

In *Run-Through* Houseman gives a curious account of Welles's mental state at this time. He writes that Welles was overcome by a sense of doom, that he was haunted by a feeling of sin, a dread of retribution that paralleled Faustus's own fears. Houseman says that he lived in panic; that at night, when his eyes closed, demonic presences that symbolized his sins closed in on him, clawing at him with all the hellish fierceness with which Faustus would be torn apart for eternity. It is hard to imagine what could have been so devastating and haunting for Welles that he would make these confessions to Houseman. Could his brother's incarceration in Kankakee be hanging on his conscience? Was he, like his brother, suffering from the agonizing strains of the Welles clan—the dire experiences with Mary Head Wells Gottfredsen.

After a struggle that had gone on for ten years, Richard Welles at last secured his release from Kankakee. He had found a legal clause in the insanity acts of Illinois that allowed him to provide his own habeas corpus, in effect giving him custody of himself and allowing him a hearing before a judge at which he could state his own case as a sane person. The hearing was successful.

Because of Dr. Bernstein, Richard had lacked proper clothing and lived much of the time in rags. One of the Sheffield family, which had owned the Sheffield House in Grand Detour before Richard's father bought it, visited Kankakee in the course of a charity tour and saw Richard, his clothes almost in shreds, working in the laundry. She was so shocked by this horrifying vision of the son of her father's old friend that she collapsed, and the incident remained on her mind for the rest of her life. Orson appears to have done nothing for Richard, probably from ignorance of the true situation; if he did help, there is no inkling of it on the insanity records. When Richard left Kankakee, his total capital was eight dollars. He was now thirty-two years old, and he had spent the best years of his young manhood among some four thousand people who were mentally ill. It is scarcely surprising that he had no strong desire to be an active part of the world, and for the next few years, he drifted from job to job. He visited his brother briefly in New York in 1937, but it was not a particularly warm experience for either of them, and Houseman, who met Richard only on that one occasion, said that Richard made almost no impression on him.

Welles was busy at the time with the radio show *The Shadow*, booming or laughing hollowly in the role of Lamont Cranston, who was certainly a melodramatic counterpoint to Faustus. Indeed, at times the declamatory style of Lamont Cranston seemed to overlay the portrayal of Faustus; Welles's moving rapidly back and forth between radio and classical drama operated to the disadvantage of both performances.

Doctor Faustus was approved by both Harry Hopkins and Hallie Flanagan; it satisfied all the requirements of morality, classicism, and high theatrical art for which the Federal Theater Project stood. It was clear to Houseman and Welles that they must now undertake a departure, both to avoid predictability and to introduce (another purpose of the project) a new work of artistic merit by a contemporary composer.

They settled on Marc Blitzstein, whose play with music, *The Cradle Will Rock*, had been put together the year before. A brilliant artist of passion and commitment, Blitzstein had written the play when consumed with the fervor of the intellectual left. Like Sidney Kingsley and Archibald MacLeish, Blitzstein was concerned with the dangers of industrial oppression in America, and in his work he dealt with a strike in an imaginary town called Steeltown U.S.A., an abstract and symbolic place observed in the Dos Passos mode. Mr. Mister, the steel mill tycoon who rules the community with a brutal hand, subdues the local editor, intellectually emasculates the president of the college, buys off the most powerful opposition, and organizes the killing of his archenemy, a leader of organized labor. The opposition to Mr. Mister comes from Larry Foreman, union organizer and radical, who defies and finally destroys him.

Blitzstein used recitative and aria, revue patter, tap dance, suites, chorals, and "silly symphony," conscripting elements of contemporary music to create a dazzling and original work that would effectively symbolize the true nature of the relationship of capital and labor. He was greatly influenced by Bertolt Brecht, whose advice led to the creation of the work and to whom the work was dedicated.

Welles had heard of *The Cradle Will Rock* from a number of distinguished figures of the theater, and after he met Blitzstein during the run of *Horse Eats Hat* he was more enthusiastic about putting on the play. There were delays; for a time the Actors' Repertory Company had planned to do *Cradle.* Then, at a dinner at the shared apartment of Houseman and Virgil Thomson, Blitzstein played, sang, and acted the entire work with extraordinary drive and power, and all agreed that the following day *Cradle* would be announced as the next major production of the group. Will Geer, a genial, shambling actor with the capacity to suggest incipient evil (as he showed later in the film *Seconds*), was cast as Mr. Mister, and Howard Da Silva was cast as Larry Foreman. Both were later to fall afoul of the blacklist.

Welles worked closely with the composer and conductor Lehman Engel. Many scenes were compressed, rewritten, developed in the give-and-take between the collaborators. Meanwhile, in Washington there was growing unease over the nature of the production and its commentary on the evils of capitalism—the characteristic economy of the United States. Lip service to the left was one thing; permission to express left-wing views on the stage was, for an organ of government, something else. (Many who had paid such lip service had panicked and turned the play down when it came to making the final decision.)

Once again Welles decided on a brave and original theatrical approach for *The Cradle Will Rock.* He stripped the stage of all scenery and painted it with light to create the powerful and vivid effect of a steeltown in turmoil. He wanted to match the austere precision and driving force of the play with the minimum of clutter—another embodiment of his neo-Elizabethan ideals. Rehearsals ran through the middle of April 1937, and the advance was promising: fourteen thousand seats were sold. The rumblings in Washington went on and on.

During this period Welles worked closely with the composer, conductor, and lecturer Aaron Copland on *The Second Hurricane,* an opera for schoolchildren, played by children and evoking in essence the spirit of a new generation of Americans. The premiere was originally scheduled for April 21, 1937, with Lehman Engel conducting. Edwin Denby, who had written the libretto, conceived the story in these terms: an aviator seeks the help of high school volunteers in flood relief (a reference to work done by schoolboys during the Depression), and four boys and two girls fly off in the plane, which is forced down by weather conditions near the river; the group fights for territorial imperatives and food, but at last, as the hurricane sweeps down on them, they learn the value of comradeship in adversity. The intent was to compose a work extremely simple and clean in style, ideally matched to its youthful theme. Denby thought that the youngest actor-director in America should be engaged to put it on, and as a result, Copland, a man of enormous charm and ugly attractiveness, went to see Welles, who was delighted with the idea; when Copland played him portions of the score, he threw up his hands and said he would accept at once. The press got behind the project, and high school performers swarmed in for the auditions. Welles enjoyed most of them and drew much of the cast, including the leads, from the Professional Children's School. Only one adult appeared in the work: Joseph Cotten, as the aviator, at a salary of $10 a performance.

Backed by Welles, Copland's supporter Mary Lescaze obtained money from such disparate sources as Mrs. Leopold Stokowski, Carl Van Vechten, and Lincoln Kirstein, and Paul Bowles played the music on the piano at the run-throughs for potential backers. Welles was considerate, if exhaustingly overenergetic, in whipping the young team into action; he placed the two choruses on the stage and the orchestra at the rear, with the conductor facing the audience. However, as time went on, even his energies began to frazzle, for he was already involved with *The Cradle Will Rock,* and he had to hand over much of the direction to Hiram Sherman. *The Second Hurricane* opened in May 1937 at the Playhouse on Grand Street for three experimental performances, followed by a radio broadcast; the reviews were mixed, but undoubtedly the work was an aesthetic triumph for all concerned. (A year later, sponsored by the magazine *New Masses,* excerpts of the work were presented on radio with commentary by Welles.)

Senators Burton Wheeler, Robert Reynolds, and Gerald Nye and others of the extreme right-wing faction on Capitol Hill were determined to quash the Federal Theater Project. Influenced by Berlin, these men, who were soon to be sold out spiritually and politically to the German Embassy in Washington, these pillars of rectitude, saw "Communist elements" infiltrating the American theater through the WPA. Indeed, their argument that the radical left was at large in the New York area was not unfounded; it scarcely helped the cause of American liberalism that those involved in the theater, instead of standing firm on their principles, tended to pretend that their aim was only to entertain and enlighten the public. So deep was the shame in a capitalist nation in espousing anything approaching a left-wing position—no matter how urgently that position might be pressed in private—and so embarrassing to many in the establishment were people

like Houseman and Welles that they and many of their associates had
to disguise their principles in showmanship and braggadocio.

In recent years Welles has commented on the intellectual bankruptcy of the authentic left, which owed its position not to Moscow, as
was so frequently alleged but to the principles laid down by George
Bernard Shaw, Beatrice Webb, Eugene Delos, and more recently Ber-
trand Russell in Great Britain: an enhancing of authentic democratic
principles of equal opportunity for men and women, black and white,
maimed and whole, ill and well; an idealist vision corrupted and ex-
ploited by the Soviet Union and driven into a corner by those elements
in the United States that correctly felt threatened and imposed upon
by them. These were the principles that would be resurrected by President John Kennedy, after they had cost innumerable artists of talent
and enterprise their careers in the McCarthy era of the 1950s.

The Cradle Will Rock was not mere entertainment, as Houseman
alleges; rather, it crystallized the very problem that was then rocking
America. Strikes were erupting everywhere in response to the brutal
ill-treatment of workers by the Gestapo-like gangs that swept through
the Ford and General Motors factories (and were mercilessly exposed
by Warner Brothers in such brilliant and forgotten films as *Black
Fury*). The repression of the workers, forcing many into ineffective
company unions, had brought about rebellion and conflict almost unprecedented in the history of American labor. As *The Cradle Will Rock*
went into rehearsal, not only General Motors but Republic Steel, an organization run on tough principles and no polite words, were being
torn apart by workers armed with baseball bats and clubs, and in Chicago the Memorial Day riots made headlines when police met union
members with tear gas and bullets. In Lansing, Michigan, factories
were closed down; the ultra-right-wing Clare Hoffman, a Michigan
congressman, led the hysteria of those on the Hill who blamed communism as a source of the problems. In fact John L. Lewis, aggressive
head of the CIO, had powerful Nazi connections, in league with the oil
millionaire William Rhodes Davis; he had visions of forming labor
unions into a federation that would spread throughout Mexico as well
as the United States, in preparation for a Nazi takeover of the
Americas.

The right-wing faction, of which Roosevelt was painfully aware
and whose influence he dared not entirely resist, represented the forefront of anti-intellectualism in America. Its members had hated the
Federal Theater Project from the beginning because it encouraged
government subsidy of enlightened thought. Now, with strikes erupting everywhere, they could label the Federal Theater Project's new

venture with Orson Welles as an example of rabble-rousing and Communist infiltration. Harry Hopkins, ill with cancer, could not sustain the pressure; nor could the determined Hallie Flanagan, who after all was a government employee. Budget cuts, each more cruel than its predecessor, began to be imposed on all WPA projects as those who resented the employment of the unemployed and abhorred the idea of a workers' theater and a workers' literature gained the upper hand.

On May 27 the Federation of Architects, Engineers, Chemists, and Technicians, the WPA branches of the Teachers' Union and the Newspaper Guild, the Artists' Union, the City Project Council, and the Workers' Alliance called a one-day strike of seven thousand WPA members in New York. Forty-fourth Street was filled with marchers protesting the cuts called for in Washington. On June 10, following lengthy debates in Congress, New York City was asked to cut the budget by thirty percent, and seventeen hundred workers were dismissed. All openings of new plays, concerts, and art galleries were to be postponed until after July 1, while the cuts and the reorganization of the Federal Theater Project took place. Further sit-downs occurred. With great daring, three hundred members of the Negro Theater Project in Harlem and four hundred members of their audience refused to leave the theater and remained there all night; on the same evening, the audience at a Brahms concert at the Federal Theater of Music refused to leave the theater until dawn.

Flanagan fought gallantly to allow *The Cradle Will Rock* to continue in production. Welles's designs for glass-bottomed floats, his simple but striking scenery consisting of multiple platforms, and his elaborate musical concepts worked out with the composer were all threatened with imminent demolition. Even after Lawrence Morris of the Federal Theater Project saw a run-through of the show and pronounced it magnificent the opening remained imperiled. Archibald MacLeish and Virgil Thomson interceded in vain. Houseman told Flanagan that he would tolerate no interference with his production. In Washington, Welles saw Ellen Woodward of the project and David Niles, WPA director of information, and wrongly insisted that the play was "not a political protest but an artistic one." This falsification of the play's true purpose, conceived and offered in desperation, was received with the indifference it probably deserved. When Welles said he would launch the production independently, Niles replied that in that case the WPA would no longer be interested in it.

Welles returned to New York in time for the penultimate rehearsal. It was a convention of the Federal Theater Project that a telegram would be sent just hours before opening night, giving formal legal authorization for the production; as the hours before the dress rehearsal wore away, there was no word from Western Union to encourage the producers. Houseman, Welles, and others connected with the production called everyone they knew to the final run-through, and many responded, including the playwrights George Kaufman and Moss Hart. Unfortunately, the performance that night encountered many technical problems: the glass wagons with their echoes of Russian agitprop theater, the complicated lighting worked out by Jean Rosenthal, and the orchestrations and vocal arrangements briskly but at times awkwardly handled by Lehman Engel caused some feeling of clumsiness and ineptitude. Yet the audience was thrilled by the fervor of the production and was carried away by the sheer daring and excitement of the occasion.

The next day, June 15, 1937, was an historic one. The precious telegram had still not arrived, when suddenly the theater came under a state of siege. WPA guards seized the building, protecting the box office from anyone who might want to buy a ticket. The precarious glass wagons, the elaborate costumes and props, and even Howard Da Silva's toupee were confiscated. Crammed into the ladies' room in the basement, Welles, Blitzstein, Houseman, and their associates holed up like a pioneer family surrounded by Indians in the eighteenth-century West; they dared not leave the building for fear of being locked out permanently. They called everybody they could think of, futilely reassuring them that their tickets or invitations would be honored and that the production would take place as scheduled. In fact it could not be, for there was nothing with which to present the play.

For a time an effort was made to arrange a separate deal with Actors' Equity, in which the play would be pulled out of the Federal Theater and presented as a Houseman-Welles production. But Equity ruled against any such decision and indeed ordered all Equity members in the cast not to appear in the production under any banner except that of the WPA. This was a shocking blow; there was no reason why *The Cradle Will Rock* could not be performed without scenery, but if the principal actors were lost, it would be a disaster.

In something like desperation, Houseman dispatched Jean Rosenthal with $10 to flag down a truck and drive around the block while Blitzstein, Welles, and Houseman tried to locate a rentable piano. Luckily, Blitzstein obtained one from his landlady, and Rosenthal picked it up. That was Marc Blitzstein's account; in John Houseman's version of the events, Rosenthal herself found the piano, and then he told her to hire a truck. She found one in the garment district, had the piano put on the truck, and on Houseman's orders began circling the theater, waiting for instructions. The piano, of course, was crucial: with it, Blitzstein could provide the music for a performance.

The piano was in hand, the problem of the musical side of the performance was resolved. It was now a question of talking to the actors, and Houseman and Welles concocted a marvelous scheme. They told the players that while Equity had forbidden them to appear on the stage, there was nothing to stop them from performing in the audience. Many of the actors responded favorably.

The curtain was due to go up at 8:00 P.M. Someone with the WPA guard hung a notice on the theater door: NO SHOW TONIGHT. At 7:00 P.M. a crowd was gathered outside the stage door made up mostly of sympathizers and including many who had bought tickets for the performance and were stubborn enough not to have called for their money to be returned. At 7:20 P.M. the actors Hiram Sherman and Will Geer played out scenes from the show. Jean Rosenthal was still haplessly circling the block with the piano. Then a theatrical real estate agent in the ladies' room, whom everyone had been ignoring as he offered various run-down theaters for their use, again mentioned the Venice Theater when he turned to leave. Everyone grew excited; they could perform at the Venice. They hired it for $100, and immediately Blitzstein, Abe Feder, and others headed for the new location. Rosenthal told the truck driver to take her to the Venice. Houseman, Welles, and the others went into the street and announced that the performance would take place at the Venice, that the curtain would be at 9:00 P.M., and that they could bring anyone they wanted free of charge to see the performance. Everybody cheered and began making their way uptown on foot, by cab, subway, and bus.

Word of these happenings spread rapidly; the commuters dragged complete strangers into the migration. Friends and relatives were called and invited to enjoy the free seats. Excited and hugely enjoying their defiance of the authorities, Welles, Houseman, and Archibald MacLeish took a cab to the Venice. Within less than an hour the New York theater world was in an uproar. Lehman Engel made himself a hero by smuggling the orchestrations out of the Maxine Elliott Theater under his overcoat, while Houseman worked to set up the Venice, which had been dark for years. According to Houseman, close to one thousand people° crowded into the house carrying sandwiches and pop bottles and the theater was flowing with laughter, cheers, and enthusiastic conversation. Feder and Rosenthal organized the lights. Blitzstein

---

° *Variety* mentioned a smaller figure.

began tinkling away at his second-rate piano. By 9:00 P.M. every inch of the theater was filled, and many people were standing at the back of the orchestra.

The players, of course, were in the audience; there was nothing on stage but the piano and the composer in his shirtsleeves, struggling with the badly tuned instrument. The theater was totally unaired, the spotlights flyblown and dusty. Houseman and Welles came forward to speak from the stage. Houseman described the problems of Hallie Flanagan and Harry Hopkins and explained why the performance had been stopped; Welles expressed his admiration for the audience in journeying uptown to the Venice and talked of the WPA "cossacks" who had taken over the Maxine Elliott. He told the story of Steeltown and described the scenery the audience would not see. Finally, Welles said resonantly, "And now, ladies and gentlemen, we have the honor to present—with the composer at the piano—*The Cradle Will Rock!*"

The curtain rose. Blitzstein, still in shirtsleeves and suspenders, began pounding away, awkwardly singing the opening lyrics written for the character of a female prostitute. (Backstage, three Broadway producers were trying unsuccessfully to get Welles and Houseman to sign contracts.) A remarkably moving moment followed. As Archibald MacLeish wrote in *Stage* magazine (January 1938), "There occurred a miracle." Singers in the cast and even in the audience, led by the actress Olive Stanton in a box, began to join in the music. MacLeish continued:

> From the first voice of the first singer the thing was evident: there was no audience. There was instead a room full of men and women as eager in the play as any actor. As singers rose in one part and another of the auditorium, the faces of these men and women made new and changing circles around them. They were well-wishing faces: human faces such as a man may sometimes see among partisans of the same cause, or friends who hope good things for one another. The whole feel of the room was of well-wishing and common cause.

It was a great evening. Marc Blitzstein breezed his way through half a dozen parts whose players had abandoned the production in fear of repercussions for acting in defiance of the government. Hiram Sherman played the Reverend Salvation and Professor Scoot (unbeknownst to Houseman and Welles, he had memorized every part in the libretto). His and many other performances were given from the boxes; still others, and the chorus, were seen from the cleared front rows of the orchestra.

For ninety minutes without intermission° the impassioned performance continued, with an unrehearsed break after Scene Six to allow everyone to catch their breath. MacLeish appeared before the second act, vividly repeating and enhancing his speech from the last night of *Panic*, reminding the audience that it was taking part in a great occasion, and praising its members for their courage and freshness of response. At the final curtain the audience went mad. It screamed, it yelled, quelling some people who made loud dissenting charges of radicalism and communism. No one who attended that night would ever forget it; not until 1:00 A.M. was the exhausted cast allowed to go home. Blitzstein, who was fragile and high-strung, was on the edge of a nervous breakdown, but Welles, still possessed of demonic energy, spent the rest of the night awake.

The next morning *The New York Times* described the occurrences of the previous night. A hastily assembled committee pulled together $2,205 to assure the production a two-week run; Helen Deutsch, press agent for the Theater Guild, posted $1,500 with Actors' Equity to cover the salaries of the actors in the event a proper commercial production could be secured. The decision was made to present the show for a fortnight at the Venice, and it opened on June 18. A restless Welles kept changing the production from day to day. Every performance was a sell-out. The front-page news coverage went on and on. On Sundays the company and crew made their way to Bethlehem, Pennsylvania, at the invitation of the steel workers' union. Many of the union members were confused by the play, whose intellectualism, despite the fact that the work symbolized the grievances of the workers, ran somewhat above their heads. Interestingly, the local steel company set up a rival show, forcing certain employees to buy tickets and to ignore the Welles production if they valued their jobs; nothing could have illustrated more clearly the validity of Blitzstein's argument.

By now it was clear that there could be no reconciliation with the Federal Theater Project, despite every effort of John Houseman to negotiate. On July 6, 1937, five days after the play closed, the government announced that it was no longer interested in the Blitzstein production. Simultaneously, and predictably, Welles, Houseman, and their associates officially resigned from the project, while *The Cradle* went on tour.

° Welles was again reaching toward a film format by eliminating intermissions and aiming at ninety-minute running times.

During that tour Welles was distracted for a time with other activities. On radio that summer he presented *Les Misérables,* Victor Hugo's tragedy, co-starring Martin Gabel, Ray Collins, Alice Frost, Agnes Moorehead, Hiram Sherman, and Everett Sloane. Welles himself played Jean Valjean, the unhappy thief who was pursued for a lifetime by the relentless Inspector Javert; Martin Gabel played Javert with sinister force. The seven-part production ran from July 23 to September 3, 1937, displaying all of Welles's genius at full stretch.*

Radio had the capacity to unleash the human imagination (later, television would all but destroy it); the listener could conjure up pictures in his head as he followed the grim story of pursuit, revenge, and betrayal. The chase through the sewers of Paris was conveyed through the clanking of irons, the rush of water, the sudden hollowness of a voice resounding through damp and brooding stone. In *Les Misérables* Welles showed an invention and power that were to emerge the following year in *First Person Singular* and later in his classic *Mercury Theater of the Air.* Music, no longer a mere accompaniment that crashed at dramatic moments and was antic at cheerful ones, now became an emotional bridge that carried the listener from one event to another with consequential lyric power. The performances were orchestrated, the voices chosen to complement each other and to be heard in counterpoint like musical instruments. Moreover, there was a powerful sense of milieu: by means of clever if obvious devices, the listener was made to feel present at the events, transported back in time on a magic carpet of sound. Millions of Americans could find themselves in the atmosphere of a repressive and cheerless Paris that was far removed from the city of their imaginations.

At this time Welles was working with the celebrated producer Arthur Hopkins on a version of *King Lear* to be presented under the auspices of Hopkins' lavish patronage. And during this period the Welleses moved with Budget the dog to a quasi-English house near Katharine Cornell's home at Sneden's Landing in the Hudson Valley, with a rent of $155 a month, engaging a cook and a gardener and buying a 1937 Lincoln limousine complete with chauffeur (like his father before him, Welles was a very bad driver). Virginia was two months along with their first child, and they expected it to be a boy and intended to call the infant Christopher. There, in the comparative peace of their small home, the couple quarreled constantly; when John

---

* Charles Laughton and Fredric March had appeared on the screen in a 1934 version of the novel; there had also been several French film versions.

Houseman visited them, he could sense the tension. Perhaps part of the problem was that Virginia was almost Welles's equal in intelligence and she insisted in holding her own in arguments; she was a strong-willed, edgy woman who refused to allow her husband to ride rough-shod over her intellectually. She was beautiful, stylish, gifted, with a first-class mind—and perhaps in his heart of hearts Welles would have preferred a mindless and submissive wife whose domesticity and lack of competitiveness would allow him to express himself without contra-diction at every turn of the conversation. Thus it was not a happy house, and what happiness there was disappeared when the plans for *King Lear* fell through for a variety of reasons, chief of which was that Welles wanted absolute creative control—an impossibility in the com-mercial theater and an unacceptable idea for Hopkins. There seemed to be only one alternative in that difficult summer, after the thrilling realization of *The Cradle Will Rock*: Houseman and Welles would have to form their own theater, where they could unleash their egos with only artistic considerations to limit them.

4

In essence, Welles and Houseman had already established a repertory company; they had linked themselves to a reliable team headed by Feder, Engel, Rosenthal, and their assistants, and they had established a style that was unmistakably their own. It was in a sense only a technicality that would take them into independent production and quickly establish them as the foremost producing team in the intellectual theater of America.

The American Mercury magazine, present in the living room at Sneden's Landing as they discussed setting up their company, supplied the name under which they registered in Albany. "Mercury" conveyed youth, speed, lightness, grace, and daring as well as flight and dazzlement; it was a perfect choice. Houseman became the president, Welles the vice-president, and the ever-reliable Augusta Weissberger the secretary. The entire capital was $100. In the suffocating heat of August 1937 the two backers, creators, and directors of the new company began the search for an appropriate venue. They settled on the Comedy Theater on Forty-first Street and Broadway, whose history went back to the nineteenth century. For years the Comedy, handsome and elegant, had been in the hands of amateurs or second-rate foreign companies; its rental was low ($175.50 a week), and the partners obtained a five-year lease on a tiny deposit. A small army of sweepers and cleaners set about disposing of the rats and spiders, scrubbing the stage, and rendering the auditorium habitable. Brooks Atkinson promised his support, and John Houseman, with Atkinson's blessing, was given space in *The New York Times* to announce his and Welles's high and serious purpose.

The *Times* of August 29, 1937, carried the bold and confident statement that the Mercury Theater would open early in November and that four or five plays would be presented each season, most of them plays of the past that had some bearing on contemporary life. The program would be flexible, beginning with *Julius Caesar;* the plays would be presented on Elizabethan principles (in the mode of *Doctor*

Faustus), achieving the appropriate speed and violence through the use of an apron stage, sound devices, music, and lighting. Other plans included George Bernard Shaw's *Heartbreak House*, William Gillette's *Too Much Johnson*, John Webster's *The Duchess of Malfi*, and Ben Jonson's *The Silent Woman*. Each play would run approximately six weeks, in repertory, so that two different works could be seen in a given week. The top ticket would be two dollars, and many seats would be priced from fifty cents to one dollar. In addition, an apprentice group would be established, known as the Studio; designed as a source of talent for the theater, it would be composed of all non-Equity extras appearing in the repertory. Outside membership would be limited to twenty-five, and the cost would be $150 for six months; the studio was sponsored by Antoinette Perry, Gertrude Lawrence, Katharine Cornell, Alfred Lunt, and Lynn Fontanne.

Now that the announcement had been made, there came the awkward matter of the financial backing. While Welles and Houseman owned seventy percent of the Mercury, thirty percent would have to be given to others in return for outside investment. It was decided to have shareholders, who would be given non-interest-bearing notes; the note holders would be repaid by commitment and promise when the theater showed a profit. Among those who invested as note holders was George J. Hexter, who had worked at the Federal Theater Project and had money of his own; Myron S. Falk, a retired builder-contractor; and his daughter, Mildred Falk Loew, who had married into the prominent theater family. Others were William Rapp of *True Story* magazine, the radio director William Sweets, the carpet heir Gifford Cochran, and a well-to-do law student, Charles Schnee. As the money came in, it was put into the theater rental, office furniture, telephones, and other equipment. With little experience, Augusta Weissberger became business manager for the Mercury. Carlos L. Israels and Arnold Weissberger were the theater's lawyers, the former representing the backers and note holders, the latter representing Welles and Houseman. Jean Rosenthal took over from Abe Feder (and one of the office girls later became famous as the actress Judy Holliday).

Unhampered by the restrictions of the Federal Theater Project— which had gotten into more hot water with its production of Sinclair Lewis's play about a fascist takeover in America, *It Can't Happen Here*—Welles and Houseman decided to make their *Julius Caesar* as devastating an attack on modern dictatorships as *Panic, Ten Million Ghosts,* or *It Can't Happen Here*. The production would become a vehicle of these embattled representatives of the left. It would be staged in modern dress, as though it were set in present-day Rome, with a Mussolini-like dictator and scenes of mass hysteria mirroring current demonstrations for the Italian leader. Marc Blitzstein was engaged to write the score and Lehman Engel to conduct and arrange it. Samuel Leve, who had worked for the Federal Theater Project, was hired to execute Welles's audacious staging ideas. Welles cast Joseph Holland as Caesar, Martin Gabel as Cassius, and Norman Lloyd as Cinna; Welles himself would play Brutus. His old friend of the Cornell tour, John Hoystradt, was cast as Decius Brutus.*

The sets were designed as bare, stark platforms with traps and ramps, presenting the actors with considerable problems of movement but evoking with abstract force the harsh nature of a dictatorial state. Jean Rosenthal arranged for them to be built across the river at the old Fox studios in Fort Lee, New Jersey, currently being used as a warehouse. The actors would wear street clothes and uniforms rented from Brooks Costumes. A platform stage was built into the audience, and uncovered steam pipes could be seen on the bare brick walls. The intention was to present the play in as undecorated a manner as its physical staging.

Rehearsals began in October, and Welles was delighted with his cast. He enjoyed the look of them in their uniforms and suits; Caesar wore a Sam Browne belt and a dark green uniform, exactly like Mussolini; the conspirators bent on the assassination of Caesar wore fedora hats turned down at the brim and turned-up coat collars, like gangsters in Hollywood "B" movies; and Brutus wore an ordinary civilian suit, not unlike that which a politician might sport during a campaign. Holland, Lloyd, and Welles all made powerful impressions at the first reading. Richard Wilson joined the company as Welles's special assistant, a post he was supposed to retain until the end of the 1940s. William Alland turned up to share with Wilson the stage work, then obtained a job as actor; later he would become the famous shadowy reporter in *Citizen Kane*.

Welles worked with even greater enthusiasm and disregard for the hours of day and night than he had under the banner of the Federal Theater Project. He exasperated, excited, and moved his cast, even those who were not used to his irrational, extravagant, and often tardy behavior. He concentrated on the secondary players, knowing with his

---

* Welles had first produced *Julius Caesar* at the Todd School, playing Cassius, Marc Antony, and the Soothsayer.

uncanny instinct that the chorus and crowd, down to the smallest and most obscure figure, had to have fully realized identities. He placed featured players among them, and he spent hours with them, recording the speeches of Antony and Brutus and having them speak specific lines in reaction. These lines were daringly interjected in the modern idiom. One member of the crowd, Ross Elliot, recalled later, "For example, when Antony spoke the first words of his speech in eulogy over Caesar's body, one of us said, 'Aw, shut up!' Another member of the mob then came in with 'Let him talk!' and so forth. It was by no means a matter of walking on and off the stage and making odd noises." So impatient was Welles to continue the rehearsals on the actual stage itself that he dragged the forty members of the company by subway, ferry, and bus to Fort Lee, where he drove them through their paces amid sawdust, loud hammering, and the yells of workmen.

Norman Lloyd remembers that in portraying the poet Cinna he wanted to provide the character of a street poet, a pamphleteer who hands out verses for a subversive political pupose; Welles had wanted a different interpretation, that of a bohemian poet, but Lloyd won the battle. He recalls that Welles would slip out of the theater during the Marc Antony oration at Caesar's funeral, have a quick drink and a bite of food at a local restaurant, then race back to the stage just at the second of his cue. On one occasion the theater caught fire; without breaking rhythm he said, in correct pentameter, "Kind sirs, please put the burning furnace out."

The dress rehearsal was disrupted by a violent mishap. Welles had reassured the cast that the traps with which, like a magician running a magic act, he had peppered the stage were perfectly safe. By an irony that everybody appreciated, he became the victim of one of them. On his way up a ramp to the stage to give a pep talk, he tripped and fell forward straight through a trap, hitting the basement floor face first fifteen feet below. Yet not even this could faze him; assisted to his feet, the groaning genius made his way forward and proceeded with the rehearsal.

The play opened on November 11, 1937. *Time* magazine said:

No gilded trappings hung from above, no canvas masonry affronted the eye of the 1937 realist. The play, up to date in dress and interpretation, was the thing. The red brick back wall was the only backdrop, the gadgets of a more formal theater being idle in the wings. The high loft, emptied of its scenery, lent itself to a grotesque play of light and shadow. Below, on a bare stage platform graded down toward the audience by three

steps, the Mercury Theater players enacted a sinister tragedy. . . .

Welles had drastically truncated and transposed parts of the play
and disposed of intermissions, in much the same way he had adopted
and staged *Macbeth*. And as in *Macbeth*, he was frank about the dangers of fascist dictatorships and the wickedness and treachery of a state
such as Italy. With the Spanish Civil War raging, with Austria already
a victim of Hitler and of its own traitorous middle class, and with a
world war looming, the presentation was very much to the point, summarizing symbolically the liberal position. Indeed, the now emascu-
lated Federal Theater could not have envisaged such a production
under its censored and drastically undermined public charter. Perhaps
conscious of the danger of drawing too much attention to the play's political implications, most of the critics, who were in sympathy with the
Mercury's purposes, concentrated on the production's impressive physical qualities.

Jean Rosenthal, like Abe Feder before her, strikingly executed
Welles's concept of light beams as part of the overall presentation—
reaching toward the techniques of the screen that were later employed
in *Citizen Kane*. The actors trooped diagonally up and down the raised
stage, through vivid slashes almost of the intensity of sunlight, advancing from the rear of the bare platform and gathering, as one critic
wrote, in "little knots around stabbing shafts of light."

Brooks Atkinson, supportive as ever, welcomed the Mercury Theater to New York, called for recognition of the original acting and producing talent it offered, and praised the stripped, honest, swift, and
vivid nature of the production as a whole. Stark Young talked of the
"boldness" and "freshness" and "the refreshing element of energy"
that were exciting and ingenious in execution. The distinguished Joseph Wood Krutch of *The Nation* wrote that "from the vague night of
dark recesses the characters emerge into the light to say their say or do
their deeds, and that is enough not merely to hold an audience tense
. . . but to send them away carrying in their minds both the meaning
and the feel of conspiracy in a tottering world."

One stroke of good fortune was that just before the *Julius Caesar*
premiere, an elaborate but disastrous production of Shakespeare's *Antony and Cleopatra*, starring Tallulah Bankhead and the silent movie
star Conway Tearle, opened and—as the critic Ruth Sedgwick reported—"died sumptuously on $100,000 worth of Egyptology and a
pyramid of adverse criticism." *Time* magazine said, "Last week, after
long preparation and a road tour, Tallulah swept into Manhattan's

Mansfield Theater in the traditional gilded brassiere and diaphanous pantalettes of the servant of the Nile ... Broadway was not surprised when the play closed after five performances." One wit remarked that "Miss Bankhead sailed in her barge down the Nile ... and sank."

The contrast between flossy, meaningless extravagance on the one hand and dedicated, austere playmaking on the other was only too clear, and the Mercury Theater was a winner. Welles's belief that thirties audiences, who loved the fast-moving melodramas and comedies of Hollywood, would want Shakespeare plain and unadorned proved to be inspired. And underneath the enterprise lay his own political convictions; for them, Houseman says, the Mercury and its productions provided "an instrument of artistic expression and a ladder to fame and power." That may have been true for Houseman, and it may have been part of Welles's ambitions, but, whatever Houseman's motives, there can be no question that Welles saw the theater as a vehicle for radical ideas and that *Julius Caesar* was as much a product of agitprop thinking as *It Can't Happen Here*, *Panic*, or *Waiting for Lefty*.

By now the consensus was that Orson Welles was the most gifted young director in the United States. Breaking with tradition, he was bringing Shakespeare to the people in a manner unprecedented since the heyday of Edwin Booth. His team may have grumbled, even fought his influence—many felt used by him or drained by his energy and power—but none could deny that he gave their lives an excitement, an edge, a force they had not had before. Above all, everyone in the Mercury, like those in the Theater Guild or the Group Theater, was dedicated to artistic achievement first and to financial enhancement second; they did not mind going hungry (even if Welles did not) in the interest of good theater.

There were always problems at the Mercury. Houseman recalls that the toilets splashed so loudly they could be heard in the theater, and perhaps this was one reason for Welles's insistence that there be constant sound effects and music throughout the production. Conditions for many members of the cast were unpleasant: the chorus of sixteen men, most of them just out of college, had to cope with being crammed into a dank and depressing pit beneath the stage that was haunted by rats, spiders, and cockroaches. Their salaries were so small that they could afford to eat only one meal a day. And devoted as they were, they came perilously close to going on strike.

It was decided to present *The Cradle Will Rock* again, at the Worklight Theater, an adjunct for trainees of the Mercury; in the meantime, Welles embarked on Thomas Dekker's *The Shoemaker's Holiday*, which served as light relief much as *Horse Eats Hat* had provided a lighthearted contrast with *Macbeth. The Shoemaker's Holiday* was an Elizabethan folderol, complicated in plot, moving across a wide social spectrum, and richly realized by the author. It had first been acted before Queen Elizabeth on New Year's Day 1600. Welles decided to recreate that event, to try to capture what he felt was the ribaldry, dash, color, extravagance, and virility of Elizabethan England. Once more he sought a freedom from "fustian" styling; he wanted the play to be busy in the best sense so that contemporary audiences could respond to it and its antic humor and gusto with excitement.

Set in the time of King Henry V, the story concerns the love of an aristocrat, Rowland Lacy, for Rose, the Lord Mayor of London's daughter. Lacy's uncle, the Earl of Lincoln, objects to the match (Rose is a commoner) and dispatches Rowland to the war in France in order to interrupt the affair. But Rowland deserts and, disguised as a shoemaker in the service of the Lord Mayor's supplier of shoes, manages to return to his loved one's arms. Threatened with death for desertion, he is pardoned by the genial monarch and weds his love. Woven into the story are several subplots, the whole conveying skillfully the essentially democratic nature of the British people, each knowing his place in society, the humblest working man on joyous terms with royalty, and each sensing himself part of a larger organism structured in terms of class yet definably English, making every individual a part of a special club. Above all, the play contained the true spirit of Elizabethan England, and Welles took on the direction of it with delight. In showing that happiness can be achieved through crossing class barriers, Welles could illustrate effectively the dangers of power that had obsessed him in his other productions. Where there was no despotism, there was joy in a ready give and take at every level of a society: such was the underlying theme of *The Shoemaker's Holiday*.

With Jean Rosenthal and Samuel Leve, Welles reworked the huge *Julius Caesar* platform stage into a set evocative of the atmosphere of an Elizabethan London. Tall wooden houses were shown in perspective, and a shoe shop, the Guildhall, the home of the Lord Mayor, and the busy markets of the city were wonderfully realized. Costumes were designed by Millia Davenport in the correct weaves and woolens of the era. Lehman Engel composed the music. In December 1937 rehearsals were at full stretch, with Whitford Kane as the shoemaker Simon Eyre, Ruth Ford as the ingenue Jane, Alice Frost as Rose, and Edith Barrett, who met and married Vincent Price during the rehearsals, as the maid Sybil. Joseph Cotten made a dashing and attractive Rowland Lacy; others in the cast were Norman Lloyd, Hiram Sherman, and Frederic Tozere. Richard Wilson, whose position as Welles's special assistant had considerably strengthened, played one of the shoemakers. Throughout the rehearsals, Norman Lloyd recalls, Welles ate obsessively while the cast was forbidden food; when one fat actress begged for a bite of the pie he was devouring, Welles screamed at her to "get lost."

Welles pulled a typically effective stunt of showmanship on Christmas night. At the end of the performance of *Julius Caesar*, still dressed as Brutus, he told the audience that anyone who wished to remain into the night would see *The Shoemaker's Holiday* in a surprise midnight performance; in the meantime, they could either go out for a late evening supper or stay and watch the scenery being changed. Half the audience left, half remained, but virtually everyone had returned to the theater at midnight. The performance, with no intermission, ran not much over an hour (*Julius Caesar* as we know had run just ninety minutes). This was again a radical break with tradition: it was customary then for a theater performance to last two and a half hours, and indeed once more a handful felt they had not gotten their money's worth. But most welcomed the chance to see a production in one sustained unbroken movement. Certainly *The Shoemaker's Holiday*, previewed that Christmas night and beginning its run on New Year's Day—338 years after its first performance—was exhilarating in its pace. The critic of *The Commonweal* wrote that "by increasing [the play's] tempo and pointing up the characters, Mr. Welles has increased its value both as a human document and as a study of Elizabethan London." Although one or two purists, led by Ivor Brown, the distinguished critic of *The Observer* of London, thought that Welles's abandonment of the play's lyricism was a mistake, Brooks Atkinson had no complaints; indeed, Atkinson particularly admired Hiram Sherman as the journeyman Firk and praised him as "the incarnation of the comic spirit of the play." *Time* magazine summed it up: *"The Shoemaker's Holiday* struck Broadway like a brisk wind." It seemed that 1938 would be a golden year; night after night the audience responded with laughter to the goings-on before the burlap curtains and the stylized perspectives of London streets, and the money began to come in.

At this moment of success, with the world seemingly at Welles's and Houseman's feet, there were nevertheless ominous signs. The repertory policy itself would soon place the collaborators in a bind. Having scheduled the rotation of plays for a given week, in the manner of the Cornell and Gate seasons, they were unable to accommodate the audience response to a hit. Thus they could give only a limited number of performances of a work that, in a normal commercial production in a theater of its own, could have earned them enormous sums of money.

As it was, the profits were considerable, but they would have been far greater if, like Jed Harris before them, the collaborators could have had several hits at once. And not only were their energies frazzled by having to manage three plays at once while planning others, but they could not sit back and watch a sustained presentation unfold over a year or two. They had to keep their colored balls in the air, and this was a considerable personal and financial strain. In an interview in *The New York Times* (February 20, 1938), Hiram Sherman remarked that "all our plays so far have been in the manner of stunts, but someday we'll be producing a play in which an actor opens a door, a real door, walks in, sits down, and begins to talk. And that'll be the end of us."

Simultaneously, Welles was busy with *Cavalcade of America* and *America's Hour* on radio; he seemed unable to be happy unless he was doing a dozen things at once. He also had the ambitious idea of presenting George Bernard Shaw's *Heartbreak House* in a conventional manner, which would be somewhat revolutionary for the Mercury. Houseman was influential in this decision; he wanted to emerge from experimental theater into the lofty regions at the top of the profession. Welles knew that Shaw, with his Fabian ideals, had been the inspiration for all that was best in American liberalism—and *Heartbreak House* was in many ways an expression of Welles's own feelings. In essence, the play pointed to the dangers of isolationism. Written during World War I, it showed how, in the words of the Shaw scholar St. John Irvine, Shaw criticized "Englishmen fiddling while Europe smoulders." *Heartbreak House* takes place in an afternoon and an evening in a British manor under the influence of the ancient Captain Shotover, retired from the navy, who lives with his daughter Hesione and her husband, Hector. Like the manufacturers of war implements in *Ten Million Ghosts*, Shotover is responsible for creating devastating weaponry (including a death ray that explodes dynamite) that will cost human lives. In his preface to the play, Shaw talks of the hopeless indifference of nice, simple, middle-class people to politics and to war; like several Russian dramatists before him, he exposes the essential weakness and evasiveness of human beings trapped in a world of inherited money and settled property. The theme could not have been dearer to Welles's heart.

Welles wanted to cut the play, which ran a full three hours on stage, and to dispense with the elaborate stage directions, which he always hated. But Shaw, in his correspondence with Welles and Houseman—some of which has been preserved—and in occasional transatlantic telephone conversations, was characteristically adamant that not a single word be altered, removed, or juxtaposed. The dramaturgy must be followed to the letter, or his authorization would be withdrawn. His royalties would not be reduced in light of the less than fully commercial status of the company; shrewdly, Shaw had instructed his New York contacts to check on the Mercury's financial position. However, his letter setting out his royalty requirements (15 percent of the gross when the receipts exceeded $1,500 a performance, 19 percent when receipts were between $500 and $1,500, and 7½ percent when receipts were between $250 and $500) was not received until the play was already in production.*

The preparations for *Heartbreak House*, discussed by Shaw and Welles in long and expensive transatlantic phone calls, were as stringent as those for Welles's other productions. Once again he wanted extreme accuracy in the settings, and the room in which Shotover lived, deliberately nautical in mode, was admirably realized by his ever-reliable team. The company had moved to the larger and more spacious National Theater, where conditions were superior for all concerned, and the current repertory flourished as rehearsals of *Heartbreak House* proceeded. A new addition to the company was the auburn-haired Irish beauty Geraldine Fitzgerald, whom Welles found fascinating. She had had a success on the Dublin stage and appeared in an attractive movie, *Turn of the Tide*; she had a fierce quality, sparkling eyes, and a beautiful figure. Intensely Irish, she had a tremendous attraction for Welles, and he was much impressed by her beauty. There was interest, too, in her son, Michael Lindsay-Hogg, today a prominent theatrical director, because of his striking resemblance to Welles.

What was unassailably certain was that Welles became the father of a daughter, Christopher, that spring. He was frantic beyond the traditions of fatherhood on March 7, 1938: *Julius Caesar* was due to open that night in Chicago, and he had to fly there to supervise; he was scheduled to meet thirteen hundred Chicago high school students and their English teachers for a discussion of "The Modern Approach to Shakespeare"; and Virginia was in a New York hospital, waiting for the baby to arrive. If he were in Chicago when the baby was born, he would never forgive himself; nor would he forgive himself if he were to miss the opening in the city in which he had grown up. At rehearsals there had been problems with Lawrence Fletcher as Julius Caesar, Edmond O'Brien as Mark Antony, and Morgan Farley as Cassius, and all

---

* Shaw had sent his terms to Pennsylvania, which he thought was a city, because the telephone number on the Mercury stationery had a Pennsylvania exchange. Not surprisingly, the letter was returned, "Address Unknown."

three actors urgently needed Welles's attention. Moreover, Chicago's Erlanger Theater presented technical problems that called for his greatest efforts. "Will stork outrace plane?" Esther Schultz asked in *The Chicago Daily Tribune*, wondering whether the baby would arrive before the plane did at Chicago airport.

Welles flew to Chicago, returned to New York, rushed to see Virginia at the hospital, then rushed back to Chicago, where he visited Maurice Bernstein. Calling at the hospital, he gasped to a knot of reporters at the front door, "Phew! What it's like to be an expectant father!" He was a guest of Tom Powers (of the *Julius Caesar* cast) at the Cliff Dwellers' Club, where he held his own against hecklers and admirers when he spoke to the members. He participated in an open forum at the Erlanger after one performance, dined with childhood friends at the Petit Gourmet restaurant, and at midnight flew back to New York after a quick interview with his old supporter Ashton Stevens. Stevens wrote:

> Whether you agreed with him or not, his opinions were surer and saltier; because they sounded like his own rather than like the last he had heard or read. He has a magnificent ignorance of the requirements of a snob. He is a restlessly constructive fellow who just won't leave the stage where he found it. I'm afraid he is a genius; but mighty good company nonetheless.

On March 27, 1938, Christopher Welles was born, and Virginia returned to the house at Sneden's Landing. Welles, after delightedly chucking the baby under her chin, saw little of her in subsequent weeks, as his work on *Heartbreak House* consumed him utterly and further flights to Chicago were necessary to resolve the continuing problems with *Julius Caesar*. According to John Houseman, Welles was unfaithful to Virginia throughout this period. Whether or not he had a romance with Geraldine Fitzgerald, there were other women who engaged his attention, among them, columnists said, the ballerina Vera Zorina. It is easy to see from Virginia's letters two years later, many of which have been preserved, her intense love for him and the bitterness she felt about his betrayal of her. Never very strong, her health declined steadily after the birth of her child, and she would soon be in danger of losing her life. Can one doubt that the anguish of Welles's promiscuity—if Houseman is to be believed on that score—caused her at the very least a series of psychosomatic ailments? A photograph by Louise Dahl-Wolfe, published in *Harper's Bazaar*, showed Orson looking uncharacteristically angelic while gazing in delight at his offspring, posed cheerfully on her mother's lap; on the face of it, Virginia appears radiant, but on closer inspection her face shows sadness in the eyes and great tension in the mouth.

Heartbreak House continued in rehearsal. Phyllis Joyce, an Australian, played the part of Lady Utterword, and Brenda Forbes played Nurse Guinness. A new member of the company, Erskine Sanford, was Mazzini Dunn, a part he had created for the Theater Guild; he would later be the flustered editor in *Citizen Kane*. Then a *Time* magazine cover story, "Marvelous Boy" (May 9, 1938), gave the ultimate accolade to Welles's flourishing career. Mentioning Welles's flat feet and asthma, his moon face, and his shambling walk, the piece was predictably inaccurate and foolish but not unkind.

Heartbreak House opened on April 29, 1938. The audience may not have been as ecstatic as those at the Mercury's previous openings, but Brooks Atkinson, despite his annoyance at the length of the play, was as respectful as ever. Noting the absence of tricks and stage devices, he commended the overall intelligence and sensibility, the wit and dramatic alertness of the approach. Atkinson found fault only with Geraldine Fitzgerald's performance, which, he said, indicated nothing more than an ability to memorize lines. Welles himself, still twenty-two, was claimed as the eighty-eight-year-old Captain Shotover; the critics agreed that he simulated advanced old age with unerring skill. A photograph from the production shows him with a long white beard, wearing a crumpled white suit and sitting bowed over at a table; the makeup is extraordinary: for even the hands are effectively marked to suggest the wrinkles and liver spots of later years.

The lesson of *Heartbreak House* was that Welles's style need not be based merely on inspired gimmickry, a collection of mannerisms and expressionist devices; he was as capable as any conventional Broadway director of handling a production in a straightforward manner. And audiences responded happily to the concentrated intelligence and vigor of the play. When the first season ended in June 1938, the Mercury had a glorious profit of $40,000.

The company planned a summer stock production of Oscar Wilde's *The Importance of Being Earnest* in Dennis, Massachusetts, to be moved to the National Theater afterward; the intent was to provide an exquisite, extremely stylized production that would contrast with the other shows. Unfortunately, Hiram Sherman, one of Welles's favorite players and perfect for the male principal in *The Importance of Being Earnest*, decided to join the cast of a new musical comedy, *Sing Out the News*, and he left the Mercury.

Welles was devastated. He collapsed with childish petulance at

Sneden's Landing, lying on his bed and groaning as though in the grip of a fatal illness. Like so many egomaniacs, obsessed with themselves and their work to the exclusion of everything else, he was unable to comprehend that someone in his company could "betray" him, could want to appear in anybody else's work or under anyone else's direction. Clearly Sherman had grown tired of being simply a creature of Orson's world and wanted to strike out on a career of his own, unbound by the inevitable restrictions imposed on a member of a stock company. Houseman suggests that Whitford Kane, Sherman's actor roommate, destined to be the source of the name *Citizen Kane*, influenced him against Welles, but the simpler explanation is likely to be correct. When Houseman was summoned to Sneden's Landing, he found Welles in a fury, grousing loudly that Sherman was his Judas or Iago and was stabbing him in the back.

Welles was lifted from his despair by the pleasing news that executives of the CBS radio network, excited by Welles's success in the theater, wanted him for his most ambitious radio presentation to date. This was *First Person Singular*, to begin on June 11, 1938, with Welles as the producer, director, narrator, and central performer of each hour-long dramatization of a famous play or novel. Welles decided to enhance the experimental techniques he had first honed in *Les Misérables;* the new venture would bring his memorable voice and imposing manner to that wide public for dramatic literature that seems virtually to have vanished from the American scene today. The quality of the dramatizations would be equivalent to that found in productions of the British Broadcasting Corporation in London and would match the excellence of Norman Corwin's admirable *Studio One* series.

With great skill in selection as always, Welles chose "Treasure Island" for his initial *First Person Singular* broadcast. He played both the narrator and Long John Silver with relish and attack. Listening to the production is still an enthralling experience. The opening, with the boy telling of his nightmarish journey and his encounters with the devilish villains, the atmosphere of wind and salt and sea, are effortlessly conveyed through an able adaptation by Houseman and a battery of excellent sound effects.

As it turned out, "Treasure Island" was pushed into second position, replaced at the last minute by "Dracula," a bolder and more publicity-worthy beginning to the series. Like "Treasure Island," it was an adaptation of one of Welles's favorite books; and again Houseman worked with Orson, often over a table at Reuben's restaurant, well into the night. It was not an easy novel to adapt. The first part, told in diary form from the point of view of Jonathan Harker, a naive young man visiting Count Dracula on a business matter in the Carpathian Mountains, was straightforward enough; then, mysteriously and without warning, the author, Bram Stoker, moved the narrative to England, employing correspondence, diary entries, and other narrative devices that broke the book into sections and all but wrecked its central emotional line. Through the force of the author's imagination the story regained its momentum and drove to a powerful conclusion. However, in radio, as in film and television, the story line had to be extremely simple, based on one premise, and with a single protagonist to represent the audience's point of view from first moment to last. This took a tremendous amount of effort and the most drastic condensation, juxtaposition and control. The results were extraordinarily powerful: "Dracula" became a masterpiece in its own right, faithful to the spirit and letter of the book (and far superior to both the trashy, camped-up stage version by John L. Balderson and the absurd, grotesquely tacky movie version with Bela Lugosi). Throughout the broadcast Welles used the same inspired devices he had brought to *Les Misérables* and would soon bring to the soundtrack of *Citizen Kane*. To this day, Welles's "Dracula" is the best performing version.

In addition to the weekly grind of scripting, producing, and directing *First Person Singular* (shortly to be called *Mercury Theater of the Air*), Welles, restless as ever, began laying out plans for the fall season of the Mercury. With the abandonment of *The Importance of Being Earnest* and the removal from the repertory of *The Shoemaker's Holiday* because of Hiram Sherman's departure, two new works were needed to fill out the cycle. The first of them was *Too Much Johnson*, by William Gillette, an actor-playwright who had made Sherlock Holmes as vivid a presence in the theater as he had been on the printed page. His version of Conan Doyle's stories, enhanced by his classic performance in the title role, had created a sensation. Like *The Shoemaker's Holiday* and *Horse Eats Hat*, *Too Much Johnson* was a "sport," a break in the high seriousness of purpose that characterized the Mercury.

The second addition to the schedule was a highly charged dramatic work, *Danton's Death*, by the ill-fated young playwright and revolutionary Georg Buechner. A denunciation of the dangers of power that was perfectly placed in the Orson Welles canon, *Danton's Death* told what happened when Robespierre assumed power during the French Revolution. The play showed how, by overthrowing an oppressive royal and aristocratic order, the revolutionaries only replaced one form of tyranny with another: thus it was a savage and appropriate comment on the rise of the so-called petit bourgeois regimes in Germany and Italy that had overthrown the old settled money class and replaced traditional government with disorder, treachery, and violence.

Too Much Johnson offered opportunities for fast-moving, energetic staging based on the techniques of silent film comedy; it was a launching pad for Welles's desire to break free of the confines of the stage itself. In all his productions he had been reaching out beyond the stage through his rejection of conventional scenery, his elimination of the intermission, his insistence on a ninety-minute production, his emphasis on the rhythm and momentum of the total performance, his use of elaborate lighting effects, and his impatient disposal of the author's stage directions. Inevitably, the logical conclusion of this policy would be to embrace motion pictures as the freest and cleanest method of expression. Welles decided to abandon convention entirely by filming part of *Too Much Johnson* and showing the film portions on stage. This was not utterly original on his part; similar devices had been used in Germany, and Florenz Ziegfeld had introduced film scenes into some of the earliest editions of his legendary Follies. Yet no one had dared to extend the film-and-stage mode to this extent, and the restlessly experimental Welles wanted to take the theater a step further.

In order to centralize his activities, he moved for a period from Sneden's Landing to rooms at the St. Regis Hotel in midtown Manhattan. There he set up a combined studio, cutting room, and production office that was run with the kind of inspired chaos typical of him—and that rapidly began to resemble the ship's cabin in the film *A Night at the Opera*, in which the Marx Brothers are joined in a tiny cabin by maids, janitors, plumbers, manicurists, and a procession of room-service waiters. There was nothing Welles liked better than busyness; there was nothing that made him more uncomfortable than silence and solitude. The fact that filming *Too Much Johnson* involved reckless, madcap chases and whirlwind confrontations delighted him. His resurrection of the movement and passion of the Elizabethan theater had been typical of him; now, using the most contemporary of art forms, he could unleash an equal amount of volcanic energy, spinning without restraint from one exciting comic episode to another.

The first of the major film segments consisted of a chase through New York. This was revolutionary not merely in terms of technique; location shooting had been more or less extinct since the silent film period, when a freer and more untrammeled mode had prevailed. With the advent of the talkies and their greater restrictions on the use of cameras and sound equipment—and the wholesale importation of playwrights into Hollywood—movies had largely reverted to theater. Welles wanted to restore the openness, freshness, and innocence of the days of the Keystone Kops, and in this too he was years ahead of his time. Audiences today laugh when characters in movies of the thirties and forties express their admiration for an outdoor setting that is only a backdrop, and we can see now all too clearly that a chase was staged against back projections. Welles would have none of this tedious trickery; he wanted to show the real New York in a way it would not be shown again until Gene Kelly and Stanley Donen's revolutionary *On The Town* in 1949.

The film material for *Too Much Johnson* consisted of a twenty-minute prologue and two ten-minute introductions to the second and third acts. It would be shot silent, then projected with a band and a sound effects team placed behind the screen (another device used by Ziegfeld in the teen years of the century). In order to accommodate this footage, Welles cut the play itself to just over an hour of stage time. The story of the play and film involved a series of pursuits: the cuckolded husband chasing the rake who had seduced his wife, an angry patriarch removing his daughter from her lover's arms, the rake's wife attempting to entrap her husband, and so forth.

In his approach, Welles drew from Mack Sennett shorts, including the delightful *Love, Honor, and Behave* and *The Lion and the Girl,* which he projected for Houseman and other colleagues in New York. He also looked at Chaplin's shorts but found them less energetic and fast-moving. Above all, he was dazzled by Harold Lloyd's *Safety Last,* in which, among other stunts, Lloyd dangled from a hand on a clock face high on a building in downtown Los Angeles. From these movies Welles learned that the best techniques of film involved rapid cutting, quick blackout lines, a minimum of complication, and one central idea pursued from first shot to last. He found an ideal cameraman, Paul Dunbar, who had worked for Pathé News; Dunbar was used to working rapidly, under any kind of weather condition, and Welles told him to recreate the very look of silent film, which he did by undercranking the camera to achieve a jerky, fantastic action at normal projection speed.

Welles cast much of his company in the picture, including Joseph Cotten, Arlene Francis, John Houseman, Edgar Barrier, and the delightful Mary Wickes, destined to play the most memorable nurses in Hollywood history. The long-suffering Virginia Nicolson Welles, using her stage name of Anna Stafford, sportingly agreed to appear in an important part. Marc Blitzstein played a French barber, and Herbert Drake, drama critic of *The New York Herald Tribune* and soon to become press agent for the Mercury, was a Keystone Kop.

Welles drove the cast to feats of athleticism far beyond their normal capacities. He began shooting in a steamy mid-July in Central Park, only to have the first day's work interrupted by rain. He was quite happy to continue the chase scene in the storm, but the horses in the sequence, terrified by the thunder, reared up on their hind legs and refused to draw the rented victorias. The hackmen would not force the horses to continue, so the entire day's work was canceled.

For three days Manhattan was lashed by driving winds and rain; afterward, Welles went back and finished the scene, then proceeded to shoot on the roof of the Washington market, where the portly Houseman, Herbert Drake, and others dressed as cops pursued Joseph Cotten as he swung from the eaves like a would-be Tarzan. Cotten had to jump from the roof to avoid an infuriated Edgar Barrier, whom he had cuckolded in the story. Just a short time before this, a suicidal youth had stood on a high ledge of the Gotham Hotel and threatened to jump at any moment; the episode, later the basis of the film *Fourteen Hours*, had drawn vast crowds. Thinking that the activity surrounding Cotten was another suicide attempt, hundreds of people gathered in the street, and Welles had to make a perilous descent from the roof to explain that what the crowd was seeing was only the filming of a movie comedy. Everyone relaxed, then laughed and applauded when Cotten jumped from a second-floor window into a horse-drawn wagon filled with cabbages, followed by an enraged Barrier.

There was no question of anyone's being insured or refusing to act in life-risking situations. Even Houseman had to engage Barrier in a fake saber duel at the edge of a two-hundred-foot cliff, with their feet slithering toward the drop at every moment; either of them could have been killed. Such were the risks that Mack Sennett had put his actors through, name players or not, and Welles would not be upstaged by his memory. It says much for the devotion of the anguished players, not one of whom had ever done anything beyond a modest game of tennis or the length of the swimming pool, that they were prepared to stretch themselves for this antic ordeal.

In the most urgent improvisation, Welles dressed up virtually everybody who could walk as militant suffragettes and marched them through the streets of the city. Another improvisation involved altering buildings to look like those of some three or four decades earlier for sequences set in Cuba. A model was built of a Cuban plantation, with a volcano made of papier-mâché and tropical plants from a local store arranged around it, the whole designed by the gifted James Morcum. The model of the plantation house was cunningly matched to the interior set, which the characters would enter seemingly from the screen itself. Fog (of dry ice) shrouded the house, and the image of a steamship appeared on a glass screen; with great ingenuity, Welles and Morcum were able to give the impression that the ship was sailing past the island. (The sequence foreshadowed the opening of *Citizen Kane*, with its evocation of Kane's castle in Florida.) The intention was to create an atmosphere of self-indulgent romantic kitsch, and by all accounts the results were striking. The music composed for the sequence by Lehman Engel was antic, bravura, and comic in mode.

Some scenes were shot in Yonkers, near the Bronx River Parkway; furniture borrowed from a local theater and an abstract version of a bedroom were pulled together to provide a setting for Arlene Francis (in a black negligee) to flirt with Joseph Cotten. In one scene Francis was shown clutching a picture of Cotten to her bosom and hiding it there, but in the close-up her cleavage did not satisfy Welles, and he cut in Augusta Weissberger's, much to Miss Francis's annoyance.

Other scenes were shot at a rock quarry in Haverstraw, near Sneden's Landing, which was also made to look like Cuba through the addition of rented palm trees and blacks wearing straw hats and colorful shirts; in these scenes Cotten rode a white horse through dirty water in a chase episode.

The shooting continued for ten days, with twenty-five thousand feet of film completed, and the editing was done at the old Pathé studios. Welles withdrew to his rooms at the St. Regis to cut the picture. And all the while he continued doing *First Person Singular*, preparing the elaborate "A Tale of Two Cities" and planning the next two or three programs.

According to Houseman, Welles went on having affairs with different women in his rooms; they had to wade through masses of film in order to reach the bed. Housekeeping was out of the question, and maids were forbidden entry to Welles's rooms. The bed sheets were seldom replaced, and dust—the curse of New York City—gathered so thick on the tables you could write your name in it. The floor was so heavy with film that it was almost impossible to penetrate to it; soon the room was like a snake cage at a zoo, with Welles in the middle of it, moving from exhaustion to exhilaration, running stretches of film through a Moviola and chortling or screaming with rage. All this work fragmented Welles's energies disastrously, and then the trouble began. Welles exhausted the financial resources of the Mercury, so painstakingly built up, in the sheer expense of making and cutting the film—and he was not even able to finish it. Then he discovered to his horror that he had had no right to make the film in the first place. The filming had been widely covered in the press, and lawyers for Paramount Pictures wrote him that they owned the screen rights and he was not entitled to show the work at all.

There was further trouble when some of the actors objected to not being paid for their work and complained to Equity; Welles tried to pass the work off as rehearsals or dry runs to allow the actors to see themselves on screen in preparation for their performances, but Equity refused to buy this and ordered that every player be paid in full, or Welles would be expelled. This payment absorbed the remaining capital, and from having been enormously prosperous, the Mercury had fallen to the edge of ruin.

Worse followed. The decision had been made to present *Too Much Johnson* at Stony Creek rather than in New York. Welles had shown a serious lack of foresight; the film could not be projected in the Stony Creek auditorium, for the local fire laws forbade the use of nitrate film in the projector because it was so highly flammable. And Houseman did not much like the results of the film—or, at the first rehearsals, the stage portion of the production, which he found "trivial, tedious, and underrehearsed." He announced point-blank that this must not be the first production of the fall season. However, Welles was obstinate and decided to open the play in the summer, ahead of the other productions. As Houseman had seen, the play was not effective, especially without the movie footage. The so-called tryout, indifferently reviewed and saved from disaster only by the theatergoing public's residual affection for its presenters, simply did not work. That fatal lack of discipline that often underlay Welles's full-blooded talents had this time proved destructive.

Even Welles in his despair had to admit he had been wrong to consider opening the fall season with this work. He went into a depression, and his asthma, always aggravated by a nervous condition, was so severe that he had to occupy a special intensive-care oxygen tent at the St. Regis. Only with difficulty could he summon the energy to work on *Danton's Death*, a play he loved; once more he decided to open up the stage and to give an abstract, terrifying force to the play's picture of the French Revolution. He also forced himself to rise to the occasion of what had now become *Mercury Theater of the Air*. The radio shows had proved greatly successful, building steadily until Campbell Soup became their sponsor late in 1938. Despite all the problems with the

shooting of *Too Much Johnson,* the collapse of his dream for filmed theater, and his illness, Welles had still managed to whip up considerable
excitement on the airwaves. But nothing he had done in that field could
possibly match the sensation he achieved that fall in the unforgettable
broadcast of "The War of the Worlds."

5

Welles and Houseman always sought a degree of variety in their radio presentations. In the fall 1938 season they offered a reworked "Julius Caesar," a stylish "Oliver Twist," an "Around the World in Eighty Days" condensed into less than eighty minutes (Welles was to produce an ill-fated stage version of this work some nine years later), "Heart of Darkness," and "Jane Eyre." (The Conrad work would be the basis of an ill-fated film project of Welles; *Jane Eyre* would be filmed in 1943 with Welles as its star and, in part, director.) Now the collaborators wanted to adapt a science fiction work, and they settled on H. G. Wells's *The War of the Worlds*, a concentrated and powerful novel in which sinister and mysterious invaders attack Earth from the red planet whose canals were then the talk of astronomy buffs everywhere.

Exhaustingly busy as always, Welles had to find a writer to make the adaptation, and he chose Howard Koch, later a co-author of the script of the legendary *Casablanca*. Koch, then a skilled but over-worked tyro, frequently produced sixty pages of script a week, condensing and rearranging the classics under the strict guidance of Houseman. He often worked a twenty-hour day, passing on his scrawled dialogue and directions to a college girl stenographer who transcribed them on an equally grueling schedule. Both Welles and Houseman were obsessed with rewriting, and often dialogue was being changed at the last minute, when Welles—working as always off the top of his head—would slash, condense, transpose, and throw the work around until the very second he went on the air.

"The War of the Worlds" was written under exceptional pressure, even for Koch. Welles was deep in rehearsals for *Danton's Death*, too distracted to help when the novel proved difficult to adapt and called for Welles's touch. Realizing that there was little characterization or depth in the story, Koch found it impossible to choose a correct mode. He told Houseman he would like to do something else, and his wife was also determined that he be relieved of the project.

An exhausted Koch took a Monday off and drove up the Hudson Valley to see his family. Thoughts of the script were buzzing through his head. He had transferred the story's setting from England to New Jersey, thus ensuring an identification on the part of millions of Americans. As he drove, he realized he had been working so fast that he had failed to examine a map of the state in order to give verisimilitude to the story of an extraterrestrial invasion. He pulled into a gas station on Route 9 and got his map. In New York the next day, he laid it out and decided that wherever his pencil landed after he closed his eyes would be the spot for the Martian arrival.

He opened his eyes. His pencil had landed on the town of Grovers Mill. It was a lucky happenstance: Grovers Mill, like Grovers Corners in *Our Town*, had just the right sound of rural America. It was also close to Princeton, where there was an observatory, and thus the character of Professor Pierson, the astronomer, could be placed at the university. The area northeast of Trenton, from Lawrenceville to Dayton, East Millstone, Neshanic, Hopewell, and Clarksville, would become the humdrum setting of a terrifying imaginary event.

For six days before the scheduled broadcast, the strain and struggle of creation brought Koch almost to a nervous breakdown. He settled on a device in which the story would be presented as an actual event, with a news announcer interrupting a program of music to report the terrifying occurrences. Koch took his cue from the famous broadcast the previous year of the burning of the Hindenburg, the German zeppelin that had caught fire at its mooring in Lakehurst, New Jersey. The announcer, in the midst of describing the grandeur of the huge craft as it settled at the mooring tower, saw the flames burst from it and the people dying, and he broke into sobs and cries of anguish on the air.

The show was rehearsed on a Thursday, recorded, and improved that night by the team under Welles's guidance. For legal reasons the names of some few places (but not Grovers Mill) had to be changed at the last minute. On Saturday, Paul Stewart, Welles's assistant (who later played the butler in *Citizen Kane*), prepared the entire aural fabric of the show. It was scheduled for Halloween, Sunday, October 30, and changes were still being made only minutes before the start at 8:00 P.M., Eastern Standard Time.

Welles made a signal for the orchestra to play the Mercury's theme (from Tchaikovsky's well-worn B-flat-minor piano concerto), then he introduced the story, speaking ominously in his best midnight-and-whiskey-sour voice: "We know now that in the early years of the twentieth century this world was being watched closely by intelligences greater than man's and yet as mortal as his own." He was followed by an announcer discussing a "slight atmospheric disturbance of undetermined origin . . . reported over Nova Scotia, a forecast of rain, accompanied by winds of light gale force." The announcer added, "We now take you to the Meridian Room in the Hotel Park Plaza in downtown New York, where you will be entertained by the music of Ramon Raquello and his orchestra." Another voice said that the orchestra music was coming from the Park Plaza (a nonexistent hotel). And then:

> Ladies and gentlemen, we interrupt our program of dance music to bring you a special bulletin from the Intercontinental Radio News. At twenty minutes before eight, central time, Professor Farrell of the Mount Jennings observatory, Chicago, Illinois, reports observing several explosions of incandescent gas, occurring at regular intervals on the planet Mars.

The announcer declared that the gas was understood to be hydrogen and moving rapidly toward the earth. Further bulletins, interrupting the orchestra, told listeners that "Professor Pierson at Princeton" had further comments to make. Pierson described "a red disk swimming in a blue sea, transfer stripes across the disk." This conventional description of the planet Mars and some deliberately dull comments furthering the description were followed by the announcement that at 8:50 P.M. a flaming object had fallen on a farm near Grovers Mill. Carl Phillips, now emerging as the chief reporter on the story, seemingly speaking from the Wilmuth farm at Grovers Mill, described the extraordinary thing that lay half-buried in a vast pit covered with splinters of a tree. "It looks more like a huge cylinder. It has a diameter of . . . what would you say, Professor Pierson?" "About thirty yards."

Phillips describes the metal as being yellowish white. A crowd is present and has to be forced back. The object gives off a hissing sound, and then Phillips describes a new and alarming development: "This end of the thing is beginning to flake off! The top is beginning to rotate like a screw! The thing must be hollow!"

Phillips sees something, or someone, crawling out of the hollow top. "I can see peering out of that black hole two luminous disks . . . Are they eyes? It might be a face. It might be . . . Good heavens, something's wriggling out of the shadow like a gray snake." He tells of the creatures emerging, the leader with a V-shaped mouth dripping saliva from rimless lips that seem to quiver and pulsate. The creature seems to be weighed down by gravity. "The thing is raising up. The crowd falls back." And now the full horror strikes home: the creatures are at large, forty people lie dead, "Brigadier General Montgomery Smith" takes charge. An announcer reports that "those strange beings who landed in the Jersey farmlands tonight are the vanguard of the invading army from the planet Mars."

By this time, panic had set in among many members of the radio audience. Those listeners had not heard Welles's introduction, which would have prepared them for the nature of the broadcast, for they had switched over from *The Edgar Bergen and Charlie McCarthy Show* after the ventriloquist and his dummy had temporarily left the air. Regular listeners to Charlie McCarthy, who would not have been interested in the more specialized Mercury Theater presentations, were unaware that they were listening to a drama; they thought there actually had been an invasion from Mars.

Thousands panicked. In Newark, New Jersey, twenty families fled their homes, covering their heads with towels and pressing handkerchiefs to their faces. In New York City several hundred people jammed railroad stations and bus terminals in search of an immediate exit from the city. One woman called up a terminal to obtain a schedule, screaming, "Hurry, please, the world is coming to an end!"

In Harlem hundreds more swept into the churches, seeking sanctuary and calling for prayer because of "the end of the world." One woman described how she ran up to her roof to look for signs in the sky and in her anxiety almost plunged to her death when she slipped and fell. In Rhode Island people stormed the switchboard of *The Providence Journal*. Electric light companies were asked to disconnect all power so the Martians would have no light to guide them. In Pittsburgh one man found his wife in the bathroom, holding a poison bottle and yelling, "I'd rather die this way than that!" As far away as San Francisco switchboards were swamped, and one woman shouted over the line to her local operator, "How can I volunteer to stop this awful thing?"

In Birmingham, Alabama, people rushed into the streets en masse; at one college the women in the sorority houses, weeping and trembling over the broadcast, lined up at the telephones to speak to their parents or other loved ones for the last time. The streets leading from almost every city in New England were filled with refugee cars. Parties stopped dead as the hysteria spread. No one seems to have listened to the end of the broadcast, when Welles explained that a dramatic presentation was all it was.

The stories of the terror were numberless. One housewife, Sylvia Homes of Newark, gave an account that illustrated the general feeling:

> We listened, getting more and more excited. We all felt the world was coming to an end. Then we heard "get gas masks!"

That was the part that got me. I thought I was going crazy. It's a wonder my heart didn't fail me because I'm nervous anyway. I felt that if the gas was on, I wanted to be together with my husband and nephew so we could all die together. So I ran out of the house. I guess I didn't know what I was doing. I stood on the corner waiting for a bus, and I thought every car that came along was a bus and I ran out to get it. People saw how excited I was and tried to quiet me, but I kept saying over and over again, to everybody I met: "Don't you know New Jersey is destroyed by the Germans—it's on the radio."

One anonymous victim of the broadcast, a senior at a Houston college, said later, "My roommate was crying and praying (as we drove off). He was even more excited than I was—or more noisy about it, anyway; I guess I took it out in pushing the accelerator to the floor." He added, "I thought the whole human race was going to be wiped out— that seemed more important than the fact that we were going to die. It seemed awful that everything that had been worked on for years was going to be lost forever."

Archie Burbank, a filling station operator in Newark, told of his experience:

All of us ran into a grocery store and asked the man if we could get into his cellar. He said, "What's the matter? Are you trying to ruin my business?" So he chased us out. A crowd collected. We rushed to an apartment house and asked the man in the apartment to let us into the cellar. He said, "I don't have any cellar! Get away!" Then people started to rush out of the apartment house all undressed. We got into the car and listened some more. Suddenly the announcer was gassed, the station went dead, so we tried another station but nothing would come on.

It is estimated that some twelve percent of the radio audience heard the broadcast and that more than half of that number took it seriously. Indeed, as Bernard Herrmann and the Mercury orchestra played the final chords at the conclusion of the show, the phone rang in the control room and the mayor of a midwestern city demanded to speak to Welles immediately. He yelled at him, "There are mobs in my streets! Women and children crowding my churches! Violence, looting, rioting! If this is just some crummy joke, then I'm coming right to New York and beat you up!"

CBS, which up to now had given Welles his head, was furious.

William Paley, its all-powerful chief, was under pressure from local bigwigs to discipline his star. Newspaper reporters besieged the lines and rushed into the studio. Officials arrived with members of the studio police and forced Welles, Houseman, and their entire team into a back office while squads of CBS staff members obtained every script and every record and either destroyed them or locked them away from public view. Somehow the press forced their way into the temporary prison in which the Mercury team was incarcerated and screamed for information: how many deaths had been caused? Had there been "fatal stampedes"? What word about suicide, riot, and murder?

In the early hours of the morning Welles and the rest of his team were released. Typically, they made their way not to their homes but to see what was going on with *Danton's Death*. Buechner's play was still being rehearsed at that hour under substitute directors; no crisis could keep the unstoppable Mercurians from their work.

So great was the panic caused by "The War of the Worlds" that it seemed Welles would be destroyed by the event. The press was largely condemnatory, in some cases attacking not only Welles but the gullible radio audience itself (thereby risking criticism from its own readers). The Federal Communications Commission discussed taking disciplinary action, and lawyers for some people who had believed the broadcast threatened to prosecute the Mercury. Luckily, the ingenious Arnold Weissberger found a clause in the CBS contract absolving the Mercury from "all legal liability resulting from the content of our show." As a result no action was possible, and the matter was allowed to pass. Yet the episode had succeeded in illustrating—as perhaps Welles had secretly intended—the extreme vulnerability of the United States at a time when Hitler had begun to ride roughshod over Europe. It was clear that America was ill prepared for anything approaching a confrontation with an enemy power. Far from marshaling, or even attempting to marshal, a coherent response to what they believed were invading forces, red-blooded Americans had fled like children before Welles's Halloween gimmick. What would happen if there were a real invasion? What would happen if long-distance aircraft allowed the German air force to bomb New York?

America had not experienced a foreign invader since the War of 1812, and it had never been bombed from the air. Because jets did not exist in that age and air travel was expensive, it was largely only the wealthy, immigrants, and students on foreign exchanges who had firsthand knowledge of Europe, and European news often got pushed into the back pages of the newspapers. Consciously or not, Welles had drawn attention to the dangers of isolationism and unpreparedness as sharply as Shaw had done in *Heartbreak House.*

Stimulated by the effect of his sensational broadcast yet shocked at what it revealed of public gullibility, Welles proceeded with *Danton's Death.* As so often before, he disposed of the intermission and most of the stage directions and trimmed the play to his favorite ninety minutes. In Welles's interpretation the play was intended to illustrate a transition from authentic revolutionary feeling to what one critic described as "military dictatorship and the degradation of liberty and equality to battle cries of international carnage." The parallel with the totalitarian systems of Germany and Russia (the latter parallel greatly distressing the Communist party in America) was explicit. In both Germany and Russia—as in the Italy exposed by the modern-dress *Julius Caesar*—people's parties had quickly become corrupted, betraying the principles of equality and democracy in an assertion of individual power treasonous to the concept of State. *Danton's Death* could not have been more appropriate in 1938, nor could its message have been less likely to be well received in Berlin and Moscow—or in certain circles in Washington. Welles engaged Stephen J. Tichachek to design the sparse scenery, composed largely of a cyclorama made of skull-like Halloween masks, picked up by the cast from costume stores and packed together so tightly they looked like the deathly contents of the Paris catacombs after the Revolution or the wholesale beheadings of Madame Guillotine.

Jean Rosenthal's lighting strikingly evoked day, night, blood, and fire. Sometimes the cyclorama of skulls became a bloody red, at other times a steely, adamantine gray; at the final curtain, as the guillotine knife descended with a sinister blaze of light, the stage and the entire theater were plunged into stygian darkness. At the center of the stage was an elevated platform, not dissimilar to that in *Julius Caesar,* and the cast rose or fell upon it as it became in turn the Chamber of Deputies, the Conciergerie, and even a tumbrel, the cart that carried the condemned to the execution block. In the last sequence the platform rose high above the stage, dominated by Madame Guillotine awaiting her victims.

Welles had never been so obsessed with a production. He did not sleep for almost two days as he dress-rehearsed the play; at other times he slept on a couch in the center aisle of the theater, ate from there, directed from there, and lay down there when he was too exhausted to stand. And the results were startling and stimulating to a degree. Unfortunately, critical taste had turned against Welles. Why? Why were the reviews of *Danton's Death* almost uniformly unfavorable? Had "The War of the Worlds" undermined his credibility? Was it because he had fooled the Establishment, and now the newspaper owners were putting pressure on their critics? Or was it the traditional need among critics to cut down the very people they had raised to the heights, like the priests of the Aztec empire who trained young men to physical perfection, dressed them in gilded robes, invited them to the top of the pyramid, and then cut out their hearts with stone knives?

The critical response to *Danton's Death* in November 1938 was brutal (and, if we are to judge by the photographs of the production, quite unfair). Only the ever-loyal Brooks Atkinson could find something to praise in the presentation. Many criticized Vladimir Sokoloff, a veteran of the Stanislavsky Moscow Art Theater, as Robespierre; they charged that his command of the English language was insufficient. "Mr. Sokoloff," wrote Stark Young of *The New Republic*, "fought so valiantly with the English language as to be something of a solo drama for himself . . . for the words stuck, clung and spit themselves beyond our normal listening habits." Young also characterized Welles's delivery of the curtain speech as St. Just as "merely stylized exhibition, arbitrary and too hard to follow."

The public proved notably indifferent to *Danton's Death*. Theater party agents, who depended on a favorable press, failed to secure the necessary numbers of tickets, and the Communist party, so often approving of the Mercury, ostentatiously withdrew its support, thereby ensuring that many radical intellectuals would not attend. The play closed after twenty-one performances, and with it went every last cent of capital that had been scraped together in the previous few months to bail the Mercury out of debt. No one can be blamed for this. Sanctimonious explanations were offered, even by the admiring Brooks Atkinson, to account for the sudden failure of the Mercury. Atkinson wrote of Welles's "whims and desires in the operation of the plays," which were supposed to have brought a company low. (And, it might be added, that had provided Atkinson with cause for some of the more hyperbolic pronouncements of his career.) John Houseman examined the situation in an essay, "Producing the Play."

The very nature of Welles' method has defeated him. The violence that transports an audience and forces it into an understanding of old values and into an intimate emotional participation in the great works of the past may also . . . fill an audience with a most infuriating and exhausting sense of discord. The spectators may have a justified feeling that they are witnessing, not one of the great plays of the past, but a personal conflict between the director and his material.

Houseman was right to draw attention to Welles's manic, frustrating excesses. Yet through the Mercury and *Mercury Theater of the Air*, Welles had revitalized and revolutionized theater and radio, giving them an excitement, a color, and a political purpose and strength they had never known before and would never know again. That he overstretched himself and in *Danton's Death* risked bucking both the right and the left should be no cause for disparagement. Even Brooks Atkinson charged him with possibly having wrecked the Mercury Theater. True, his extravagance, his insistence on nightlong rehearsals with a fully paid cast, his wild *follies de grandeur,* drained the Mercury's coffers. But the determination to give of his best is surely moving; and, despite Houseman's statement that the only purpose of the Mercury was to bring its creator(s) success and fame, one cannot deny that Welles made more than a few useful points about the threat of fascism in Europe, and this alone justified the Mercury's brief career and gives him a permanent place in the history of the theater.

Another fling at Shakespeare was imminent. For years Welles had planned a condensation of Shakespeare history plays under the title *Five Kings.* He had a craving to play Falstaff, and here it must be said that his purpose was more self-centered than sensible. He began laying out a scheme for *Five Kings* while continuing his career in radio. *Mercury Theater of the Air* became *The Campbell Playhouse,* sponsored by the Campbell Soup Company and handled by the Ward Wheelock advertising agency under Wheelock and the inexhaustible Diana Bourbon. Welles, Houseman, and Howard Koch provided the scripts, Ernest Chappell the commercial announcements, and Niles Welch the regular announcements. Bernard Herrmann, the eccentric and irascible conductor and composer, continued his work for Mercury as the maestro of the orchestra.

Beginning in December *The Campbell Playhouse*'s time slot was Friday, 9:00 P.M. to 10:00 P.M., replacing the Sunday hour in which *Mercury Theater of the Air* had appeared. From "Heart of Darkness" (which had followed "The War of the Worlds," "A Passenger to Bali," "Pickwick Papers," "Clarence" (from Booth Tarkington), and "The Bridge of San Luis Rey," the team moved on to its first presentation under the new banner, Daphne du Maurier's "Rebecca." Welles was the difficult hero, Max de Winter, and Margaret Sullavan his nervous bride; Agnes Moorehead provided an effective menace as the sinister housekeeper, Mrs. Danvers.* The program included an interview with du Maurier in London; she recalls today that she was delighted with the version.

On December 16 Welles appeared with the English comedienne Beatrice Lillie in "Call It a Day" by Dodie Smith; Christmas week featured "A Christmas Carol," in which Hiram Sherman was reunited with Welles, who played Scrooge. The final production of 1938 was "A Farewell to Arms" by Ernest Hemingway, in which Welles had the exciting experience of co-starring with Katharine Hepburn. She was so taken with him and the show that she sent him a large bouquet of red roses and a thank-you note the following day. Welles went on to do Elmer Rice's "Counsellor at Law"; "Mutiny on the Bounty," which Virginia Welles co-adapted with Houseman and Koch, and which included an interview with a specialist in the *Bounty's* history; "Arrowsmith" with Welles and Helen Hayes; "The Green Goddess" with Madeleine Carroll; and "Royal Regiment," adapted from the novel by my godfather, Gilbert Frankau, starring Mary Astor and featuring an interview with the author from London. Others in the series were "The Glass Key," "Beau Geste," "Twentieth Century," "Showboat," "Les Misérables" (again), "Private Lives" with Gertrude Lawrence, "Our Town," and "Victoria Regina" with Helen Hayes recreating her famous stage performance.

During all this activity Welles continued to prepare *Five Kings.* In the middle of rehearsing "Black Daniel," the story of Daniel Webster, with Joan Bennett, Welles announced at a commemorative luncheon on April 24 (Shakespeare's birthday) that the chronicle plays in the new format would be presented in association with the Theater Guild. The Theater Guild would supply the backing and much of the sixty thousand subscription list; the production would tour before opening on Broadway. Burgess Meredith was cast as Prince Hal, John Emery as Hotspur. The three acts would be divided into thirty-two scenes, the action taking place on a large revolving stage that kept circling "like a Lazy Susan on a breakfast table," according to one account. The intention was to carry out a plan of continuous action without scene-shifting; once more the lighting would provide atmospheres of gaiety or gloom. One part of the scenery represented London, the other the bat-

---

* Welles's first-person approach, with Margaret Sullavan narrating, matched that of the novel and inspired David O. Selznick to create a precedent by following suit in his 1940 film version.

tlefields; Jean Rosenthal wrote in *Theater Arts Monthly* (June 1939), "A basic castle setting made up 'London' and was placed on one third of the revolving stage together with a street running through the center and a large open court at one end and a narrow alley at the other. In addition, a basic tavern set made up the other part of the 'London' set." For the battle scenes the stage revolved; the actors fought or marched on platforms and ramps that became the respective fields of conflict."

The Mercury Theater and the Theater Guild prepared this elaborate experimental production in Boston while "Royal Regiment" was in rehearsal for broadcast. *Five Kings* was badly organized and confusing, in part because Welles seemed to have lost control; according to Houseman, his drinking now averaged one to two bottles of brandy or whiskey a night, and his sexual affairs were further dissipating his energies. Rehearsals (in the ballroom of the Claridge Hotel and in various rehearsal halls in New York City) had been chaotic and often disastrous, marked by Welles's frequent lateness and seeming inability to wield the influence and energy he had hitherto demonstrated. Lack of money was another problem; the Guild exerted extraordinary pressure on everyone. The big turntable was a headache, for it tended to get out of control. Suddenly Welles became more erratic and even accused Houseman of poisoning him. It was scarcely the best atmosphere in which to open the production out of town.

On February 24 Welles appeared in "State Fair" with Burgess Meredith on *The Campbell Playhouse*, and the author, Phil Stong, appeared with them. On Monday, February 27, 1939, *Five Kings* opened in Boston without a proper dress rehearsal; Welles's idea of running the show with two intermissions proved to be a disaster. The laborious, heavyweight production lasted until 1:00 A.M., and by the time it had finished, two-thirds of the audience had left the theater. The Theater Guild directors, led by Lawrence Langner, were extremely depressed and disturbed by what they took to be a fiasco of major proportions. Critics unanimously agreed that the play was not yet ready for Broadway. The correspondent for *The New York Times* wrote that "depth of characterization was missing . . . the performance has still to acquire polish and assurance. And the revolving stage must be tamed. . . . [*Five Kings*] will need hard training." *Time* magazine said that while Welles had slashed much that was dull from the royal cycle of plays, he had also ripped much that was vital; Falstaff was "often good fun, but seldom Falstaff."

After an uncomfortable week in Boston that included a horrendous moment when Langner was presented with a $15,000 bill for golden time* caused by Welles's notorious all-night rehearsals, the play shifted to Philadelphia. It took ten boxcars to accommodate the scenery and costumes. Langner and the other Guild directors, extremely annoyed with Welles by this time, insisted the production be cut by forty minutes. Even though it was shorter in Philadelphia, the show was a disaster. Welles's taste for the extreme, the extravagant, and the baroque had alienated even his strongest admirers in the company, and in Philadelphia he did something unconscionable. Just before the opening in Philadelphia he radically shifted all the positions of the cast and all the lighting arrangements of Jean Rosenthal. The dangerous lack of control that was soon to mark his career had manifested itself.

The reviews in Philadelphia were equally bad, and Welles feared that *Five Kings* might not make it to New York. He began investing his savings in the production, switched scenes again, replaced actors, and flew to Chicago to try to persuade the First National Trust and Savings Bank that it should release to him the rest of the trust left by his father, which was not due to be paid until May 6, 1940, his twenty-fifth birthday. Understandably, the bank refused. Houseman gave him no support at all; their relationship had deteriorated drastically. Moreover, the now burdensome *Campbell Playhouse* was still grinding on. In spite of his out-of-town problems, Welles managed to drag himself through broadcasts of "The Glass Key," "Beau Geste," and "Twentieth Century" while Houseman worked gallantly to sustain the series at a high level. In this impossible period, with his life seemingly drained away, Welles received—completely out of the blue—an amazing offer.

He had a keen admirer in George J. Schaefer, production head of RKO-Radio Pictures in Hollywood. Schaefer was a man of considerable skill, intelligence, and style, one of the rare sensitive souls in a cold and brutal industry. He felt that Welles would be a major addition to the prestige of the studio, one of the smaller in Hollywood, with a record of quality production as exemplified by the immortal *Gunga Din* and the Fred Astaire–Ginger Rogers musicals. After weeks of negotiation with Arnold Weissberger, he drew up a contract that contained several remarkable provisions: Welles would receive $100,000 for the first film, which he would produce, write, direct, and star in, the subject of which he was free to choose, and over which he would be granted a unique autonomy. He would also receive a unique twenty percent of the profits. For the second picture, he was to receive $125,000 plus twenty-five percent of the profits. No other director in the talkie pe-

---

* Double-time pay called for by union rules for late-night work.

riod had been granted the right of final cut of his work; Welles alone
had secured through his lawyer that privilege. Even he found it hard to
believe that he had been made such a glorious and unprecedented proposal. Whether or not this was a publicity gimmick, the studio was
firmly committed to him by June, and he began to make plans to go to
California with Houseman, who, though much disaffected with him,
unhesitatingly agreed.

The two men set out for Hollywood in July. Welles stopped off
briefly in Chicago to present and appear in a theatrical version of *The
Green Goddess*, which he had already done on radio. It was given as an
RKO circuit vaudeville show, and everything went wrong with it; even
a film sequence he had shot in New York was accidentally projected
backward. The fiasco seemed to set the seal of disaster on an impossible
year.*

Welles and Houseman moved into the Chateau Marmont Hotel just
off Sunset Boulevard for several weeks. Welles hated Hollywood—the
palms, the brassy light, the vulgar opulence—and Hollywood ignored
him. Despite concentrated effort on a possible first project, Conrad's
Heart of Darkness, Welles continued to plan for another season of *The
Campbell Playhouse*. This was crazy; he would have to fly to New York
every week to do it. Meanwhile, *Heart of Darkness* occupied his days
and evenings. Once again he saw the possibilities for comment on the
misuses and corruption of power.

---

* In *Run-Through* Houseman describes a curious incident. As Welles and he
passed the Bismarck Hotel, Welles pointed to an alleyway at the back, saying,
"That's where they brought my father out—feet first." It was then that he told
Houseman his father had killed himself; Houseman says Dr. Bernstein falsified the
death certificate.

6

Nineteen thirty-nine became a nightmare. That year Welles won the TWA prize for the most traveled passenger, logging more than 300,000 miles in the air between Los Angeles and New York. Flights were grueling in those days; the coast-to-coast trip took about eighteen hours, and when the weather was bad, the plane had to land until it cleared. Welles made the round trip every week, going over the *Campbell Playhouse* scripts with Houseman in New York, flying to Los Angeles to work on *Heart of Darkness*, then flying back to New York a week later for another radio presentation.

The pressure from the Ward Wheelock Agency to get out of the RKO deal and go back to New York to live was endless. On July 28 Welles cabled Wheelock that his contract with RKO was "irrevocable" and he saw "no reason" why Campbell Soup "should not allow him to originate his shows from California."

He moved from the Château Marmont to a large house at 426 Rockingham Drive in Brentwood, thereby adding to his exhausting activities the problems of setting up house. Wheelock constantly peppered him with complaining cables. The executive had understood, he said, that *Heart of Darkness* would be made before September, thus releasing Welles for the fall radio season, but now it would not be made until December. Wheelock threatened injunctions against the studio. Weissberger, who was about to leave the law firm of Riegelman, Hess, Strasser and Hirsch for his own offices, was working day and night to settle the differences between Wheelock and Welles. On August 1 he urged Welles to resolve the matter once and for all, and Welles did so. Yet Wheelock seemed unable to realize that Hollywood broadcasts would be as acceptable as Broadway broadcasts, and no one would care where they originated.

In August, Wheelock, evidently worn out by his struggles with Welles, handed over the matter of dealing with him to his associate, Diana Bourbon. Her letters—antic, sometimes explosive, filled with energy—practically leap off the pages even today. From them she emerges as a woman of extraordinary determination, intelligence, and steely nerves, a woman hard pressed in her dealings with a recalcitrant genius. She harassed him, wheedled him, flattered him, and came close to abusing him as the harrowing production schedule rolled on with "Ah, Wilderness," "Peter Ibbetson," and "Jane Eyre."

So rattled was Welles that he was even fighting with Weissberger that month, complaining about his warnings and subtle attacks on the agent Myron Selznick's range of responsibilities. There was a problem over the casting of "Algiers." Hedy Lamarr had been in the film version, which was a huge popular success, but MGM had banned her from the radio because of her foreign accent and poor acting ability, both of which would be exposed when her beauty was not visible to the audience.

After much suffering, Welles made a deal with George Schaefer on *Heart of Darkness* on August 28, 1939. On September 13 Welles was deeply involved in work on the project. Two days later Schaefer advised Welles from Europe that he was beginning to have qualms about *Heart of Darkness*—less than three weeks after he had agreed to go ahead with it. He wrote that in a Europe submerged by war, people were reluctant to go to the theaters; the unwritten implication was that serious movies would have a hard time of it if there were no continental audience to supplement the less sophisticated American audiences. Welles was asked to pare the *Heart of Darkness* budget and to build the entertainment value of the film as high as possible for the American public.

Welles set about pasting up the novel page by page in a large book, dictating dialogue from the paste-up to his secretary, noting different ways to present each scene, then sketching details of camera angles, with descriptions and drawings of each character, the total growing from 254 pages of script to 800 pages in the breakdown. He settled on the technique of telling the story in the first person, and he began with a sequence in which the audience was given a lecture on photographing the picture from a subjective point of view. (A similar lecture on the soundtrack was contained in Walt Disney's *Fantasia* the following year.) He would show a canary cage with a greatly enlarged human face behind it, the mouth filling the screen: this was the canary's-eye view. The audience would then be shown the world from the character's view. Welles would play both Marlow, the seeker after truth in the African jungle, and the mysterious ivory trader Kurtz, who not only symbolizes fascism by lording it over a native tribe but refers directly to Hitler in the dialogue. By giving the camera the eyes of Marlow, Welles sought to convey a vision of river and jungle that would drive the audience forward into a strange and exotic adventure. And this new experiment in film would at the same time use the character of Kurtz to alert the audience to the danger of fascist dictators.

In his anxiety to please, he cabled Schaefer sometime in mid-September to assure the executive, who was now in New York, that "every cent would be counted twice" in the spending on the picture. No single luxury would be indulged; there would be provision only for absolute essentials. Innumerable changes in the method and approach would keep the cost of the picture down. The budget-cutting clearly took its toll on his nerves; on October 12 he rushed off a letter to Diana Bourbon that was filled with annoyance at the questions and comments in her notes, angry at criticisms of his approach, and upset by critiques of "Algiers," which she had suggested was ruined by the sound effects of North African street scenes ("And goddammit, don't accuse me openly or covertly of sabotaging the [Campbell] Playhouse"). He fiercely defended his decisions in "Algiers" and expressed annoyance that Diana's complaints had come to him "through third persons." So rapidly was the relationship with Campbell deteriorating that, as he flew to New York to do "Liliom," CBS was flatly refusing to pay his rent on the house in Brentwood.

Welles was also bothered with demands and complaints from Maurice Bernstein. In a letter of October 30, Weissberger wrote that Dr. Bernstein wanted reimbursement of $1,233.76, which he had advanced to Welles as his guardian; so determined was Dr. Bernstein to collect this money (which he had already collected from the Chicago bank) that he sent Weissberger the canceled checks that he had preserved for over a decade. Orson telegrammed Dr. Bernstein that a letter with the money would follow, but Dr. Bernstein wrote an especially obnoxious note later in October ("I have been in a terrible fight with the mailman who said there was no letter from you"). Could he please hear by November 1, because his examination before the California board was on November 15. (The implication was that he needed money for the fare.)

Dr. Bernstein was already well off in his thriving career as a bone deformity specialist and surgeon and a society physician in Chicago, and he certainly did not need his hard-pressed protégé's financial support in the move. He slimily reassured Welles that Orson need not bother about his "imposing upon you or taking advantage of you"; he just wanted some help "until settled and earning." He added, "Although I may not burn up California, I can always earn enough to make a living." Then, "What you spend in one venture, I can live on for life." He said that he himself could supply the basis for "a new venture": a play about him. Maybe friends could suggest prospects for him in California. He could not go back to Kenosha, and Chicago was driving him to distraction. He begged, "If you will not write, phone or wire me."

Not content with harassing Welles, Dr. Bernstein pressed Herbert Drake, the Mercury publicist, to dun money from certain of Dr. Bernstein's former patients who had moved to California. On November 7 he grumbled that he was still waiting for a phone call from Orson. Meantime, Welles produced "The Magnificent Ambersons" for radio and was laying out "Mr. Deeds Goes to Town" and "A Christmas Carol"; and he was struggling to get *Heart of Darkness* through the front office, starting photographic tests again with several of his favorite actors, led by Everett Sloane and Norman Lloyd. He was also busy on a script for *The Smiler with a Knife,* based on a novel by the British poet and critic C. Day Lewis, who used the pen name Nicholas Blake for a series of entertaining thrillers.

The Smiler with a Knife was based on the life of Sir Oswald Mosley, whose blackshirt brigades suggested to many a fascist takeover of Great Britain; Welles turned the story into a comedy-thriller in the Hitchcock vein. The hero and the heroine (a daughter of the attorney general) discover under odd circumstances a clue to the existence of a fascist plot similar to the Christian Front movement's attempted coup d'etat against Roosevelt that year. The madcap heroine determines that a sinister but charismatic society figure rather like Howard Hughes is the leader of the revolutionary conspiracy (in one sequence the villain imprisons her in an iron lung). The script—witty, episodic, fantastic—is marvelous; it seems decades ahead of its time, and it could be filmed today. (One scene took place at the Todd School.) However, it was overlong and the political parallels in it were undoubtedly much too risky for a jittery movie industry terrorized by right-wing senatorial investigations. The theme of a fascist takeover (usually Lindbergh was nominated as a potential president by the North American fascists) was certainly the obsession of the left at the time.

While Welles was working on *The Smiler with a Knife,* Dr. Bernstein at last got the money he wanted and sent off a fanciful version of Welles's life to Herbert Drake for publicity purposes. Little or nothing of it could be used. And again he requested money: "I personally think that it would be a great stunt for him. You know how people feel about crippled children, the old homestead and mother. Orson always figured on spooky, scairy [sic] things, and it would do him good to show his big admiring public that he has a tender side to his bearded nature."

Dr. Bernstein passed the California state exams and revisited California at Orson's expense at the end of November. Welles's financial affairs were then worse than ever. In a long, extraordinary memorandum to Welles's assistant Richard Baer on November 27, Weissberger pointed out the ghastly state of Welles's finances. He said that while most Hollywood big money earners were on stringent budgets and were told exactly what they could spend, Orson refused to conduct his affairs in that way. He incurred expenses before determining whether he could afford them, and thus he was always in the red. The delay in *Heart of Darkness* was bad because it left him insolvent; he could not draw more money until he started production.

Welles never repaid the Mercury backers from his RKO contract as he had promised. When William Sweets, one of the backers, wrote to Houseman on November 22, 1939, Houseman was obliged to explain that Welles had sunk $50,000 into the Mercury in a futile attempt to save it, and no repayment to Sweets could be made.

By sheer effort Weissberger had forced Columbia Artists to hold out from their advances enough to pay Welles's immediate expenses. The lawyer constantly tried to get Schaefer to make an advance on movie money, but it was impossible to do so, even to the tune of a thousand dollars, because Schaefer could not be sure he would get the money back. Weissberger ordered Baer not to obtain local loans, as this would complicate the issue and could be dangerous. Weissberger warned Welles that the delay in payment on *Heart of Darkness* would create a very great stringency. It "must begin soon."

Baer wrote Weissberger of Welles's extraordinary demands for money and the fact that he had to support John Houseman on Orson's income as Orson's employee; the rent from the house was due, and it was difficult to find even fifty dollars in cash. CBS had made huge advances and had not been repaid because of Welles's "vicarious habits." Baer had had to besiege CBS with frantic letters and telegrams to get the rent money. He added that Welles fully realized the seriousness of his financial position. He was living on money earned from radio, much of which was going to pay his and Mercury's debts. But he refused to cut down on his standard of living; Baer felt that Weissberger should do his utmost to obtain loans, even for two-week periods, as Welles was flat broke.

In November, Campbell and CBS at last relented, and Ward Wheelock agreed that Orson could move the *Campbell Playhouse* operation to Hollywood. Welles arranged to have some of his favorite actors, including Agnes Moorehead, George Coulouris, Joseph Cotten, and Everett Sloane, transferred to Los Angeles. Work recommenced briskly for *The Campbell Playhouse.*

In the meantime, Welles was becoming involved with the beautiful, high-cheekboned actress Dolores Del Rio. A descendant of the grandee conquistadors of Mexico and related to a Zapata revolutionary general, she had the bearing and manner of an aristocrat. Born Lolita Dolores Negrette in 1905, she had been married in the 1920s; her husband, Jaime Del Rio, died in 1928. She starred in *Flying Down to Rio* (with Fred Astaire and Ginger Rogers), and she had made headlines by rescuing a child from drowning. In 1930 she married the distinguished MGM art director Cedric Gibbons, whose sumptuous white sets presented a world of glamour and luxury that was synonymous with the MGM style. He and Dolores had enjoyed what was often described as a fairy-tale marriage; they lived in an elaborate art deco house in Santa Monica that had tubular steel stair rails and huge, beautifully furnished rooms alive with colored glass screens and brilliant lamps, a house in which Cedric Gibbons expressed his eccentric, kitschy genius to the full. It was well known in Hollywood that on the nights the couple felt romantic, they would stage a Romeo-and-Juliet scene in which Dolores would lean over the balcony that dominated a secret staircase, and Gibbons would ascend the stairs to perform his marital duties.

By 1938 the marriage had soured, the couple having grown tired of one another. Orson and Dolores met at a party at Jack Warner's; Welles had always admired her and once followed her out of a New York nightclub just to stare at her. Their relationship took fire at once. Despite his exhausting travel schedule, his financial agonies, and his fights with CBS, Welles still found time for a full-blooded romantic affair. They made a dazzling couple, and Gibbons added fuel to the fire by expressing bitterness at what was going on.

Virginia Welles took the situation badly. She was in agony, painfully hurt, even though her marriage to Orson was over in the physical sense. She could not bear to think of losing him, and when she set up divorce plans, gallantly telling reporters that she did not blame him because he was a genius who worked twenty hours a day and had no time for marriage, she was breaking apart inside. A great consolation to her was Geraldine Fitzgerald*

Dr. Bernstein was still a nuisance. On November 29 he wrote Her-

---

* Ironical if gossip about Welles's earlier relationship with Fitzgerald were true.

bert Drake that Orson had promised to call him, probably on the money issue, but had not; as a result the good doctor had had very little sleep, followed by bad dreams. ("If you should hear of my sudden death, you will know that no one is responsible but Orson, however I will haunt him in his dreams.") He was still going on about money at the beginning of December. Weissberger was unsuccessfully pressing Welles to collect money loaned to Burgess Meredith and Charles MacArthur, the playwright husband of Helen Hayes.

On December 16 the official separation agreement between Virginia and Orson was drawn up: if Virginia remarried and took up residence outside the United States, she would be able to have Christopher with her during custody periods, provided she pay for the child's travel to and from her father; Virginia would have $500 to cover the railroad fare to Reno (to obtain her divorce) and the attorney's fees there; Orson must pay at least half her rent and he must take out $50,000 life insurance with Christopher as beneficiary and an equal amount with Virginia as beneficiary (provided she did not remarry); Virginia was to receive $500 a month allowance.

By mid-December *Heart of Darkness* was canceled. The budget had reached just over a million dollars, and this was far beyond the studio's resources; the references to fascism and Hitler were unacceptable; and there were casting problems. Welles began signing actors for *The Smiler with a Knife,* among them Ray Collins, John Emery, George Coulouris, and Everett Sloane. On December 16 Baer memoed Weissberger that Welles continued to profess ignorance of his finances and that there was great stringency in trying to cut costs. "There is staring us in the face the simple fact that it is a full-time job to get money from Orson." It was a full-time job to get money from Burgess Meredith as well. Two days later Weissberger was writing Baer about Orson's extravagance. Coming east in September, Orson had "ordered the purchase of an airplane," believing it would cost less than $5,000, even though he had no funds with which to buy it; he dropped the idea when he found that the upkeep would cost $20,000. Weissberger urged Baer to cut servants' salaries to the bone and reduce household expenses; bills were coming in at "eight hundred dollars a week, a tremendous amount of money for a bachelor's living expenses." That same week, Orson ("Ort") Collins Wells died in Chicago; Welles still owed Wells money that he had borrowed in 1932.

The fights with Diana Bourbon continued, and in fact cancellation of *The Campbell Playhouse* was imminent. Welles refused to allow one of Bourbon's favorites, Irene Dunne—whom he did not admire—to appear in anything. Meanwhile, Bourbon opposed his dear Gerry Fitzgerald because she was not known in the provinces. Finally, he was forced to accept Irene Dunne because, he wrote Bourbon, she had "millions more fans than I" and Fitzgerald had no mass public.

Two days after a joyous Christmas with Dolores Del Rio, Welles had to go to New York for a strenuous conference with Bourbon, and he announced he would be using a private plane despite the expense and the lack of insurance. He was talked out of this only with difficulty.

Dr. Bernstein, now living at the Chateau Marmont on Welles's meal ticket, wrote him at the outset of 1940, "I understand from Henson, the undertaker at Kenosha, that . . . your father's grave was disturbed. When they dug him up, they found him holding a copy of *Radio Mirror* and *Time* magazine." This grotesque touch of humor was followed by an expression of desperation; Dr. Bernstein lied that he had "only $700" between himself and oblivion, and he must have good clothes, an apartment, and money for a year, as he had nowhere to turn. He would never impose, but he knew Orson could help him without great sacrifice. "You have helped many stranded actors who meant nothing to you. I hope that I mean more than they did to you."

He added more touches of personal humor. He said Orson's great-grandmother was involved with Spanish pirates, and he provided a poem ("He's a ham and somewhat of a cad") about Welles that found an echo in the song about Kane sung by the chorus girls in Welles's film of the following year.

A few days before Christmas 1939 a meeting had been held in a private dining room at Chasen's restaurant in Beverly Hills. Welles, Herbert Drake, John Houseman, Richard Baer, Richard Wilson, and others discussed the problems of *The Smiler with a Knife*. After dinner Baer read out the notice from RKO that until the script was completed and approved and a shooting date set, all salaries of Welles's Mercury team would be stopped. Welles said he would pay Moorehead, Sloane, and the others, but it was pointed out to him that he had no money to pay them. Albert Schneider, Welles's manager, had the unpleasant duty of conveying to him this fact, a fact of which he was already firmly apprised. He was furious; he charged Schneider with having stolen the money. And this despite the fact that Weissberger had been informing him daily of his ruinous extravagance.

Welles screamed and yelled at the group, blaming them collectively. When Houseman asked him what he would do about the actors, he replied sharply, "What would *you* do?" Houseman advised him to level with them, to tell them that all the money had gone. Welles said he had never lied to his Mercury people, that Houseman had lied to them and was a crook. According to Houseman, Welles picked up a burning Sterno dish heater that had been used for the steaks and threw it at him drunkenly. It whizzed by his head and hit a curtain. Welles threw another, and the curtains caught fire; then he threw two more.

According to Welles, he upset a service trolley and the fire in the chafing dish caught on a curtain; the fire was extinguished with a soda siphon. Welles screamed "Crook!" and "Thief!" down the stairs after Houseman.

Welles followed up this onslaught with a four-page telegram. Houseman left the next day by car for New York. Stopping in New Mexico, Houseman wrote Welles that he felt no reduction in his affection for him and said he did not want to see their partnership "follow the descending curve of misunderstandings and mutual dissatisfactions along which I see it so clearly moving." He said he intended to go back to New York and that he would like, "one day, again to produce plays together." He expressed nostalgia for the Mercury and said that "the present situation is hopeless and must be changed at once for both our sakes."

7

Welles's financial affairs were in still greater disarray as 1940 began. Virginia obtained her divorce in Reno on February 1. In his new independent law offices in New York, Arnold Weissberger was fretting over ways and means of balancing the accounts. Meticulous as always, he insisted on paying off as many debts as possible, but Welles constantly required new funds to support his way of life. He insisted on having a houseful of servants in the manner of the moguls, and they included Charles, an imposing, carefully silent butler; a maid; a cook; and Alfalfa, a chauffeur and man of all work, whose role at the wheel Charles sometimes—to Alfalfa's irritation—usurped.

A consolation as always, Dolores Del Rio was the one magic note in his troubled life. Her beauty and composed, serious temperament relieved by flashes of humor were an inspiration and a joy. When Welles had to leave her to go to New York at the beginning of February for conferences with the RKO board, he was exceptionally edgy and out of sorts.

For years one of his favorite havens was the restaurant "21," where he was known to the staff and where he spent prodigally beyond his income. At lunch with Houseman on an early February day they discussed what he might do next, now that his two projects for RKO were firmly on the shelf. They knew that Herman J. Mankiewicz was interested in writing a film about William Randolph Hearst, the grand and notorious newspaper tycoon whose support for Hitler had made him a target of the American left. Hearst and Colonel Robert McCormick of *The Chicago Tribune* had been among Franklin D. Roosevelt's strongest critics on the isolationist front line. Hearst had organized a famous fake interview with Hitler by his correspondent Karl von Wiegand, in which Hitler was supposed to have reassured the Western world on the subject of his intentions; this infamous episode had greatly annoyed one of Welles's most admired figures, the liberal journalist and editor George Seldes, and others of similar persuasion, including I. F. Stone and Albert E. Kahn.

In view of the fact that *The Smiler with a Knife* had just been stopped, allegedly because of casting problems but more definitely because of its anti-Nazi content, it is surprising that Houseman and Welles considered the Mankiewicz idea. Given Welles's political outlook and that of Mankiewicz, any film portrait of Hearst that they devised would be not only unflattering but distinctly colored by a left-wing viewpoint. Now that Europe was at war and Roosevelt was fighting the isolationists, such a movie would draw considerable criticism in Congress. Indeed, the right-wing senators Burton Wheeler and Gerald Nye were even then charging that Hollywood was making anti-Hitler movies that could provoke Germany unduly in a time of peace with America. No such considerations inhibited the two collaborators, who decided to go to Los Angeles and talk the story out with Mankiewicz.

They flew to California in late February, and Houseman preceded Welles to the witty, bitter, grousing, and miserable Herman Mankiewicz's home at 1105 Tower Road in Beverly Hills. The writer had been injured in a car crash and lay abed with his left leg in a large white cast like the Man Who Came to Dinner. But even in his bedridden state he was cantankerously excited. Always a vigorous salesman of himself, he had pressed the idea of the Hearst story with Welles weeks before because he saw in it an opportunity to break free of the hackwork that had weighed him down for so long. Movies like *Escapade, My Dear Miss Aldrich, The Emperor's Candlesticks,* and *It's a Wonderful World* were depressing examples of manufactured studio screenplays, written without enthusiasm. The one exception was *John Meade's Woman,* which contained elements of a criticism of riches in the story of a tycoon who suffers from personal isolation and loneliness in his pursuit of wealth and power. The movie was mediocre, but it offered more than a glimpse of its author's political leanings. Earlier in the 1930s he had written a fairly uncompromising critique of Hitler in a script about the rise of the Nazi party; this script was suppressed in view of the fact that Hollywood had substantial investments in Germany.

As Houseman expressed Welles's desire to revive the Hearst project, Mankiewicz warmed to his theme. He spoke of his personal knowledge of William Randolph Hearst and of his experiences at dinner parties at Hearst's mansion, San Simeon. He retailed many anecdotes, some true, some invented, of the royal figure of newspapers, and Houseman dutifully or fascinatedly attended. Mankiewicz reminded Houseman of an idea he had discussed with him before, that of presenting a life story seen through many different eyes so that the audience could have a portrait in the round. He had planned to make a version of the life of either Howard Hughes or the criminal John Dillinger in this manner, showing each from various points of view; now, in his excitement over the Hearst idea, he spoke of presenting Hearst's life in a similar approach.

Fired by Mankiewicz's enthusiasm, Houseman realized that this failed writer had enough in him to make a comeback with this bold and audacious idea. Houseman called Welles from Mankiewicz's bedside and told him with characteristic sonority of his pleasure in Mankiewicz's response. Immediately Welles jumped in his Ford, and Alfalfa drove him to Tower Road. In the following days Welles discussed the script with Mankiewicz, and a deal was quickly set: Mankiewicz would write the screenplay, using Welles's ideas, with Houseman supervising, and Welles would come in at a later stage to edit, condense, and add to the screenplay he had inspired.

There were reasons for this rather surprising altruism on Welles's part. Normally he would have insisted on being present at every stage of the writing, but at that time he was distracted by personal problems and the need to make some money immediately by embarking on a lecture tour. Mankiewicz decided that Hollywood residence offered too many distractions, and he and Houseman, accompanied by a secretary and a nurse, took off to the ugly little town of Victorville in the high desert northeast of Los Angeles. There, in a shared bungalow at the Campbell ranch, they argued over the correct approach, and when the approach was agreed upon, Mankiewicz dictated to a secretary, Rita Alexander (later supplemented by Frances Schenck).

Sarah Mankiewicz, the writer's wife, and William Alland visited Victorville from time to time and went away with pages for Welles to read. He was not pleased; he found them dull and wordy. *The Campbell Playhouse* was absorbing his attention, and the notes and telegrams from Wheelock or Bourbon in New York were even more irritating than usual. He had to supervise the scripts, cast, and produce the shows—a grueling weekly routine—while at the same time preparing his lecture tour and revising for Harper the 1934 acting editions of Shakespeare that he had worked on with Roger Hill. As usual, he was averaging two or three hours' sleep a night, sustaining himself on massive doses of Benzedrine; yet he still earned the devotion of the somewhat neglected Dolores Del Rio.

There was the constant radio work, the fielding of creditors, the long discussions with Weissberger and the letters to and from Weissberger's office concerning the IRS close-in on Mercury, and there was Richard Baer, constantly reminding Welles of money problems and hazards. So severe was the financial pressure and the struggle of getting into the studio from Brentwood that finally he gave up the house there. The landlord, Paul Leviton, was extremely annoyed in the wake of Welles's departure; he complained of damage to the property, broken Wedgwood china, shattered vases, a carpet chewed up by Welles's dog, stained furniture, a swimming pool mattress ruined, a dozen highball glasses broken, even a cologne bottle shattered, and curtains, venetian blinds, a velvet bedcover, blankets, and sheets all rendered virtually unusable.

Baer and Weissberger wrangled bitterly with Leviton to get the charges reduced to less than five hundred dollars. When at last the bill had been paid, Baer's remarks about it were savagely unprintable. Under Weissberger's pressure, Welles moved considerably down the social scale to 8545 Franklin Avenue, a pleasant, unostentatious Cape Cod house with a white clapboard front and eaves, high in the Hollywood Hills.* Reached by a narrow winding road, it was perhaps chosen because it was so difficult to find. Alfalfa and Charles between them used up as much as $150 a month in gas driving Welles back and forth on his journeys to RKO, CBS, and Dolores's house. As if Orson did not have enough to contend with, Virginia gave him further problems. She was so ill from some undisclosed ailment, according to one of her pleading letters to Weissberger, that she had only a fifty-fifty chance of recovery. She demanded and got the Ford even though she was in the hospital and could not drive it; Welles had to give it up and buy himself another—and Charles had to have his own car.

Welles was even more fretful over an inept series of articles by Alva Johnston and Fred Smith in *The Saturday Evening Post*, "How to Raise a Child: The Education of Orson Welles, Who Didn't Need It," which contained the usual nonsense about his nine aunts. Welles shared the manic dislike of all show business people for life stories that they themselves do not edit, control, and censor, and without a shred of reason or sense he threatened the editor of the *Post*, Wesley Stout, with a libel suit. Welles demanded retraction of the entire contents of the articles, a demand to which the editor understandably refused to accede. When Welles telegrammed a thunderous insistence on an apology, Stout slapped him down with a reprimand, telling him that coercion was certainly not the correct way to obtain a retraction. Welles had to abandon his threats.

---

* Oddly, John Houseman lived there later in the 1940s. It was owned by Sidney Toler the screen's Charlie Chan.

Virginia seemed to grow worse. In note after note she wrote of going east with Geraldine Fitzgerald and her husband, but she was too sick to be moved. She complained about doctors, nurses, and income tax demands. So constant were the problems concerning her that, tired of dealing with them, Welles's secretary, Miss Walthers, resigned and Katherine Trosper took over.

Still fuming over the *Post* articles, Welles picked up a book by Professor Hadley Cantril of Princeton on "The War of the Worlds" broadcast, and he had scarcely gotten to page three when he exploded with anger. He dashed off a wild letter to Cantril on March 26, grumbling about "a serious error" in the work that was "detrimental to my reputation." His beef was that Howard Koch was given credit as author of the script, when Koch had been "merely a member of the writing staff." In fact, Welles said, grudgingly scattering praise where it was not due, John Houseman and Paul Stewart were responsible. He demanded that an erratum slip be placed in all printings (he meant copies, with a correction in future printings) crediting him with being the sole author. Cantril refused, and once again talk of a lawsuit rang the rafters at Franklin Avenue. This hatred of giving credit to anyone else was typical of Welles; his ego could not or would not tolerate the idea of anyone's sharing, in that highly collaborative industry, the applause for a famous and world-shaking achievement.

On April 3, with great impatience, Welles gave up the house on Franklin for no discernible reason other than financial pressures. Weissberger compelled him to economize by taking an apartment at 11009½ Strathmore in West Los Angeles and abandoning the household staff. (Alfalfa worked for him from time to time, not always with salary.) Virginia was forced to take a cut in alimony, and the maid, Rona Graves, was talking about unpaid back salary. Welles had to draw on his trust fund in Chicago and dispose of securities. And Maurice Bernstein was still demanding money, insisting on a refund of $1,300 he had expended on Orson's education. Weissberger told Orson that, despite his earnings from RKO of more than $70,000 plus expenses, he had only $4,700 left on April 9. On top of everything else, Cantril was threatening a lawsuit because Welles had attacked his book publicly, and he was getting affidavits from Koch, Houseman, and others in support of the accuracy of his book.

In early April, Welles headed for Kansas City and points east, lecturing and firing off telegrams to United Press International, which had allegedly misquoted him as speaking slightingly of Hollywood. On April 13 he was still fighting with Cantril, accusing him of relying on Anne Froelich, Houseman's former secretary and now Koch's secretary. There were grumblings of a conspiracy and charges that Houseman's affidavit was as worthless as Froelich's because Houseman was about to produce a new play by Koch on Broadway (a pure fantasy of Orson's). He redoubled his demands that the book be changed in his favor.

Welles traveled through the Northwest and across the country, speaking informally about acting, telling stories, inviting hecklers, reciting speeches from Shakespeare, and in general setting out to shock and amuse. It was an exhausting trip, and Welles was dogged by worries. One faint ray of light was that Virginia had started to talk about remarrying; she was involved with Welles's friend the writer Charles Lederer, who, ironically, was the nephew of Marion Davies, the mistress of William Randolph Hearst, whom Mankiewicz and Houseman were busy slaughtering in their script. The sorely pressed Welles certainly appreciated this touch of humor in his life, and more certainly he looked forward to being relieved of alimony and child support payments, for Lederer was conspicuously rich. When Orson returned to Los Angeles at the end of April, Houseman went to Hollywood to confer with him.

Soon Virginia was asking for a lump sum settlement in advance of her marriage. Welles responded that such a settlement would make him a miserable loser, and why should he be obliged to present her with a dowry? His curious reasoning showed an abandonment of responsibility to his former wife and his child; he gave no inkling of enthusiasm for paying for Christopher's upbringing. Virginia gave up her plea, and somehow Welles persuaded her to take a further cut in alimony and to pay her own hospital bills.

Only his articles and lectures kept Welles from outright bankruptcy as his debts far outran his frail capital. Virginia, obsessed with property, pressed for various books, records, pictures, china, silver, glassware, and linen drapes from the old apartment in New York. Oddly, Welles refused to pick up the $1,350 owed him by John Houseman or to take Houseman off salary, nor would he collect $200 owed him by Burgess Meredith. Houseman wrote rather ungratefully to Virgil Thomson on May 2, 1940, "It really does not seem five weeks that I've been here. . . . I am treated with great respect and kindness by my studio, but my employer [Welles] is an egomaniac and a megalomaniac. His present mood is one of endless procrastination. God knows when he will start making the picture with this new company of his."

Welles telegrammed Weissberger to pay no bills for the time being without his permission, to give up the notary offices in New York and fire the staff, to have record checks rushed to him with lecture fees without deducting debts where possible, and to cash in the long-beleaguered trust fund in Chicago.

Money, money, money: the agony continued day and night. In May $10,266.95 was shelled out to the IRS and money was repaid on loans from CBS. In June came the shock that every cent from the lecture tour had gone. Virginia was bitter and furious at Welles's failure to support their child. In a threatening letter to Augusta Weissberger she wrote, "The joke is on me too long, and I will find a lawyer to agree with me. (I'm sorry if I sound sinister, but that is the way I feel.)" Arnold Weissberger was annoyed. He slapped her down with a short note telling her all bills had been paid and, in effect, to stop her whining.

It was an ugly, tense month, and there was little relief when at last Mankiewicz and Houseman returned to Hollywood with the screenplay, which they called *American*. The script was somewhat unwieldy and stodgy, as Welles had found on one brief visit to Victorville, and indeed it adhered too closely to the lives of the tycoons who had inspired it to have an independent vitality of its own: it smelled of the lamp. The present script was the second draft, and Orson decided that with a supreme effort it could be worked into a satisfactory film.

The screenplay covered seventy years in the life of a tycoon, and its best feature was its disillusioned, hectic portrait of power and its misuses. In the first draft there was a long episode in Rome in which Kane stays in a lavish Renaissance palace and disports himself with a party of pimps, homosexuals of both sexes, and nymphomaniacs; in this palace Kane gets the idea of buying a failing newspaper for fun, thus forming the basis of his empire. There were scenes in the White House, of Kane's honeymoon in the Wisconsin north woods,* of Kane's school days and early roisterings. In one sequence a young admirer of Mrs. Kane was found dead in the grounds of Kane's palace in Florida, named Xanadu, and this recalled the old canard that Hearst had caused the death of the director Thomas H. Ince when he became convinced that Ince was having an affair with Marion Davies. There was a reference to the Christian Front's attempted coup d'etat against Roosevelt in the killing of Kane's son Howard during an attempt to seize an armory, and in this there was a reference to the hearings in Washington and New York on the Christian Front attempt on the New York State armories.

American was simplified in its second draft, but the script still had direct parallels with Hearst's life. The characters of two Kane associ-

---

* William Randolph Hearst had an estate in the region that was much discussed in Kenosha.

ates, Bernstein (for Maurice Bernstein) and Jedediah Leland,° were based on Hearst's business manager S. S. Carvalho and on Ashton Stevens, the Chicago columnist and critic who as we know was a friend and supporter of Welles. Stevens read and approved the script and later visited the set to see himself portrayed by Joseph Cotten, and he wrote of the visit in his column. The business of building the newspaper empire was close to that in Hearst's own life. Both Hearst and Kane were only children, born in 1863, both were expelled from Harvard, and both obtained their fortunes from a mineral mine.

Hearst attacked President McKinley in his paper; Kane attacked President Monroe. The famous telegram exchange between Hearst and the artist Frederic Remington was retained almost exactly. (Remington, covering the Spanish American War of 1896, cabled Hearst: "Everything quiet. There is no trouble here. There will be no more. I wish to return." Hearst replied: "Please remain. You furnish the pictures; I'll furnish the war.") When Kane's guardian banker, Walter P. Thatcher, grumbles that the newspapers are losing a million dollars a year, Kane says, "I'll have to close this place—in sixty years." The response is drawn from Phoebe Hearst's comment on learning that the papers were losing the same amount: "At that rate, he could last thirty years."

There are parallels also in the character of the political boss Jim W. Gettys (named after an acquaintance of Welles, a trustee of Todd) with Boss Charles W. Murphy, a political operator who fought Hearst when Hearst ran for governor of New York; Walter P. Thatcher is a caricature of J. P. Morgan.† Kane's politics reflect Hearst's, beginning with a Jeffersonian emphasis on free speech, attacking corruption in big business, and later turning to fascism. Sometimes the parallels are startling: in 1889 Hearst's *Examiner* reached 62,000 circulation on Sundays; in *Kane,* the circulation reaches the same figure. Again and again the story echoes the character and spirit of its subject. The parallels are not merely exploitative but serve a purpose: to expose the moral corruption caused by riches, fame, and unlimited power. In the early drafts of the script some of the parallels are so close that the legal dangers involved would have been insuperable. For example, Hearst worshipped Abraham Lincoln, and Mankiewicz and Houseman placed Kane in the Lincoln Room of the White House, gazing transfixed at Lincoln's portrait. The character of Marion Davies was greatly distorted in the pa-

---

° Jed Harris, producer, and Leland Hayward, agent, were well known to Welles and Mankiewicz.

† John Houseman questions this in his memoir.

thetic Susan Kane, but the blond hair and the voice were similar. Later Welles would add touches from other people's lives, among them the descent of Evelyn Nesbit Thaw, the well-known actress who was involved in a famous shooting incident at Madison Square Garden and became a miserable nightclub entertainer, the debacle of Ganna Walska in Chicago, and Edith Mason's addiction to her Italian conductor-coach husband.

The origin of the crucial element in the story, Rosebud, the name of the sled that was the one innocent and beautiful thing in Hearst's life and is consumed in the final shot of the picture, burned as a symbol of all Kane had lost, is a subject of speculation. Mankiewicz always said that Rosebud was based on a bicycle lost when he was a child. In 1942 he was sued, or threatened with a suit, by a woman who claimed she had been his mistress in the 1920s and that he had called her Rosebud. Welles maintained that Rosebud was the name Marion Davies gave to her nose (or her private parts). In the special edition of French *Vogue* for December 1983, Welles, discussing his late father, said that a horse that had won the Kentucky Derby was named after his parent.* This is not true, but a list of Derby winners (which includes Macbeth II and Joe Cotton) shows that the winning gelding in 1914 was Old Rosebud.

Mankiewicz added one touch from his own experience. Many years before, he had had to write a review of a production of *A School for Scandal* for *The New York Times*. The star was Gladys Wallace, wife of Samuel Insull, who had built the Chicago Opera House. He began with the words, "Miss Gladys Wallace, an aging, hopelessly incompetent amateur, opened last night in," and then fell asleep at his typewriter, overcome by the demon drink. The same incident occurs in the movie when Kane's associate Leland passes out at his instrument.

Welles began working on the script on June 1, applying bold, characteristic strokes. He switched lines from one character to another, transposed scenes, altered and then dropped the Rome sequence, sharpened the characterizations, and cut several episodes (a dinner scene at Rector's in New York, the honeymoon in Wisconsin, material dealing with Bernstein in Xanadu). He added the opera scenes, drawing on his memories of Chicago and the Ganna Walska scandal. In every way Welles improved the screenplay, steadily reducing it from three hours to just under two. He slashed through a subplot dealing

---

* As we have seen, there *was* a well-known racehorse named Dick Welles, a sibling of Ort Wells; in *Citizen Kane* a reporter suggests that Rosebud might have been a racehorse.

with an attempted assassination of Kane, added and then dropped a shipboard scene with Kane's first wife, and in this third draft gave impact to the character of Susan. The resulting story was more intimate and less expansive than the original.

Much of Welles's feelings of bitterness toward Virginia were exposed in the scenes in which Kane angrily attacks Susan. Welles's assault on Houseman at Chasen's is echoed in the violent outbreak of anger in which Kane throws the perfume bottle at Susan (an identical bottle was one of the smashed items listed at Brentwood) and in Kane's scream downstairs at Gettys.* As the two collaborators had intended, there was much of Welles in the portrait, particularly in the early scenes: Kane loses the Rosebud sled and his mother at the age of eight; Orson's mother died when he was eight. Like Kane, Welles at an early age struck his friends and colleagues as being strangely isolated from them—using them, manipulating them, sparking them to great attempts, yet essentially cut off from them by his ego and his prodigious talent in a world that was in the last analysis his own.

Welles's ruthlessness, like Hearst's, consumed, enhanced, and disposed of everyone in sight. And he suffered from that because there was a point at which he, like Hearst, could not be reached. The difference between them was that Welles was an impoverished artist writing about wealth from the point of view of the angered and embittered intellectual left, while Hearst looked down at the world from a position of supranational power. One was a liberal, the other a fascist; yet with great wizardry—and despite the bold pen of Welles striking through one revealing passage after another—Mankiewicz and Houseman worked an implicit comment on their great and good friend into the warp and woof of the bold narrative called *John Citizen, U.S.A.*, then, finally, *Citizen Kane*.

Welles, starting June 18, reworked the script with Mankiewicz. Their revised screenplay was completed on June 24; it ran to 156 pages with 118 scenes. In May, before starting on the rewrite, Welles had been in New York to attend the annual RKO sales convention at the Waldorf-Astoria Hotel, where he skillfully announced the work in progress in a manner designed to conceal its revelatory theme and titillate the salesmen with the prospect of a potential winner. The Production Code office in Hollywood received the script in July, and the motion picture code administrator, Joseph I. Breen, shortly to join

---

* Welles persistently denied the parallel, saying he drew the scenes from an unproduced playscript.

RKO for a brief spell, declared the script acceptable on condition that the brothel scene was cut and some other trims were made. Certain direct references to Hearst were taken out because some people at the studio, following Welles's first reading of the material to George Schaefer, saw potential legal problems. Schaefer was torn between the excitement of a prospective money-maker that would justify his questionable investment in his young protégé and the fear that the story was too bold, too close to the truth, and too left of center to be acceptable to a naive and conservative industry and mass public.

That summer was undoubtedly the most significant of Welles's life. Virginia had married Charles Lederer in Arizona and moved to Lederer's house on North Elm Drive in Beverly Hills. She continued to press Welles for money, but her demands were less seriously entertained now that she had a husband. When Welles called the house to inquire about Christopher, Lederer was rude and belligerent.

By contrast, Lederer was extremely mild and gentle when he received the script from Mankiewicz, who, behind Welles's back, had asked him to see whether anything in it would offend Marion Davies. Lederer replied that he saw no reason to believe she would be upset. (According to Pauline Kael, Lederer in fact forwarded the script to Hearst, but this cannot be correct, or there would have been retributive action by Hearst's people at this time instead of later.)

Welles kept Mankiewicz officially on the RKO payroll, paying him a thousand dollars a week through the Mercury/RKO accounts; he tested Joseph Cotten successfully as Leland; he gathered details of Hearst circulation figures and of newspaper office buildings and layouts for the art department; he tested Ruth Warrick and liked her for the part of the first Mrs. Kane; he went to battle yet again with Virginia, who had returned to the hospital; he began hiring the team that would create a masterpiece; he read the script to George Schaefer. Of course he himself would play Kane; anyone who had dared to question that casting would have been a fool.

He loved to use the Mercury players, and consequently he launched several of them on movie careers. This was one of the rare films cast almost entirely with newcomers to the screen. George Coulouris, the gifted British actor whom he had brought to Hollywood, had made two movies when Welles hired him to play the saturnine, Morgan-like banker, Thatcher. The difficult and edgy Everett Sloane was cast as Kane's business manager, Bernstein. Ray Collins became the political boss, Gettys. Agnes Moorehead, who had first met Orson when he was five, was ideally cast as Kane's tragic mother. Erskine Sanford became Carter (named after Jack Carter), the old editor of the collapsed newspaper Kane assumes. Paul Stewart took the role of Kane's butler. William Alland was Thompson (echoes of Virgil Thomson), the reporter who explores the story of Kane, and the narrator of *News on the March*, the *March of Time* parody that comes at the beginning of the film. All these actors had had rich stage experience, but with the exception of Coulouris, all were strangers to the screen. Welles carefully instructed them in screen acting as opposed to acting for the stage. For weeks now he had been screening one movie after another (among them the films of John Ford*), learning screen rhythm, speed and momentum, the indispensable flow of editing, the dreamlike images, and discovering how the camera eavesdropped on lives as though it were a silent and invisible observer of emotion.

Welles went beyond the Mercury to find a remarkable, totally unknown player. Her name was Dorothy Comingore, who, when Welles met her, was called Linda Winters. A discovery of Charles Chaplin, and probably a girl friend of his, she had appeared only in crowd scenes and was living in obscurity. Welles met her at a party, and with his usual instinct for talent he saw at once that she would be perfect as Susan Kane. Now every part had been ideally cast.

From his long theater experience, Welles knew that casting was two-thirds of the battle in preparing any theatrical presentation. But he also knew that motion pictures demanded enormous visual craftsmanship, that merely to mirror great acting would not be enough. From his master, John Ford, he had learned how each subject calls for its own visual style. In Ford's case that style ranged from the bare and austere approach of *Stagecoach* to the highly mannered and heavily Germanic high-contrast black and white of *The Informer* and *The Long Voyage Home*.

The cameraman of *The Long Voyage Home* was Gregg Toland, who had achieved, through deep focus, by shooting directly into lights, using ceilings made of muslin, and arranging scenes in which characters were isolated against darkness in brilliant pools of light, a visual chiaroscuro rather like that of German silent films and those German woodcut novels (especially Otto Nückel's *Destiny*) in which the story was told entirely in pictures. Welles saw how Toland's approach to a story of ships and seamen could be applied to a story of power and loneliness. When Toland said that he wanted to work with him, Welles was delighted. Toland decided to use the Germanic style of *The Long Voyage Home* in *Kane*.

---

* Especially *Stagecoach*, a model of economical screen narrative.

Samuel Goldwyn had Toland under contract and disliked loaning him out (he was in demand by the Goldwyn star Merle Oberon and had just won an Academy Award for *Wuthering Heights*). But Toland was determined to free himself, and he appealed to Goldwyn to loan him out. To Welles's delight, Toland brought with him the talent of his entire team, his operator, his assistant cameraman, and the rest of the crew.

Welles hired his old friend and colleague Bernard Herrmann to compose the musical score, including the fake opera *Salammbô* (suggested by Welles and drawn from Flaubert's novel), whose motif was a parody of Massenet's *Thais*, an opera in which Hearst's first love, Sybil Sanderson, had appeared (as had Edith Mason Bernstein). Houseman put together the libretto from Racine's *Phèdre*. Fortunately, the art and sound departments of RKO were superb. The ambience of Kane's world was recreated with great economy using existing sets, some of them from the classic *Gunga Din* and from *Son of Kong* and *Mary of Scotland;* the famous long shot of Xanadu recalled the castle in *Snow White*. Even the music incorporated existing copyrighted themes; the *News on the March* theme had been heard in *Nurse Edith Cavell*, which Welles's friend Herbert Wilcox had just made for RKO.

A main concern of Welles was makeup. He was fascinated by the studio's resident makeup artist and head of the makeup department, Maurice Seiderman, a White Russian whose father had been a wig-maker for the Moscow Art Theater. Seiderman had won a children's drawing contest, and that had earned him his Moscow Art Theater position. He had fled the Russian Revolution and settled in the United States, where he had worked on Max Reinhardt's celebrated 1924 production of *The Miracle* in New York and with the distinguished Yiddish Art Theater. Welles fastened on him at once. To play Kane, Welles had to age from twenty-five to seventy-five, and the other characters also had to age in the course of the film. With his great knowledge of makeup—indeed, his obsession with it, for he hated his flat nose—Welles was fascinated to see evidence of Seiderman's skills. Seiderman had an intimate knowledge of anatomy and the process of aging and was acquainted with every line, wrinkle, and accretion of fat in aging men and women. Impatient with most makeup methods of his era, he used casts of his subjects in order to develop makeup methods that ensured complete naturalness of expression—a naturalness unrivaled in Hollywood.

For the duration of the shooting Welles would see himself transformed each morning into one of the last five of the seven ages of man. The ordeal began at 5:00 A.M., and when Welles was playing the older

Kane, it continued for as long as three hours. At night the makeup had to be removed, and the procedure did terrible things to the natural skin and beard that had been growing under the makeup during the day. Sometimes peeling off the layers of plaster and jellylike substances— Russian vodka was used to liquefy and remove the material—was especially harrowing. Seiderman made six artificial chins, three noses, eye patches, a false hairline, a bald pate, a graying lacquer, false veins and wrinkles, a makeup suggesting liver spots, and body padding to evoke a middle-aged spread.

Welles was given special contact lenses covered with a network of red veins, and he could imagine himself as he would be forty-five years hence, a bald, wrinkled old man (actually he would age quite differently). He was delighted to the point of laughter with the results, and he was even more pleased when he could remove the gruesome intimations of mortality and rediscover his young, smooth-faced, and virile self.

According to Welles, all those associated with the film, and the studio files (though Pauline Kael denies it), the early scenes of *Citizen Kane* were passed off as tests. Allegedly, Welles was afraid that if the studio brass realized the picture was in production, they might have been tempted to close it down. Actually, such a motive was implausible because Welles had already had the script approved at every level. In fact the tests, done in the usual way, were so good that the decision was made to include them in the picture. This was commonly done in Hollywood; for example, when Betty Field was shot in costume tests for *Kings Row*, the tests were included in the picture.

Production started on July 29, 1940, with the scene in the *News on the March* projection room in which the film magazine producer assigns Thompson, the reporter, to find out why the dying Kate uttered the word "Rosebud." Soon after this Welles shot the scene in which Thompson meets the broken-down Susan Kane in the nightclub, one of the best episodes in the picture. Immediately afterward Welles directed the scene of the picnic at which Kane bursts out in rage, the Chicago hotel room scene (shades of the Bismarck!) where Susan reads aloud the critical attacks on her opera debut, a shot of Kane talking with Hitler, Kane going to Susan's apartment when she has a speck in her eye, and the lightning-swift wedding scene. These scenes were all still listed as tests in the production reports. Officially, the picture did not begin shooting until August 1, when Welles, through Herbert Drake, advised the press that they could come whenever they wanted and watch the great work in progress. Louella Parsons and Hedda Hopper both wanted to be first on the set; the rival vultures fluttered their feathers at the prospect of seeing the birth of an alleged master-piece.

On July 31 Louella gurgled in her column in *The Los Angeles Examiner*, "I can hardly wait until tomorrow at five P.M. to see the great Orson Welles in action." Apparently she was blissfully unaware that the movie, despite many trims, still emphatically pilloried her boss. The next morning Hedda said in her column in *The Los Angeles Times*, "I wouldn't miss the christening for the world." However, neither columnist turned up on the appointed day. Louis B. Mayer of MGM, who must have gotten wind through Hearst of the subject of the picture, scheduled a preview of the Clark Gable vehicle *Boom Town* on August 1, and since his word was law, both columnists attended that screening rather than the *Citizen Kane* shooting.

When Louella did turn up a few days later, Welles cleverly entertained her at a five-course lunch in his dressing room, which had been the dressing room of Gloria Swanson and was still decorated with red satin in the manner of a brothel boudoir. When Louella, who was no fool, pressed for details of the story, Welles waffled. "It deals first with a dead man; you know, when a man dies there is a great difference of opinion about his character. I have everyone voice his side and no two descriptions are alike." She demanded to know whether the script dealt with Hearst, and he denied it. She was so completely taken in by Welles's charm that she believed him. Louella was impressed by Welles's statement that he had lived near her (and Ronald Reagan's) home town of Dixon, Illinois, and in her column on August 25 she gurgled about his being a "hometown boy making good." Hedda visited the set and was supportive, though she was careful not to write too much that would echo her deadly rival.

On August 26 Herbert Drake sent Welles a memorandum on Herman Mankiewicz's viewing of some early cut footage of *Kane*. Oddly, Welles has since had the highest praise for Mankiewicz's writing of the scene in which Bernstein was interviewed by Thompson, but Mankiewicz did not like the way it was played, and he told Drake on the telephone, "Everett Sloane is an unsympathetic-looking man, and anyway you shouldn't have two Jews in one scene." (Presumably he was referring to William Alland as the reporter Thompson.) Mankiewicz wanted the Atlantic City cabaret scene reshot because he was not pleased with the looks of Dorothy Comingore, who had been made up to look old and unattractive. Mankiewicz felt that there were not enough close-ups and the presentation was "too much like a play." He was upset with most of Welles's changes. Yet in every way Welles had improved on his original material.

Each day of work was more exciting than its predecessor. With the aid of Toland, Welles created one dazzling image after another, taunting, pricking, and tantalizing the great cameraman to go beyond anything he had ever attempted. With his astonishing grasp of the language of cinema, Welles added to it a new vocabulary of his own, and he revolutionized the soundtrack overnight. Sound, no longer a mere accompaniment to the image, became an electrifying element in itself. As he had done in radio, Welles used sound ironically, dramatically, with vivid emphasis, enhanced, subdued, tossed around in a manner that only deep experience on the air could have made possible. Above all, the movie magically dissolved the heavy techniques of talking pictures in a miraculous succession of fluid visual effects. The film's content was more or less journalistic, its style richly poetic. The childhood sequences in the snow were perhaps Welles's finest achievement, mingling deeply felt sentiment with images that are reflected in the glittering, snow-covered hut contained in the crystal paperweight that the dying Kane lets slip from his hand.

With economy, drive, and youthful vigor, the movie rushes forward, sometimes tragic in mode, more often comic, the figures composed in the frame often like those in a comic strip—the funnies that Welles loved so much. Antic and searching, at times cheating by showing events that the characters who tell the story could not have seen, moving from burlesque to moments of blank despair, the picture resembles a kaleidoscope, the splintered essence of the American experience.

Welles drove his actors hard. Sometimes he would drag them through a hundred takes and more in order to get the precise effect he wanted. When the butler tells the reporter that he can explain the Rosebud mystery, walking through the great echoing vastness of Xanadu, Welles had the two actors repeat their lines fifty-seven times. The scene with Joseph Cotten in the hospital, close to death, was done in 108 takes. A tiny moment such as Thompson's calling in his story to *News on the March* after he sees Susan in the nightclub was dragged out for a whole day of work. In the scene in which the newspaper editor is pushed out of the *Inquirer* after Kane takes it over, the actor playing the editor, Erskine Sanford, broke down under the pressure. But others, led by Agnes Moorehead and Joseph Cotten, never complained and indeed vibrated to their friend's relentless yet devoted handling. Adopting his stage techniques and the manner of normal conversation, Welles encouraged the actors to overlap each other in speaking, and in this Mankiewicz's dialogue breaks were useful.

Sometimes Welles allowed his own feelings to be released. In one scene, when Kane leaves the apartment building following a bitter confrontation with Boss Gettys, Welles was so carried away that he slipped and fell down the stairs and sprained his ankle. For an entire week he had to shoot around his own character, using a wheelchair, and then when he appeared again, he had to work to conceal a limp. Another actor with something to conceal was the pregnant Dorothy Comingore, and it took all of Toland's wizardry to hide her condition.

In the furniture-breaking scene Welles unleashed himself with unprecedented fieriness; he set up four cameras to shoot the sequence, knowing that he must cover it from every angle and could not repeat it many times. William Alland recalled later, "Orson staggered out of the set with his hands bleeding and his face flushed. He almost swooned, yet he was exultant. 'I really felt it,' he exclaimed. 'I really felt it!' "

Paul Stewart remembered an episode that resembled the fire at the Sheffield House:

> I'll never forget the day Orson shot the burning of the sled. One of the stages at the Selznick studio had been made into the warehouse with a working furnace. The scene had to be just right because the audience had to see the sled go in and the word Rosebud consumed in flames. When the ninth take had been shot, the doors of the stage flew open and in marched the Culver City Fire Department in full fire-fighting regalia. The furnace had grown so hot that the flue had caught fire. Orson was delighted with the commotion.

Joseph Cotten remembered that he played the part of Leland between the New York and road tour presentations of *The Philadelphia Story*. In his drunk scene he was concerned to avoid the usual clichés of such sequences. Welles decided that exhaustion would be the appropriate condition, so he kept Cotten up until 3:00 A.M. and Cotten was stumbling over his lines. He shot throughout the night, until Cotten gave exactly the right tone of being worn out; Welles had been driving him for twenty-four hours without interruption.

As if Welles was not busy enough making *Kane* and fielding debtors and Virginia with equal determination, he worked in other directions as well. On August 30 he began seeking the support of churchmen of various denominations for a plan to make a movie of the life of Christ. He wanted to use a simple, rustic American setting with plain American folk, in the form of a passion play; he did not want to use star players or even members of the Mercury Theater, and he envisaged a bare, austere style that was as far removed from *Citizen Kane*'s as *Stage-*

coach's was from *The Long Voyage Home*'s. The response was guardedly sympathetic; church leaders, including Fulton J. Sheen, wanted more details, and obviously they were wary of publicity that might suggest either that they were indifferent to a monumental idea or that they were supportive of an undertaking that many would consider blasphemous. Cecil B. De Mille had gotten away with treating this theme in *King of Kings*, but Welles emphatically did not want anything approaching such a laughable venture. It is doubtful that he could have brought the idea off, and after much correspondence during and after the shooting of *Kane* he characteristically grew tired of it and abandoned it.

Meanwhile, Mankiewicz was furious that Welles was claiming sole credit on the script, and he had gotten in touch with Houseman in New York and insisted that Houseman support him in any lawsuit that Mankiewicz might bring. In Mankiewicz's and Houseman's view, Welles had written no more than ten percent of the script, and the changes he had made were no greater than those any self-respecting director would make to any screenplay.

Amazingly, Welles continued working on the acting edition of *Macbeth* for Harper during the final weeks of work on *Citizen Kane*. Once the movie was completely shot—only eleven days over schedule and not much over budget—he turned over the editing to the talented Robert Wise, who admirably handled the challenge. Wise was especially effective in preparing the newsreel, *News on the March*, in which he created an impression of a vast mass of film footage drawn from many periods; in some cases he even scratched the film deliberately by dragging it over the cement floor of the editing room to give it a look of age and wear and tear. He did a fine job with Susan's disastrous opera tour, ending it on a shot of a fading cue light. This crude but effective symbol terminated a montage that owed everything to Wise's talent.

Wise also gave the movie much of its extraordinary fluency by using brilliant radiolike linking devices that at one stroke overcame a decade of clumsiness in the narrative form of many talking pictures. In October, while the picture was still unassembled, he left on an extended lecture tour of Omaha, Cleveland, Toledo, Dallas, San Antonio, Houston, Oklahoma City, and Tulsa. Not only did he need the money, he was also avoiding the draft. The studio and Herbert Drake made every effort to conceal the fact that Welles was petrified by the thought of going into the army. Even though America was not at war, public feeling had been dragged by Roosevelt to the firm position that any ablebodied man should be in uniform. Anyone who dodged the call-up was considered either a sissy or a coward or both.

Welles clearly feared that if he were drafted, in view of his lack of formal education he would be a mere private. His earning power would disappear, his career would end just as it was starting—and he would be totally unsuited to the discipline and knockabout life of the armed services. He wrote pleading letters to Weissberger, begging him to explain what could be done. On September 27 Weissberger wrote him that since he had a dependent child he might be eligible for exemption; in addition, if he were forced to break his contract with RKO, he would throw many people who depended on him permanently out of work. On October 24 the matter still needled the young genius, who advised Weissberger that because Charles Lederer was now helping to support Christopher, a deferment on that ground would be harder to achieve.

Troubles mounted. Mankiewicz continued to threaten his lawsuit, and efforts to dissuade him with warnings that his legal position was weak failed entirely. The life of Christ idea was crumbling. Work on the *Macbeth* edition was pressing. When Orson wanted to borrow $3,000 from RKO or CBS or Campbell, it was not available, and the money to meet the expenses of his tour had to be scraped together with difficulty. Virginia and her husband insisted that Welles pay $28 a month to the school where Christopher was enrolled. Welles was so distracted that he repeatedly called the William Penn Hotel in Houston to be sure they were holding a room for him, but when he arrived in Houston he went to another hotel and then had to pay both bills. He canceled his appearances in Tulsa at a moment's notice and was billed $600 for canceled reservations. Richard Baer wrote Weissberger on November 25, "Going off . . . at the end of the picture is a problem. Welles made at least 80 to 100 long-distance calls to me, and bought $200 worth of unnecessary tickets."

Welles returned to Hollywood for the dubbing of the singer Jean Forward, who was deliberately encouraged to sing badly as the failed opera star in *Kane*. He also was close to the recording engineer James G. Stewart, and he insisted on special sounds, especially when a white cockatoo screams angrily from its perch at the moment Kane walks out of Susan's life.* Although he had been away for much of the editing, Welles was deeply involved in the use of the track; in a sequence in Madison Square Garden he enhanced the realism, which had been undermined by the use of visual cut-outs in lieu of an audience, to simu-

---

* He often claimed his father owned a cockatoo, or in some versions a parakeet, and rescued the bird from the Sheffield House fire, a story denied by those who rescued him.

late a vast audience by having an impression of ten thousand people on the track.

Welles took special interest in the last part of Bernard Herrmann's work on the music. Unlike most movie scores, which were simply lush symphonic accompaniments to the images, the music for *Kane* was devised rather like that accompanying a ballet. There were two main motifs: a four-note figure on the brass that illustrated Kane's power, and the Rosebud theme, a vibraphone solo that recurs whenever Kane is overcome by sentiment for the past. Perhaps the loveliest moment in the score is when the reporter Thompson reads the pages of Thatcher's diary in the echoing library: a sad melody blends into a brightly innocent flutter of woodwind and strings, evoking images of Kane's childhood—whirling snow and an impertinent clash with the banker-guardian. The music throughout is an integral part of the movie and a reflection of Welles's musical upbringing. At the beginning it is grim and full of foreboding as we see the Disneyish window of Xanadu. When the ceiling light in the death chamber of the tycoon is snapped off to indicate death, the camera moves to an interior with an extraordinary break in the trend of the melody, which itself suggests the extinction of the human personality. Wonderful too are the brass bands and wild musical numbers that accompany Kane's rise to power, linking montages with comic, vibrant enthusiasm, as in Welles's radio shows. At times the effect is more operatic than the opera theme of some episodes warrants. The versatility is never extraneous or unnecessary; the rhythm of the editing is matched by the rhythm of the music itself.

Gregg Toland did not complete *Citizen Kane;* during the final weeks his crew had to take over because he was needed under his Goldwyn contract. But every foot of the finished picture is stamped with his special style, controlled and enhanced in every possible way by Welles's dynamic genius.

8

The inescapable Dr. Bernstein continued to pester Welles with pleas for money, claiming every cent he had paid out for his upbringing and needling Welles to use his influence to obtain openings for him in the medical profession in Los Angeles. Dr. Bernstein behaved as though he were a struggling young physician who had to fight for every patient; his sour and charmless letters, laced with excessive romantic praise for Orson's every action, make very disagreeable reading.

John Houseman was then in Los Angeles, pressing Welles to undertake the direction of a Broadway stage version by Paul Green of Richard Wright's currently successful novel, *Native Son*. The novel, written with a power and drive that to some extent overcame its questionable moral position, told the story of Bigger Thomas, a vigorous, muscular black man driven by hate, a wild animal at bay, who was perhaps too overt a symbol of oppression and anger to achieve a convincing reality in his own right. When he accidentally smothers a white girl and then has to saw off her head to get her body into a furnace, when he makes love to his girl friend afterward and then kills her by smashing her face with a brick and dumping her down an airshaft, it is hard to retain even a shred of identification with him. Yet that is part of the author's intent; he is saying that we who lead safe and respectable lives, whether white or black, cannot understand the consuming hatred and desperation that society provokes in an embattled male animal who does not know how to make a living. Houseman and Mankiewicz (who had briefly optioned it) had considered adapting *Native Son* while they were working in Victorville. Houseman hoped that a successful production of this controversial work would help to recoup the substantial losses sustained on *Five Kings*, and he wanted to bring together several actors from the Mercury who had appeared in *Kane* as well as Jean Rosenthal and Jimmy Morcum.

The distinguished dramatist Paul Green, who lived in Chapel Hill, North Carolina, where he was a local institution, read Richard Wright's novel in April 1940. Wright had at one time lived in Chicago, and he had boisterously supported the public presentation of Green's pro-black one-act play *Hymn to the Rising Sun*. Following the publication of *Native Son*, Wright's literary agent in New York, Paul Reynolds, asked Green if he was interested in dramatizing it. Green said he was not; although there were aspects of the book he admired, he was appalled by what he thought was an unnecessary degree of brutality, and he refused to believe the scene in which Bigger Thomas burned the girl in the furnace because it seemed to him that her body would have to have been not merely decapitated but chopped up before being committed to the flames.

Later the producer Cheryl Crawford approached Green, and once again he declined. But gradually he felt a little warmer toward the project, and when John Houseman went to see him in Chapel Hill, he at last agreed, on condition that Wright travel from Mexico and work with him. Green also asked that he be allowed to make the Communist elements in the play comic, and he wanted to alter the character of Bigger Thomas so that Thomas no longer seemed to be a mere victim of circumstances but was at least partly responsible for his moral decline and his violent activities. Wright wrote from Mexico agreeing to these conditions (which was rather surprising in view of his leftist commitment to the theme of crime as the result of environment, and his current membership in the Communist party). Presumably, the thought of achieving Broadway fame overcame other considerations for Wright, and this confirms one's feelings about the morally questionable character of his admirably written novel.

Wright traveled via his brother's home in Chicago to Chapel Hill that June and, with suggestions from Houseman, began working with Green on the adaptation. In the severe heat of July and August, author and playwright toiled together at the University of North Carolina and in Green's cabin. Green visited the prison at Raleigh and talked with the warden to learn the procedure for an execution, and he visited Death Row. The warden told him that most men died with resignation and that some were even eager to die. He told Green of the death chant traditionally sung by the convicts when one of them went to the chair, and recalled a criminal who, when placed in the chair, cried, "This is the happiest day of my life." Green saw eight condemned men doing jigsaw puzzles on the floors of their cells.

There were problems during the writing. When Wright tried his hand at one scene on his own, it turned out to be entirely novelistic and lacked the elements of drama. Local prejudice built up against Wright's presence in the town, and the university, influenced by the prejudice, opposed Wright's using the campus. One of Green's cousins arrived with a gun, intending to shoot Wright down, but Green pleaded with his relative and succeeded in calming him.

Work on the script continued in drenching rain that fall, the war news from Europe providing a melancholy overcast. By November the script was completed, and Houseman dropped by to offer suggestions.

Having sent the script to Welles in Hollywood, Houseman returned to New York. Welles called him there and, despite his misgivings about Green's interpretation, and his sure feeling that he would have to change much of the script back to the novel, told Houseman he had decided to go ahead. The venture appealed to Welles for several reasons. First, he would use it to sort out his differences with Houseman and restore an association for which he had an understandable nostalgia. Second, he would have a chance to express his feelings for the blacks and their oppression in America. Third, he would match what he anticipated to be *Citizen Kane*'s huge success on the screen with an equivalent theatrical triumph.

But he could not start on *Native Son* immediately. The *Kane* matter had to be cleared with the press, and Dolores Del Rio, who was finally preparing for her divorce, needed his sustenance. And yet another project had excited Welles's restless attention: Arthur Calder-Marshall's *The Way to Santiago* struck to the nerve of his personal concerns and revived the theme and something of the matter of *The Smiler with a Knife* and the story of Charles Foster Kane's son (in the first draft of the *Kane* screenplay). The novel dealt with a plot by Nazi agents to overthrow the government of Mexico, a plot engineered by the diabolical but beautiful Lionel Transit, who has risen from the slums of Shanghai to assume the leadership of a Falangist clique. Transit is associated with the heavy-drinking General Torres and his mistress, Concepción. A journalist named Jimmy Lamson seeks to expose the plot.

Just as *The Smiler with a Knife* had been based on two attempted coups d'etat, *The Way to Santiago* drew on historical fact. In Mexico, General Almazán had tried to upset the 1940 polls with bloodshed and violence, and in this he had been supported by the American labor leader John L. Lewis and the oilman William Rhodes Davis, both of whom had substantial interests in sustaining Nazi alliances in that region. The dashing Lionel Transit is first cousin to Anthony Chilton, the good-looking villain of *The Smiler with a Knife,* and both recall Errol Flynn, who played a similarly crucial role in fascist activities in Europe and the Americas. A familiar subject arises in *The Way to Santiago* when General Torres is asked, "And once a year you'll have dinner with . . . William Randolph Hearst at San Simeon, I suppose?"

Welles began to work sporadically on the script, starting and discarding drafts without the kind of emotional commitment that was called for by the material. Meanwhile, Houseman was still working with Paul Green and Richard Wright on the script for *Native Son.*

Welles found some relief at Christmas in entertaining his friends and Dolores, with whom he was now living in West Los Angeles. The house was filled with flowers and sparkled with the lights he had arranged with bravura. The Christmas tree decorations were of his own making. All that was lacking was snow, and no doubt, if he could have arranged for the special effects department to provide some, he would have done so. Among the guests at the Christmas party were Maurice and his third wife Hazel Bernstein, and on January 2 Hazel wrote to thank him for everything and for "the sweetness of Dolores."

The new year opened on a note of foreboding. On January 3 there was a secret rough-cut screening of *Kane,* without music, for *Life, Look,* and *Redbook.* But word of the screening inevitably leaked through the press department, and the *Hollywood Reporter* announced that morning that Welles was showing the picture. Hedda Hopper called to say she was coming no matter what. Herbert Drake telegrammed her, "Come if you must," but added that he did not want her to see the movie at this rough stage. Somehow Louella Parsons failed to get wind of the screening.

The reactions at the screening were varied. *Look's* critic, James Francis Crow, said, "A most unusual picture and one of the finest I've seen." Dick Pollard and Douglas Churchill were fascinated. But Hedda hated the picture; as the screening ended she told Welles, "You can't get away with this"—and he replied, "I will." Bitter though her enmity was for Louella, she was furious at what she told friends was "the vicious and irresponsible attack on a great man." A philistine to the end, she wrote in her column that the picture was "a dubious box office prospect," and she complained that the photography was old-fashioned and the writing corny.

On January 8 Welles wrote Louella Parsons that a piece in *Friday* magazine that week carried "a vicious lie." He assured the columnist that he had called the editor and told him that the picture was not about Hearst and that there must be a retraction. The character of Kane was totally fictitious, he told Louella, and any similarities, "though unavoidable, were not intended." He denied the statement that "Louella Parsons may be surprised to find out that my picture is about her boss." He suggested arranging a lunch at which he would show her the picture and prove his point.

On the same night that Louella talked to Welles, she finally got word from San Simeon that the picture was about Hearst; why the information had been kept from her for so long is unclear. By midnight that night the order had gone out that not one word of RKO publicity could appear in any Hearst newspaper, nor would any RKO advertising be accepted. Louella was deeply upset because she had been taken for a ride by Orson, who had indeed brilliantly tricked her when he had called her to the studio. Furthermore, she was convinced that Hedda was in on the deception, for in her blindness (and her refusal to meet Hedda) she failed to see that Hedda for once was very much on her side.

Hearst's attack on Welles would include a campaign against the employment of foreigners in the movie industry; in other words, Hearst would attack Hollywood as a whole, blaming it for making the picture and accusing it of harboring Jewish refugees from Hitler. The pro-Nazi G. Allison Phelps, whom Jewish committees had exposed for his contacts with Berlin, made a vicious broadcast smearing Welles. Louella Parsons worked day and night. She called Nelson Rockefeller, asking him in his role of majority shareholder in RKO to abandon both Welles and the picture. She told George Schaefer he should give up on the movie immediately. And she demanded a screening of it. Accompanied by two Hearst lawyers and her chauffeur, she swept into the RKO screening room, saw the picture with mounting horror, and swept out again before it was over. (Her driver-butler, Louis Collins, risked his job by stopping to tell Welles, "That was a right fine picture.")

She telegrammed Hearst immediately to tell him that he had been libeled, the two lawyers having refused to make the call. Hearst insisted that RKO hold up the release. There were threats on every side. Louella called movie leaders Joseph Schenck, Y. Frank Freeman, Darryl F. Zanuck, David O. Selznick, and Jack and Harry Warner (the Warners refused to talk to her). She then called Will Hays, in charge of the industry's morals, telling him to stop the picture because a rule in the Production Code said that movies could not be made about living people. She told Louis B. Mayer, who as head of MGM was the most powerful figure in the industry, "Mr. Hearst says if you boys want private lives, I'll give you private lives." In other words, the Hearst press would expose the personal scandals of the moguls, starting with Mayer himself. In her hysteria Louella called every member of the RKO board of directors and threatened that "fictionized" stories of their lives would appear in the Hearst papers and magazines. She flatly forbade W. G. Van Schmus, head of Radio City Music Hall in New York, to run the picture; since Nelson Rockefeller owned the theater and panicked at her words (or sympathized with them), she won that battle.

Hedda Hopper wrote that as a result of the Hearst campaign, "there will be a lot of heads that formerly were accustomed to satin pillows reposing in baskets." She doubted that *Citizen Kane* would ever be shown in public.

Herbert Drake was frustrated in his efforts to promote Welles's cause; he wanted to lead a crusade that would place the independent and liberal Hollywood element behind Welles, but the big battle was going to be fought among the money boys. Clearly every effort must be made to support Schaefer in his annoyance at the pressures being brought upon him. Drake was further handicapped because Perry Lieber of RKO publicity, annoyed at not being invited to the first preview, had washed his hands of the matter. Orson made Drake promise not to lose his temper until the issue was settled. Then Drake was accused of precipitating the Hearst matter by announcing that *Kane* was Hearst's life; this, he wrote an associate in New York, was "a dirty lie, a base canard, a vile accusation, a vicious flight into the realms of imagination."

According to Charles Lederer, Hearst was not at all disturbed by the movie himself, but his son William Randolph Hearst, Jr., was upset about it, as were a number of apple-polishers in the Hearst circle. Welles has claimed that there was an attempt to frame him on (unspecified) criminal charges. And there was another element: an attack on the picture would boost circulation. Louella herself cannot have been oblivious to this fact. Although she was sincerely shocked by what she called (in her 1961 memoirs) "a cruel, dishonest caricature . . . done in the worst of taste," she also had a shrewd idea that the controversy would attract readers to her column. And Hedda must have suspected that her own comments would add to the excitement. Already *Kane* was being sacrificed on the very commercial altar it had set out to desecrate.

One cannot ignore a further possibility: that, as during the "War of the Worlds" fracas, Welles relished the enormous publicity that would accrue from a major controversy. George Coulouris has said that Welles admitted to him that he hoped he would be attacked in order to make him even more famous. However, that likelihood is undermined or at least rendered insecure by the highly ambiguous tenor of Welles's notes and letters. They indicate that Welles, though possibly stimulated by the controversy, was petrified that the picture would not be released.

On January 10, 1941, he called Arnold Weissberger in New York to ask if Hearst could get an injunction; the lawyer advised him that Hearst could not. However, Weissberger cautioned Welles and Drake that they must constantly reiterate that the picture had "nothing to do with Hearst." On January 14 Weissberger told Orson he should issue a public statement "denying as unequivocally as possible that the picture had any relation to Hearst." Mud was being slung on every side; on January 17 Drake was threatening through the grapevine to dig up Mexican birth certificates of twins born to Marion Davies if Hearst continued to create trouble. (That little scandal never surfaced; Davies was never revealed to have had illegitimate children.)

Schaefer's attitude was that all this was something of a storm in a teacup. However, he knew the matter would ultimately rest with the controlling stockholders. If any attempt were made to stop the picture, Schaefer could no doubt force it through the board by using the argument that Welles would sue for interference with contractual agreements if *Kane* were not released. However, in a note to Welles on January 20 Weissberger cautioned that Schaefer might prove to be a broken reed, for his position at the studio was rapidly weakening. "His easygoing nature is a problem, and you will have to strengthen him with legal action."

In the meantime Louis B. Mayer contacted Nicholas Schenck, head of Loew's, Inc., the parent corporation of MGM. He asked Schenck to offer Schaefer the entire cost of the picture if RKO would destroy the negative and all prints. Schaefer resisted, but he knew that if he went to his board, he would be forced to accept. So, very courageously, he committed himself to going ahead with the release. And he was no fan of Mayer. The MGM boss had tried to force him to employ one of Mayer's circle as Hollywood vice-president of RKO in 1939; Schaefer had refused, and Mayer was furious. That tiny incident may in itself have saved *Citizen Kane*.

Van Schmus of Radio City Music Hall crumbled at last and canceled the *Citizen Kane* premiere set for February 14. Meanwhile, Welles took a bold step: while in New York for work on *Native Son*, he showed the picture to the RKO executives and directors—at Radio City Music Hall. It was a daring move, but so convinced was Welles of the excellence of his film and his power to enforce the showing that he risked his career and won. It was decided to go ahead and release the movie in April. Simultaneously, Welles issued yet another bulletin to all media denying that the picture was based on Hearst.

Welles began to calm down. He worked on *Native Son*, holding long discussions with Houseman on the final version and the casting. Staying in one of the grand art deco suites at the Waldorf Towers, he was tireless in his enthusiasm even as he kept his fingers crossed that there would be no last-minute reversal on *Kane*. He also worked on

The Way to Santiago and planned a trip to Mexico to research it. He began casting *Native Son* at the beginning of February, and his Mercury team—Ray Collins, Everett Sloane, Paul Stewart, Erskine Sanford, and others—rallied round. Black actors were drawn from the days at the Lafayette, among them Canada Lee, Welles's choice to play Bigger. Gifted with a magnificent physique and a compulsive, fierce energy, Lee was a daring choice for the part when a more famous actor (such as Paul Robeson) might have been chosen. Welles was captivated by Lee, and once more he saw the burning talent in him.

For Welles, the chief problem lay with the Paul Green adaptation. Green had given the play a lyrical, poetic, and religious overtone that Welles believed the brutal savagery of the book did not call for. Even though further revisions were made, Welles was not entirely satisfied. As rehearsals began, Green struggled, he wrote in his diary, "with Welles, Hauseman [sic] and Wright to make the play come out with some sort of moral responsibility for the individual." He wrote that his collaborators were determined to cut out a scene in which a state-appointed lawyer tries to understand Bigger Thomas "and prepare some grounds for defense, and where the family and family preacher set their guard on Bigger's lost but unyielding soul." Green was offended by Welles's decision to cut some singing, even though Green's trip to Raleigh had proven it was ethnically authentic. Green was also upset that Welles was using "left-wing, left-wing propaganda complete. But since Wright was on their side, I yielded. After all, his novels, his characters, and after this only the play mine."

His most intense objection was to a striking but in his view tasteless final effect in which Canada Lee was stretched in a cruciform position behind the bars of the death cell, thus presaging his electrocution and giving him what Green felt was a spurious Christ-like connotation.

Houseman called Green to a meeting with Wright and Welles at the theater, and Green demanded that his own ending be restored. Houseman said it was out of the question, that Green had deliberately distorted the play. The Paul Green Foundation will not confirm or deny that Green walked out angrily from a rehearsal, as John Houseman claims in *Run-Through*.

Forced to cancel his trip to Mexico, Welles again became panicky about *Citizen Kane*'s fate. He had a terrible night on March 6, 1941, one of his rare occasions of outright hysteria. His letter to George Schaefer is totally manic: he complains that he sat up until 4:00 A.M. calling Schaefer, that when at last he reached him he had been received only with generalities. He writes that he could not believe Schaefer was deliberately avoiding him. He could only suppose he was pursuing some policy "the nature of which must be kept secret." He adds, going totally off the rails, "as regards *Kane,* I'm the only person I know who has any faith in you at all" and that in "your new program of evasiveness" only "a very real affection and trust" could ever "sustain that faith." The letter continues in a similar vein, Welles charging Schaefer with all kinds of inadequacies. Welles concludes, "*Inter alia,* my nights are sleepless and my days are tortured."

He was at last reassured when a New York booking was found at an RKO-owned theater, the Grand Old Palace in Times Square, in the very heart of the theater district. And he was cheered by a telegram from his beloved Alfalfa in Hollywood, who joked that, on the occasion of the first night of *Native Son,* "Willie Hearst joins me in wishing you the greatest of success."

Welles's staging of *Native Son* was by all accounts as bold as his making of *Citizen Kane.* One of the few things on which he agreed with Paul Green was the elimination of intermissions, his customary practice. And he went a step further in not issuing programs, irritated as he was by people lighting matches or cigarette lighters in order to examine their programs in the dark; instead, ushers handed out slips of paper stating that playbills would be provided after the performance.

According to his customary mode, Welles used light and darkness and sound effects (or faces isolated in darkness) with the same originality and power that had gone into his still unreleased picture. He introduced many special touches that Green, who had grave misgivings about the presentation, had to admire. When a gum-chewing newspaperman closes in on Bigger Thomas, Welles had the actor playing the reporter remove the gum from his mouth, stick it on a wall, and smash it with his fist, thereby symbolizing his crushing of Bigger like a bug. In the scene in which Bigger kills the young girl, Welles had the actress dressed in long black stockings that, when her legs writhed in the air during the struggle with Bigger, made them look like long black snakes in the light.

The trial scene, which was in many ways a precursor of the trial scene in *The Lady from Shanghai,* was played as though the audience was the courtroom crowd. In a setting of liver-colored brick, the tenement apartment of Thomas's family seemed simply an extension of the auditorium. When the police cornered Bigger in the warehouse, the uniformed men appeared in the balcony and in the boxes; they fired directly at the stage, and the theater exploded with shouts and flashlight beams. The scene that Green dreaded most was the one that thrilled the audience more than any other. This was the climax, in which Thomas stood behind bars with his arms outstretched in a cruciform position, telling the audience, "See what you've done to me, you've crucified me." This statement, coming directly from Welles's liberal sensibility, was not forgiven by Green. Nor could Green accept the fact that Welles put up the sign "Orson Welles's NATIVE SON" outside the theater—or that Richard Wright would tolerate such nonsense.

The play opened to an enthusiastic public and strong reviews at the St. James Theater on March 17, 1941. Essentially a compromised melodrama drawn from a great novel (and a travesty of Green's version), it served the purpose of drawing public attention to the ill-treatment of blacks. What undermined the play was that without the intense power of Wright's narrative (and the moral correctiveness of Green's adaptation) the play looked like a plea for support for a criminal, and this played into the hands of such antiliberal critics as Grenville Vernon of *Commonweal*.

But whatever anyone might say about the glorification of a killer or about the elements of communism that were falsely said to have been inserted in the play—some Communists had walked out of the previews because of what they took to be a betrayal of their ideals—*Native Son* was an outright triumph for both Welles and Canada Lee. No one who saw the play would ever forget the acting of this former stableboy, jockey, and amateur lightweight champion. All the electrifying power and hatred he had concentrated in him was unleashed on stage, and many hardened Broadwayites literally cheered the thunderous force of his performance. Welles's impassioned direction, the inspired use of the apron stage, the marshaling of action, and the controlling and timing of the dialogue were the expressions of a fiery genius at full stretch. Brooks Atkinson of *The New York Times* proclaimed *Native Son* "the biggest American drama of the season," thereby setting the seal of triumph on the occasion. And it was typical of Welles that he could not resist a private joke: much to the despair of Wright, Green, Herbert Drake, and all those who were trying to keep the content of *Citizen Kane* a secret until the film's release, Welles had somebody place a child's sled bearing the name Rosebud on stage in the opening tenement scene, where it had no business being.

The congratulations poured in, and RKO splurged $50,000 on two-color, full-page advertisements for *Kane* in the national magazines. Their slogan—"It's terrific!"—soon became the general slogan for the picture. Some magazines leaked reviews of a movie the public still could not see. John O'Hara, then at the height of his fame as a novelist, said in *Newsweek* that "your faithful bystander reports that he has just seen a picture which he thinks must be the best picture he ever saw."

Look magazine extolled "bold theatricalism . . . musical and photographic eloquence . . . spellbinding narrative." *Life* said *Kane* was "good and then some. Few movies have ever come from Hollywood with such powerful narrative, such original technique, such exciting photography." *Time* talked of "the most sensational product of the U.S. movie industry. It has found important new techniques in picture-making and story-telling. . . . It is a work of art created by grown people for grown people."

Welles was cheered by these statements. In Hollywood, Cary Grant, Barbara Hutton, Samuel Goldwyn, David O. Selznick, and William Wyler, along with Welles's new friend King Vidor, saw and were fascinated by the picture. Director Leo McCarey announced that he was abandoning ninety pages of a script to start again, so overcome was he by the excellence of the movie. The picture made everyone feel at once thrilled and ashamed. Welles's subsequent claims that he was without friends in Hollywood because of the nature of the work are utterly without foundation; he was surrounded by adulation, not least because many directors and producers were delighted at the annoyance of their hated bosses, the moguls.

Back in New York, Welles fought for an early release date, and at last the press previews took place in early April. The acclaim for *Native Son* may well have accelerated matters. As though determined to rock the boat yet again, Welles launched a radio play, "His Honor the Mayor," suggested by the title of a George Ade story; it dealt with the efforts of a small-town mayor to allow a Communist meeting to take place under the provisions of the first amendment, even though he is opposed to communism. The Hearst chain, supported by the American Legion, attacked the broadcast on CBS and charged it and other productions of The Free Company with being "un-American and tending to encourage communism and other subversive groups"[*]

Of course when Hearst began charging Welles with Communist leanings, the attack gave Welles untold new publicity. Everyone knew that he was not a Communist but a Roosevelt liberal, and when on April 19 a Production Code certificate was at last issued for *Kane*, Welles's path to victory was firmly set.

He postponed his trip to Mexico for several months, fielded charges that he had excessively accumulated bills for personal clothing sup-

---

[*] The Free Company was a group of writers formed under Attorney General Robert H. Jackson to attack foreign propaganda in America; it was led by Roosevelt's speechwriter Robert E. Sherwood, William Saroyan, Maxwell Anderson, and other literary figures.

plied to *Citizen Kane*, dodged still more money requests from Dr. Bernstein, and went for medical examinations in order to determine his draft status. He was found to have a series of Job-like physical problems: not only the flat feet that made his shuffling walk unnerving to some and his old problems of hay fever and asthma, but chronic myocarditis and angina (both painful diseases of the heart) and arthritis and a bifida of the spine. The doctors also found evidence of fractures and ankle dislocations; evidently he had not completely recovered from his fall downstairs on *Kane*. It was recommended that he have a complete rest.

The world premiere of *Citizen Kane* occurred at the Palace on May 1, 1941. It was a festive occasion and Dolores Del Rio shared it with him. Despite the fact that the movie had by no means been made for the man in the street, Herbert Drake had worked overtime with the RKO people: Times Square was jammed, and the four-story neon sign announcing the picture flashed and glowed above an enormous crowd. This was the big moment of Welles's career; there would never be another like it.

Three ages of Orson: aged 5, aged 36, aged 67. (Photo 1, Charles Higham Collection; Photos 2 and 3, Phototeque)

Orson's terrifying great-grandfather, Wisconsin district attorney and powerful lawyer, Orson Sherman Head. (Kenosha Historical Society)

Right: Mary Head Wells Gottfredsen, aged 80, reading Mary Baker Eddy's *Science and Health.* She lived to hear Orson accuse her of being a black magician. (Kenosha Historical Society)

The rarest of all Welles photographs. In a picture taken in Sigrid Jacobsen's garden, the following can be seen (left to right): Welles's father Richard, Sigrid, visiting neighbors, Orson's mother Beatrice, Orson aged 7, and Dr. Maurice Bernstein, later Orson's guardian. (Charles Higham Collection)

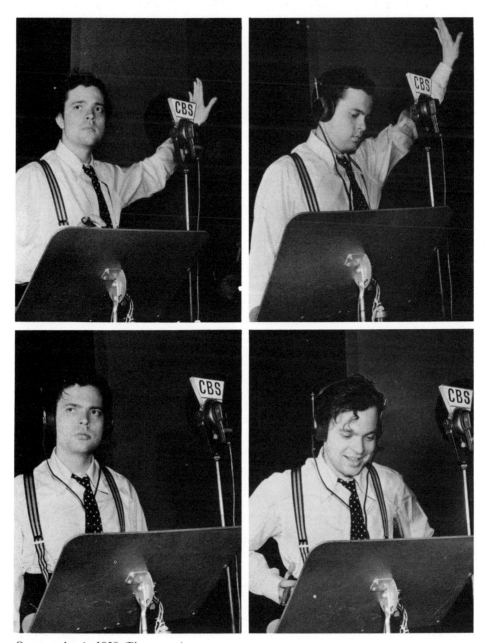

Orson on the air, 1938. (Phototeque)

Welles's design for *Twelfth Night,* Todd School production at Woodstock, 1933. (Lilly Library)

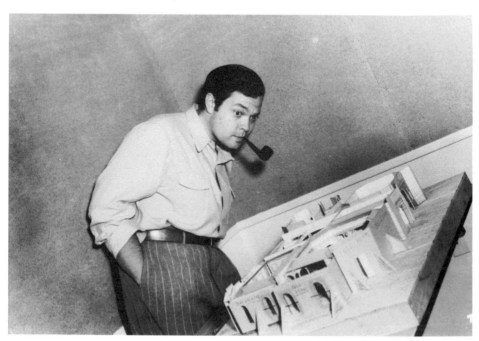

Orson brooding over a set for *The Magnificent Ambersons.* (Charles Higham Collection)

Joseph Cotten, Orson, and Erskine Sanford in *Citizen Kane.* (Charles Higham Collection)

Welles as Charles Foster Kane: the election campaign scene. (Charles Higham Collection)

Orson and Joseph Cotten in *Citizen Kane.* Note the muslin imitation skylight. (Charles Higham Collection)

Dorothy Comingore doing the jigsaw puzzle in *Kane.* Her short-lived career tragically echoed that of Susan Kane in the movie. (Charles Higham Collection)

The welcome-home party in *Kane;* (left to right): Everett Sloane, Orson, Joseph Cotten. (Charles Higham Collection)

Orson directing a scene from *The Magnificent Ambersons*. (Charles Higham Collection)

The great Agnes Moorehead (foreground), Tim Holt, Dolores Costello, and Joseph Cotten in a funeral scene from *Ambersons*. (Charles Higham Collection)

Above: Welles on the *Ambersons* set with his devoted assistant Richard Wilson. (Charles Higham Collection)

Left: Orson in a publicity shot, playing samba records in preparation for his ill-fated epic, *It's All True.* (Charles Higham Collection)

Part of the dazzling samba sequence from the tragically unfinished *It's All True.* (Lilly Library)

Orson and his first wife Virginia
Nicolson in the mid-1930s. (Lilly
Library)

Left: Orson with his baby daughter
Christopher, at Sneden's Landing, New
York, in the late 1930s. (Lilly Library)

Welles in Hollywood, 1939. (Phototeque)

The clock tower scene in *The Stranger.*
For years Welles had a nightmare that
winged statues like the one on the right
would come to life and pursue him.
(Charles Higham Collection)

Orson with his girl friend the Mexican star Dolores Del Rio at a nightclub in the early 1940s. Visible in the background is Herbert Marshall. (Phototeque)

The mirror scene from *The Lady from Shanghai:* Rita Hayworth in six images. She agreed to pretend a reconciliation after their separation to help him make the picture. (Charles Higham Collection)

Alexander Korda visits the set for *The Lady from Shanghai* to chat with Rita and Orson. He and Welles tried unsuccessfully to work together on several major projects. (Lilly Library)

A party on board Errol Flynn's yacht, the *Zaca,* in Acapulco harbor during the filming of *The Lady from Shanghai;* (from left to right): Flynn, his wife Nora Eddington, Rita Hayworth, Orson, unidentified, and William Castle, associate producer. (Charles Higham Collection)

With his third wife, Countess Paola Mori Di Girfalco, aboard the Italian liner *Andrea Doria*, 1955. (Phototeque)

As General Dreedle, on location in Mexico for Mike Nichols's *Catch-22*, Welles is interviewed by Peter Bogdanovich for an as yet uncompleted authorized biography. (Phototeque)

Welles with Jeanne Moreau on the set of *The Sailor from Gibraltar*. (Phototeque)

As Falstaff in armor. (Charles Higham Collection)

The old Charles Foster Kane. Welles aged quite differently. (Phototeque)

As Cesare Borgia in *The Prince of Foxes*. (Phototeque)

Orson in *Macbeth*, shot at the home of cheap westerns, Republic Studios. (Phototeque)

Makeup test still for the film project *Heart of Darkness* from the novel by Joseph Conrad. (Charles Higham Collection)

In *Chimes at Midnight* as Falstaff, one of Welles's favorite roles. (Charles Higham Collection)

As Sheriff Hank Quinlan in *Touch of Evil.* (Charles Higham Collection)

Orson during filming of the 1969 film of *The Southern Star.* (Phototeque)

In *Get to Know Your Rabbit* Orson played an eccentric magician, one of his favorite real-life roles. (Phototeque)

Orson in a scene from the BBS production *A Safe Place.* (Phototeque)

9

An anxious Orson Welles did not sleep the night of the *Citizen Kane* premiere. Yet the reviews surpassed his expectations. Bosley Crowther in *The New York Times* said, "Far and away the most surprising and cinematically exciting motion picture to be seen here in many a moon . . . cynical, ironic, sometimes oppressive, and as realistic as a slap." Howard Barnes wrote in *The New York Herald Tribune*, "The motion picture stretched its muscles at the Palace Theater last night, to remind one that it is a sleeping giant of the arts." *Time* gushed, "Lush with the leggy beauty of Publisher Kane's teeming love-life, grotesque with his wholesale grabs of Europe's off-scourings." Cecilia Ager of *PM* said, "Seeing it, it's as if you never really saw a movie before." William Boehnel wrote in *The New York World Telegram*, "What matters is that *Citizen Kane* is a cinema masterpiece—that here is a film so full of drama, pathos, humor, drive, variety and courage and originality in its treatment that it is staggering and belongs at once among the great screen achievements."

The intellectual weeklies were by and large on Welles's side. A rare mixed review was Otis Ferguson's in *The New Republic*; Phillip T. Hartung went overboard in *Commonweal*: "He saw and he conquered. And *Citizen Kane* is the proof."

Back in Hollywood, Welles was rejoined by Dolores Del Rio, who had secured her divorce from Cedric Gibbons in January and had been very little seen in New York during those crowded weeks. The Los Angeles premiere at the El Capitan Theater was sensational; all Hollywood was there. *The Hollywood Reporter* backed down from its previous attacks, and the editor, W. R. Wilkerson, published an apology in his editorial column on page one. Clark Gable led the applause by telling Erskine Johnson of *The Los Angeles Daily News*, "Gosh, now I have to go back to making those lousy A pictures." Erich von Stroheim, Gilbert Seldes, and Pare Lorentz joined the chorus of praise. But the film historian Richard Griffith, writing in *The Los Angeles Times* (May 12, 1941), said that "though the attempt is praiseworthy, the results are shockingly unsatisfying"; the broadcaster and columnist Ed Sullivan described the movie as "cruel and unnecessary"; and Eileen Creelman of *The New York Sun* snapped, "It is a cold picture, unemotional, a puzzle rather than a drama."

Meanwhile, Welles was as busy as ever. He was fighting off charges from the Hearst papers that he was associated with the alleged Communist waterfront leader, the Australian Harry Bridges, whom Senator Burton Wheeler and others of the extreme right were trying to deport, while at the same time, ironically, Russia banned *Kane* because it portrayed a tycoon with sympathy. He was still battling the accusation that he had overcharged for the use of his own clothing in *Kane*. He was struggling with the draft problem. And he was working on a story about the career of the French mass murderer Désiré Landru, known as Bluebeard. Later he discussed the notion with Charlie Chaplin, and Chaplin decided to use the theme for a black comedy that became *Monsieur Verdoux*—and paid Welles $5,000 for the privilege. (Welles often falsely claimed that the entire story of the movie was his own invention.)

Perhaps in part from the strain of all the activity surrounding *Kane*, Welles was feeling ill. He had painful backache, foot and ankle strain, a hernia, and asthmatic rales in his lungs. He was x-rayed and his stomach palpated by Dr. Kenneth Davis. Another physician, Dr. L. Dudley Bumpus, again declared him unfit for military service, and that decision was confirmed by the draft board. This was a relief, and Welles had to make an effort to pretend he was sorry.

When *Citizen Kane* went into general release, the public failed to respond to the excellent reviews and proved indifferent to the picture. Virtually every theater where the movie was shown suffered from its exhibition. Welles was desolated to read that losses at the Palace in New York alone amounted to just over $18,000. A $12,000 loss was shown at the El Capitan in Hollywood. (The picture finally lost $160,000 but earned its money back through reissues.)

According to Hearst's biographer Ferdinand Lundberg and others, Hearst and Marion Davies saw *Kane* in San Francisco during the week of May 27, entering and leaving the theater unobserved. Asked what he thought of the movie, Hearst, who was furious, replied, "We thought it was a little too long." (Marion Davies later denied that they had seen the film.) John Tebbel, another Hearst biographer, wrote that "contrary to legend, Hearst rather enjoyed seeing himself portrayed on the screen." A third biographer, Frederick Swanberg, said "Hearst was able to joke about *Citizen Kane*." He added that Hearst had a print of the film, and only Marion Davies pronounced it grotesque.

The Hearst press continued to make no mention of the film, and the major distribution chains failed to accept it. The distributors were nervous about the prospect of litigation from both Hearst and Mankiewicz, who had had a bitter struggle to secure his proper credit as co-author of the screenplay and was still talking about taking action beyond his Writers' Guild arbitration. The Warner's, Paramount, and Loew's circuits all declined the picture, and it was only when Schaefer threatened Warner with a conspiracy suit that Warner's crumbled. Reports of dismal audience response filled *The Motion Picture Herald.* The comment from the Iris Theater of Velva, North Dakota, was typical: "Stay away from this. A nightmare. Will drive 'em out of your theatre. It may be a classic, but it's plum 'nuts' to your show-going public."

When Welles completed the first draft of *The Way to Santiago*, renamed *Mexican Melodrama,* and presented it to RKO, the studio bosses objected to the sensitive political content of the script, as they had done with *The Smiler with a Knife.* In view of the impending failure of *Kane* at the box office, George Schaefer did not dare press his luck. And when the story was submitted to the Mexican government, it naturally refused to cooperate in a venture that would show the extent of Nazi influence within its borders. Welles's attempt to make a bold anti-Nazi picture in a time of American peace with Germany had failed again. And not to be overlooked was the fact that, as we shall see later, RKO's largest stockholder, Nelson Rockefeller, for all his lip service to anti-Nazism, had substantial investments in German-owned companies both in Mexico and south of the Panama Canal.

Welles took on yet another film project that summer: *Journey into Fear,* from the novel by Eric Ambler, which dealt in a more trivial manner with the theme of Nazism. It was the story of an engineer in Istanbul, Howard Graham, who meets (aboard a steamer on the Black Sea) a succession of bizarre and eccentric characters, including a fascist villain who represents the rise of Nazi power in the Middle East. Welles set to work on a treatment and, mindful of the failure of his two political scripts, kept the Nazi elements to a minimum. Ben Hecht wrote the first draft but never quite completed it, and Ellis St. Joseph and Richard Collins worked on a revised draft. Welles talked of hiring the actor Thomas Mitchell to do yet another draft, but he abandoned this idea and wrote it himself with Joseph Cotten, whom he cast in the leading role in mid-July. Dolores Del Rio was cast opposite Cotten; having been idle for some time, she was delighted with the prospect of working under Orson's direction.

Welles also agreed to develop a film called *Pan-American* that would illustrate aspects of life in North and South America. This was the plan not of Nelson Rockefeller, as has frequently been stated, but of Ourival Fontes, minister of propaganda and popular culture of Brazil. He proposed a multifaceted picture of Brazilian life to John Hay Whitney and Walt Disney during their South American trip in October 1941. President Getulio Vargas was equally enthusiastic about the project, and the Brazilian government's Motion Picture Division would provide complete facilities. The film would be distributed by RKO at a charge of twenty percent of the gross sales, or at cost, whichever was lower, and all overhead would be charged at cost against actual studio expenditures. RKO would be guaranteed by contract up to thirty percent of the cost (to a limit of $300,000) by the Inter-American Affairs Committee.*

Nelson Rockefeller, the head of the Inter-American Affairs Committee, clearly saw that *Pan-American* would effectively help to oppose the Nazi anti-American influence in Brazil. But his public stance was a sham. Indeed, so cynical was Rockefeller's approach that he placed advertisements attacking Nazism in Nazi-controlled newspapers, in order to provide the owners with revenue—and he was rapped on the knuckles by President Roosevelt for doing this. Later he was to keep the Chase Bank branch in Nazi-occupied Paris open for the duration of the war, which facilitated the direct supply of funds, transferred from South America. In addition, he allowed the Standard Oil headquarters in Caracas, Venezuela, to be leased from a Nazi corporation, and it shipped oil through Switzerland in 1943 and 1944. The creation of *Pan-American*, now retitled *It's All True*, was, like the advertisements in Nazi papers, a front for Rockefeller's true purpose. Welles knew nothing of the truth and fell for the plan.

Ironically, Walt Disney—the only Hollywood executive to receive Hitler's authorized filmmaker Leni Riefenstahl when she visited the movie colony in 1937—was also hired to head up a propaganda film cementing North and South American relations. The result was the entertaining but infamous double disaster of *The Three Caballeros* and *Saludos Amigos*, in which Donald Duck was seen dancing all over the Andes. Like the Disney project, *It's All True* was to be framed by the traditional music of the Latin American countries.

Welles wanted the North American segments to include *Love Story*

---

* Welles and Schaefer agreed that it would cost $600,000; subsequently denials by Welles and others notwithstanding, that sum was to be spent by Welles before half the picture was completed.

by John Fante, about a typical young American couple who live out a fantasy: a bricklayer pretends to be wealthy in order to impress his bride, they spend their wedding night in a borrowed expensive house, and then he tells her the truth. Duke Ellington, Louis Armstrong, and other jazz greats would appear in another North American story, *Jam Session* by Elliot Paul, which would tell the story of jazz through episodes of Louis Armstrong's life. (The story of the samba would similarly be told through the life of some as yet unselected figure of Rio.)

Welles also planned at that time *The Magnificent Ambersons*, from the novel by Booth Tarkington, which he had presented on *Mercury Theater of the Air* on October 29, 1939. As though he did not have enough on his hands, he was struggling to produce books and records in the Todd Shakespeare series. On July 29 he optioned the rights to two stories by the documentary filmmaker Robert Flaherty. *The Captain's Chair,* for the North American segment of *It's All True,* was about a Hudson Bay trader; *Bonito, the Bull* was based on a traditional episode in which the president of Mexico spared a bull in a corrida in answer to a boy's plea. David Stuart was hired to work with Elliot Paul on the *Jam Session* script, now retitled *The Story of Jazz.* Stuart, the manager of the Jazz Man record shop on Santa Monica Boulevard in Hollywood, had no experience in screenwriting but knew most of the history and was personally acquainted with many of the major jazz figures.

In New York, Canada Lee, who frequently fought in private the same battles against whites that he fought on stage, was about to embark on a national tour of *Native Son* when a car dealer charged him with larceny. It was alleged that he had tried to sell an automobile on which he had not made a payment. Weissberger had a hard fight to keep Lee from going to prison; after a protracted court struggle, he was let off with a caution, and only a concentrated effort suppressed the story.

There was further tension in the financial negotiations with Duke Ellington over the music for *The Story of Jazz.* In the end, Ellington got $11,000 to supply and arrange appropriate music; Welles's meetings with him were sporadic, for Welles was very busy in early September. With his usual impetuousness, he decided after months of planning to write his adaptation of *The Magnificent Ambersons.* He accepted an invitation from King Vidor, who had warmly befriended him on his first arrival in Hollywood, to stay with him for two weeks on his yacht moored at Wilmington. During this visit, uninterrupted and unharassed, Welles put together the screenplay. As before, he adhered closely to the text, adding only a considerable enhancement of the character of Aunt Fanny Minafer, the frustrated spinster who wanted

Eugene Morgan and lived in anguish in the Amberson house like Mary Wells Gottfredsen.°

The Magnificent Ambersons, published in 1918, was part of the trilogy *Growth,* which pictured life in a midwestern city that was a disguised version of Booth Tarkington's Indianapolis. It won a Pulitzer Prize, and it remains, along with *Penrod* and *Penrod and Sam,* a moving record of the simple world of boyhood. The central figure of *Ambersons* was the explosive George Minafer, the arrogant young man who gets his comeuppance and learns humility through confronting the greater sophistication of European society. Beyond sharing the same first name, George Minafer and Welles had in common a Midwestern upbringing in a town that moved from the horse and buggy to the machine age within a decade—and the presence of an automobile manufacturer, Eugene Morgan. Welles claimed that Tarkington was a friend of his father and a frequent visitor to Grand Detour, and he said that Eugene Morgan was modeled on his father. There is no substantiation for either claim; Tarkington did not visit Grand Detour, and a careful search of his papers at Princeton shows he did not base Eugene Morgan on Welles, nor did he, so far as can be determined, know him. But it is probable that the fantasy-spinning Richard Welles told his son of the acquaintance.

Welles's affection for the story sprang from his father's imagined reminiscence as well as from a deep knowledge of the world from which the story emerged. George Orson Welles and George Minafer were both whippersnappers, disobedient and rebellious, who yearned for the big city; both were overly fond of cake and other rich foods, were roly-poly figures in their teens, and were accused of being sissies. Both were given to displays of bad temper, and there is no mistaking the resemblance in their individual conflicts with their families: Orson's hatred of Mary Wells Gottfredsen, and perhaps his uncles, is reflected in George Minafer's fights with the frustrated Aunt Fanny, who yearns in vain for Eugene. Furthermore, neighbors in Grand Detour recall that Orson liked strawberry shortcake, George's special fad, more than anything; it was all the rage in those days. And undoubtedly Welles drew on memories of his mother in the portrait he developed of George's mother. Her death while George is still a young man can only be said to mirror the death of Beatrice Welles when Orson was eight.

Welles began making bold sketches for the picture in Hollywood,

---

° There is an indirect reference to Badger Brass: she loses her money on a newfangled automobile lamp.

working closely with the gifted art director Mark Lee Kirk and the costume designer Edward Stevenson. Although both men were able to bring from the research department considerable information concerning the interior of the Rudolphsheim-like Amberson house as it would have been at the dawn of the automobile age, the 1905 motor buggy that was not far removed from the early Nash machines on which Richard Welles worked, and the customs, modes of clothing and hair, and items of decoration from a kitchen boiler to the mansion's grand staircase, Welles himself supplied details from his own experience that surpassed those of his collaborators. He even produced a nostalgic reference to the icehouse at the Sheffield House in a winter sequence shot in a similar building in downtown Los Angeles.°

A passage in *Ambersons* that had inspired Herman Mankiewicz was recreated. In Welles's favorite scene in *Kane*, Bernstein recalls having once seen a girl in a white dress on a ferry—and the image has haunted him the whole of his life; for the film of *Ambersons*, Welles found the equivalent: Jack Amberson remembers seeing a girl at a depot, crying, a girl he never forgot.

Welles began to cast the picture, testing and selecting Dolores Costello as Isabel Amberson. She had been married to John Barrymore, the idol of his youth, and he was fascinated to meet her, exchanging many thoughts with her, memories and evocations of the great actor, who was performing drunkenly at the same time in second-rate Hollywood films, and who for some reason Welles liked. Joseph Cotten was selected for Eugene Morgan; Tim Holt, whom Welles remembered from *Stagecoach*, was ideal as the handsome but already plump George Minafer, and indeed he looked rather like a small-boned, slighter version of Welles. Agnes Moorehead was the only possible choice for Aunt Fanny; and Anne Baxter was admirably cast as Eugene Morgan's daughter, Lucy. Richard Bennett, father of the actresses Joan, Constance, and Barbara Bennett, appeared as Major Amberson.

Welles drew not only on his own recollections in preparing the film but on the appearance of old photographs, with their use of silhouettes or oval frames within frames, and he drew on the silent movies he had seen in his childhood. By mid-September many beautiful designs had been worked out, and Welles was in exceptionally good spirits, delighted by everything his colleagues gave him.

Now his chief distraction was setting up *My Friend Bonito*. Welles

---

° This was a filmmaking custom in snowless Los Angeles; *Lost Horizon* had been photographed in that same building, the director Frank Capra evoking a wintry mountain range and windswept passes within its confines.

engaged his friend Norman Foster, who was bilingual in Spanish and accustomed to Mexican conditions, to fly to Mexico and prepare the film. Foster was to cast the picture and shoot second-unit work that would include backgrounds of the ranches and footage of the birth of the bulls, their branding, their preparation for the corrida, and the boy who would train them. Foster worked doggedly, selecting the warmly appealing Jesús Vásquez (affectionately nicknamed Hamlet) as his star and casting the respected Domingo Soler as the boy's mentor. He prepared—often with a few greased palms—for the cooperation of the Mexican authorities; the able Joe Noriega, a Mexican movie expert and coordinator, would take care of the countless problems normally encountered in Latin American countries. Through most of August, while Welles was preparing *Ambersons,* Foster was working with Noriega to smooth the path.

Then the Canada Lee case flared up again. Following a change in staff in the district attorney's office in New York City, Lee was again charged with selling the car that carried an encumbrance. Arnold Weissberger bailed him out so that he could appear in the play on tour.

Hazel Scott was hired to play jazz for *It's All True,* and Welles wanted the celebrated artist Oskar Fischinger to do an animated cartoon in which the sounds of jazz would be matched by food and utensils jumping in unison. Elliot Paul would write the script to accompany the dancing knives and forks.

Shooting on *My Friend Bonito* began in September. Al Gilks started as cameraman, then had to report to Washington on October 13 for secret work connected with President Roosevelt's covert preparations for war. Floyd Crosby took over. The second unit in Mexico was struggling bravely under severe financial restraints applied by the studio. Welles was in Mexico October 14–17, accompanied by Dolores Del Rio, to watch the preparatory shooting at the Rancho Atenco. He was cheered by the evident efficiency of the film crew in Mexico, and he returned to Hollywood with footage that he ran at the studio on the night of October 17. He cabled Foster that the footage was wonderful, marvelous, very exciting, "beautiful as anything you saw in your life," and appointed him co-director of *Bonito*—"And God bless you."

A new legal problem loomed on October 17, 1941. One Harry Silverstone charged Welles and Mankiewicz with libel because in the script of *Kane* a man of that name was said to have murdered his wife; after dragging on for some time, the case was thrown out of court.

Welles began rehearsing the cast of *Ambersons* for a total of five weeks, discussing with each actor the characters and their role in the story, their homes, their schooling, their backgrounds and the society in which they lived in the script. Originally he recorded the players as though they were on the radio, then played back the scenes for comment; he thought he might have the actors match their lip movements to the recorded sound, but the tests did not work well. He played the recording for Joseph Breen, briefly in charge of production after being the film censor for years, and George Schaefer; both were impressed.

Unfortunately, Welles could not get Goldwyn to release Gregg Toland, who was busy with another picture, and it was not until the last minute that, acting on a suggestion by Toland, he chose Stanley Cortez (brother of the silent film star Ricardo Cortez). By chance Cortez was at RKO doing tests that month, and he watched Welles in the rehearsals. Welles's new manager, Jack Moss, told Cortez that Welles might use Toland's crew from *Kane* without having an official cameraman on the picture. Cortez asked Moss if he could do the job, and Moss mentioned him to Welles. After running some of Cortez's films and the tests, Welles offered the position to Cortez, and Cortez accepted.

To this day Stanley Cortez remembers his excitement at the challenge. The shooting began on October 27. He was extremely talented but—to Welles's annoyance—as slow as Toland was fast, and he had a literalness to which Welles did not warm. However, his work was fine, and Welles was satisfied with the look of the dinner party scene with which he and Cortez began the movie. Cortez achieved a shimmering, rich, dark look that Welles rejoiced in; Cortez claims that Welles threw his arms around him when he saw the rushes.

Filming the sleighride scene indoors was a challenge for both director and cameraman. For twelve days cast and crew worked in below freezing temperatures. The lighting bulbs exploded in the cold, and the 4,000-watt arcs melted the snow. Welles asked for a Currier and Ives look; the art department supplied a cyclorama of snowy Indiana countryside by feeding 5,000-pound cakes of ice into a cruncher. Welles, who hated the cornflakes-dipped-in-gypsum snow used in most movies, told the magazine *Modern Screen:* "Phony snow just won't do. I want the real thing, so that we can make snowballs and people can get smeared with it and have it drip."

Welles wanted to move the camera in long, unbroken shots through the house, to create a symphonic effect; Anne Baxter remembers how, in order to achieve this, furniture, mirrors, and even walls had to be moved on rollers, hinged and shifted about as each movement of the players was timed with a stopwatch. Baxter says she was so inspired by the director's genius that the difficulty of this never fazed her.

As the shooting continued, Cortez's slowness again aggravated

Welles, who still missed the speed, decisiveness, and lack of fuss incarnate in Gregg Toland. Cortez's fiddling with lights drove him to the brink of fury. Toland was selfless; Cortez, cut from the same cloth as his brother, was deliberate and enjoyed being center stage. But Welles was a dreamer, a biographer of his own past as well as Tarkington's, and all he wanted was someone to convey his vision without an intervening ego—and Cortez got in his way. He knew Cortez would have to go, even though everything he did was as magnificent as Toland's work on *Kane*.

In *The Magnificent Ambersons* the images flow miraculously along: the film carefully renders an American past, creating with affection a world as formally nostalgic as a cameo brooch. A tram stalled near a house, its horses champing; snow on eaves and heavy on winter's bare trees; the shine of a window where a woman stands listening tenderly to the tripping melody of a serenade; a hat fixed in a cheval glass; faces shining with the glow of cold and voices raised as a horseless carriage jigs away on its journey under a shaking tasseled canopy while a sleigh forms more delicate swooping parabolas in the snowbanks nearby: the early part of the film has a cool lyricism, the mood of a Frost poem. But the second half is even richer in its deep shadows and wintry colors, as the swarming darkness of the Amberson mansion presages death for Isabel Amberson Minafer, for her husband, and for Major Amberson, who is the house's most formidable living ghost. As each door closes, whether or not it bears a glistening black wreath, it seems to close forever on all possibility of escape. As each white face fades away in the night, we seem to be watching the interment of corpses and hearing their last requiem.

The film is composed in scenes in which the actors are given theatrically visible exits, but they are not "merely" theatrical. They serve a purpose: they show that the figures in the film's formal dance are forever retreating into shadows, into death. It is a film of vanishings, as when two knots of people, one in the foreground, the other "rhubarbing" in the background after the Amberson ball, move out into the windy night, leaving the polished hall to its shadows as the musicians pack up their instruments. The Morgan Motor, too, vanishes over a hill past a giant wintry tree, and an iris-out blots its image forever, to be followed by a black wreath tied to the door of the Amberson house.

Throughout the film people are leaving, drifting away like leaves before the wind. In the ballroom scene the dancing figures seem to recede into infinity, an effect achieved in part by the judicious use of mirrors. Upright struts and pillars constantly create frames within the frame, so that the people seem to be fixed like moths on plates, fluttering and trapped. A variant on this method occurs in Isabel's deathbed scene, when the shadows of the bedstead and the lace curtain trap her in a web of doom, and a sudden, shocking change of light into near darkness (as someone draws the curtains) firmly involves her in death.

The soundtrack has the effect of isolating the people in the film, of withdrawing them from us. Voices are constantly heard "off"—not quite an innovation, since William Wyler had used the method in *These Three*—the device being more extensively employed here than before. Just as we constantly see people framed in uprights, half-glimpsed through doorways, or reflected in mirrors and windows, so we hear their muffled voices through doorways or in the far distance of rooms, floating down a stairway or mingled with the measures of a dance or the hiss and clang of a factory. It is part of the film's evocation of a deathly atmosphere that, apart from Aunt Fanny's whine, everyone should speak in subdued, sad, falling tones, their words having a dying fall in a film of endless dying. Echoes of Rudolphsheim, of a child's footsteps and an early bereavement.

There are curious lapses in this lovely elegiac work. In the early passages that illustrate in montage the passing of the years before George Minafer's birth, we see George himself fully grown, in a boat with his mother, who looks no younger than she does in the main body of the film. Agnes Moorehead is seen among the Greek chorus townspeople, commenting on the Minafers' behavior—an astonishingly slipshod touch. (Similarly, in the projection room scene in *Kane*, Joseph Cotten and other members of the cast could be seen among the reporters in the near-darkness.) These lapses illustrate the more private, quirky side of Welles's art.

During the shooting of *The Magnificent Ambersons* Welles managed to do *The Lady Esther Show* on CBS and ran rushes of *My Friend Bonito* along with those of *Ambersons*. As she had done during the filming of *Kane*, Dolores Del Rio lovingly insisted on picking him up at the studio at night and taking him out for big meals; she recalled later that he would eat prodigiously, returning visibly stuffed, his stomach swelling, to do more work.

Fueled by oysters, steaks, and ample wine, Welles sent Norman Foster cable after cable, criticizing him for not keeping in touch, jocularly expressing jealousy of Foster's wife, Sally (sister of Loretta Young), who had joined him, complaining of fuzzy close-ups of Jesús Vásquez, calling for fuller close-ups of sweating faces and "smoking, burning flesh, Yum-Yum!" at the branding and for more footage of the blessing of the animals. One telegram read, "Yes shoot national holiday, yes shoot visit, yes go on shooting. I love you dearly." By the end of November, Foster was sick with dysentery and there were delays on top of delays caused by weather.

On December 2 about an hour of *Ambersons* had been finished. Jack Moss ran it for Joseph Breen, who memoed Welles, "The material we saw was really excellent, and although you know me to be a chronic kicker, in this instance I have naught but praise—from my heart. God love you." These were cheering words from the industry's most notorious scold, now in uneasy occupancy of his executive position at the studio.

On the same day there were ill tidings from Mexico. Foster was not only sick, but facing worse weather, camera trouble, red tape, and an accident in which the government censor had fallen off a train and broken his arm. A rancher helping the unit also fell from a train, this time fatally, and another helper was almost fatally gored at a finca, or training ranch. A wrangler, stripped by bandits, had one ear cut off and his face slashed with a knife. Indeed, bandits constantly threatened the unit; everyone feared an ambush when a truck stalled on the muddy, rainswept roads.

When at last they began to shoot the bullfight, they had nothing but headaches. Rare moments of sunshine had to be snatched on the wing; most of the time there was a hellish scenario of icy rain and fog and dripping pine trees and lava running from small volcanoes that seemed to be in permanent eruption. Because of the weather, the bulls were often testy and ticklish. In the blessing scene the children shivered, coughed, and sneezed, huddling miserably against the church wall to keep out of the wind. Sally Foster got influenza, and at one stage the unit had to clear out of a ranch and sleep on cots in broken-down rooms in an abandoned hacienda where the windows were shut tight and could not be moved. At 4:00 A.M. a foreman's drum rattled loudly to call a few peons to go out into the fields at dawn, and no one could sleep after that.

Welles, fretful to a degree, was consoled by a telegram from Schaefer that praised the completed hour of *Ambersons* and was especially admiring of Agnes Moorehead's performance. That performance had not been easily achieved: Welles had driven the actress to hysteria with his countless takes—a leaf he had taken from William Wyler's book.

On December 7, a Sunday, came the news that Pearl Harbor had been bombed. For three days Welles directed as though in a dream, unable to concentrate on the rushes from Mexico or to deal with the problems of rain and mud and red tape. That Simon and Schuster had rejected his introduction and script of *Citizen Kane* for publication in book form seemed unimportant then.

In December, Welles was deeply concerned with the matter of three Soviet citizens, Luigi Longo, Franz Dahlen, and Heiner Rau, former members of the Republican forces in Spain, who had been arrested in Vichy, France, and were to be turned over to occupied France for delivery to the Italian and German governments. Welles was convinced that if they were handed over, they would be arrested. He appealed with telegrams directly to President Roosevelt and Secretary of State Cordell Hull—a fact that, had it come to light, would have played into the hands of those who accused him of being a Communist sympathizer. But the telegrams were not made public, and the three men were handed over and disappeared.

On December 11 it was settled that the moment *Ambersons* was shot and in rough daily assemblages, Welles would fly to Brazil to cover Carnival in Rio, February 14–17. He had in mind telling (through the eyes of a child) the story of the samba, the South American dance music that was then sweeping the continent, following the rapid movement of dancers and musicians from the slums above Rio, the notorious favelas, to world recognition. Bruno Cheli, the RKO manager in Rio, had secured the commitment of the Brazilian government all the way up to President Vargas, and enormous coverage could be guaranteed in the Rio press and on the radio, especially if Welles arrived with Dolores Del Rio.

Under the pressure, Welles began to rush his work on *Ambersons,* and there were clashes with Cortez because of the revised schedules. He was working from 8:00 A.M. until late at night and driving his cast hard. Meanwhile, he corresponded with Roger Hill about subsidizing a chair of drama at the Todd School; he was planning volumes of the Mercury Shakespeare series and 78 rpm record albums; he was busy with *The Lady Esther Show;* and he was working on *The Story of Jazz,* with Duke Ellington, Elliot Paul, and David Stuart. And now Welles made a serious mistake.

He decided to go ahead with the much-delayed *Journey into Fear,* using the script he had written with Joseph Cotten in July. Cotten and Dolores Del Rio would star, and Welles selected Jack Moss, who had never acted, as the sinister silent villain. He began to prepare for the picture, talking with the actors and generally devising with the cameraman Karl Struss a cramped, grim, somber look for the film. He even appeared in the picture with a false nose and an astrakhan hat as Colonel Haki, a Turkish police chief. It was obvious that he would have a nervous breakdown if he kept up the pace, especially when he was due to leave for South America. Then, just when he should have gone to Joseph Breen and told him that Mercury was appointing Norman Foster the official director of *My Friend Bonito*, he foolishly recalled Foster from Mexico. Instead of giving *Journey into Fear* to another director, he insisted that Foster take it over.

Much as he loved Orson, Foster was angered, shocked, and maddened by this disastrous mistake to the day he died. *My Friend Bonito* was firmly on its way to being a masterpiece, while *Journey into Fear* was a badly written jumble, devoid of artistic merit. Foster had never had a chance to prepare it or to read the script. Stopping *My Friend Bonito* in mid-production meant that all the weeks of agonizing work— the sicknesses, the delays, and the great artistic achievement—were discarded like a toy tossed aside by an impetuous child. Foster made embarrassed explanations to the members of his Mexican network and left the country he loved with the tatters of the unfinished work in his hands.*

The day after Foster returned to Hollywood, December 23, *My Friend Bonito* was officially canceled for an indefinite period, and on December 26 Richard Wilson advised Foster of the change of assignment. A bad-tempered and irritable Foster began work on *Journey into Fear.* He directed without enthusiasm, covering his irritation by following Welles's master plan for the crowded, throbbing scenes aboard the oceangoing ship that formed the focus of the action.

Welles was running from set to set of *Ambersons,* dashing over to *Journey into Fear* in his false nose and fur coats, arranging for additional scenes of *Ambersons* to be shot by other hands, working on *The Lady Esther Show* (which meant going to the CBS studios), and generally driving himself and everyone else into a frazzle. Yet he managed to get his shots in preparation for the trip to Brazil, to have a medical examination, to see the consul about his passport arrangements, and to make travel reservations. There were also incredibly complicated plans for shifting an entire unit (rare in those days) to another country, along with secretaries, assistants, press agents, and other members of the Mercury/RKO entourage.

---

* The Mercury brought the unhappy Jesús Vásquez to Hollywood and installed him in a Catholic school.

10

Somehow clambering out of his problem with *The Lady Esther Show* by promising that he would deliver broadcasts from Rio, Welles began wrapping up *Ambersons* in the last week of January. He would have to leave to his editor, Robert Wise, the task of assembling the final footage. The film was over budget and schedule: $1,013,760.46 against a planned $853,950. Due to the rush of making it, camera crane noises had ruined parts of the soundtrack and those parts had to be redone. The sets cost, at $137,265.44, three times more than *Gone With the Wind,* and twice what was budgeted for. Bernard Herrmann's scoring and the intricate sound recording and dubbing could not be finished under his personal supervision. He had in mind that Wise would take the final cut to Brazil, where Welles could deal with it. If only he had allowed his second unit to shoot in Rio until he was ready, as he had done with *My Friend Bonito,* he might have saved much of the agony that was to follow.

But he was in a hurry, and the idea of Rio excited him. He began telling people the fib that he had been conceived in Rio. He wanted to see Carnival. He wanted to enjoy the publicity that he was promised would greet him on his arrival. And he would be not merely a Hollywood director but a semi-political figure, an emissary of democracy.

Augusta Weissberger would accompany him as his personal assistant, along with another well-established secretary, Shifra Haran. In mid-January fifty thousand feet of Technicolor film were flown in, with twenty-five thousand more to come at the end of the month. On January 22 Richard Wilson and a large entourage of technicians flew via Miami to Rio. Stranded in Belém because of a mishap in supplying funds or tickets, they had to be cabled money for their immediate expenses. This first group included, in addition to Wilson, Elizabeth Amster, secretary; Edward Pyle, operator; Joseph Biroc, operator; William Howard Greene, first Technicolor cameraman (a representative of the Technicolor company); Harry J. Wild, cameraman; Ned Scott, stillman; and several minor figures.

On February 4 at 11:10 P.M. Welles left Los Angeles on American Airlines, Dolores remaining behind to work on the tedious *Journey into Fear,* which was already over budget. Welles hated flying, and this flight was utterly exhausting. The plane stopped in Fort Worth and Nashville before arriving in Miami more than twenty-four hours after it departed. The plane then went on to Puerto Rico and various island airports, and it was not until three days later, at 3:55 P.M., that the cold (in those days airplanes in flight were very chilly) and tired passengers arrived. Indeed, even this miserable journey was possible only because of the influence of Nelson Rockefeller. The bulk of air transportation was taken up at that time by the Pan-American Conference in Brazil, at which the Under Secretary of State, Sumner Welles, was a prominent figure. And the trip was undertaken without passports, which were still in preparation when Welles arrived, not yet having been cleared by the formidable Ruth Shipley of the Passport Division in Washington.

Rio was packed because of the conference and the approaching Carnival. Hotel rooms were at such a premium that most of the crew had to be housed at a second-rate hotel; it was only with a supreme effort that the RKO people found Welles a suite at the luxurious Copacabana Palace Hotel. He arrived to brilliant skies in the wake of a heavy tropical rainstorm that had thrown most of his unit around in their plane; now the giant thunderclouds had cleared and the airport was jammed with well-wishers and fans whipped up by the local office.

As he was driven through the streets, Welles was stunned by the spectacle. Rio was a blaze of tropical colors, its sidewalks alive with teeming cafés, its air filled with the scream of sirens, police cars jamming every thoroughfare. The view from his suite was astonishing. As far as the eye could see stretched the azure waves of the Atlantic Ocean. The vast sweep of the crescent-shaped beach with its white sand and its hundreds of sculptured bodies was dominated by the figure of Christ on the great peak, the funicular railway that was spun like a silver filament across the lush, green mountain, and the crawling slums that covered the hills. Planes trailed signs announcing Brazilian beer or rubber tires. White skyscrapers glittered in the light. The music of the samba reverberated along with the scream of sirens and auto horns.

Rio in 1942 was the most exciting city on earth, and Hollywood seemed a million miles away. Exhausted though he was, Welles was still only twenty-six and eager for adventure and fun. When he walked out of the hotel, with people staring at him in fascination even though he was not yet a celebrity in Brazil, he was greeted by a wall of breathtaking heat. In accord with local protocol he wore coat and tie, and this meant he had to shower several times a day because he became soaked with sweat in a matter of minutes (and the water ran warm from the taps and sometimes not at all). In meetings with Richard Wilson, his special assistant Robert Meltzer, and the camera people, he learned that problems already existed. Several technicians had arrived without equipment, which had been delayed on board ship. Many were struggling with red tape and import controls. Others were suffering the effects of typhoid shots that they should have had in Hollywood. The studio troubleshooter, Lynn Shores, was a grumbling veteran who created problems for everyone and disliked Welles from the outset. Welles was kept busy attending receptions, giving interviews, and appearing on radio. Two Rio newspapers carried a life story of Welles that included the usual number of mistakes. King Momo of the Carnival and the star Grande Otelo met with Orson and were cast. Some of the crew came down with bad sunburns after rushing out onto the beach to get a quick tan to compete with all the gorgeously dark brown people.

Welles was in a bad temper that first week. He shouted at his publicists because he claimed there were not enough people at his receptions. The ship carrying the lights was delayed, and there was a desperate and futile search for their equivalents that extended even to Buenos Aires. Finally the unit secured antiaircraft searchlights, the electricians working overtime to adapt them for use in the picture.

Welles cabled Drake about his annoyance at the lack of publicity and announced in an interview that he would make *Mexican Melodrama* with Dolores after all and would finish *My Friend Bonito* himself in Mexico. Meanwhile, Herbert Drake warned the RKO publicist in Rio, Tom Pettey, to be circumspect. Orson, he said,

> has certain unpleasant habits, such as reading your mail. . . . Don't mind him any if he is rude. He regards it as a time-saving expedient. You will find it difficult to get a logical answer from him about what he is going to do. He trusts always his genius and/or charm to get him out of any situation. Sometimes the irresistible force meets the unmoveable object. At such times, go in the bomb shelter.

By February 14, with Carnival in full swing, the crew was struggling against heavy odds. Welles had dysentery but managed to attend a press conference at the Tijuca tennis club on February 13. The next day, still feeling terrible, he remained on his feet to continue shooting Carnival scenes. The streets were filled with revelers and celebrants wearing a fantastic array of masks and costumes, each one more surreal than the last. In the darkness, as the crowds became increasingly fierce and intense, the six army searchlights were manned by eighty Brazilian officers and soldiers supervised by the electricians. It was almost impossible to move through the thousands of dancing, jigging, screaming people, and often members of the crew became lost in the crowd. The soldiers failed to understand the needs of the unit, and every shot had to be made in black and white as well as color in case the color film might be damaged or scratched.

Welles spoke on the radio (partly in Portuguese), met with the press, attended a gala ball, and filmed the arrival of King Momo, the dazzling parade on the Avenida Rio Branco, a masked ball in Petropolis, and people whirling through the beachfront areas. On the third day, the sky was overcast and rain threatened, and the humidity made everyone feel they were living in a fever swamp. Welles did not sleep all night, and his dysentery weakened him; finding a toilet was an ordeal with the crowds of people and little knowledge of the city. He hated the *Life* magazine team that dogged him everywhere, taking pictures of him making shots. In his distress he even skipped a press conference at the end of Carnival.

By February 23 Welles was in even worse shape. He forced himself to attend a ceremony at which he accepted prizes for *Citizen Kane* for best picture, actor, and director. In filming he struggled with mist and fog that suddenly blanketed the beach. By February 28 there were huge thunderclouds and severe rain.

He also had to contend with the difficulties of working with William Howard Greene, who had been imposed on him by Herbert and Natalie Kalmus of Technicolor. And he was vexed by four reels of *Journey into Fear* that had arrived for examination and did not look good. Norman Foster was bombarding him with questions, and he could answer few of them. Some of his scenes as Colonel Haki had to be redone, so he faced the prospect of getting a heavy fur coat and a false nose from Hollywood and then dressing up for the replacement shots.

On February 25 pickup photography—shots that had not been completed following Welles's dismissal of Stanley Cortez on New Year's Day—was finally finished on *The Magnificent Ambersons*. Robert Wise advised Welles that the print would be shipped to him to look at.

Schaefer cabled Welles on February 27, urging him to cut the print of *Ambersons* as soon as it arrived. As it happened, the picture was still being shot; some of the scenes that had been rushed were unsatisfactory and had to be redone. Welles cabled Jack Moss on February 28, with the rain beating steadily outside his suite, that he was worried about the delays in *Ambersons* and wanted it shot on triple shifts; rubber noses, mustaches, and eyebrows should be rushed to Rio; Dolores should view the rushes of *Journey* as his representative.

On March 1, as the rain continued, Schaefer cabled that *Ambersons* must be ready for the Easter season because it had cost over a million dollars and had to make its money back quickly.

In the meantime, Welles was preparing another panel in the *It's All True* collection. This was the story of the Jangadeiros, four fishermen from Fortaleza on the hump of Brazil, who in 1941 had sailed their primitive, seining paiva tree-trunk raft, the *São Pedro*, 1,650 miles without a hull or a compass, through shark-infested waters, to Rio to bring word of their wretched working conditions to President Vargas. The fishermen had created a sensation when they sailed into Rio harbor after the harrowing journey, and they became national heroes of Brazil overnight as they were escorted—*Kon Tiki* adventurers before the event—through the streets in triumph to the presidential palace.

Welles was thrilled by the story as only he could be thrilled, and on March 5 he, Robert Meltzer, and Augusta Weissberger flew by Beechcraft to Bahia, Recife, and Fortaleza to meet the Jangadeiros. Two days later he returned to Rio with the raft fishermen. Humorous, tiny, and quaint, their bodies hard as steel, their minds quick and mercurial, the Jangadeiros were marvelous, and Welles loved them as they loved him. They were installed in glory at the Copacabana Hotel, and Orson worked with them on the script during the rainy days that followed. The struggle to obtain a studio was a difficult one; it was not until March 12 that Lynn Shores managed to pin down the Cinedia Studio for several weeks.

With the rain drumming steadily on the windows of his suite, Orson worked, laughed, and drank with the fishermen, and soon the story line was laid out. Welles made a second trip north for research and returned to find that the studio was refusing to allow him to shoot the Jangadeiros episode in color. This was absurd; it would mean that parts of the picture would be in black and white, parts in Technicolor.

The weather continued bad, the mist and rain making work impossible until the third week in March. Welles filled the time by reviewing the script, preparing broadcasts, and running more footage of *Journey into Fear*. The studio, nervous that *My Friend Bonito* would be lost for good, sent Joe Noriega back to Mexico to make additional shots.

On March 15, the cut print of *Ambersons* arrived in Rio, too late for Welles to do much with it. He cabled Wise to make changes—but these were impossible at this stage. Then a bombshell struck. On March 17 *The Magnificent Ambersons* was previewed in Pomona, California, on a bill with *The Fleet's In*, a lighthearted musical, and it was badly received. In every way the timing was wrong for *Ambersons*. Now that America was at war, the public was oppressed by fear; there was scarcely a family that did not know a man in the service, and every ablebodied youth was being conscripted. People were looking for escape, for fun and laughter at the movies. A long, heavy, serious motion picture about death and dying, a spinster's sexual frustration, and a boy's cruel impudence, much of it taking place in the dark, was not what Americans wanted, and to many critics the film's concerns seemed trivial in view of world events. George Minafer, as played by Tim Holt, was not a sympathetic figure, and the public could not identify with him. The preview audience was restless and impatient, irritated by the slow pace and unamused by the comic touches. When Richard Bennett delivered his speech about the decline of the Ambersons, symbolizing the vanishing of a pre-machine age America, the audience laughed at his slurred diction; the scene in which Aunt Fanny sat with her back to the boiler, directed by Jack Moss, caused quite a few to walk out. Wise cabled Welles, "The picture does seem to bear down on people"; he himself did not particularly care for it.

The audience comment cards were unfavorable (one said that Welles must have been frightened in the cradle to have made such a movie). Schaefer cabled Welles, "never in all my experience in the industry have I taken so much punishment or suffered as much as I did at the Pomona preview. . . . [The audience] laughed at the wrong places, talked at the picture, kidded it . . ." After *Five Kings*, this was the second major setback of Welles's career. Undoubtedly much of the film would have to be retaken. Welles cabled suggested changes, but they were not made.

Another blow fell that week. A new executive, Charles Koerner, was now in charge in Hollywood, the admiring Joe Breen having returned to his job as industry censor. Koerner was in a fury because two players, Everett Sloane and Eustace Wyatt, had to be brought from New York for reshootings on *Journey into Fear*.

On March 24 Welles cabled Jack Moss that he would not accept any cuts in *Ambersons* suggested by Moss, Robert Wise, or Joseph Cotten; that he could make changes only if Wise came to Rio with the print; that he was sure a new scene Wise had shot would not be satisfactory and must be redirected by Norman Foster. He wanted the scene in the kitchen in which Aunt Fanny cries out, "George, George," to be redubbed; concerned with the laughter it provoked, he wanted the scene played in a more subdued tone. On March 26 he suggested further changes and cuts running to some eight pages. Robert Wise says that he could not follow them comfortably. Little was done about them.

Welles tried to prop himself up by announcing, in a press release issued by Tom Pettey, that he would "shoot the conquest of Peru"—a classic case of whistling in the dark.

A more exhaustive report from Wise cast Welles into an even deeper depression. And Schaefer cabled him that he was against, finally against, shooting the fishermen sequences in color, and there must be no argument about this. (Schaefer was under grave pressure from his executive board.)

In Hollywood the *Ambersons* retakes were in progress. Robert Wise and his assistant, Mark Robson, had left their families and holed up in a motel, working twenty-four-hour shifts to, in Robert Wise's words, "keep the audiences in the theaters." Scene after scene was sliced through, transposed, or replaced in order to make the picture tighter, speedier, more understandable. In desperation, Welles cabled them on April 2, 1942, to ask for a happy ending. He suggested that the end titles show Agnes Moorehead blissfully playing bridge with her cronies and the late Isabel Amberson looking young in a locket; Tim Holt and Anne Baxter would be seen in an open car, happy and gay, followed by a shot of the microphone and the announcement that the picture had been produced, directed, and written by Orson Welles. This shocking telegram refutes Welles's allegations that the idea of a happy ending was imposed on him by the studio.* During the *Citizen Kane* post-production he had panicked that the picture would never be released; we can now see that he had panicked again.

A further annoyance was Dr. Bernstein's cabling him to send a thousand dollars immediately by Western Union ("Very imperative, Love B").

Holy Week delayed the shooting when the weather at last improved. Welles tried to have Foster and Wise flown in from Hollywood, and in the midst of these futile efforts he was planning yet

---

* A different happy ending was shot by his team without his approval.

another movie. This was *Green Mansions* (later to be made by Mel Ferrer as a vehicle for Audrey Hepburn), and Welles was sketching out possibilities for the script while he fenced with the daily emergencies of Rio.

At the Academy Awards in Hollywood that month, Welles shared with Mankiewicz the Oscar for best screenplay. On the best picture award, *Kane* lost out to his idol John Ford's *How Green Was My Valley*. On April 5, Welles dashed off a note to Mankiewicz saying that he had wanted to wire him after the dinner, "You can kiss my half." And he offered Mankiewicz an appropriate retort—"Dear Orson: You don't know your half from a hole in the ground."

There was no reply to this letter.

Meanwhile, the Carnival footage, both actual and recreated, had gotten totally out of hand. Grabbing at straws, Welles asked Wise (letter of April 6) to prepare a script from the footage he was sending. It was a futile request; Wise was no writer, and anyway, he says today, he could make nothing of the material, which was simply a jumble of what was essentially travelogue stuff. Tom Pettey wrote Herbert Drake on April 7 that "if all the film we've shot was laid end to end, it would reach to the States, and there would be enough left over to serve as a marker for the Equator. As for the film story, only God and Orson know; Orson doesn't remember." Pettey added that Welles was spending his days shooting costumed people batting balloons and throwing confetti, that he directed from a cane-bottomed rocking chair that was liable to turn over at any moment. He suffered from loose bowels and "the disposition of a teething baby." For lunch he had spaghetti, black beans, and cheese; at night he went to the casino to gamble, and after midnight he wrote ("or so he said"). Money was very short, and Augusta Weissberger's job was to keep Orson in cigars, which were constantly being stolen. Word had just arrived that Wise could not come to Rio because of government wartime priorities.

The local RKO branch was overdrawn in its accounts by April 9 and could give Welles almost no money. Welles's behavior became more erratic. He fought bitterly with Pettey over every interview, skipped appointments without warning, and seemed to provoke the press deliberately, when before he had at least pretended to be friendly toward them. Pettey wanted to quit, he was so depressed by having to turn out ridiculous press statements to cover for the problems Welles faced. His releases have the look of rush and desperation; they contain a typical mix of hyperbole, concocted stories, and would-be amusing episodes (Welles splashing his colleagues with water from a fountain, Welles treating the fishermen to a display of magic).

The crew grumbled increasingly about the slow pace of the work. For days on end, as he shot scenes at the Municipal Theater, Welles was ill with dysentery. Then, fighting mist and rain, he began shooting sequences in the favelas, the hideous slums that crawled up the hills over Rio, where he wanted to show the origins of the samba. Shooting amid piles of garbage and wading through excrement thrown down from the hillside, haunted by vultures overhead and surrounded by rats and roaches, Welles and his crew were jeered and pelted with beer bottles by slum inhabitants who resented having their misery recorded on film. Priests interceded in an effort to have the company withdraw, but Welles stubbornly pressed on.

On April 12, with three months of shooting in the can and still not one proper linking scene to indicate a story line, Welles cabled Schaefer promising cost cuts. He said he had bent to orders that the raft scenes be in black and white; in fact, he was secretly shooting them in color, which Schaefer did not discover until weeks later. He complained of arbitrary treatment from RKO that had caused him serious embarrassment and loss of time and money. Disaster, he warned, would be the inevitable consequence of further needless assaults on his authority. He was upset that RKO wanted to cancel the scene in the Urca casino; that was to be the grand finale of the Carnival sequence, a big production number in which the samba would find its apotheosis. The sequence was soon canceled.

Schaefer cabled back that he had been trying to reach Welles for four days only to be told he was out, even though the operator said she heard Orson's voice. He denied angrily that he had forced Welles to abandon color for the fishermen scenes and said that black and white had been mandatory from the beginning. The Urca casino scene would be canceled because Welles wanted the casino rebuilt at a cost of $25,000. Schaefer said that the *Ambersons* situation was threatening, and he added that it was "painful to send the cable" because Orson was such a "stickler for quality," but he was coming to the conclusion that Welles had "no realization of money spent or problems of recouping costs."

On April 15 Welles replied that black and white was impossible for the raft scenes; as for *Ambersons*, there had been cast illness during its making and had a "criminally slow cameraman."* He had worked day and night to finish the film and did not consider its cost excessive.

On April 16, with rain still slowing work on the film, Schaefer ca-

---

* The much maligned Stanley Cortez.

bled once more, adamant about costs and about knowing when the picture would be finished. Why, for example, had Orson spent a total of $33,000 in March alone? He added ominously, "We can't go on, even if we have to close down the picture."

On April 18 Welles cabled further revisions in *Ambersons* to Robert Wise, none of which Wise could understand. Following a shaky preview of *Journey into Fear*, Foster wrote suggesting changes. Instead of taking care of them, Welles flew to Buenos Aires to receive the Argentinian best picture award for *Kane*. He was astonished to find that Buenos Aires, with its wide avenues and polished cultural life, was almost like a European city.

He returned to a series of violent arguments with the RKO official Lynn Shores. Shores fought the whole fishermen episode and Welles was infuriated. His behavior became still more erratic. He would disappear from location for long periods. Some days he started shooting at 11:30 A.M. (unthinkably late by Hollywood standards), broke for lunch at 12:30 P.M., returned at 1:30 P.M., and stopped at 5:30 P.M., refusing to work at night. He complained that Robert Meltzer and Dick Wilson sat in morose silence at meals, while he puffed blackly at his cigar.

By early May Welles's energy seemed to have picked up. As he approached his twenty-seventh birthday, the crew was busy shooting the voyage of the raft fishermen—defiantly, in color. He was giving lectures, going to cocktail parties, and shooting samba dancers at the Rio tennis club. Voodoo practices were being filmed on a closed set, and there was considerable fear of trouble from the Macumba priests. There were days when everything seemed to be going well, and then, according to Tom Pettey, Welles would "pick up a gal and vanish in his car for hours"—or get into a row with the person nearest to him—with the result that everything went badly for the rest of the day. His dictatorial tactics upset the Brazilian supplementary crew, and he fired an assistant director. (Lynn Shores restored the man to the payroll and used him in the local RKO office.)

A detailed report on Welles, sent by the Rio executives to Hollywood, was extremely unflattering.

On May 7 Welles cabled Maurice Bernstein on the doctor's birthday, a day after his own, asking about such lost items as a cap and picture of Lincoln given to his maternal grandfather, Benjamin Ives. He mentioned that he had heard no more from "a certain party" (Dolores Del Rio), and in a reply on May 14, Dr. Bernstein advised him not to stir up "those particular embers." He reported that he had visited RKO, that out of one hundred thousand feet of color film, only twelve thousand feet could be used (presumably because of damage), and that the studio was upset by the seemingly arbitrary mingling of black and white with Technicolor film. He attacked Welles's circle of associates as "climbers and flatterers." He repeated a story told him by W. R. Wilkerson of *The Hollywood Reporter*, that Schaefer would not renew Welles's contract, "so you should now make plans for the future." He attacked Moss and others "who have sucked you dry" and added, "You STILL need a guardian." He said, "You have little to show after your tremendous successes." And he had news of Alfalfa, who had come in looking like a lost goat but was brown and well after a trip to Phoenix.

Dr. Bernstein neglected to mention other serious developments. In the wake of Joseph Breen's return to his old job as industry censor, a power struggle was under way in New York between the three principal interests in the studio: Floyd Odlum, president of the hundred-million-dollar Atlas Corporation, who had saved the studio from bankruptcy in 1939; Nelson Rockefeller, for the Rockefeller Group; and Colonel (later General) David Sarnoff, head of the Radio Corporation of America. Odlum was opposed to Welles and Schaefer and supported the recently appointed executive Charles Koerner, who was equally opposed to Welles. Rockefeller and Sarnoff supported Welles. By the beginning of June, Odlum controlled forty-seven percent of the company, and Rockefeller and Sarnoff resigned from the board. Representatives of the company prepared to go to Rio to close down *It's All True*.

Then a tragedy clouded Welles's future with RKO. On May 19, shortly before 9:00 A.M., the raft carrying the fishermen was towed out into a misty Guanabara Bay in preparation for the recreation of the raft's entry into Rio harbor at the end of the fishermen's epic journey. A large wave caught the launch that was towing the raft and snapped the tow lines, and the raft rolled over in the swell. Two of the fishermen started to swim to shore while two others managed to right the raft. Jacare, the leader, weakened in the water and called for help, then vanished. According to newspaper reports (but not the studio reports), the water was infested with sharks, and one shark was locked in battle with an octopus. Newspapers, including *The New York Times* and the Rio press, said that a shark took Jacare. The raft turned over again, and the remaining fishermen helped beach the raft. Some days later a shark was washed up on the coast; the fishermen said that human bones and teeth in its stomach might be Jacare's.

RKO's Phil Reisman was in Rio running interference for the studio and doing his best to protect Welles. The shock of Jacare's death and the demands from Hollywood to close the picture down pushed Welles to the wall. He made a deal in which $10,000 was desposited by RKO in a Rio bank in Richard Wilson's name to cover more production costs, the sum not to be touched by Welles; the unit would be given a silent Mitchell camera, forty thousand feet of black and white film, and a new cameraman, George Fanto.

On June 8, under extreme pressure, the Carnival sequence was finished. Most of the unit left for Hollywood. There was some tension in Rio over the death of Jacare and the filming of voodoo practices. On June 16 Welles was back in Fortaleza to film the sequences of the raft fishermen's preparations for the journey south. Another fisherman replaced Jacare. Welles's team, pared now to Fanto, Wilson and his wife, Elizabeth, and Shifra Haran, recreated the life of the fishing community, beginning with the men leaving the port at dawn in search of food. In the mood of Flaherty, Welles evoked the warmth of communal living, the building of native huts, the making of lace, the cooking of fish in handmade ovens, the construction of a raft by lashing together five tree trunks. The funeral of a drowned fisherman allowed striking silhouetted shots of the mourners against the sky. Although the equipment was late in coming from Rio, the team performed magnificently. Meanwhile, the recording for the samba numbers was going on in Rio under Meltzer, and Welles cabled a lengthy memorandum from Fortaleza crammed with remarkable details about Carnival history. He said he was enjoying Fortaleza with one tripod camera, another camera and a half, two broken-down reflectors, and a crew of two. "The work is hard and healthy, and I feel excited and hopeful about it all."

Welles was impressed with Fortaleza and the natural beauty of the people. But again he was dogged by ill luck: George Fanto's locally enlisted assistant was injured while filming on rocks in a storm. Moreover, the Office of the Coordinator of Inter-American Affairs emphatically was tired of the entire project. The executives told Lynn Shores in Rio that they did not want to pay for Welles's transportation back to Rio, or to Chile and Bolivia, and "the sooner he got out of there, the happier they would be." The newspapers told of Welles's having thrown furniture into the street from his hotel. Rain was rusting his equipment. The U.S. embassy was increasingly critical of Welles. Yet the unit pressed on to Recife and Bahia to film the raft putting into port for supplies on its way to Rio.

All this material remained undeveloped when it was shipped to Hollywood. By the end of July 1942 Welles's work was allegedly done; the Carnival footage had been completed, and so had most of the raft fishermen scenes. The original budget of over half a million dollars, had long since been exhausted and very little of it showed on the screen.

The studio dislodged Schaefer immediately, and Floyd Odlum decided to cancel the whole effort. Like Disney's *Saludos Amigos,* the venture was a setback to the North and South American relations it had purported to cement. Indeed, the death of Jacare—a national hero—allegedly due to a motion picture company, the anger of the voodoo priests, and some anti-American sentiment combined to leave a bad taste in the mouths of many Brazilians. Welles did not help matters by posing as a doctor and attending a medical conference at the headwaters of the Amazon; this gag, though no doubt innocent enough, added to impressions of his irresponsibility.

On August 6 Welles arrived in La Paz, Bolivia, on his way back to America from Brazil via Peru. He was met by the executive secretary of the CIAA Committee, who had other tasks to perform at the airport but still found time to greet Welles. Allan Dawson, first secretary of the U.S. embassy in La Paz, reported later to Secretary of State Cordell Hull in Washington:

[Mr. Welles] was rude and expressed dissatisfaction that he had not been met by a ranking person from the Embassy proper. Not knowing of this incident, an officer of the Embassy asked an American newspaper correspondent who had an interview with Mr. Welles to tell him that the Embassy would be glad to be of any possible assistance to Mr. Welles if he would get in touch with it. The message was delivered and the correspondent reported that Mr. Welles showed marked indignation and said textually, "Goddammit, what do they mean by not having anyone up to meet me?"

This behavior certainly earned Welles no affection in Bolivia, and most people were glad to see him go. According to State Department files, he was also rude and high-handed with officials in Lima, Peru.

Returned to Hollywood, Welles found that his world had collapsed around him. *The Magnificent Ambersons,* screened for the trade in Los Angeles on June 30, 1942, had had its world premiere on July 1 at the Pantages on Hollywood Boulevard and the RKO Theater on Hill Street in downtown Los Angeles—on a double bill with *Mexican Spitfire Sees a Ghost,* starring Lupe Velez. There was no invited audience; the picture opened without ceremony. However, RKO did place expensive four-page advertisements in both *Variety* and *The Hollywood Reporter* to announce the opening, and the ads had original designs by Norman Rockwell. The choice of Rockwell, the most famous optimistic perpetuator of American domestic mythology, was an unhappy attempt to give the film a degree of respectability and an image of sunny good cheer. A motion picture that dwelled on the dissolution of the pre-automobile age, the deaths of many characters, and the frustration of a lonely spinster was dressed up to look like sheer Rockwellian nostalgia. The powerful Bosley Crowther's review in *The New York Times*, along with *Variety's* review, set the seal of failure on the film, and it lost $624,000, a colossal sum for those days.

Bosley Crowther wrote with his usual clumsiness on July 1:

> Without stars and with much gloom, Welles has a picture that's distinctly not attuned to the times and probably will be just as dismal at the B.O. as the story is on the screen. . . . On top of the slow and constant jerking on the audience's feeling for hatred, the focal point of that emotion is so inconsequential as to be ludicrous. With a world inflamed, nations shattered, populations in rags, with massacres and bombings, Welles devotes 9,000 feet of film to a spoiled brat who grows up as a spoiled, spiteful young man. It's something of a *Little Foxes*, but without the same dynamic power of story, acting and social preachment. . . . The woe [is] piled up. . . . The picture [is] virtually entirely in dark and shade. It's somber and unattractive. . . .[Welles] actually has very little to be proud of, nor has Booth Tarkington, who wrote the best-selling novel on which this film is based.

Crowther's review doomed the film as much as the automobile age had doomed the Ambersons. It was a review that plunged a dagger into the heart of Welles the artist.

11

Back in New York in the fall of 1942, Welles was at his lowest ebb. At twenty-seven he had already sunk to the depths.° *Ambersons*, cut to ribbons and partly reshot, had not even been seen by him in its final version, and he had no say regarding its release or distribution. *Journey into Fear*, a failure from every point of view, was still being patched up and reshot in October, when Welles was in New York for talks with George Schaefer's replacement, N. Peter Rathvon. For years Schaefer remained bitter and angry because Welles never contacted him after that courageous man, who was dedicated to Welles's welfare, was forced to resign in part because of that very commitment. Vernon Harbin, a studio executive, confirms Welles's ruthlessness in abandoning Schaefer. In fairness to him, he may have been so impatient over the waste of time and effort on *It's All True* that he had reached the point of no return with *Ambersons*.

Incredibly, a memorandum of October 20, 1942, from Welles to Nelson Rockefeller indicates that 20th Century–Fox was willing to take over *It's All True*, but Welles felt he must turn down the offer because it could affect his independence. He suggested to Rockefeller that he wanted complete freedom in the future, and the Fox offer would mortgage that future. He met with Rathvon and argued that the fourth story of *It's All True, The Story of Jazz*, could be dropped and the Mexican part, *My Friend Bonito*, completed; the whole could then be released with *Saludos Amigos!* Rathvon rejected the idea.

Welles was busy once again with radio, addressing broadcasts to South America and doing the Lockheed Aviation show *Ceiling Unlimited* for the war effort. In November he met with Rockefeller, who

---

° One consolation was that the hated Mary Wells Gottfredsen had died in July, at the age of eighty-eight, while Welles was in Peru on his way home. She left only her house: all her money had gone; she willed books to Orson and his brother, who now worked as a night janitor in New York, oddly enough at the Negro Theater Project headquarters.

urged him to make any deal possible on *It's All True* because "the future of everybody concerned was mortgaged by it."

Determined to obtain the film himself, Welles asked Rockefeller if he might buy a percentage of it; he wanted to use it as collateral for a loan from RKO. This matter was in abeyance when, having little or no money, Welles agreed to undertake the leading role of Edward Rochester in *Jane Eyre* for Darryl F. Zanuck at 20th Century–Fox. By then he had foolishly told Zanuck that he could not accept the deal on *It's All True*.

He moved into Fox at the beginning of January 1943, insisting on having an office as well as a dressing room so that he could broadcast for the *Hello, Americans* series and script a documentary while he was making *Jane Eyre*. He stumped through the part of Rochester with a false nose and ample use of his booming voice, giving little characterization to the role. But he succeeded in certain sequences, particularly that in which he is confronted on his wedding day with the presence of his demented first wife, whom he is forced to reveal to his bride. In sequences in which Rochester is haunted by his agonizing past he achieved an unexpected edge of suffering in his playing.

The film's chief interest lies not in Welles's performance, physically powerful though it was, nor in the resolute but pallid performance of a much too pretty Joan Fontaine as Jane Eyre, but in the stylistic elements that evoke the very atmosphere of *Kane* and *Ambersons*. Although the director, Robert Stevenson, a charming and genteel Englishman who later made *Mary Poppins*, insists that Welles had nothing whatsoever to do with the direction, the physical evidence is quite to the contrary. The whole first half of the film is Wellesian to a degree, and it ideally captures the rich Gothic flavor of Charlotte Brontë's novel. The opening, with a terrified Jane as a child, her vicious aunt played by Agnes Moorehead, and her aunt's fat, Orsonian son, has a handsome, brooding look and a narrative power that, backed by Bernard Herrmann's characteristic score, matched those of *Ambersons*. Later, in the scenes of the cruel and repressive Victorian school, when Jane (Peggy Ann Garner) and her friend Helen (Elizabeth Taylor) walk in punishment with flatirons in the rain, the direction intensifies under Welles's inspired influence. Henry Daniell as the diabolical headmaster Brocklehurst is a totally Wellesian creation, albeit the dialogue by Aldous Huxley is drawn verbatim from the novel. In its second half the movie becomes more conventional, more or less an imitation of William Wyler's *Wuthering Heights* in mode.

Robert Craft and Vera Stravinsky confirm that Igor Stravinsky was engaged to compose a score for *Jane Eyre*—and Welles had something to do with this. Clearly he had not forgotten seeing the composer during the Stravinsky tour of 1925, when Stravinsky brilliantly conducted the Chicago Symphony. The composer did some work on the music but could not come to terms with Zanuck, and the unused themes later emerged in his *Ode*.

On February 26, as production of *Jane Eyre* continued, Welles wrote a friend in Rio, Fernando Pinto, that his quarrel with RKO had assumed "virtually Homeric proportions." At last they had let him see *It's All True*, and he used his earnings from *Jane Eyre* to develop the footage in the laboratory. He hoped that after it was recut another studio would buy it (a direct contradiction of his refusal of 20th Century–Fox's offer); if not, he would release it himself. He added, "I have a degree of faith in [the picture] which amounts to fanaticism, and you can believe that if *It's All True* goes down into limbo, I'll go with it." He wrote later that he was "thrilled by the Carnival footage and the raft fishermen material." Apparently Welles succeeded in securing a share in the picture, and later this enabled him to obtain a loan from RKO. Suddenly his ego asserted itself, and he decided he wanted to be listed as associate producer in view of his major creative influence on *Jane Eyre*, but Zanuck would not hear of it.

In 1942 Welles wrote an introduction to the Mercury Printing Company's own published account of the famous Sleepy Lagoon case, in which seventeen Mexican-American boys were accused of assault and conspiracy to commit murder, and guilty verdicts were handed down for twelve of them. The affair brought out much of the latent racism in America, and the Los Angeles newspapers whipped up public feeling by talking of crime waves among Mexican-Americans. Welles vigorously opposed this hysteria.

His private life limped along during this period. He was living now at 7975 Woodrow Wilson Drive in the Hollywood Hills, a modest address far removed from the lavishness of Beverly Hills. He had a short-lived affair with Lena Horne, which because of the miscegenation issue was kept out of the papers. Horne was tough, bitter, brilliantly talented, but rebellious and unhappy in a Hollywood that largely misused her. She and Welles suffered from the fact that she was married, to the humble and subdued Lennie Hayton. Welles had liked her in her one good film, *Cabin in the Sky*, in which she and the great Ethel Waters appeared to striking effect. Lena had spent much of her childhood on the road and had left school at sixteen. Yet her mind was first class and her passionate nature well-nigh irresistible. It was unfortunate that Welles did not buy *The Story of Jazz*, rework it with Lena Horne as the star, and direct it, using Ellington and Armstrong.

Instead he spent his time wrangling with Zanuck, insisting that he have top billing over Joan Fontaine in *Jane Eyre*, and working on a script of *The Little Prince*, the fantasy by Antoine de Saint-Exupéry (which was filmed thirty years later by Stanley Donen). He turned down the leading role of the priest in Zanuck's *The Keys of the Kingdom*, a version by Lamar Trotti of the best-selling novel by A. J. Cronin, to be directed by John M. Stahl. Had he appeared in the movie and influenced its direction, it might have been memorable; with Gregory Peck as the star, for all its fine craftsmanship it emerged as a humdrum epic relieved only by a few vividly realized sequences in China.

Welles appeared as a magician in the film *Follow the Boys*, and the following month he produced his one-man circus and magic show, in which he plucked dollar bills out of oranges, read minds, extracted rabbits from hats, and sawed film stars in half. His assistants were JoJo the Great (Joseph Cotten) and Calliope Aggie (Agnes Moorehead). He went through dozens of costume changes each night, hugely enjoying the experience and reliving, like an oversized child, the experiences of the tent shows he had staged at the age of eight in Grand Detour.

He also appeared with Claudette Colbert in the tedious movie *Tomorrow Is Forever*, in which he played without enthusiasm in order to earn money.* He was being pursued by Virginia Lederer once again for failing to maintain his life insurance, of which his daughter was beneficiary, and Christopher's own insurance.

Sometime that summer he met Rita Hayworth, whose exquisite figure, perfectly chiseled features, dancing ability, and melodious speaking voice had propelled her to international fame by 1943. In a city filled with beautiful women, she was among the most beautiful, an authentic goddess possessed of an especially sweet, shy, gentle nature and an intelligence that was often ignored because she was so attractive and lacked self-confidence. On the screen she exuded erotic appeal and a bold, sexy, extroverted persona; in private she was simple, uncultivated, so soft-spoken as to be almost inaudible, sensitive, and gifted with a self-deprecating sense of humor. Certainly she represented no threat to a colossal ego such as Welles's. In every way, he felt, she was perfect for him; not only was she devastatingly pretty, she was not at all challenging or brassy—as so many Hollywood women were in their efforts to compete with men.

To Welles's credit, he saw beyond Rita Hayworth's beauty to her

---

* It was a great success; following the success of *Jane Eyre*, it made Welles bankable as an actor.

talent as an actress. Born (her birth certificate shows) in Brooklyn on October 17, 1916, she had begun dancing at the age of twelve with her father and mother, Eduardo and Volga Cansino. In her first movie, *Dante's Inferno*, she appeared to striking effect in a tango sequence aboard a ship at sea just before it caught fire, a deliberate mirroring of the SS *Morro Castle* disaster in 1934. Under the direction of Howard Hawks she was excellent as a promiscuous wife in *Only Angels Have Wings*, and she had been fine in a similar role in *Tales of Manhattan*. As the temptress Doña Sol in *Blood and Sand*, she memorably seduced the bourgeois bullfighter Tyrone Power. She exuded vitality, charm, and a ruthlessly self-indulgent sensuality that no one in her era quite matched.

Welles found himself in bed with the object of every red-blooded GI's dream. Somehow it was appropriate that he, the quintessential dreamer, should find in his own life the image of a dream.

But Rita was involved with Victor Mature, the Kentucky-born son of a Swiss immigrant scissors grinder, who had emerged from the Pasadena Playhouse three years earlier to achieve instant success in such films as *The Shanghai Gesture* and *My Gal Sal*. He had met Rita during the shooting of *Blood and Sand*, when he was under contract to 20th Century–Fox. There was much criticism of their affair, chiefly because Mature, a man of shrewd wit and intelligence, disliked columnists and made no attempt to flirt with them. When he enlisted in the coast guard and was sent to Connecticut, Rita's boss at Columbia, Harry Cohn, did his utmost to end the relationship. Nevertheless they attended the premiere of *Tales of Manhattan* together.

It was while Rita was separated from Mature by three thousand miles that she met Orson at a party given by Joseph Cotten. Welles asked her out to dinner the next night, and with a laugh and throwing back her hair, she accepted. Cohn was furious. He hated Welles and everything he stood for, and he forbade him to visit Rita at Columbia. But as their relationship began, Rita was fascinated and so was Welles. They fell in love.

Rita was determined to live up to the extraordinary personage to whom she was committing herself. She began studies of the arts and philosophy, and she joined the magic show: Welles sawed her in half night after night. One night she confided to Joseph Cotten's wife, "People are staring at me. They think I'm dumb." "They're staring at you all right, darling," Mrs. Cotten said, "but it's not because you're dumb."

Yet not even Rita Hayworth could totally ease the pain of the ruination of *Ambersons* and the abandonment of *It's All True*. Welles was in poor health, out of work except for radio, bored and restless, believing that his career was finished at twenty-eight. Much as Rita's work excited him, it was humiliating that the columnists, led by the ferocious Louella Parsons, treated him simply as the escort of a star. When Rita made *Cover Girl* in May 1943, he was fascinated; the movie, directed by Charles Vidor, was inventive with its brilliant use of mirrors and was filled with energy, drive, and rhythm. It was during the shooting that Welles began his engagement to Rita. Despite Louella Parsons's bitter attacks (she publicly advised Rita not to go ahead), Harry Cohn at last yielded and, delighted by Rita's latest box-office results, agreed to her marrying Welles.

The impetuousness of the affair was typical of Welles, and Rita, no less typically, was looking for emotional security following a disastrous marriage to Edward Judson, who had alleged criminal connections. His treatment of her had been so appalling that even the most scurrilous columnists forebore to discuss it in detail. Rita, shy, nervous, frozen at parties, her spirit withdrawn and secretive, was as far removed from Orson as anyone could be; yet his attraction to her beauty, and her attraction to his forcefulness and intellect, drove them into a relationship to which neither was properly attuned.

The marriage took place on September 7, 1943, before Judge Orlando H. Rhodes at Santa Monica Superior Court. Rita was in the middle of shooting *Cover Girl,* and the studio publicity department had cleverly timed the nuptials to coincide with the wedding scene in the picture. A nervous Welles behaved like a klutz at the ceremony: he forgot to take the ring out of the box and had to struggle to open it; he was trembling so much he could not get the ring on Rita's finger until at last the impatient judge said firmly, "Hold her finger with your other hand." He obeyed, and Rita broke into a flood of tears. They kissed several times, mostly for the cameras, until finally the best man, Joseph Cotten, said, "Orson, you've got lipstick all over your face!" and everyone burst out laughing.

Welles wiped off the lipstick with a large pocket handkerchief and took Rita to the elevator. The thirty seconds they spent in it before reaching the street constituted the full length of their honeymoon. Rita had to drive at once to the Columbia Studios in Hollywood, where she shot the white wedding scene for Charles Vidor. That night she appeared at the magic show to be sawed in half.

For a time the couple lived in Welles's house on Woodrow Wilson Drive. Rita rose at dawn to go to the studio, and at night there was the magic show; it was not until *Cover Girl* finished shooting that the couple had time to get to know each other. There was no question that

Welles—who like all fabulous monsters was fascinated by innocence—was captivated by Rita's sweetness of character and purity of nature, the rarest of all qualities to be found in Hollywood, especially among motion picture stars. He was intrigued by her father and mother, who had been professional dancers; the Cansinos had strong and appealing personalities, and they got along well with Orson. Once the picture was done, Rita could sleep till noon; at night she and Orson gave intimate dinner parties for their friends. The Cottens were the most frequent visitors.

Orson found Rita's femininity amusing: her concern about her right eye, which she imagined drooped and looked lopsided; her worry about her glorious hair, which she brushed fanatically to try to control; her fussing over the cost of clothes for public appearances; her discomfort at being stared at in public; her hatred of interviews; and her intensity in training with the Mexican bullfighter Fernando López, who was teaching her the movements of bullfighting. Welles, who had a smattering of Spanish, enjoyed listening to Rita speak with her grandfather in their native language. Above all, he loved her quietude and serenity, the fact that she seldom displayed temperament (something her father had taught her). She was incapable of being high-handed or difficult, yet she could not easily fake the constant interest in Orson's every action that her egocentric husband demanded.

The best times were the evenings the couple went to out-of-the-way Mexican restaurants—and their trips to Mexico, which they both loved for the raffish atmosphere. Of course, watching Rita was always wonderful because, even when she read the funnies in bed with her morning coffee, giggling at the comic strip "Terry and the Pirates" (whose principal characters resembled her brothers in the army), she looked irresistible.

The house on Woodrow Wilson became a little cramped. When Rita was pregnant, the couple moved to 136 South Carmelina Drive in West Los Angeles, a house with a swimming pool that was more commensurate with Rita's star status. The house was bought in her name, and indeed most of the money they put into it was hers. To help bolster Welles's financial position, Rita loaned him $30,000 without interest. But it was impossible to save him from insolvency, for his debts were too heavy and his ignorance of investments fatal even with Arnold Weissberger's guidance. Hollywood gossips insisted the marriage could not last, and the chorus was led by Louella Parsons, who attacked Welles at every opportunity. Indeed, when Rita married Orson, Louella discontinued her coverage of Rita's activities and stopped seeing her, which pleased Rita. Yet her column continued to fire tiny barbs, among them the canard that Welles had first met Rita in a restaurant, walking up to her and announcing, "I am Orson Welles."

It is difficult today to grasp the extent of the power that such columnists had in the 1940s. So great was Louella's influence that, despite Hedda Hopper's return to Welles's team and her support of him, Louella kept most people in Hollywood from hiring Welles. Oddly enough, Louis B. Mayer of MGM was an exception. He offered Welles the chance to direct Sienkiewicz's epic *Quo Vadis*; Welles turned it down. He was unsuccessful in getting *The Little Prince* off the ground chiefly because the studio chiefs had not forgiven him for *Kane*—and because they were afraid of Louella. The commercial disaster of *Ambersons*, followed by the ruination of *It's All True*, reduced him to the level of being merely the Brain who married Rita Hayworth.

Rita kept on working. In early 1944 she planned to film *Pal Joey* with Gene Kelly, to be directed by Victor Saville, but Louis B. Mayer refused to loan Kelly out to Harry Cohn again, and the project collapsed. When Darryl Zanuck, at Orson's suggestion, offered Rita the starring role in *Laura*, Cohn in turn would not loan her out. Instead, Cohn cast her in *Tonight and Every Night*, a story about the dancing stars who performed throughout the bombing of London. She would come home to West Los Angeles filled with excitement from her meetings with Victor Saville and the choreographer Jack Cole, showing Welles the costume sketches by Jean Louis and captivating him with her enthusiasm.

Soon the work on the picture proved grueling. Cole was a martinet who drove the remarkable cast—Rita, Gwen Verdon, Carol Haney, Bambi Lynn—with a fanatical intensity. Rita had never worked this hard before. Cole controlled Rita more severely than Welles did. He looked at her figure and realized that despite her beautiful thin arms and legs, she had a belly that was largely due to excessive eating, a fault exacerbated since her marriage. For breakfast she regularly ate several eggs, bacon, fruit, toast, jam, and coffee; at night she had a large dinner of Mexican food. Jean Louis worked heroically to cover up the problem. Sometimes, he recalled to her biographer, John Kobal, she came to fittings with her feet bleeding from the grueling dance sessions. Welles was worried about her.

In the evenings an utterly exhausted Rita often simply fell into bed and went to sleep. When she had enough energy, she complained about Harry Cohn, who had her followed everywhere by a woman detective, spoke about her slightly behind her back, and had her dressing room bugged so he could hear every word she said. She hated his dourness, his lack of polish or grace, his calling her a "dumb broad" and attacking Orson as "a washed-up so-called genius."

To add to her weight problem, Rita began to look pregnant as the filming continued. She developed an odd aversion to the smell of paint but otherwise showed none of the temperament that stars tended to display when carrying a child. Her lack of vanity, her total profession-alism, continued to please everyone, including the rigorous Jack Cole, and she was devotedly faithful to Welles despite enormous pressures not to be. The picture was entertaining and well made (though com-pletely false in its portrait of England), and Welles was delighted with her performance.

Despite his fondness for her and his pleasure in knowing that there would soon be a child, Welles was restless at being out of work and embarrassed that he was now simply fodder for the fan magazines.

On May 18, 1944, the lawyer Carlos L. Israels, representing the holders of the original issue of non-interest-bearing Mercury notes, sought repayment of the $30,000 Welles had promised to pay from his RKO contract—a promise he had not kept. Israels advised Arnold Weissberger that the note holders had a valid claim because Welles had violated his fiduciary duty in wasting the corporate assets. Israels, acting on behalf of Myron S. Falk, Mildred Falk Loew, and George J. Hexter, warned Weissberger that there would be a lawsuit unless the partners were satisfied.

Welles tried to buy the notes for $2,500, but Falk and the others declined. At a meeting of Weissberger, Israels, Falk, and Hexter, Falk raised the isue of what Welles ought to do "from a moral standpoint." Arnold's surprising reply was that Welles was a "son of a bitch" and could be expected "to act accordingly." The matter was finally settled for a nominal sum.

In 1944 Welles found something to occupy him: the Roosevelt re-election campaign, to which he decided to commit himself. However, his plans for embarking on a nationwide promotional tour on behalf of the president were delayed by Virginia Lederer, whose husband Charles was now in India with the army air corps. She was furious at Welles's failure to provide for his daughter Christopher, and having failed to obtain a response to her complaints, she took him to court in May, charging him with abandoning his promises under their divorce agreement. She said that one of the/stipulated arrangements was that Welles would make a will leaving $100,000 to Christopher if Virginia remarried, but Welles had not done so. She maintained that Welles had not made Christopher sole beneficiary of the insurance policy since she had become Mrs. Lederer, though she had frequently and persistently asked him to do so. She stated also that Welles had paid only $133 a month for his daughter's support; the rise in the cost of living and the need for education and music lessons had rendered the allowance insufficient. She claimed that Welles was earning $10,000 a month and was well able to do what she wanted. She also asked for $10,000 in attorney's fees and $250 in court costs.

Welles delayed appearing in court several times, but on June 28, after a trip east to assist in Roosevelt's campaign, he appeared before Judge Stanley Mosk in Los Angeles. He stated his willingness to pay for his daughter's care and said that he was in difficult straits financially and had been ill for several months. His lawyer, Charles E. Millikan, told the court that the demand for $10,000 in attorney's fees was ridiculous. Welles's business manager, Jackson Leighter, testified that Welles had earned only $80,000 in the last financial year and was $65,000 in debt "through show venture losses." (What these losses were cannot be determined—unless they refer to retrospective payments on *Five Kings*.) Leighter said that Welles's net income was now $2,000 a month and that he could not afford to make higher payments. However, Judge Mosk ordered Welles to increase his payments, and the attorney Max Gilford was awarded $900 in legal fees.

On May 11 Welles had attended a Washington conference on governmental matters; on May 18 the secretary of the treasury, Henry Morgenthau, Jr., wrote that he was sure Welles would be "wonderful in the fifth War Loan Drive." That week Welles became a consulting expert in the office of the secretary of the war finance division. He was now a dollar-a-year man for the duration.

He worked on special radio shows for the Treasury, in part with the aid of the left-wing writer Donald Odgen Stewart. There were collisions; on May 18, following Welles's radical editing of one script, Stewart wrote him, "One doesn't saw a writer in two so conveniently—I think you owe me something more than a telegram." Welles was too busy to respond. On May 20 he opened the fifth War Loan Drive with an hour-long radio symposium of American eloquence on the subject of democracy from Thomas Paine to Thomas Wolfe. The program featured Charles Laughton, Lionel Barrymore, and John Huston (among others) speaking of "the deepest causes and highest purpose of the war." He summoned the support of Leopold Stokowski, Oscar Hammerstein II, and Bernard Herrmann and delivered a message from General Dwight D. Eisenhower. Welles even found time to respond to Stewart before plunging into an elaborate broadcast known as *The Texarkana Program* on June 3. In Texas he appeared with Walter Houston, Agnes Moorehead, Joseph Cotten, Danny Kaye, and Joe E. Brown to call upon public support for the war effort. In a Hollywood short-wave cut-in, Lionel Barrymore, Franchot Tone, Laird Cregar, Charles Laughton, Ray Collins, Paul Muni, and others spoke of the importance of democracy. Welles supervised the audio montage. On June 27 Secretary Morgenthau sent a letter of appreciation.

In the midst of this activity Welles began to plan the film *Don't Catch Me,* a thriller in the Hitchcock mode. He threw a lavish party to raise support for Roosevelt, but many invitees declined to come, among them Humphrey Bogart and his wife Mayo Methot and the Fred Astaires; apparently, outside his own circle Hollywood still considered him controversial.

Welles was also busy that year writing for the magazine *Free World,* a left-wing publication devoted to the cause of democracy, the winning of the war, and the consolidation of the free peoples. Louis Dolivet, a Frenchman of wealth and distinction and a key supporter of the Free French, who was on the board of the magazine in New York, was responsible for Orson's contributions. One of them, "The Habits of Disunity" (May 1944), began, "The great events in the world are Russia's victories. Our liberal press is full of everything else." Welles went on to discuss the Soviet role in the Mediterranean, saying that Moscow had been found improperly guilty of diplomatic intervention in the Anglo-American occupation government in southern Italy. Churchill, coming out squarely for Italian Royalism, had suffered less from liberal criticism. He added, "Our pride assumes that the Italians hope for more from us than they hope for from Russia. And we really shouldn't be sorry if Russia chooses now to compete cheerfully in power politics with us and on the terms of our own foreign policies." He continued, "Russian foreign policy is everywhere called enigmatic, everywhere decried as nationalistic—everywhere blamed for being self-interested and cynical."

He wrote that "our maneuverings in the name of expediency don't excuse—perhaps do explain—Russia's. . . . In Moscow, if they are more bitterly, they are not more professionally cynical than we are in Washington." He said, "The Soviet Union deserves criticism, but just now we can't afford to be critics. We're too busy, or we should be, helping the Soviet win this anti-fascist war." He spoke of the "insanely divided, helplessly sectarian" left and how the right was gaining advantage over it. He spoke of "the liberals" being "too long wedded to failure, and they are still perversely in love with it." He said, finally, more in sorrow than in anger, "Liberals must learn to be at least as intolerant of their own impotence as they are of its international results."

This odd and somewhat confused essay was typical of the work Welles contributed to *Free World*. At times he seems to say that where all is corrupt and misguided, the Russians should not be singled out as exceptions to the rule; at other times he suggests that a cynical expedient should be encouraged in which Russia is supported in order to win the war. Evenhandedly attacking both right and left, he seems to leave himself in a position of confident democratic nihilism, neither fish nor fowl in terms of his political position. This kind of expansive moral denunciation and exhortation leaves the reader with little but shreds in his hands.

In an editorial, "Race Hate Must Be Outlawed" (July 1944), he seemed to be on safer ground. He pointed out that the war was being fought against the very causes of racial hatred and that the fight was against the denial of man's equal dignity. He made no direct mention of the Holocaust, which had already been revealed by *The New Republic*, yet the implication was clearly there.

> Race hate isn't human nature; race hate is the abandonment of human nature . . . the Indian is on our conscience, the Negro is on our conscience, the Chinese and the Mexican American are on our conscience. The Jew is on the conscience of Europe, but our neglect gives us communion in that guilt, so that their dance [sic] is even here the lunatic spectre of anti-Semitism. This is [to be] deplored; it must be fought, and the fight must be won.

These were brave if ill-written words indeed at a time when many people in America were still avoiding the Jewish issue and few were prepared to consider their own guilt, a time of moral righteousness in which the conquest of Germany and Japan was seen as the act of a clean and guiltless America. If Welles's intention was to ruffle feathers in both the Democratic and the Republican parties, he achieved his purpose.

He was back in the pages of the magazine in August, in September, and intermittently thereafter, but he was handicapped by a somewhat confusing prose style in which he seemed to be tossing off ideas to a secretary. The ideas were morally unexceptionable but stylistically ineffectual. And they reached only a limited audience; like many liberals guided by the spirit of Henry Wallace, he failed to penetrate deep into the American psyche. He wrote of Roosevelt:

We have always protested Roosevelt's policies, both foreign and domestic, when we have found them in disagreement with our principles. We now recognize that the Roosevelt persuasiveness may be bulwark enough against Republican Toryism, but we affirm that more is called for today from the leader of the American democracy. We expected that more will be forthcoming. We do not hesitate to go on record that American progressives in this election have no choice but Roosevelt.

In October, Welles fell ill from a series of intestinal problems. He faced another court action from Virginia because he had failed to meet the court's award of support for Christopher. Yet his public moral position remained immaculate: He was planning to visit with the president in Washington on October 23, and he would speak at the Roosevelt campaign meeting. Hannah Dorner of the Independent Voters' Committee of the Arts and Sciences for Roosevelt made the arrangements for that meeting with presidential assistant David Niles.

On October 23, while an indisposed Welles was at the Waldorf-Astoria in New York discussing a play with Donald Ogden Stewart, President Roosevelt cabled him from the White House: "I deeply appreciate everything you have done and are doing. I have just learned that you are ill, and I hope much you will follow your doctor's orders and take care of yourself. The most important thing is for you to get well and be around for the last days of the campaign."

Welles replied two days later that "this illness was the blackest of misfortunes for me" because it had stolen away so many days from the campaign; he could not think that he had accomplished a great deal, but he well knew that this was the most important work he could ever engage in. "Your wonderfully thoughtful and generous message reached me at exactly the moment when the doctors and I had decided that I couldn't do anything but get worse. Your wire changed my mind. I promise to take your good advice, but I still hope to be back on the road by next week." Following Roosevelt's reelection in November, Welles received another communication from the president:

I may be a prejudiced spectator who had a special interest in the action, but I want to thank you for the splendid role you played in the recent campaign. I cannot recall any campaign in which actors and artists were so effective in the unrehearsed realities of the drama of the American future. It was a great show in which you played a great part.

In the December number of *Free World* Welles wrote of the glorious cause of freedom that the vote for Roosevelt supported. He spoke of the vote's being a rebuke to reactionaries and the triumph of liberalism, and he reminded the reader of his two months of travel during the campaign. "Your editor comes out of [this] campaign convinced that liberalism is no longer a small voice. It is loud and sure. In 1944 it can be heard above all other voices in our nation." He ended on a triumphal note: "We are sure that the next four years are going to be great years ... difficult, glorious, hazardous, triumphant years. We face those years with the best hopes Americans have ever had the right to hold. As world citizens, we march into the first bright days with the most perfect pride."

The mantle of prophecy proved to be ill fitting. The immediate postwar years resulted in the reconstitution of Nazis in Germany during the Truman administration, the restoration of the power of the right, the advent of blacklisting and the J. Parnell Thomas committees, the origins of the McCarthy era, the emasculation of the liberals and the destruction of the kind of theater for which Welles stood.

Welles's domestic life was enhanced on December 17 by the birth of his daughter Rebecca (named for a character from Sir Walter Scott). He continued to move in the arena of semi-amateur politics, and he again met Franklin Roosevelt on the presidential train in December. As 1945 dawned he continued his work for the president and on behalf of the *Free World* Congress, the fourth installment of which was to take place in March. He also prepared a special reading edition of the Bible.

1 2

Despite a huge income in 1944, Welles was desperate for money by December. He had paid for his campaign travels himself, and apparently he was still struggling with debts from his disasters. *It's All True*, consisting of thirty-seven boxes of negative Technicolor and black and white film and positive prints, lay in storage in Salt Lake City, and Welles, using this footage as collateral with Nelson Rockefeller's help, succeeded in obtaining a loan of $197,500 from RKO and a businessman named Jay M. Nercesian. On December 15 he delivered to RKO and Nercesian a promissory note for the full amount of the loan. He agreed to repayment in installments, $100,000 before September 1, 1945, and $97,500 with interest on or before September 1, 1946. To secure payment of the promissory note and all other sums, he delivered to RKO a chattel mortgage on personal property described as all the negative fillm photographed in the course of *It's All True* and all positive prints and literary, dramatic, and musical matter.

On May 22, 1946, RKO was to bring an action against Welles in the state of Utah, demanding foreclosure on the mortgage executed by him. Welles had failed to make repayment of any part of the loan. As a result, the studio took the thirty-seven boxes of film, and Jay M. Nercesian claimed some of the material. Thus Welles lost *It's All True*—which he could have cut and assembled at any time between late 1942 and 1946—to RKO for good. For years since then he has said that the studio improperly took the material from him and junked it.[*]

Just before Welles surrendered the footage once and for all, the cameraman Russell Metty offered to arrange the available footage for potential backers, who could then buy it and allow Welles a free hand to cut it; Welles was to explain the film to the audience in an introductory talk, recut it in its entirety, and provide a coherent narrative. The

---

[*] Much of it was sunk in the Pacific; the rest was given by Paramount, which had obtained it, to U.C.L.A. Film Archives in 1985.

screening was arranged, the backers were present, but Welles, who had forgotten all about it, did not turn up. It was a grave embarrassment to Metty and perhaps the second most serious mistake Welles ever made.

The six-year-old Christopher's Christmas present to him in 1944 was a sketchbook in crayon, "Work and Play," that showed her mother gardening, her "father" (Lederer) feeding chickens, her mother falling off a chair, and her sister's (presumably Rebecca's) cat refusing to jump over a stick. There were also a fairy story about an apple tree and many colored drawings and expresions of love. Welles sent her toys for Christmas and apparently visited her, but his chief attentions that month were lavished on Rita and Rebecca.

On January 8, 1945, Arnold Weissberger wrote Welles to summarize his financial problems, which were worse than ever despite the fact that his total income for 1944 was a staggering $208,553. Of that, $170,000 came from radio, $10,000 from the Treasury show for Morgenthau, $7,710 from royalties on books, and $20,000 from his appearance in *Tomorrow Is Forever.* Yet the debts of the Mercury and the year's delay in making *Kane* had left him with a crushing burden. Carlos Israels and Myron France, attorneys for the Mercury, were still struggling to pay off the outstanding amounts. So desperate was the situation that Weissberger forwent his fees for the year until Welles should have the funds with which to pay him.

Welles now began writing a column for the then liberal *New York Post,* in which he dealt with politics, added touches of phony autobiography, and discussed the end of the war. Welles's column reflected the influence of George Seldes, whose newsletter *In Fact* exposed neo-Nazism in America on every page. On February 8, 1945, Welles alerted the reader to the existence of Nazi-influenced German-language newspapers that praised Franco and Mussolini and defended Ireland for refusing to deny asylum to Nazi leaders. In another column he denounced the attempts being made in several quarters to stop the Nuremberg trials. He wrote of Nazi infiltration in Mexico, of sinister attempts to plot against the Russians, of the suppression of blacks and Jews, and of plans for postwar reconstruction that would restore Nazis to power in Germany. His liberalism was impressive enough to cause whispered accusations of communism in certain quarters, and of course this delighted him. Producing these columns, which were interlaced with maxims and recipes, at the rate of two or three a week while still suffering ill health, Welles was hard pressed indeed, and Rita felt more and more estranged from him.

During this period Welles received his first serious film offer in some time: the producer Sam Spiegel had bought from the writer Victor Trivas a story about a Nazi war criminal who escapes Germany at the end of World War II, slips through Argentina and Mexico, and finally hides in a small town in Connecticut, where nobody suspects who he is. He marries the daughter of a supreme court judge, disposes of a former colleague who threatens to reveal his identity, and fights a battle of wits with a war crimes commissioner sent to expose him. The work was a prophetic one, for many war criminals entered America and lived seemingly ordinary lives; the issue was not raised seriously until the 1970s.

When Spiegel approached Welles to offer him the part of the Nazi, Welles was tempted and finally accepted; any story that revealed the horror of Nazi racism would be agreeable to him, even though he would have to play the villain. Spiegel did not want Welles to direct the picture, and in fact he had expected John Huston, whom he engaged to work on the script with Anthony Veiller, to undertake that task. But Welles, eager to work again, asked Spiegel point-blank to let him direct, and Spiegel realized that if he refused, he would not get Welles to play the central role. He understood the risk involved and knew that he would be criticized by everyone in Hollywood for taking it, but he decided to go ahead.

In the meantime, Welles was busy writing his *Post* columns and coping with the drawn-out courtroom battles with Virginia. Radio work never ceased to occupy him. He adapted, narrated, directed, and acted in the CBS *This Is My Best* series from March 13 through April 24, at last using his much-loved "Don't Catch Me" and (for the second time) "Heart of Darkness," a vivid and striking substitute for the film he had longed to make. There was talk of his appearing on Broadway, acting and directing *King Lear,* but the extensive discussions with the producers Paul Faigay and Oliver Smith were to no effect. The Mercury Bible project failed to take off; his agent, Helen Strauss, reported that despite every effort by the William Morris office, Dial and Doubleday had declined it. The consensus, Helen wrote on February 27, was "that it contained nothing new and that its attempt to tie in with present history was nothing more than the average minister does every day of the year." Lippincott agreed, and William Morris gave up its efforts to sell the property.

On March 10 Theresa Helburn of the Theater Guild offered him the part of Leontes in *A Winter's Tale,* but he had to turn it down because his radio work was too pressing. He recorded speeches of American presidents for Decca, losing a battle with Decca's Jack Kapp to do the introduction in Latin. He also recorded *The Song of Songs* of Solomon for Decca (a collector's item today).

His columns, now syndicated, ran into trouble almost from the outset. Like the *Free World* editorials, they tended to be muddled and politically too far to the left to appeal to a mass audience, particularly in his native Middle West. On March 23 Robert M. Hall of the New York Post Syndicate wrote that a number of newspapers had canceled the column and readers had not demanded reinstatement; publisher interest was shrinking as a result, and the column was in danger.

Orson and Rita had moved yet again and were now living at 347 Fordyce Road in Brentwood. Rita was not in good health; shortly after Rebecca was born, Rita's mother died at the age of forty-five of peritonitis. Rita's father, who slept in the library of the Welles home, was distressed by Welles's habit of working late at night. By the time the war in Europe ended in May, Rita and Orson were living in separate rooms. She was continually feeling weak and crying a great deal; Orson was busier than ever.

On March 21 Orson reached a new agreement with his former wife over Christopher. He agreed to maintain a $71,000 insurance policy with the child as beneficiary, to pay $200 a month for her support until she became twenty-one, and to make provision in his will for Christopher's inheriting $100,000 from his estate, less the insurance payment, provided that his estate could offer that amount. Charles Lederer was still in India.

In mid-April an irritated Robert Hall of the New York Post Syndicate claimed that Welles had fallen behind with deliveries. But he flattered and coaxed him, expressing his admiration for *This Is My Best* on radio and for Welles's broadcast tribute following the death of President Roosevelt. Later that month there were rumblings of dissatisfaction from the sponsor of *This Is My Best*, and indeed the network was fretful over the choices Welles was making for the show. At the end of the month Welles was in San Francisco to attend an economic summit meeting on postwar affairs and problems on behalf of *The New York Post*.

Rita was at work in May on *Down to Earth* (a musical sequel to the fantasy movie *Here Comes Mr. Jordan*), in which she played the muse Terpsichore, who descends to live among mortals. The film, directed by Alexander Hall, occupied her for most of the summer while Welles was busy coping with the constant dissatisfaction of Robert Hall at the Post Syndicate. On May 19 Hall wrote that most subscribers were dissatisfied with the column and there had been many cancellations; it was surely unfair that the Post Syndicate should be losing $200 a week in fees; and would Orson please reduce his fee accordingly? Hall complained that Welles had failed to supply new and strong material on politics and suggested that he write more about Hollywood, the theater, radio, and the arts—the fields for which the average reader knew him.

On May 30 a distracted Welles wrote Hall that he could not adjust to the fact that his column was a flop. He had been told that it took a long time for a new feature to catch on, and he thought six months was not a long time. He banked on Hall's willingness to stick by him; he had counted on his confidence, and now he was asked to take a cut—with the implication that he was lucky not to be fired outright. Welles reminded Hall that the column cost him much more than he was paid for it and that he had thrown over big opportunities to do it. Working on it took a major toll of him. He was not interested in writing about anything but politics. Petulantly he added, "I think I can do as well as [Dorothy] Thompson, and you don't. You think I can do as well as Elsa [Maxwell], and I don't. I know I can't because I don't want to."

It was an unfortunate letter. His subscription to Geneva Cranston's Washington news service that gave him most of his material cost considerably less than $200 a week, and he had no other offers at the time. Certainly he could not have written a gossip column about Hollywood; even if he had been inclined to do so, it would have meant breaking the rule that show business people, like members of the Mafia, will do anything except snitch on each other.

His column in danger, Welles was struck by an even more severe blow: he was fired without warning from *This Is My Best*. He was given no written notice, but Wayne Tiss of CBS and Arthur Pryor of BBD & O (the sponsor's agency) were suddenly unavailable to him, and his calls were not returned. In frustration, Welles took the matter up with one of the agency people in the corridors of CBS. The man was drunk, and there was an argument when Welles asked to meet David Titus, an agency representative, at the Brown Derby in Beverly Hills to discuss the matter. When Welles began to shout, the representative agreed to arrange the meeting.

Titus was unable to help. A rehearsal of "Don't Catch Me" was called for the next week's show, and after an hour of preparation word came that cast and crew were dismissed. Welles suggested replacing the drama with "The Taming of the Shrew" starring Rita Hayworth—a reckless idea since it was the allegedly highbrow nature of the program that was causing the difficulties. Three hours after he made that suggestion he was told he was fired. Among the charges against him were that he had been running over budget and that there had been problems with his statement that "the sponsor was only in the control room because I invited him." In a note to Arthur Pryor on May 30 he wrote, "I think you should know . . . what this affair has cost me in the radio business. The cost to my own feelings is the most painful part of it all."

A run-down and depressed Welles left for New York in June 1945. He was so exhausted that he barely put in any work on preparing a Museum of Modern Art exhibit of his career, and he talked only desultorily with potential backers about making a movie of *Native Son*. He kept up his subscriptions to Geneva Cranston's Washington newsletters with a kind of despairing knowledge that they would soon be useless to him. No money was coming in. On June 11 he told Cranston that his doctor had given him the choice between absolute quiet without working on his column and admission to a hospital. To his horror, he learned he had hepatitis, the disease that had killed his mother at the age of forty. Feeble as he was, he managed to attend, as a writer for the Post Syndicate, the International Monetary Conference at Bretton Woods, New Hampshire, where plans for postwar economic solidarity in Western Europe were being formulated.

In his sickness he became possessed by odd dreams. He envisioned reviving *My Friend Bonito* and cabled Norman Foster in Mexico City that he would try to get there to work on reviving the story. Typically, he did not follow through. Roger Hill wanted him to come to Woodstock to address the students, but his illness made the trip impossible. Evidently he did not tell Hill the details of his condition, for Hill cabled him on June 19, "Now an unrecognizable and spineless Welles says he can't [come]. Where is the bright lexicon of youth? I await a new wire from a spirit renascent." Welles had already flown back to California for a complete rest.

The long-suffering Robert Hall of the Post Syndicate agreed to continue paying Welles for at least a time. But he urged him to widen his range along the lines of a recent Welles column on the comedian Jack Benny and his sidekick Rochester. In a long letter on June 25, Ted Thackery, editor and general manager of the *Post*, asked Welles to bear in mind that he was not addressing "a small, specialized audience of intellectuals." If he felt there was a gulf between him and the common man that could not be bridged by common words, he should turn his talents to pure science, "which does not have a greater good for the greater number as its determining whatever that might mean." He urged Welles to have

patience, patience, and above all patience, with your fellow craftsmen whose purpose in life, if any, is to assist you. Even when you feel their counsel is wrong, consider it, even if only to discard it, since, right or wrong, their opinions are, by the very nature of things, certain to be representative and therefore a clue to the unfinished business always ahead of us.

At last there came relief: *The Stranger* was pulled together by Sam Spiegel, and Welles was assigned to direct. Welles wanted Agnes Moorehead to star as the war crimes commissioner delegated to trace the whereabouts of Kindler, the Nazi mass murderer who has hidden under an assumed name in a Connecticut town, but Spiegel insisted on Edward G. Robinson for the role. Robinson was in a sour mood, only reluctantly taking on the part, and convinced from his first meetings with Welles that the director's genius was in abeyance. Be that as it may, Welles was committed to designing and preparing the picture.

Welles hired Russell Metty, who had worked with him at RKO, to do the photography. Powerfully built, brusque, and rude to a degree, Metty had the appearance and manner of a longshoreman and the soul of a great pictorial artist; he was fast, skillful, and adroit. Welles also hired Perry Ferguson, the art director on *Kane,* to recreate a Connecticut village. Under Welles's supervision, Ferguson built a 124-foot clock tower that was at the center of much of the action. Ferguson's team discovered an appropriate clock that had been in the Los Angeles County Courthouse until 1922 and since then had lain in the cellar of the Los Angeles County Museum; Welles had it hoisted by cranes in two sections and reassembled in the tower.

The scenes in the tower gave him the greatest technical challenges. Metty recalled years later that the tower was boxed in on all four sides and the walls could not be removed to allow for the cameras. The tracks on the tower itself, set around a number of German clock figures, had to be greased to allow for the movement. In shooting a sequence in which Welles and Loretta Young had a tense meeting on a ladder, Young, one of Hollywood's toughest actresses, had to hang by a rail without a net over a steep drop. What the insurance people thought of this has—perhaps fortunately—not been recorded.

The picture was shot in thirty-five days without incident. Loretta Young, Norman Foster's sister-in-law, says that she may not have agreed with Welles's politics, but she certainly admired his talent. The opening scenes of *The Stranger* are the best: the war crimes commissioner allowing a war criminal to escape so that the fugitive can lead him to a concentration camp colleague; the hounding of the fugitive through a deeply shadowed South American port; the photographing of the fugitive by a passport cameraman who sends him to the war criminal in Connecticut; and the early sequences in the Connecticut town, with a fat storekeeper chortling at a radio comedian while the war crimes commissioner asks probing questions that will led him to his quarry.

There are typical Welles touches throughout. The radio comedian is almost inaudible, but when the soundtrack is taped and played back slowly, one hears a very Wellesian line of humor: "The hotel room was so small, every time I closed the door, the knob got into bed with me. You know how cold brass doorknobs are on a winter night." When Inspector Wilson follows the fugitive Meinike into the gymnasium of the Harper School for Boys, Meinike stuns Wilson with a blow from a practice ring. On the walls, virtually invisible to the naked eye unless the film is run slowly, are pennants reading HARPER VS. TODD. And after Meinike stuns his pursuer, he leaves by a door marked with the sign, "Use the apparatus at your own risk."

The picture declines in quality as it goes along, stumbling badly in a scene at a dinner party in the home of the Nazi war criminal's father-in-law, when Kindler discloses his feelings for the German people. It is impossible for us to believe that he would blow his cover after having gone to such extraordinary lengths to maintain it. Welles has taken a leaf out of Hitchcock's book; in *Shadow of a Doubt* there is an almost identical situation: the mass murderer Uncle Charlie, who is staying with his folks in a small California town, recklessly discloses his feelings of hatred for rich old women. Indeed, *The Stranger* in many ways resembles *Shadow of a Doubt*, both in theme and in style. Welles's performance as Kindler is powerful and effective and to some extent overcomes the many flaws in the writing; the direction has a conventional spareness, cleanness, and narrative drive quite unlike anything else in Welles's work. The paper chase sequence in the woods, in which the college students' cheerful athletic movements are contrasted with a grim confrontation among the trees, is well directed from first shot to last, proof positive of Welles's unfaded ability to extract the most from a dramatic episode.

Despite his preoccupation with *The Stranger* that fall, Welles managed to find the time to write his *Post* column, but at last the work on the picture canceled it in November. And by now almost all the syndicate buyers had deserted him. Rita completed *Down to Earth* and began dating the popular singer Tony Martin; this irritated Welles and made him determined to reunite with her. However, on December 5, when he returned from a trip to New York in a last effort to save his column, she announced a separation. After one night at home Welles left for a Sunday broadcast from Treasure Island in San Francisco Bay. He returned on December 17 to give an exclusive interview to the columnist Florabel Muir of *The Hollywood Citizen News* on the subject of his collapsing marriage. He told her he was gloomy and hard hit by Rita's withdrawal.

> I love Rita for what she is exactly. I don't want to change her one little bit. Now why is it that a girl will marry a guy, knowing what he is, having no illusions whatever, and then never be satisfied until she has made him over entirely on a new plan of her own? I could tell Rita I would change my ways, that I'd be home every night for dinner at a certain hour, and I might even succeed over a period of months in living up to a letter of my agreement, but she would think I was sacrificing myself and that I was acting a part. Rita looks and acts like a friendly, gentle, gay little thing, but in reality she has a will of iron. I hope she will not act too hastily in discussing our status with lawyers.

He added that he had urged Rita to go to the desert and think things over before making a move; he said he would certainly pay for Rebecca's upbringing in the event of a divorce, and he would expect to have custody for six months of the year.

While in Northern California on another trip, Welles telephoned Rita in Palm Springs and agreed to talk with her in Hollywood. They met at Chasen's, the scene of Orson's battle with Houseman six years earlier, and they had a fight in public that caused considerable excitement in the newspaper columns. After that Rita was adamant about making no further attempt at a reconciliation. In an atmosphere of extreme tension, they met at a lawyer's office to settle the details of the separation. Welles diverted himself with a trip to New York and a date with Natalie Thompson, former wife of the actor Robert Hutton, at El Morocco. Rita was busy completing her Wellesian *film noir, Gilda,* during those painful weeks of December. Louella Parsons, relentless as ever where Welles was concerned, gushed, "My heart goes out to the little Hayworth girl."

Welles had other troubles. He was being sued by the actor Franchot Tone for unpaid salary allegedly agreed to on December 26, 1941, for Tone's appearance in *Mexican Melodrama* with Dolores Del Rio. Defending the case cost Welles a great deal of money; Rita was sympathetic, and for a moment or two it seemed there might be a reconciliation. Then Welles's temperament drove them apart again. Welles flew to Mexico for a vacation shortly before Christmas.

In the first week of 1946 he traveled to New York to speak on behalf of Eleanor Roosevelt's American Committee for Yugoslav War

Relief while his attorney Loyd Wright was discussing with Rita and her attorneys the division-of-property arrangements in the legal separation. On January 16 Elizabeth Chamney, Rebecca's nurse, wrote Welles that Rebecca was developing rapidly and was very wise, keenly alert, and happy as always; she was now walking and had cut her molars. Chamney enclosed two photographs of the child standing by the Christmas tree.

Welles spoke at the Madison Square Garden rally on employment practices on February 28 and began talking about running for Congress; at the same time, at the Waldorf Towers, he was seeing Cole Porter, the brilliant composer whose talent was then at low ebb. Remembering his musicals at the Todd School,° Welles had taken it into his head to do a musical production of one of his favorite books as a child, *Around the World in Eighty Days*. Welles approached Porter, who admired him, to ask him to work on the music; Welles himself would write the script and appear in the production, to be called *Around the World*.

Simultaneously, Welles was busy discussing with the stocky, cigar-chewing producer Michael Todd a version of *Galileo*, the play by Bertolt Brecht, which he wanted Charles Laughton to star in. This production would recreate an early draft by Brecht, written in 1938 as a symbolic picture of oppression of the intellect under fascism; the parallel with *Galileo*'s treatment by the Inquisition was obvious. But Welles was edgy about Brecht's material and, excited by the idea of *Around the World*, set it aside temporarily.

While Welles continued his discussions with Porter, Frank Bilcher, an attorney for Rita Hayworth, wrote Loyd Wright that Rita was pressing for a settlement agreement. Bases for the settlement included the repayment by Welles of a $30,000 debt plus interest, the sum to be paid in full or, failing that, in installments. Rita should get a share of all rights and stories bought by Welles during the marriage; a property they had bought in Carmel should be divided; child support and alimony payments should be guaranteed. Welles had to agree to most of these provisions, but he balked at giving Rita half the earnings he might have from *Around the World*.

Welles was trying to raise money in April. Cole Porter was very expensive, and a star of any magnitude would cost a fortune. Mike Todd agreed to put up $40,000. Welles began sketching out plans for

---

° *It Won't Be Long Now* and *Finesse the Queen*.

the production, working with the set designer Robert Davison and the costume designer Alvin Colt with impassioned determination. He wanted to assemble an entire circus on the stage, a dazzlement of acrobats, tightrope walkers, and trapezists; he wanted to show a train speeding acroos the West, an Indian massacre, and a bridge collapsing; he wanted movies interlaced with physical action to recreate the mood of silent serials with storms at sea, bank robberies, and episodes in Chinese opium dens. He would show Jules Verne's hero, Phileas Fogg, being carried off by an eagle, and he would have a native princess shoot at the eagle from the theater aisle, causing it to lose some feathers. Idea piled on idea with reckless, unbridled extravagance. More money was raised from the producer William Goetz and from Alexander Korda, who held the European rights to the title of the story. By the time their money had been spent on the production, there was nothing left for a starring cast, so the decision was made to forgo big names. Welles hired little-known performers, including Alan Reed, Arthur Margetson, Mary Healy, Julie Warren, and Larry Lawrence. He was pleased with them, but he scarcely had time to see them in action.

Porter wrote the songs far too quickly and badly. "Should I Tell You I Love You," "If You Smile At Me," "Look What I Found," and "Pipe Dreaming" were quite devoid of the sparkle and charm associated with Porter's recent hit, "Panama Hattie." Welles passed the songs for production either because he was too awestruck by Porter's reputation to demand new numbers or because he was so completely occupied with raising money and taking on every aspect of the production that he let his normal standards slip.

Another effort was made to raise cash: he would film the thriller *If I Die Before I Wake* by Sherwood King, a Columbia property that William Castle was supposed to direct with Franchot Tone as the star. On April 26 Richard Wilson cabled Lolita Hebert at the Mercury offices in Hollywood to "try desperately to get *If I Die Before I Wake* to Harry Cohn [boss of Columbia Pictures] immediately. Perhaps Franchot Tone has book. Tell him we need it for picture deal." Welles's version of this was that in desperation he had called Cohn with the idea of filming a pulp novel he had seen in the ticket office of a theater, called *The Lady from Shanghai*. But *If I Die Before I Wake* had been published in 1938, and no paperback edition existed until 1962.

Sherwood King had written *If I Die Before I Wake* in Chicago in 1937, in a five-dollar room in a boardinghouse. Since he could not afford the rent, he made a deal with his landlady. Each week, Scheherazade-like, he would read a chapter of his book to the guests, and if the guests were unable to solve the mystery, he would go rent free. They did not solve it; he went rent free; and he stayed on.

Throughout mid-April there were rehearsals for *Around the World*, which opened in Boston on April 27, 1946. It had not been properly scripted, nor did it have more than a confused and episodic character; the vast sets, rich costumes, immense cast, and conglomeration of movie and stage scenes failed to add up to a coherent creation. The action moved from the interior of a bank in London to Hyde Park, to Phileas Fogg's flat, to the London Whist Club, to Charing Cross Station, the docks at Liverpool, the English Channel, Paris, the Spanish border, Barcelona, and the Mediterranean. It went from the Suez Canal to a jungle railroad in India, a section of the great Indian forest, the pagoda of Pilagi, a telegraph station in the kingdom of Bundelcund, a jungle camp in the Himalayas, a street of evil repute in Hong Kong, an opium hell in the same city, the China coast, the inland sea of Japan, Yokohama, and the Oka Saka Circus.

As if this were not enough, the action proceeded to a bordello in Lower California, a San Francisco depot, a Lizard Gulch stagecoach station, a train passing through the Rocky Mountains, a perilous pass at Medicine Bow, a water stop on the Republican River, the peak of Bald Mountain, the frozen plains of the West, New York harbor, a London jail, the interior of Fogg's cell, and back to London, with the audience carried into the interior of a lurching hansom cab.

One idea cost Welles Mike Todd's backing. (Later Welles claimed that Todd did not have the money in the first place.) Welles wanted a scene in the West in which Fogg struck oil; Todd objected that it would cost an unheard-of amount of money to do, and the oil would ruin the costumes and sets. When Welles laughed off this complaint, Todd backed out, leaving Welles with costumes in hock; it was only when the Korda money came through, along with the nearly $200,000 that Welles raised on the chattel mortgage of *It's All True*, that the show could be got on the road.

Why did Welles gamble every cent he had—and his future—on this extravaganza? Chiefly because he hoped not only to have a vast commercial success but to recreate his Todd School musicals and the world of the silent serials that had captivated him as a child. He wanted to unleash his childhood love of circuses, sideshows, and fun fairs. He had heard of the legendary production of *Around the World in Eight Days* at Niblo's Garden in New York some sixty-one years before and he wanted to emulate its use of photographic effects, sliding platforms, and public address systems (employed again by Erwin Piscator in his German concoction *Hoppla wir Leben!*). He also hoped to go beyond the famous *Hellzapoppin'* of the comedians Olsen and Johnson, which had been a smash hit in New York earlier in the forties.

Welles miscalculated completely; without good songs, without brilliant lines, all the fantastic changes of scene as Phileas Fogg made his eighty-day trek were insufficient to fascinate an audience. In Boston, Arthur Margetson fell ill and Welles had to take over the principal role at a moment's notice (he had been playing the lesser part of Inspector Fix, Fogg's pursuer from Scotland Yard, replacing Alan Reed, who had fallen out earlier for personal reasons).

The show moved on to New York and opened at the Adelphi Theater on June 11, 1946. The reviews were mixed; Wolcott Gibbs of *The New Yorker* called it "a damn good show! Like nothing you've ever seen before," and John Chapman of *The Daily News* said it was "wonderful, exciting and funny, grand, gorgeous and goofy." But Brooks Atkinson gave thumbs down to the project, making it brutally clear that, for all its spectacle, the show lacked anything approaching a decent book. Cole Porter (who was not present at the first night) had to lend $2,500—a drop in the ocean—to try to save the day, and Welles initiated a stunt in the hope of attracting publicity: piqued by a review that said the show had everything but the kitchen sink, he carried a sink onto the stage for his curtain speech on certain nights. On June 15 he went on ABC radio to speak of his feelings about the lame public response.

> The theater has never been so poor in my lifetime. But this is always true right after a war. Not that there aren't many deserved hits on Broadway right now. Nor is *Around the World* the antidote. On the contrary, *Around the World* is made up of very old stuff—things that have enchanted me from the time I saw them under canvas, in a one-ring circus in the theater or a carnival. It's like hanging around the toy displays at a department store around Christmas time. Or going out and buying out a whole toy store [a direct reference to his father filling his toy house with toys in grand detour].

He added that he would see the show many times, perhaps once a week, if someone else were putting it on. But "I have perverse tastes . . . I haven't liked a musical since the old Ziegfeld days, when they had really funny men and lush women . . . not that *Around the World* is a musical comedy—it's an extravaganza—musicals today are too smart . . . too chic. Perhaps that is why we of the Mercury were greeted in some critical quarters with salvos of abuse." He said that because there were critics who liked the offering, and with the help and generous support of audiences, perhaps the much-bedeviled show may be, "in spite of all the hexing and heckling it's had, an authentic hit."

Despite letters from the playwright John van Druten, who described the show as "enormous fun," and Joshua Logan, who spoke of an evening that was "fresh, witty, magical, exciting," the lack of a story combined with the rapid movement and the difficulty of clarifying the relationships of the characters drained the interest of audience after audience. "Wellesappoppin!"—as *Around the World* became known—collapsed quickly, carrying with it *It's All True,* virtually all of Welles's savings, large sums of Korda's money, and whatever Mike Todd may have left in it.

Smarting from his losses, Welles returned to radio to earn a living, and in this hour of need he showed himself to be difficult once again. He had still hoped to stage *Galileo,* but he had been so distracted by the imminent disaster of *Around the World* that he had failed to give sufficient attention to the Brecht play. Charles Laughton was prepared to go ahead with *Galileo,* but Welles procrastinated and then foolishly had Richard Wilson write Laughton a long letter on Mercury Productions stationery, expressing annoyance that Welles would not be able to do the production single-handedly, that Laughton, Brecht, and even Mike Todd would have a hand in it.

Laughton was furious. Elsa Lanchester recalled years later the intensity of his fury, which is borne out by the letter he sent Welles on July 25. Laughton wrote that he did not appreciate Welles's habit of using a third party to do the calling. He said that his contract with Todd was not the same as Welles's; that he was not going to put up with procrastination; that he was under the impression that all three were going to collaborate on the production; that "you are an extraordinary man of the theater, and therefore I flatly do not believe that you cannot function as a member of a team."

Welles replied on July 27 that the problems of doing *Galileo* would be major because of his *Around the World* commitment. He said he had had to put *Around the World* ahead to make room for *Galileo* in the following season. It had been difficult to persuade Cole Porter to rush the project through, then Todd had run out of money and the project had been abandoned. "In order to clear the boards for *Galileo* and no other reason we rushed into the thankless business of presenting and in the main financing ourselves this damned costly behemoth of a spectacle." He wrote that he was determined to do *Galileo* and would even give up the financial side to ensure a deal. He said he would be willing to start rehearsals in August, but he was concerned that Laughton would not be available. He said that *Around the World* had cost him more money than he would be able to make for some time, and he spoke of the crushing weight of his disappointment.

In the end Welles dropped out of *Galileo,* and it was produced by John Houseman at the Coronet Theater in Hollywood on July 30, 1947, backed financially by T. Edward Hambleton and directed by Joseph Losey, who, like Welles, had been associated with the Federal Theater Project. *Galileo* opened in New York on December 7, 1947, to a very bad review by Brooks Atkinson but to very enthusiastic audiences. By then Brecht had appeared before the House Un-American Activities Committee and had had to leave the country.

From Los Angeles on July 29, 1946, Cole Porter telegrammed Welles at the Adelphi Theater, where *Around the World* was grinding to a close: "All my sympathy goes out to you, for you have made more than human efforts to keep our poor little show running so long."

During this time people kept turning up who wanted to pay for *It's All True* to be finished and cut. Among them was B. K. Goodman, a Chicago investment specialist, who tried without success to call Welles. Of course Welles had already lost the property. In August, Michael Curtiz and Jack Warner of Warner Brothers offered Welles the lead in *The Unsuspected,* a melodrama of which the principal character was a radio personality not unlike Welles, a sonorous ham of the airwaves who presents a program of fictionalized and recreated murder cases; the announcer himself commits murder, using complicated recording devices to conceal his crime (the device was parodied the following year by Preston Sturges in the film *Unfaithfully Yours*). Welles was dissatisfied with the script and, though he was tempted by the money, held back despite his admiration for Curtiz and the knowledge that the part was written for him. At last he surrendered the role to Claude Rains.

In his radio programs Welles devoted himself to attacking racial prejudice, which was then resurgent again in the South. He focused on the case of Isaac Woodard, Jr., a veteran of World War II who had signed an affidavit with the Department of Justice that he was permanently blind as a result of a brutal beating by the police in the town of Aiken, South Carolina, on February 13, 1946. Woodard had joined the Blinded Veterans Association in New York City, whose director was a former bomber pilot, Lloyd Greenwood, who had been injured by flak during a raid on Vienna in May 1944.

On August 10 plans were made for a Woodard benefit performance by stars of stage, screen, and radio at Lewisohn Stadium under the aegis of Joe Louis, the heavyweight boxing champion, and the contralto Carol Brice. The benefit was expected to raise $22,000 to allow Woodard to enter the restaurant business. Two hundred army veterans would serve as ushers for the occasion. In a passionately delivered broadcast on August 14, Welles supported the benefit and branded the wickedness of the blinding. The same day's *New York Times* announced that the Aiken newspaper, *The Standard and Review,* had received a telegram from the Division of Public Information in Washington exonerating the city from blame in Woodard's blinding. It said that, "on the basis of information received to date, the location of the assault on Woodard is not Aiken, South Carolina." It was signed by Leo M. Cadison, deputy director of the division.

As a result of the broadcast the mayor of Aiken demanded a retraction and a public apology. Welles responded angrily on the air the next day: "The burden of proof lies with you, Mister Mayor. You should have addressed your demand for a retraction to Sergeant Woodard. But it would have to be sent in Braille, Mister Mayor, for Isaac Woodard has no eyes."

On August 18 *The New York Times* revealed that Woodard had been arrested and beaten in Batesburg. Batesburg Police Chief Leonard T. Shul told an Associated Press reporter that he was called to a bus one night in February to arrest Woodard because he was drunk and disorderly. He said that when Woodard tried to take away his blackjack, he grabbed it back and cracked it across his head. He denied point-blank that Woodard had been handed over to the police at Aiken or that his eyes had been gouged out by clubs. The FBI confirmed Shul's statement.

ABC was furious with Welles because the network was threatened with a slander suit by the Aiken mayor and police and he still refused to retract. On August 18 Welles attended the delayed benefit before 20,000 people at Lewisohn Stadium. Mayor William O'Dwyer, in a speech read for him in his absence, said he felt "horror" at the act of race hatred and confirmed that he would do his utmost to prevent the occurrence of such events in New York City. He carefully did not name the town in which the attack on Woodard had taken place. In a memorandum to Welles on August 20, the broadcast division of ABC and its president, Adrian Samish, jointly expressed concern that Welles did not submit scripts before broadcast time; if he continued to act in this manner, he would be cut off the air.

By this time Welles had become interested in an actress named Barbara Laage, and the columnists were murmuring about a romance. Over a weekend at Catalina Island, Welles had somehow managed to throw together a script for *The Lady from Shanghai*, based loosely on *If I Die Before I Wake*, which William Castle yielded up on the condition he be associate producer.

The story was like a madman's flytrap or a Rube Goldberg invention. At the center of it was the Irish sailor Michael O'Hara (Welles intended to play the role), whose political sympathies lay with the loyalists in the Spanish Civil War. Like Welles, O'Hara rejoices in being eccentric and poor, hates the rich, and sees through and condemns all corruption. Wandering in Central Park, he rescues a woman from attackers; she is Elsa Bannister, the wealthy wife of a successful trial lawyer, and she hires him for a yacht cruise from New York to San Francisco via the Panama Canal and Acapulco, during which she makes him the victim of a complicated murder plot.

O'Hara is the only sympathetic character in the story. Arthur Bannister, the physically and psychologically crippled and impotent husband, is a grotesque parody of the sort of trial lawyer of the Wells and Head families from which Welles's father was descended. The wife is a Circe, luring innocent men to their doom. Bannister's partner Grisby is a neurotic monster (Welles modeled him on Nelson Rockefeller) who is trying to arrange his escape to a Pacific island to avoid the results of an atomic catastrophe. Even the crew of the yacht are grotesques. Yet Welles drew up a blueprint for a marvelous chiaroscuro of violence and terror in which the story, meaningless in itself, became an expression of his liberal sympathies and a springboard for a series of virtuoso visual effects.

Welles freely adapted the novel, eliminating only the fact that Bannister had been injured in World War I and removing the homosexual undercurrent of the story, in which Bannister used muscular young men, whom he watched with envious and desirous fascination, to make love to his wife and to serve him in various capacities for money. Certainly the structure of the story is basically the same, a fact that has escaped the attention of most critics who have written about the film. Yet once again Welles utterly transformed a work through his manic vision.

On August 19, 1946, Joseph Breen, once again in charge of the Motion Picture Production Code, rejected Welles's script (then called *Black Irish*) because O'Hara encouraged the evil Elsa Bannister to commit suicide to escape justice. Welles rewrote the script so that she committed suicide on her own initiative. (In a later draft, and the final film, she was shot by her husband.)

On August 22 Breen rejected this rewritten script because Welles had failed to satisfy his requirements. Welles distracted himself by doing a version of *Moby Dick* on radio. He was also busy fielding Cole Porter, who was demanding the return of the money he had loaned Welles for *Around the World.*

In September a number of creditors appeared in Welles's apartment in New York seeking money. They included an old friend and factotum, Shorty Crivello; William Goetz; and Cole Porter. He began negotiating with Alexander Korda on versions of *Salome* by Oscar Wilde and *The Master of Ballantrae.* Rita, perhaps sensing Welles's desperation, suddenly broke off her affair with Tony Martin and said she would reconcile with Orson to make *The Lady from Shanghai.* She clearly felt that she needed at least to try to save her marriage for the sake of Rebecca, who was now fatherless. Welles, pinch-hitting as a speaker for Henry Wallace at the National Citizens' Political Action Committee rally in Providence, Rhode Island, announced that he was delighted with Rita's decision, and he flew back to Hollywood the following week to begin preparing the movie. Rita was cast as the murderess.

The decision was made to shoot the picture in Mexico and in San Francisco, with the final pickups to be done at the Columbia Studios in Hollywood. As always, Welles worked closely with his cameraman, art director, and designer. Consulting with the cinematographer Charles Lawton, Jr., he settled on low-key interior lighting and natural light sources, using comparatively few reflectors for exterior scenes. He would achieve transitions from indoor to outdoor sequences without stark contrasts; by using natural light for exteriors, it would be possible to model facial features as dramatically as those indoors. Wide-angle lenses would be used to distort the faces of the villains. In an aquarium scene the lights would come from sources simulating those in the tanks; the tanks themselves would be shot separately at the Los Angeles Zoo, enlarged, and matted in to achieve the powerful effect Welles wanted. He could then match aquatic creatures to the thoughts of O'Hara and Elsa as they kissed and whispered in the near darkness.

For the sequence in Central Park after O'Hara struggles with the muggers who attack Elsa, Welles prepared the longest dolly shot ever seen on the screen: Lawton, with his camera on a twenty-foot crane, had orders to keep Welles and Rita Hayworth continually in focus as they rode three quarters of a mile in an open horse-drawn carriage. With Stephen Goosson, an experienced studio craftsman, Welles designed a set more elaborate than the tower set in *The Stranger:* a San Francisco fun house with a hall of mirrors and a 125-foot zigzag slide that was forty feet wide and twenty feet deep and had a dragon's mouth thirty feet high; the slide began at the studio's ceiling and ended in an eighty-foot pit. The cameraman and his operator rode the 125-foot slide with the camera on a mat to give a subjective view of O'Hara's plunge into the papier-mâché abyss. The mirror maze, designed by Welles, was itself a marvel of art direction; it contained 2,912 square feet of glass—eighty plate glass mirrors, each seven feet by four feet, accompanied by twenty-four distorting mirrors. Lawton could shoot through them because they were one-way mirrors. Very little of the long sequence in the fun house appeared in the picture after the studio cut it.

In September, Welles read a film script by Ben Hecht° based on Edmond Rostand's *Cyrano de Bergerac*, which Korda wanted Welles to make. Tense and excitable as always during the preparation of *Shanghai*, Welles pushed his driver so hard as he swung around a corner in Hollywood that his car collided with Dick Powell's. Throughout the preparations he was continually cabling Korda in London, and after much discussion he said he would seriously consider doing *Salome* from the script by himself and (later) Fletcher Markle. On September 27 he agreed. Welles and Markle's script makes interesting reading: it began with Oscar Wilde seated in a café in France following his exile and ruin, and over an absinthe he discusses with admirers the theme of his play. Welles cabled Korda on September 28 that he would not allow Cecil Beaton, who would have been perfect, to do the costumes; Beaton wanted to use a careful art nouveau approach rather like that of Aubrey Beardsley, but Welles wanted a more realistic approach, and he recommended the remarkable Pavel Tchelitchew. He said he was not interested in doing *Mine Own Executioner* from the novel by Nigel Balchin. That day it was announced that José Ferrer would appear in a version of *Cyrano*, so that plan was dropped. Welles added that he wanted to do a movie version of the Bible.

On the same day Welles cabled Errol Flynn in Acapulco, seeking to charter Flynn's fabled yacht, the *Zaca*, for one month starting October 1 for $15,000 including port rental, tender rental, and crew salaries and finances. Flynn agreed to cover the insurance on both vessel and crew. The crew, of course, must be Flynn's own, and firmly guaranteed—a decision that Welles would regret. It is ironical that Welles, a liberal, would want to do business with Flynn, whose role in the Spanish Civil War, unbeknownst to Welles, was just the opposite of that taken by the Irish loyalist sailor whom Welles would portray in the film.

In the cables to and from London there was much talk of Eileen

---

° Rewritten later by Charles Lederer, with whom Welles was reconciled.

Herlie, a buxom, somewhat mature-looking actress who had appeared as Gertrude in Laurence Olivier's *Hamlet,* to play the part of Salome. Welles was aggravated by the suggestion. He believed she was much too stolid, phlegmatic, and middle-aged for the part, which called for a voluptuous temptress, someone like Barbara Laage—of course! While distracted with this problem of casting, and calling Herlie "Helier" in his cables (he deliberately misspelled the names of people of whom he did not approve), he was busy recording the narrative for the opening sequence of *Duel in the Sun,* a flamboyant David O. Selznick melodrama in which Welles's friend and colleague Joseph Cotten appeared with Gregory Peck and Jennifer Jones. Welles's voice, more richly resonant than ever, added a pleasantly minatory element to a sequence in which the camera dwells on blood-red rocks and harsh, crimson skies and the narrator tells of the doomed Pearl Chávez, the Mexican half-breed whose passions ruined all men who came in touch with her.

Welles refused screen credit for the narration, believing that the work he had done was insufficient to justify the credit—or so he said. Perhaps he sensed that the movie would qualify for a Platinum Turkey award and did not want to be associated with it.

Breen was distressed about *Salome.* He wrote on October 6, "It shows Herod desirous of Salome, his stepdaughter and niece; Salome kissing the severed head of Iokanaan (John the Baptist) is perverse and unacceptable." By now Welles was so firmly committed to Barbara Laage that he insisted Korda cast her as Salome and "Helier" as Herodias, wife of Herod, who ordered the execution of John the Baptist. But Korda was determined to have Herlie, and he insisted that Welles reconsider.

That week there was an outcome in the Isaac Woodard case. Despite the fact that Welles had gotten the city wrong, his broadcasts had helped the NAACP in its quest for the persons who had blinded the black Southerner. The result of the full-scale investigation prodded by the NAACP was that Leonard T. Shull, police chief of Batesburg, South Carolina, made a confession and was sentenced to one year in prison. Welles cabled Attorney General Tom Clark to urge a longer term for Shull, and while this effort failed, at least some justice had been done.

With Barbara Laage, Rita Hayworth, Charles Lawton, and a substantial crew, Welles flew to Acapulco on October 17 and checked into the Casablanca Hotel. In 1946 Acapulco was a virtually unspoiled tropical port that was only just opening up to tourism on a large scale. The magnificent harbor lined with rich plantings of trees, the beach fringed with palms, was one of the places on earth that lived up to the allure of the travel posters. The mountains, plunging steeply into the bay, and the contrast between the raffish squalor of the downtown section and the mansions of the very rich created a typically Latin American ambience of corrupt physical beauty. Acapulco was not Rio, but in an austere postwar era it overflowed with sensual appeal, and Welles and Laage were fascinated by the port.

There was trouble from the very beginning. Rashly, Welles began the picture during the hurricane season, and the weather was often dark and rainswept, as it had been in Rio. Rita, who, like Welles, suffered from sinus problems, was listless and headachy in the sticky heat. She fretted over the loss of her long hair, which Welles had shorn, and worried that as a bleached blond she would not look attractive on camera. He tried to cheer her up with a party at the Hotel de las Américas, with thirty bottles of champagne opened for the guests. Shorty Crivello and the celebrated restaurateur and impresario Teddy Stauffer ran the elaborate occasion, and the total cost was well over a thousand dollars. Virtually everyone who mattered in Acapulco, including Errol Flynn, was present.

As shooting began, the insects, the financial problems, and the many cables and memoranda from the studio irritated everybody. At night poisonous bugs swarmed around the arc lights and blotted them out in a crucial picnic scene. A storm blew up, keeping crew members on the shore. Nevertheless Welles continued, echoing here and there, and later in the Hollywood-shot fun house scene, the German classic *The Cabinet of Dr. Caligari*, which he had run at his house the night before he left Hollywood.* He had wild new ideas for the trial scene, which was to be shot later. He cabled the Museum of Modern Art in New York to rush him a photograph of the staff of the *Inquirer* newspaper in *Citizen Kane* so that he could cast the same actors as the jury in *Shanghai*—a crazy idea, since it would have meant an all-male jury. The museum replied that they had no such still. Evidently Welles did not feel comfortable enough to approach RKO for it; later the museum sent the still, but by then he had changed his mind.

Welles arranged an English tutor for Barbara Laage, who spoke only French, and fended off Cole Porter, who demanded that money be withheld from his salary to pay off the balance (then about $1,500) of the *Around the World* loan, which was being repaid at the rate of $250 a week. Welles owed other sums as well and was being billed by Loyd Wright for outstanding fees. He had to pay Fletcher Markle, who was

---

* Most of the Caligariesque footage was cut from the finished film.

in Acapulco working on the *Salome* script. Laage was on his payroll, and so was Shorty Crivello, who had loaned Welles $4,000 for *Around the World*—and that was all of his savings. And then there were Rita's maid, her hairdresser, her doctor, and her nurse.

Welles, who could not bring himself to exercise, was having steam-baths and massages in order to lose weight. Errol Flynn was constantly drunk, and there was a horrible episode in a bar when Flynn discovered that the bartender was Jewish. Calling him "a filthy kike," Flynn dragged the man over the bar by his collar and beat him to a bloody pulp. In spite of this incident, Welles remained friendly with him. But Richard Wilson had nothing but trouble with Flynn from morning to night. He fretted like a fishwife over the slightest spot or scratch on the *Zaca.* He joked, cajoled, needled, threatened, and blackmailed everybody, complaining about the deal made with him, claiming that something (as Richard Wilson put it in a memorandum) had been "put over him." Finally, in a spirit of cooperation, Wilson promised to advise all charges for damage to Flynn's insurance company. Later, when Flynn sent Welles an enormous bill filled with unnecessary charges, Welles found to his horror that Flynn had never insured the vessel for third-party use, even though he had included the cost of that insurance in the bill.

The choice of San Francisco in mid-December was as ill-advised as that of Acapulco during the hurricane season. San Francisco in winter, though intermittently sunny, was as often damp, chilly, and miserable. At the Fairmont Hotel, Rita suffered from constant colds. The company spent Christmas in the city. Rita had a sore throat, there was camera motor trouble, and then there was a Hollywood strike: pickets held up the scene in which O'Hara meets the lawyer Grisby in an underground garage. Dr. Bernstein, to whom Welles had not spoken for years, and of whom he was clearly tired, wrote a wheedling letter to try to reinstate himself in Welles's favor. He said that he saw Rebecca often and had taught her to say Pookles, his old nickname for Orson; he enclosed a letter in pencil from Christopher, thanking Orson for a blackboard and mentioning a trip to see Charles Lederer's aunt (and Hearst's mistress) Marion Davies at San Simeon, where the lady had given her a doll and some clothes. Christopher admitted she had been carsick over her mother's coat on the long, winding drive up into the mountains. In the P.S. she thanked Orson for games, a jump rope, and a muff.

At the beginning of 1947 Richard Wilson cabled Hugo Schaaf, Welles's business associate in New York, that Orson had absolutely no money. ("We must first get a picture of what he needs and then it must be borrowed or raised somehow.") Apparently what little Welles had

had gone for expenses in Mexico and San Francisco and to pay off his debts on *Around the World* and the Mercury.

He shot the aquarium scene and the fun house scene, yet he was so unwell that he had to have inoculations from Lillian Reiss of Dr. Bernstein's office in Beverly Hills; she would arrive at the studio and wait until he could leave the set. He was also having shots for a trip he was planning to England for *Salome* with Korda. At the same time, Rita was applying for transit documents to London, and this led to rumors that the couple had been reconciled.

Welles was aggravated in that last week of shooting *The Lady from Shanghai* by the news that Chaplin was beginning the comedy *Monsieur Verdoux*, which was apparently based on the idea of the Landru case that Welles had discussed with him and then sold to him in 1941. Ann Rosenthal at William Morris was unable to find the contract Welles had made with Chaplin, so he could not sue Chaplin for a share in the picture and residuals.

Then *Salome* was postponed for a year because of Korda's mercurial habits. In New York, papers crucial to aiding Welles's desperate financial plight (they related to loans he had been given) were lost on a train between White Plains and Grand Central Station, and despite harrowing efforts, Wilson was unable to trace them.

Other offers were in the wind. There was talk of Welles's doing a remake of Frank Vosper's melodrama *Love from a Stranger*, which had starred Basil Rathbone and Ann Harding, but this came to nothing. There was talk of doing *Cyrano de Bergerac* for Korda or *Moby Dick* for Warner Brothers; they too fell through. He considered doing *Evidence*, a story by Isaac Asimov, but this did not work out. He planned to take Christopher to England despite objections by Virginia and Charles Lederer, but he was overruled by the court when he applied for Christopher's passport. Virginia promised to take Christopher to Europe to visit him.

In February, Welles encountered his first major trouble with the studio. Harry Cohn and his assistant Jack Fier° were convinced *The Lady from Shanghai* would be unreleasable, and when at last Welles began working on it with the crusty editor Viola Lawrence, she was obliged to report that the footage was a jumbled mess. True, there were brilliant passages, but much of the material was disturbing to an experienced Hollywood cutter, and Lawrence insisted that Cohn see

---

° Welles put up a notice in the Columbia commissary reading, "We have nothing to fear except Fier himself." Fier replied with another notice, "All's well that ends Welles."

the footage. She and Cohn were almost hysterical because they felt
Rita had been rendered mousy. So narrow were their concerns that the
artistry of the movie as a whole meant nothing to them; they saw the
picture only as a disastrous treatment of the studio's biggest star. They
demanded close-ups of Rita and some of the other characters, and they
wanted an added sequence of Rita running down a colonnade that
would make sense of one episode. This was shot second unit at the 20th
Century–Fox ranch by arrangement with Darryl Zanuck.

Welles hated shooting the close-ups that were required in any
movie with a big star, and indeed these shots are the least impressive in
the film. The story itself had never made sense, and Cohn and his story
department and producer Virginia Van Upp should never have let
Welles's script go through as it stood. Viola Lawrence recalls that the
cutting continuity in script form had to be spread over Van Upp's office floor and reconstructed like a jigsaw puzzle. At one stage the intention was to frame the entire story within the trial scene, but not
even this made sense.

The fact was that *The Lady from Shanghai* was a totally surrealist
work, excitingly personal (yet another liberal onslaught on the corruption of riches, with Mike O'Hara as mouthpiece) and almost willfully
uncommercial. Few viewers could identify with a left-wing Irish rene-
gade like Michael O'Hara; women were used to identifying with Rita,
but how could they identify with a cold-blooded murderess? The supporting characters, all brilliantly played, were too exaggerated and baroque to appeal to the average American. Sequence after sequence of
the film was lost on the public.

Today the movie seems even more stimulating, daring, and dazzling than it did in 1947. The satirical style, the commentary on riches
and corruption, are as intensely Wellesian as ever, and the execution is
startlingly confident and assured. The picture is outstanding in the
Mexican sequences, in the picnic scene (where Bannister, Grisby, and
Elsa lie in hammocks in the heat and exchange smart remarks), in
O'Hara's speech about the sharks, with indirect references to the Ja-
Care episode in the trial scene, which is explosive and dynamic in both
its visual and its aural styles, in the sinisterly charming aquarium episode, and above all in the confrontation in the hall of mirrors. There
the images of the combatants refracted in panels of glass, the husband's
canes reflected again and again in a series of vertical panels, then his
face and Elsa's, the alternation of full-length figures with bizarre close-
ups, all combine in an episode as poetic and unreal as the aquarium
scene.

The music, composed by a studio contract man, Heinz Roemheld, was uneven, and Welles hated it. In a memorandum to Harry Cohn that ran to nine pages, Welles complained about the music, deliberately calling Roemheld "Heinzman." He said he hated the "Disneying" use of a theme tune throughout—the time-honored device of Hollywood composers, who signaled a character or a situation by means of recurring themes in a technique familiarly known as "Mickey Mousing."

Welles was annoyed that the echoing footsteps intended for atmospheric scenes (particularly in the garage sequence in San Francisco) had been abandoned for music. He grumbled that the music was terrible in the sailing montage sequence, when he had gone to such lengths to provide the actual sounds of wind and water. He was upset that the music drowned out crucial lines and that the radio commercial played on deck in one scene simply faded instead of jumping in startlingly to provide an aural shock. He was angry that in the picnic scene the hubbub of Mexican voices in the background had been abandoned, along with the Mexican music that had been recorded on the spot. He hated the dubbing and the confused narration in the fun house sequence, which had been chopped up from bits and pieces of the track. Most of all, he objected to the use of music in the shoot-out in the hall of mirrors; he believed it utterly distracted from the impact of the scene.

In May 1947, sick and despairing over what he though was the ruination of his movie, Welles was living at 451 Ocean Drive in Santa Monica, overlooking the sea, working on *Cyrano de Bergerac*. He decided to do a production of *Macbeth* at the Utah Centennial Festival in Salt Lake City (scene of the loss of *It's All True*), and he engaged a radio actress with whom he had worked, Jeanette Nolan, to play Lady Macbeth opposite him. He staged the production with his customary panache, and Herbert Yates, head of Republic Pictures (which specialized in trashy "B" movies), who had decided to act as a patron of the arts—perhaps because of his conscience—offered Welles the chance to make a movie version of the Salt Lake City production. But the conditions were strict: he would have to shoot the film in three weeks at a cost of no more than $800,000. It was the kind of challenge that Welles—or one side of him—liked. He talked to Tallulah Bankhead about playing Lady Macbeth on the screen but later reverted to having Jeanette Nolan repeat her stage performance.

The Utah Centennial Festival production was widely talked about. It had bagpipe players emerging from darkness, marching through the audience, and moving into the street; phosphorescent lights exploded in a blue blaze, and witches seemed to float above the audience. The tone and manner of the production were not far removed from that of the "voodoo" *Macbeth* of 1936.

In order to do the picture, Welles turned down an offer from Herman Shumlin, the Broadway director, to appear in New York with Gertrude Lawrence in a version of *The Web and the Rock* by Thomas Wolfe. He also missed the chance of doing another opera with Marc Blitzstein. The shooting of *Macbeth* involved extreme cost-cutting at every turn. The brooding, damp castle was expertly managed, achieved with great skill by Welles and the art director Fred Ritter, whose previous experience had largely been with third-rate westerns. The scene in which Banquo's ghost appears was achieved with the utmost economy: instead of using mirrors or distorting lenses, Welles had a piece of clear optical glass twelve inches square placed on a stand before the camera, then he smeared Vaseline around the edges of the glass and shot the actor Edgar Barrier through it.

Unfortunately, Welles did not use as much ingenuity on the sound-track. He insisted on employing a device in which a public address system delivered the words of the text (prerecorded by the players) and the actors had to synchronize their lip movements. Jeanette Nolan recalls that the effort to do this was appalling. Moreover, she says, the track had to be recorded three times, once in heavy Scots accents, once in British accents, and once in American; when the three had been blended together, the track was almost incomprehensible. Nolan remembers that the crew became increasingly irritable with Welles; the schedules were grueling, and work continued well into the night. Welles indulged his humor by casting the actor Brainerd Duffield in drag and two Goldwyn glamour girls as the witches. They perched on papier-mâché crags, holding forked sticks and emoting heavily. Welles's daughter Christopher appeared as Macduff's child.

Recently restored with loving care to Welles's original specifications by Robert Gitt of UCLA, *Macbeth* can at last be seen in its proper form. It is a handsomely made and quite skillfully edited film. The opening, with the witches fashioning from swirling clay the face and fate of the Scottish king, is especially powerful, accompanied by the brooding score of Jacques Ibert. The movie creates a world of its own, another expression of Welles's extraordinary talent—a world of rain, fog, and stones that seem to sweat with corruption; a world of violence, cruelty, and evil unrelieved by light or comfort. We explore a labyrinth that effectively mirrors Macbeth's own mind. The flaws in the picture are chiefly in the performances. These, Welles's included, seldom rise above the amateur; in his effort to make the film under budget and on schedule, he evidently lost control of the performers. He gave all his skill and imagination to such sequences as the advance of Birnam Wood: a black skyline, smoke, clouds, mist, and a forest that slowly changes into threatening spears. The finest element of the picture is its sense of doom, which, along with the recurring refrain of the corruption of power, is the most consistent feature of all Welles's work. Above all, *Macbeth*, with its succession of brutal murders and its sense of hopelessness, is a film about death and suffering as well as (again) the corruption of power. For all its many flaws, this meager production is among Welles's most fascinating and most personal creations.

On July 18, 1947, while Welles was preparing for his trip to London, which he would make even if *Salome* was not ready, Herbert Yates wrote to congratulate him on the job he had done. But before long voices were raised in protest at the studio. Those who hated and envied artists of any kind were in full cry against the production, and Welles's signing of Jacques Ibert was bitterly attacked. The decision was made to take the picture out of Welles's hands and recut it, clarifying the soundtrack in the process.

Fretful over this, Welles was only partially cheered by a handsome package of theater tickets from Korda for London shows including *Finian's Rainbow* and *The Medium*—tickets he never used. He was still struggling with the Franchot Tone suit. In making a deposition that month, Welles was asked whether there had been a discussion between him and Tone, and he said there had been. Asked who else was present, he snapped angrily at Tone's lawyer, "The busboy at Romanoff's!" (In fact the meeting had taken place at the Brown Derby.) Asked whether the meeting had taken place in the spring, summer, fall, or winter (Tone knew it had been in January 1942), Welles threw up his hands and said, "We live in California. It is hard to determine the seasons!" He denied any obligation whatsoever to Tone, and the case dragged on for over a year before it was settled out of court.

José Ferrer's *Cyrano* was postponed, and, with typical impetuousness, Welles and Korda decided to make that picture first, with a script co-written by Charles Lederer. In the meantime, one of Welles's favorite characters, the jolly White Russian émigré actor-director and friend of Darryl F. Zanuck, Gregory Ratoff, wrote him from Rome that he should come and make a version of the life of the eighteenth-century charlatan Cagliostro. The idea intrigued Welles; the script by Charles Bennett (who had written the excellent films *Blackmail* and *Ivy*) amusingly caught the flavor of Cagliostro's tempestuous career, and the fact that Cagliostro was a magician would give Welles a chance to demonstrate one of his favorite talents. Without telling Korda what he was up to, he had secret discussions with *Cagliostro*'s producer Edward Small during the first half of September. He also spent time with his friend Claude Terrail, the owner of the three-star Tour d'Argent in Paris, who was visiting him, and with another guest, Louis Dolivet.

On September 16 Jerome Hymans of Commonwealth Pictures Corporation in New York offered to buy *It's All True* from RKO if Welles could come in and finish it. Richard Wilson informed Hymans that seven reels were cut and one demonstration reel prepared by Joe Noriega was ready. But Welles had no control over the property, and RKO had lost interest in it. Welles was ill and under Dr. Bernstein's care all that fall, and his sickness delayed his trip to Europe.

In mid-October Welles received a letter from Melvin D. Hilgenfeld, president of the California College of Mortuary Sciences School of Education for Embalmers, who sent him a list of the requirements for admission to the college and for earning an embalmer's license after two years of apprenticeship. Apparently Welles decided not to pursue the matter.

13

In the fall of 1947 Welles was poised on the edge of what would be
a long sojourn in Europe, interrupted only by excursions to the United
States. His career as an artist-director was in a calamitous state, and so,
because of his spending, were his finances. He also saw the prospect of
decreasing freedom in Hollywood in the advent of the McCarthy era.

The first whisper of the ax came on October 13, when Melvyn
Douglas (his wife, Helen Gahagan Douglas, was a member of Congress
from California and a distinguished liberal) sent Welles a clipping from
The Denver Post in which the actor Frank Fay, starring in *Harvey*, was
said to have charged Welles with being "red as a firecracker" and to
have named James Cagney, Frank Sinatra, and Will Rogers, Jr., as
Communists. The situation deteriorated as the House Committee on
Un-American Activities moved in on the industry. On October 21
Welles was summoned to the home of William Wyler to discuss the
trend of events in Washington. The Committee for the First Amend-
ment, assembled that afternoon, included Wyler, John Huston, Anatole
Litvak, Paulette Goddard, Burgess Meredith, and Philip Dunne.

At a further meeting on October 24, attended by Billy Wilder,
William Wyler spoke: "This industry is now dividing against itself.
Unity must be recaptured or all of us will suffer for years to come. Your
aid is required in this critical moment. . . . This is more important than
any picture you ever made." Welles explained that he was happy to
support the committee but that his commitments would take him to
Europe almost at once. Since Korda was still delaying on *Cyrano* and
Salome, he decided to sign the contract to do *Cagliostro*. He was visited
by members of the California Un-American Activities Committee that
week, and asked whether he was a Communist. "How do you define a
Communist?" he inquired. "Someone who takes all your money and
gives it to the government" was the reply. Then the I.R.S. must be
eighty-seven percent Communist," he replied. In New York he met
briefly with Roger Hill to discuss various projects; he left *Macbeth* in
limbo. The picture had to be redubbed, and his presence at the redub-

bing was essential. The matter of Jacques Ibert was still in the air because of financial difficulties, and Welles was needed for the scoring
sessions with the composer. The cast, struggling with playbacks, also
needed his guidance. Jeanette Nolan says that his decision to leave
created another problem: makeup and wigs and clothing would have to
be sent to him in Rome so that he could direct himself in matching
scenes.

With Barbara Laage, Welles left for Rome via Ireland, where he
cabled Richard Wilson from Shannon Airport on November 4 to rush
makeup prepared by Maurice Seiderman (whom he called Silverstein)
and health belts (devices designed to make the wearer sweat off a
waistline) to London, where he was booked into Claridge's. The
makeup did not turn up at Claridge's, and on November 6 he left for
Rome without it. It had been held up in customs at Heathrow; it was
delayed again in Rome. On November 7 Wilson wrote him at the Hotel
Excelsior in Rome that the makeup was safely on the way and "the
noses can be used seven or eight times if Orson is careful in removing
them." More noses would be sent, and "you can rip your daily nose off
with abandon." Seiderman provided instructions for thinning the
makeup with alcohol or ether.

As Welles began his preparations for *Cagliostro*, Richard Wilson
coped with the problems he had left behind. Wilson was desperate for
money for Welles and himself and tried without success to get an advance for a book of short stories that he would edit under Welles's
name. Technical equipment was being hocked at the same time the
stimulants Proloid and Dexedrine were being rushed to Rome for
Welles.

On November 20 Wilson wrote Orson about taking him a partial
print of the picture and material for "looping" matching sequences in
sound in Rome; the editor Louis Lindsay would accompany him. Wilson was suffering the screams and threats of studio executives who insisted that Welles would be charged with back interest and tax on the
negative because of delays in the film's release. But every cent that had
been made available by Edward Small, *Cagliostro*'s producer, had already been spent; there were no funds to pay for Wilson and Lindsay
to go to Rome. Wilson had a constant struggle to match up the accounts and had to fight to run the soundtrack through or to show footage in the projection rooms. On November 20 Wilson emphasized that
he had just barely been able to calm Republic over the matter of
Welles's leaving before the dubbing was done; the following day he arranged for Lindsay to go to Rome with the print.

Welles immediately began cutting the picture with Lindsay in Rome and dubbing some of his lines, working through the night and then filming all day. *Cagliostro* fell apart completely in the clumsy hands of Gregory Ratoff, who failed to rise to the occasion. Lacking the necessary visual style, he nevertheless did not call on Welles to help him, except in a brief montage sequence that shows the Orsonian touch. The result was an overblown and contrived production totally without merit.

Concerned at the great distance between him and his daughters, Welles cabled Herb Willis of Republic to buy gifts for Rebecca and Christopher and for Hazel Bernstein, Virginia Lederer, and Mrs. Joseph Cotten.

Welles spent Christmas in Rome, Barbara Laage drifted away, and when 1948 began Welles was still immersed in the shooting of *Cagliostro*, now retitled *Black Magic*. His co-star, Nancy Guild, recalls that he was excessively fretful and edgy during the entire period of the production, suffering from the lack of sleep and his concern over *Macbeth*. On February 10 Wilson wrote that he was facing hysteria, snideness, sarcasm, and threats in addition to the adamant thwarting of plans. The business affairs of Mercury were in ruins, with insolvency, no proper bank account, and loose ends everywhere. Waiting desperately for Lindsay to return from Rome with *Macbeth*, Wilson was broke and worried about earning a living, not knowing what his future would be "in relation to your own known or unknown plans." He was pressing for a version of *Othello* in color but was not getting very far; Warner's was still holding back on *Moby Dick*.

In Rome, Gregory Ratoff, well out of his depth and arguing with Orson daily, was on the edge of a nervous breakdown and talking about "a temperamental heart." Welles suddenly took off for London in the middle of shooting to discuss the long-delayed *Cyrano* with Korda.

In March the wretched *Black Magic* still dragged on, becoming more embarrassing and amateurish every day. Wilson flew to Rome to pick up the print of *Macbeth* and to discuss the *Othello* project with Welles. He told him that Mercury had moved out of Beverly Hills and into more modest offices on Sunset Boulevard in Hollywood.

During Wilson's visit, Edward Small, who liked Orson despite all the problems, told him he had had to cancel *Othello* because of the political situation in Italy; the Communist and fascist rioting would make it too difficult to do the film. There was talk of doing *The Merchant of Venice* or *Macbeth* at the Edinburgh or Salzburg festivals, but Wilson was unable to raise a bank loan to finance the productions. He told

Welles hair-raising stories of his fights with Robert Newman of RKO and Charles K. Feldman; he said that Arnold Weissberger "had had to struggle with everything and everybody."

Staying on in Rome after *Black Magic* had limped to its conclusion, Welles cabled Korda that he was working hard on *Cyrano* as Wilson flew to Hollywood with the print of *Macbeth* for the scoring for a June release. (One of Wilson's notes of about this time says he was sitting in Hollywood waiting "for records of Orson breathing" to arrive from Rome.)

Macbeth was released in the summer to very bad reviews and had to be rerecorded yet again over a period of several months. Edward Small withdrew from *Othello*, leaving Welles to think how best he might undertake making it himself.

In May, Welles flew to Hollywood briefly to try to produce a satisfactory final print of *Macbeth*. By this time he had fallen in love with the twenty-two-year-old Italian actress Lea Padovani, who had appeared briefly in *Black Magic* and who would later be a sensation in Edward Dmytryk's *Give Us This Day* (from the novel *Christ in Concrete*). She had had a strong career on the Italian stage; she was currently appearing in a season of Noël Coward in Rome.

Welles was still married to Rita, and their divorce would not be declared final until November 1948. Nor had he entirely shaken Rita out of his mind; Lea Padovani later told friends that this was extremely painful for her. And her pain was increased later in the summer when Welles was in the south of France, all work on *Macbeth* completed, and reporters noted that he was staying with Rita at the Grand Hotel in Antibes; they were seen having dinner together in the restaurant. When Francesco Rico, a reporter for the Nice newspaper *L'Espoir*, approached Welles in a nightspot at Garoupe Beach and asked him about a possible reconciliation, Welles screamed at him, "Beat it, or I'll break your face."

As a result the rumors expanded. It was said that Rita had canceled a dinner date to go out with Welles and that the couple had taken a taxi to the Fishermen's restaurant in Napouli, a village up the coast. A tire had blown, and the car went off the road; they had to hitchhike back to Antibes. Followed everywhere by reporters and fending them off irritably, they had dinner at the Pam-Pam in Antibes, which specialized in American food, and nightclubbed until 4:00 A.M., when Rita collapsed with exhaustion and Orson carried her to the waiting taxi. As customers left the nightclub, reporters asked them about the couple and were told that when midnight struck, Orson had embraced Rita and kissed her on the lips.

Welles was asked to appear in *The Third Man* for David O. Selznick and the British director Carol Reed, which would be shot in Vienna in mid-September. Welles was offered the part of Harry Lime, a mysterious criminal in the war-ravaged Austrian capitol. Welles was delighted to learn that Joseph Cotten, who remained one of his closest friends, would play Holly Martins, an American writer of adventure stories who plunges into a maze of intrigue when he tries to find the truth about Lime. The Italian Alida Valli, Selznick's latest contract star, was cast as the intriguing Austrian actress Anna Schmidt, who plays a crucial role in the action. The part of Harry Lime was tailor-made for Welles; he was even allowed to add a brief speech of his own in which Lime, high up on the Ferris wheel of the Prater (the amusement park in Vienna), talks cynically of the sum total of Swiss achievement: "the cuckoo clock."

Welles was in admiration of Carol Reed. And he was glad to have the work, for he was busy preparing *Othello* and needed every cent he could earn. In fact he had already begun sporadic shooting on sums raised from a variety of sources by the fall of 1948, and the serious work would begin after the completion of *The Third Man*.

Just before the shooting began in Vienna, Welles had a wave of panic: the part of Harry Lime was too small. He turned up on location as Reed was preparing with cameraman Robert Krasker to film the scene in which Lime is pursued by the police through the sewers. Welles was not dressed for work, and Reed was shocked. Welles said he was feeling ill, having just gotten over influenza, and could not go ahead; he was very sorry, but he could not make the picture after all.

Reed, with his entire crew and cast standing by, urged Orson to change his mind and to play the scene because otherwise it would cost Selznick a fortune, delay the picture, and possibly put people out of work. Welles was impressed with Reed's determined manner and gave in. Yet the smell of the sewers and the intense damp worried him, subject as he was to asthmatic seizures and sinus attacks, and only with reluctance did he change into Harry Lime's clothes and, unathletic as always, descend awkwardly the narrow iron stairway into the sewer. He played the sequence with intense discomfort, then, perfect though he had been, insisted it was not good enough. The long-suffering Reed stood back while Welles talked with Robert Krasker, suggesting angles and a use of shadows that greatly enhanced the sequence. It was not Reed's custom to shoot many takes, but Welles wanted at least ten repetitions of every scene; on several occasions he also told Krasker precisely how he wanted to be lit. Captivated by his performance, Reed accepted everything. Once again Welles was influencing the direction of a film he appeared in.

When Welles flew to Shepperton Studios in Britain to shoot additional sequences, he was very much on edge, acutely aware that Rita had finally given up on him and that Lea Padovani was still in anguish. Moreover, he hated looping dialogue, matching his voice to lip movements on film, and he exploded when Lady Clarissa Churchill, wife of Sir Anthony Eden, came onto the set with a giggling collection of debutantes and young men about town. He froze in the middle of a scene and angrily demanded that they leave, thus causing him a serious loss of prestige with both Winston Churchill and Eden.

The movie was a success, not least because of the haunting zither score by Anton Karas, which provided a nerve-jangling accompaniment to the action. For years afterward, whenever Welles entered a restaurant that had an orchestra or a pianist, the musicians were inclined to strike up the *Third Man* theme. And in 1951 Welles was offered a series on British radio, *The Adventures of Harry Lime*, which he handled with aplomb.

He looked for more work that would help finance *Othello*, for which he began hunting new locations in the late fall of 1948. He was offered the movie *The Black Rose*, to be made in 1949, in which he would appear with Tyrone Power and Cecile Aubry. He flew to Italy to make *Prince of Foxes* in November; he played Cesare Borgia and influenced the director Henry King in many scenes.

His fascination with Lea Padovani continued, and she says their relationship was the most committed and impassioned affair of her life. When he told her he wanted her to play Desdemona in *Othello*, she was astonished; not only did she speak very little English, she was not a Shakespearean actress even in Italian. But she was captivated by him, as most women were, and she could not resist his force. He signed her to an exclusive contract to begin at the end of her Coward season and installed her in Casa Pilozzo, his rented villa at Fregene, an enormous Italianate folly in the Mussolini tradition that had been built by a member of the Mussolini government. It struck her as ironical that Welles, a liberal, would be resident in the home of a Mussolini general.

With an actress who was also a voice coach, Padovani lived in this vast house for several months while people came and went at Welles's invitation but he seldom turned up. Finally she and the coach, tired by many hours of rigorous training, went to the mountains for a vacation. Welles arrived at the hotel like a great shadow, frightening everyone and announcing that the voice coach had embarked on an unauth-

orized vacation with her pupil and was dismissed. He presented Padovani with a ticket to London, where she would be given further training. Thus she was as much his slave as Susan Kane was her husband's.
Welles's ego would not tolerate Signorina Padovani not being able to
speak perfect English and be convincing in Shakespeare.

He began shooting *Othello* in Venice, making her go over her lines
again and again. Now that they were together in separate suites at the
Europa Hotel, their passion developed. According to Padovani,
Welles's statement to the Cannes Film Festival director and writer
Maurice Bessy that she had revealed to him "the depth and keenness of
lovemaking" was true. She also agrees with other statements he made
to Bessy, that she destroyed him, minimized him, that with her he was
no longer himself, and that he accepted everything at her hands.
"During the nine months that I spent with her I paid for everything
that I'd ever done to women for twenty years."

Padovani believes she was blind in her headlong feelings. She and
Welles were engaged to be married; he gave her a ring that she has
preserved to this day. But she was in love with another man at the
time, a man who was a member of Welles's personal staff on *Othello*.
She says that that man had a terrible physical hold on her and that she
was in agony moving between him and Welles, who never knew what
was distracting her. Her other lover demanded that she leave Welles.
In what she now believes to have been the greatest mistake of her life,
she told Welles she would have to break off the engagement.

Welles was hysterical with rage. There was a struggle between
them, and she struck him on the head with a heavy doorstop of the kind
to be found in most Italian hotels. His head was injured and he fell to
the floor. At the last moment she broke free in terror and ran to her
suite, where she told her maid to pack at once. They fled the city,
never to return to the picture.

She remembers that she met Welles in Harry's Bar in Rome some
time later; in a theatrical gesture of remorse, he knelt cumbersomely in
the crowd and kissed the hem of her skirt.

Perhaps what bound Padovani most closely to Welles in those delir-
ious and excruciating months was an episode in which they came to the
very edge of death together. Having to fly from Rome to Turin for a
children's benefit, Welles could only get a tiny plane, and Padovani,
who had merely gone to see him off, found herself coaxed into making
the trip with him. They were flying above hills when the pilot suddenly
became agitated and announced that they were out of fuel. Padovani
recalls that she held tightly to Welles's hand, which felt like a huge

block of ice in hers. He sat absolutely rigid and told the pilot, very calmly, "Bring the plane down," like a talking corpse. The pilot followed these seemingly obvious instructions, and the plane landed in a field among cows. At that moment, Padovani says, she and Welles looked at each other: they had been to the brink of oblivion. The experience was reflected later in Welles's film *Confidential Report*.

At Christmas 1948 Welles concentrated more seriously on *Othello*, using his earnings from acting and what little he had been able to scrape together from his miserable financial dealings in America. In the crucial role of Iago he had cast his old friend and colleague from the Gate Theater in Dublin and the Woodstock summer of 1934, Micheal MacLiammoir. Over the years he had remained intermittently in touch with MacLiammoir's partner, Hilton Edwards, and he was convinced that through Edwards he could talk MacLiammoir into acting Iago.

One problem was that MacLiammoir had no liking for motion pictures; he told the present author that Hollywood was "a collection of shacks at the end of a poisoned rainbow." Like many stage performers, he felt that motion pictures represented slumming. He was also concerned that Welles had already filmed bits and pieces of *Othello* in Venice, with Padovani as Desdemona and an Italian actor playing Iago. Welles assured Edwards that the Italian actor was hopeless, and he spoke warmly of Lea, whom he was busy trying to mold by dying her hair blond and driving her, Professor Higgins–like, through her English lessons.

In Paris on January 26, 1949, Welles cabled MacLiammoir, who was sick in bed in Dublin following an attack of influenza and a nervous breakdown: "Dearest Micheal Enthusiastically repeat offer made me to Hilton You play Iago with me in *Othello* film Can you come to Paris to arrange things When can you come I will try to come to Dublin if you can't come to Paris Love to you both Orson."

Edwards was so concerned about MacLiammoir's health that he delayed showing him the wire. When Welles called to beseech Edwards to have MacLiammoir accept, he did not help matters by reassuring Edwards that, despite his awareness of MacLiammoir's "fast-departing youth and borderline condition," he wanted him "to do a test." His "American associates," Welles said, wanted to be sure that MacLiammoir would photograph well on screen; in fact there were no "American associates"—they were Welles himself.

When Edwards finally showed MacLiammoir the telegram, the actor waved it away. He hated to leave the Christmas show at the Gate Theater, and he did not feel he could go to Paris to do a test. But the doctors advised MacLiammoir to make the trip because it would improve his nerves and his health to have a change of scene. MacLiammoir was further encouraged to go by the fact that his house was intolerably upside-down: dry rot had been found in it, and the building was being torn apart in the search for the source of the problem. To escape from the hell of noise and the people tramping around would certainly be welcome.

On January 29 Welles at last spoke with MacLiammoir on the telephone. MacLiammoir groaned that he was sick and was not sure he could make the trip; Welles assured him that as soon as they met he would be "revived." Welles swept aside all other excuses: when MacLiammoir said he was too old for the part of Iago, Welles said that he himself was too old for the part of Othello; when MacLiammoir said he had never played Iago, Welles countered, "And I have never played Othello"; both ruefully admitted they had gained weight, and Welles said, "We'll be two chubby tragedians together"; when MacLiammoir expressed his unease about being in movies, Welles told him he was "born for movies"—which appalled MacLiammoir as a theater snob. MacLiammoir said he did not see himself as a villain. Welles screamed, "Fuck! You're the biggest villain around in everyone's eyes but your own and Hilton's!" MacLiammoir was certain he could not play the part.

Edwards pressed MacLiammoir to accept, and MacLiammoir, moaning that no one wanted him, that everyone wanted to get rid of him, that he would have a dizzy spell or a collapse, began to pack for Paris. Welles was delighted; he knew that no one could match his old friend in the part.

MacLiammoir arrived in Paris on February 7, and Welles sent his Austrian secretary, Rita Ribola, to meet him. When they reached his rooms at the Hotel Lancaster, Welles was standing in the doorway, looking almost as he had fifteen years earlier. The two men embraced and danced around the suite with its crackling log fire before talking enthusiastically of the past. When MacLiammoir said it was amazing that Welles had not changed very much, Welles said, "Only nice people change. Louses like us never do!"

In order to get MacLiammoir into a relaxed mood, Welles took him to the Méditérranée restaurant for lunch the next day and sent him with a chauffeur for a drive through the Bois de Boulogne. MacLiammoir was put on a diet and ordered to have a massage every day to tighten up his body.

Charles Lederer turned up at the Lancaster with a new *Cyrano* script, accompanied by Virginia and Christopher. With their former bitterness forgotten and all attempts to make Orson pay child support shelved, Charles and Viginia were now close friends of Welles and gave him constant moral support. Christopher brought gifts of crayon drawings. There were very pleasant evenings that February with Mac-Liammoir, the Lederers, and Welles's favorite cutter, Louis Lindsay, who had patched together a more or less releasable print of *Macbeth* and would take care of the daily rushes of *Othello*.

Welles and MacLiammoir began work during a rainstorm on February 9, their readings accompanied by workmen banging away in the background. Welles constantly reassured MacLiammoir about Lea Padovani and her insecure command of English: if she did not progress sufficiently in time, he would have her dubbed.

Welles never ceased living it up; there were constant luncheon and dinner events with the Lederers, Lindsay, MacLiammoir, and other friends. Yet he worked hard with the art director and designer Alexandre Trauner. Trauner, who had created the mise-en-scène for the classic film *Les enfants du paradis*, was a man of great brilliance and acuity whose sketches exactly mirrored Welles's vision for *Othello*. The film was to be shot in Rome, Venice, and Nice, and Trauner was instructed to match his designs to actual locations.

Robert Coote, later famous as Colonel Pickering in *My Fair Lady*, arrived to play Roderigo, and Coote, MacLiammoir, and Welles moved happily through a number of test readings. Welles fought constantly with his long-suffering secretary Rita Ribola, whose habits of doing her nails with a file, murmuring in German under her breath, and constantly making notes about nothing in particular irritated him. He even disliked her wearing slacks on a Sunday—an odd reversion to his Episcopalian upbringing in Wisconsin and Illinois. In fact, judging from MacLiammoir's diaries, Welles treated Mlle. Ribola abominably, bullying and harassing her to the point that it is extraordinary she did not resign. Welles's tension increased with the appearance of an unidentified Dutchman in a flapping overcoat and fluttering tie who gave an impromptu audition for the role of Roderigo, which had already been cast.

Welles showed considerable flair (learned from Alexander Korda) in handling backers for *Othello*. While he could rely on his fame and charm to carry the day, he knew well that lavish amounts of the best food and wine, uproarious anecdotes, and plentiful laughter and fun could melt all but the stoniest heart. Even though his collateral was nonexistent and his promises were notoriously unkempt, he understood that moneyed barflies could be drawn to his web by alluring suggestions, intriguing ideas, and captivating hopes. All but a few fell for it; all but a few lived to regret it.

One evening early in March, Welles gave a dinner party for several prospective Desdemonas of various nationalities, mischievously playing one off against the other as he addressed MacLiammoir in all seriousness about his conception of Iago. It was Welles's typically wicked joke to tell MacLiammoir that the secret of Iago's character was that he was sexually impotent and that Iago's impotence made him jealous of Othello's virility; Iago, he said, was consumed by hatred of life because he did not enter into life. Welles equated the inability to have an erection with moral weakness and criminal hatred. It was an interesting concept, not necessarily borne out by the text but feasible in terms of drama. However, Welles's discourse was pointed in that MacLiammoir, though certainly not impotent, was surrounded that night by nubile young women whom he carefully avoided and later studiously ignored. Gobbling a large piece of sturgeon, then ordering a second course and a third, Welles maliciously embroidered his theme. Later he told MacLiammoir that "of course" he "hadn't meant to suggest" that the Irish actor's casting was due to "his sexual impotence." MacLiammoir was more or less reassured by this example of Welles's humor.

By March 9 rehearsals were well advanced. (Welles had to move fast because he was due the following month in North Africa to appear in *The Black Rose* as a Chinese military commander, a veritable Xanaduvian.) The emphasis of Welles's direction was on Iago's jealousy, his mean and angry feeling of sexual incapacity. MacLiammoir wrote that he was impressed with

> Orson's design for the growing dependence of Othello on Iago's presence, the merging of the two men into one murderous image like a pattern of loving shadows welded. . . . He is speaking many of the lines . . . with a queer breathless rapidity: this treatment, with his great bulk and power, gives an extraordinary feeling of loss, of withering, diminishing, crumbling, toppling over, of a vanishing equilibrium; quite wonderful.

Impressed though he was, MacLiammoir remained uneasy as ever about the restrictions of the screen. He was also made a little edgy by his friend's attacks on the British, with whom Welles had been dealing unsatisfactorily on the financing of his film; Welles grumbled about them for their love of tea (especially with milk), their language, their drafty rooms.

On March 11, 1949, Welles's friend Maurice Bessy arrived at the Lancaster with Cecile Aubry, a new choice for Desdemona.* She had given a good performance opposite Michel Auclair in Henri-George Clouzot's movie *Manon*, based on the classic novel. In that picture Aubry had played a childish, selfish, spoiled girl like an overgrown child who, with mindless erotic sensuality, had lured a handsome and animal youth into a liaison that resulted in disaster for both of them. Welles had been captivated by her sexual appeal and by the unthinking drive that had propelled her acting—acting by instinct, acting of extraordinary caliber. Blond, round-faced, still in her teens, Aubry was very striking but had no talent for Shakespeare. Her voice projection, breath control, and use of rhythm were unsatisfactory, as MacLiammoir noted in his diary; and all her charm and style could not help her with the lines of Shakespeare.

It was an absurd idea to have a French actress play Desdemona in English, just as it would have been to have an Italian Desdemona. But Welles, ever the victim of impulse, flew in a voice teacher and script director, Lee Kressel, to instruct her in English speech. He worked with Aubry all day while Welles sulked, and at night, often at an impossible hour, Welles would rehearse her. Aubry lasted exactly two days. Unable to cope with the English, she resembled (as Lea Padovani had before her) Susan Alexander Kane learning to sing; thoroughly flustered, she decided (she recalls) she had a contract for *The Black Rose* and departed in a whirl of temperament. Welles called the long-suffering Rita Ribola and verbally flayed her for not having signed Mademoiselle Aubry to a contract.

There followed a long series of auditions for Desdemona. Why Welles did not send to England for any one of a number of fine actresses is unclear; one possible explanation is that he found British actresses cold and dispassionate. The best that were available, led by Margaret Lockwood, Phyllis Calvert, and Valerie Hobson, would have been not only too expensive, under contract, and perhaps busy, but also not warm enough. He wanted a woman who at once was voluptuous and could speak verse perfectly. The challenge was almost too great; Welles in his despair filled the time visiting nightclubs, eating and drinking until all hours.

Welles behaved with manic eccentricity during March. When he and MacLiammoir drove past a line of people waiting to see *Manon*,

---

* Since she was cast in *The Black Rose*, Welles figured she might make *Othello* at the same time.

with Cecile Aubry's face glowing from the photographs on display, he screamed at the crowd, "Don't go in there, folks, don't go in there!" He refused to sleep, and he threw tantrums where Ribola was concerned (like Sheridan Whiteside bellowing at his nurse, Welles gave her nicknames, the most brutal of which was Miss Mud).

The auditions went on and on. At last, on March 20, the White Russian director Anatole Litvak, who had known Welles since Hollywood in the early 1940s, turned up at the Ritz Hotel bar and suggested Welles look at Betsy Blair, who had appeared as a wordless, unhappy mad girl in Litvak's picture *The Snake Pit.* Litvak was dating her at the time, and Welles liked her instantly. But the money had run low again as a consequence of Welles's uproarious living in Paris, and for a time it seemed there might be not enough left to hire Blair. Even the promised funds on *The Black Rose* did not seem to offer sufficient security, and Welles thought he would have to go to the British again to try to raise money.

At the end of March, after many changes of mind, he was finally ready to commit himself to *The Black Rose*, which he had to do now for the money. Anxious that he would lose MacLiammoir's services while he was in Morocco making the picture, he wanted MacLiammoir to go to Rome and stay in his newly rented villa at Frascati. MacLiammoir did not have the strength to disagree. At the beginning of April Welles flew to London to sign his contract for *The Black Rose*, the shooting to begin in May in the Moorish desert. Not a foot of *Othello* had yet been filmed.

MacLiammoir returned to Dublin. While Welles was meeting with the director Henry Hathaway he was also conferring intermittently with Ernest Borneman, a former Canadian Film Board and Unesco film unit director who had suggested that *The Odyssey* of Homer would make a good picture. Welles had encouraged him to go ahead and do a script, and when MacLiammoir moved out of the villa at Frascati, Welles moved Borneman in and asked him to bring his family to Rome to live with him. There Borneman worked on the script with little or no money, finding the villa badly run and heaped up with unpaid bills. Thus Welles used the villa as a kind of halfway house for those people he wanted to keep on hold regardless of their personal comfort while he proceeded with whatever work he had in hand.

In mid-April Welles was in Morocco, planning to continue *Othello* there while making *The Black Rose*. The location was at Meknes, and Cecile Aubry was the star. It took all his acting ability to cope with her, and it took all her willpower to cope with him. Edward Toledano of *The New York Times* visited the set at Meknes and saw that the crusty veteran Hathaway took no nonsense from Welles or anyone else as he tackled the formidable task of shooting among braying camels, jittery French police, and flocks of sheep and goats. Hathaway hated to be interfered with or interrupted, and he worked extremely fast. Welles lumbered about in his elaborate costumes as Bayan the Conqueror, nearly suffocating from the heat inside elaborate breeches, a soft tanned leather tunic, and a mink-lined brown Russian leather coat that contained three hundred skins, hung from shoulder to toe, that was so heavy it took two husky male wardrobe assistants to lift it onto Welles's shoulders. As if this were not enough with the temperatures close to a hundred degrees, Welles wore a spiked Saracen helmet of steel inlaid with a brass design, a veil of chain mail around its edges, and a high-standing ring of mink encircling the headpiece. It was rather like walking around inside an oven. And Welles carried 230 pounds, about forty pounds overweight for his height of six feet, two inches.°

Some days the temperature reached 120 degrees, and in the afternoon a sirocco blew out of the desert to sandblast Welles, Cecile Aubry, Tyrone Power, and the others. The four thousand Arab extras who swarmed about were often unruly, and the crew lost some precious articles in thefts. In a sequence at the palace of Sherif Moulay ben-Zidan, with hundreds of yards of matting over the mosaic tile floors to protect them, the heat had to be augmented by huge lamps powered by six generators. Further sequences were shot in Marrakesh, Foreign Legion outposts in South Morocco, and the Tinrir Oasis. Orson endured his suffocating costume day after day; even the costume designer Michael Whittaker felt weighed down by Welles's costumes, and he only had to carry them.

Filming the battle scenes of *The Black Rose* at Ouarzazate in the desert was a colossal task that involved the transportation of two hundred tons of equipment, including lighting apparatus, spears, twelve thousand arrows, shields and bows, 150 tons of cable, and the cameras.

Throughout the grueling filming Welles was writing Edwards and MacLiammoir (to his frustration, he found there were no telephones)

° While he was in North Africa, Welles had to give a deposition in a New York suit brought by Ferdinand Lundberg, author of a biography of William Randolph Hearst, who charged that Welles and Mankiewicz had plagiarized his book. Mankiewicz denied under oath that he had had access to the book, but four copies were found to have been in his library, and he was lucky to escape perjury charges. In fact, the early drafts of the *Kane* screenplay are filled with libel of Hearst. The case was settled out of court.

and peppering Borneman with messages as the harassed writer began to run out of money in Rome. Rita Ribola flew all over the map keeping everybody calm—or so she thought. When Welles wired him on May 14 to come to Casablanca around May 20, MacLiammoir could not believe that Welles intended to rehearse in a desert or to shoot *Othello* among Moroccan palm trees and mosques. MacLiammoir flew to Madrid and then to Casablanca. Welles was out in the Sahara on location, and Frank Bevis, production manager of *The Black Rose,* said that he was not expected for three weeks. The two men had a sharp quarrel; MacLiammoir wondered what on earth he was doing in Morocco. Ribola explained that Welles had cabled him—but the cable must have missed him, hence the misunderstanding. Then Welles cabled him from the desert: "Dearest Micheal I'm so sorry but Miss Mud will provide you with large sums of money, and why don't you visit Fez? Rabat? Marrakesh? Morocco is such a great country—now you *know* it's great." Later Welles suggested that MacLiammoir go to Rome to try on his costumes. MacLiammoir was furious.

Ribola did her best to pacify MacLiammoir while Welles went on acting in the agony of the desert location. Rain poured down, and suddenly Welles took it into his head to fly Borneman from Paris via Rome to work on the script of *The Odyssey.* Then MacLiammoir was dispatched to Paris and on to Rome, where Robert Coote and Michael Lawrencé (he was to play Cassio) were waiting for Welles to get moving. Betsy Blair arrived and soon joined them in affectionate recriminations directed at their astonishing mentor; all of them had given up lucrative assignments for this insanity. By early June the cast was in Mogador, a wildly beautiful but overcrowded city.

One of the features of Morocco is the extraordinary intensity of the light. But that year there was a restless feeling about the place, what Alexandre Trauner describes as an insupportable wind that could not be endured for long yet blew incessantly, causing a fine silting of sand from the desert. In Mogador Welles had found a fifteenth-century Portuguese fortress and citadel, with towering walls and battlements overlooking the sea. There he would recreate the island of Cyprus that is the setting of *Othello.* There he had everything from enormous metal bells to bronze cannons that had turned green with the seasonal rains, and the Atlantic lashed the black rocks of the coast, creating unforgettable visions. Even the exhausted MacLiammoir was dazzled by Mogador and by Welles's torrential welcoming gesture as he rose from his table at the Beau Rivage Hotel to embrace MacLiammoir passionately.

Once again Welles mesmerized the beleaguered actor, besieging him with complaints about money, clothing, and the gruesome desert location. On June 10, after all the delays, there was a rehearsal of Iago and Cassio, and later, Iago and Roderigo. The costumes had been held up by financial problems, so an entire new wardrobe was rushed in from Spain. Welles was dressed in armor and a long black cloak; Mac-Liammoir wore a yellow leather jerkin and armor, including breast and knee plates. Because of the shortage of costumes, Welles decided to have the murder of Roderigo take place not in the street but in a steambath, with the actors dressed only in towels. The result was one of the best scenes in the film: the camera snakes through stone passages past steaming pipes and wet towels, black masseurs bear oil jars through the vapor fog, and Iago is seen stabbing Roderigo through slats in the walls.

At last something had been filmed; finally something had been done on *Othello* beyond the talk and travel and squandering of funds.

Because he knew Morocco, with its strong Portuguese influences, Alexandre Trauner was able to dress up the interiors of houses and castles in a manner equivalent to that of the period. He says that, like Welles, he was not interested in pure historical accuracy; it was far more important to achieve an effect that was striking on the screen, since nobody knew what Cyprus was like in the fifteenth century anyway. Although a man of discipline with a love of planning, Trauner adapted readily to Welles's powers of improvisation. He notes that Welles approached scenes in *Othello* very much as Eisenstein did his epics of Russian history. He saw "like a painter, and many of his drawings and sketches for the movie resembled those of Eisenstien himself."

Trauner says that few studio sets were used. Apart from Emilia's chamber and a particularly large doorway that framed Othello in one scene (both constructed at the Scalera Studios in Rome), virtually everything was done in actual houses. He was constantly amazed at Welles's ability to match scenes shot far apart in time and space. For instance, Trauner worked with a grille that cast a network of shadows, and this, built in Morocco, was made to match exactly the shadows in a studio in Rome. As the filming progressed, he warmed more and more to the atmosphere of improvisation in which he worked. When the costumes failed to arrive from Florence, Trauner had other costumes made by obscure Jewish tailors working out of tiny shops in the Moroccan cities. Needing a chain for Desdemona's ornamented purse, he used a lavatory chain from a hotel. At last the Italian-made costumes arrived, but they were all heavily embroidered and elaborate, and he and Welles decided to stay with what they had: clothes, which better suggested the roughness of Othello, his people, and his time.

Frequently during the shooting Welles would disappear on a quest for money, often returning empty-handed. A Moroccan named Tenoudji finally supplied the cash to complete the Moroccan footage, but while they were waiting for the money and for Welles, the crew and the cast sat around the hotel. They had all their meals in the hotel restaurant because there was no money for eating elsewhere, and Orson told them to order the most expensive dishes so that they would seem to be rich. The wealthy mother of George Fanto (a cameraman of *It's All True*), who was a guest at the hotel, supplied the company with money for drinks and cigarettes.

During what Trauner looks back on as the adventure of making *Othello*, he and Welles began preparing two other movie projects that never got off the ground: *The Thousand and One Nights* was to have been filmed in Morocco, and test shots were made for a version of *The Merchant of Venice*. In the long years of work on *Othello*, Trauner was impressed by the contrast between the power of Welles's visual and dramatic approach to pictures and his strange insecurity, his tendency to hesitate even in the face of his own inspiration. He was, Trauner says, a man who "destroys himself continually. When all goes well, he will find an excuse which will immediately throw everything he has done into question. When all the money is available to finish a picture, he will find a reason to delay the picture before the negative is complete." He adds that Welles fiercely resents any such appraisal; when Trauner tried to discuss it with him, Welles angrily swept it aside.

When location work on *The Black Rose* was concluded, Welles had to go to England to shoot further scenes of that film. In Mogador the splendid locations, the windswept beach, and the blazing sunshine had inspired everyone, even when the complications seemed endless: Robert Coote's fear of heights, seen in the sequences shot on a scaffolding; the sudden, unexpected sun-blindness of MacLiammoir; Welles's irrational hatred of the birds that constantly hovered above; MacLiammoir's contempt for screen acting. The big jealousy scene in which Othello says, "Villain, be sure thou prove my love a whore," was shot on a watchtower above black rocks, wild waves, and a screaming wind. When the wind increased, it was so violent that the two men had to hang onto a cannon to keep from falling off the battlement, and their words were blown away in the wind, making it impossible for each to hear the other or to be recorded. Not even the arrival of Hilton Edwards from Dublin calmed MacLiammoir completely.

Welles was dissatisfied with Betsy Blair as Desdemona; he found her too cool and fragile (qualities he should have noticed earlier) and sent her to Paris while he decided what to do. Welles's screaming fits kept everyone in an uproar. Trying to settle arguments between the actors over the size of their rooms, he yelled through the bar of the hotel that if only he could keep everyone quiet, "I would sleep on the kitchen table." Finally, feeling ill and announcing that money had run out again, Welles left for Casablanca. Coote and others were sent to England, the Italian technicians were sent to Rome, and MacLiammoir and Edwards were to proceed to Welles's villa in Frascati.

The two men returned to Venice and were left stranded by Orson. He flew Fay Compton (who played Emilia) to Venice and fired Betsy Blair, replacing her with Suzanne Cloutier, a pretty French-Canadian actress. Once again he had resisted selecting a British actress to play Desdemona. Cloutier looked stunning on her first day of work in Venice on August 24, 1949; Welles was fascinated by her and began reshooting all the Desdemona sequences. He shot around the Grand Canal and at the Palace of the Doge, and he filmed the scene of raising the alarm at Brabantio's house. A vacationing Joseph Cotten arrived, and Welles immediately cast him as a senator in one sequence. Joan Fontaine, who was then appearing with Cotten in the film *September Affair*, decided that she too must be in the picture despite her annoyance with Welles over *Jane Eyre*; even at the age of thirty-one she looked surprisingly convincing as a page boy.

Welles was testy and nervous during the new weeks of work in Venice, and his irritability proved infectious: members of the cast began screaming at one another, and more than once the shooting broke up in disarray. During one mortifying dinner party with the cast gathered in the garden of their hotel, Welles, consuming one lobster after another, screamed in anger at Coote and MacLiammoir because he had not managed to secure a shot with them to coincide with a gorgeous Venice sunset.

Throughout the shooting Welles shifted from intense displays of affection, in which he smothered his cast with kisses and embraces, to more and more ferocious outbursts of anger. There may have been calculation in this: by both attacking and adoring his players, he kept them in a constant state of overexcitement that was appropriate to the feverish mood of the film. Suzanne Cloutier, who became known as the Iron Butterfly, fascinated everyone. MacLiammoir describes her in his diary.

> She is indestructible. She will discuss herself tirelessly for hours at mealtimes in French or English, in a faintly *gilded*, clipped drawl (like sunshine on snow) without pausing for breath. She will, with or without the attention of an audience, interrupt,

declaim, misquote, advise, question, beg for advice, recount, flatter, boast, invent, be amusing and embarrassing but never stagnant: even when she is silent you know that, like a cat, an immense activity is in progress.

Welles called her Schnucks. The shooting shifted to the island of Torcello. The magic of this enchanted isle temporarily soothed everyone's mood. But that happier mood disintegrated when cast and crew were transferred to Rome and luggage and props were temporarily lost en route.

In the deafening noise of Rome—a bedlam of motorbikes, cars, buses, and taxis—Welles was again nervous and testy. Scenes were shot in the studios, where the cast had to match sequences to scenes shot on exterior locations. This was an especially difficult task because Welles took bits and pieces from his various versions and reshootings and made the actors move in and out of scenes as they had done months before. MacLiammoir believed that Welles was unable to get through to Cloutier when giving her direction; this drove Welles mad, since he was used to absolute obedience and sensitive responsiveness on the part of every member of his cast. He was somewhat relieved of his tension by the arrival of his daughter Christopher with Virginia on September 15. They joined Welles and MacLiammoir at a restaurant near the Appian Way, where Christopher did imitations of Ethel Merman, John and Lionel Barrymore, and Orson himself; to her father's ecstatic delight. Later she went to the studio and expertly imitated both Compton and Cloutier. It was a disappointment to Welles that Christopher did not follow up on her early acting talent; soon afterward she and her mother left for South Africa, where Virginia was to marry a businessman resident there, Jack Pringle. Welles did not see Virginia or Christopher again for years.

A scene in which Othello struck Desdemona across the face presented a real problem. The effect Welles wanted required that Cloutier not flinch before the blow; yet every time his hand moved, she looked understandably terrified. It took hours to secure an ideal shot.

The shooting in Rome dragged. Again the money ran out, and once more work was suspended. MacLiammoir and the others wondered, they told Welles, whether *Othello* would ever be finished. MacLiammoir and Edwards had no alternative but to return to Dublin, their personal finances and those of the Gate Theater in disarray. They had been paid so little, and so little had happened with the theater, that not only their personal bank accounts but also their meager properties were threatened.

Welles scarcely helped matters by writing from London's most expensive hotel, Claridge's, to inform them that there was no money to pay them with. His was a typically outrageous approach that gave no thought to writing from a more modest address, much less staying at a more modest address as a gesture toward economizing on production costs. On September 25 he wrote, "Unfortunately I have no rich close friends here, and the rich ones are close in the wrong sense of that word" (that is, tight with their money). He did manage to scrape up 25,000 francs to send to Dublin to ensure that his cast would not disappear for good.

Edwards wrote Welles at Claridge's on September 29.

Our affairs require the immediate expenditure of £2,000, and Micheal and I would be grateful if you could let us have this in Dublin while we are over here, as you suggested. We would also be grateful if you could arrange to let Micheal have the balance of his *Othello* money to date in whatever currency is most convenient. Micheal would prefer it, perhaps foolishly, to be in sterling, but if this is not possible then whatever currency suits you best.

Edwards suggested that their London agent, John Findlay, act as go-between. Welles replied from Claridge's that he could do nothing. Moreover, he dangled a useless promise: MacLiammoir would play Brutus and Edwards would direct a version of *Julius Caesar*. Yet even to contemplate such a project with *Othello* unfinished was sheer professional insanity. (Later Welles tried to interest John Houseman in the project, but Houseman was already involved in a Hollywood version of the play with Marlon Brando and James Mason.)

The relationship between Welles and MacLiammoir and Edwards declined sharply. The two men had given undertakings to their bank for an overdraft, based on MacLiammoir's receiving payment for his work in *Othello;* now bankruptcy threatened, and their theater itself was imperiled. They sent embarrassing telegrams to Welles, begging him to find a solution to their problems and asking for a promissory note or a more concrete proposal on their involvement in *Julius Caesar*. On October 4 Hilton Edwards wrote:

Our situation over here is not dissimilar from yours; the fact that it involves considerably smaller sums of money is equalized by the fact that our potential earnings are smaller, and this makes us more than ever sympathetic with your difficulty, but we want you to appreciate ours as well. The intolerable part of the whole business is that we are forced to appear tough with you, whereas in fact we are only asking you to fulfill a portion of your undertaking so that we, in turn, may keep faith over here.

Ignoring this letter, Welles cabled MacLiammoir and Edwards on October 11, "Arranging purchase pounds need you Micheal soonest love Orson." The next day he assured them, "Arranging payment as fast as possible repeat fast as possible so please advise Findlay to drop threatening tone all love Orson."

The threats from MacLiammoir's London agents continued. Incredibly, Welles issued a contract for Edwards to direct *Julius Caesar* while he was supposedly raising money to complete *Othello*. It proved small consolation to the partners in Dublin. Welles took off for Rome, still without paying them, and they cabled him at the Scalera Studios, "Have burned our boats here and accept your asurance you will do best at earliest moment to relieve our difficulties and will both come whenever you say as you know perfectly well stop."

On October 14 the partners, still unpaid, were urgently called to Rome to recommence work. Their London agent informed them that Orson would not meet with him during his stay at Claridge's and that the position was hopeless. But so great was the couple's loyalty to Welles that MacLiammoir went to Rome and was followed later by Edwards. And they proceeded on to Morocco for further work. Once more the affairs of their theater fell into disarray.

It seems as though everybody connected with *Othello* had lost their senses in their determination to complete this extraordinary picture. Once more there were the arguments, the reconciliations, the frenzies, the threats, the ecstasies, the follies. Once again no one connected with the picture knew what would be happening from one day to the next. Orson carried everything in his head, somehow sustaining the cast's energy despite the fact that most of them were broke and the efforts of MacLiammoir's London agents to get a response to their letters and telegrams were fruitless.

On February 2, 1950, Welles splurged on an elaborate birthday party for Hilton Edwards in Mogador; but this provided only a momentary break in the ordeal of matching one shot after another to scenes filmed as long ago as the previous July. On February 19 Welles shot the most startling and powerful sequence in the picture: Iago, a prisoner in a cage hanging on a creaking chain, is hauled hundreds of feet up in the air at the Mogador castle walls. MacLiammoir wrote later of the ordeal.

This [is] Orson's invention and I have been dreading it for months ... felt much more inclined to yell "Help, help!" but refrained, and went whirling up about a dozen times, to immense delight of the Arab population who gathered in their hundreds to see the show, their favorite part of it being each descent when the cage with me in it was plunked slowly and unsteadily into the water. Faint applause whenever this happened, but respectful silence on my upward flight. Profoundly unpleasant morning.

The unpleasantness was increased by Welles's still having not paid MacLiammoir or Edwards, and the ghastly situation offered little hope of improvement. They were housed in substandard accommodations while Welles stayed in the best hotels. Often there were air flights or drives in a dilapidated automobile from one location to another; the heat was consistently unendurable. And during all this Welles was planning yet another film that would involve the partners: a version of the Sheridan LeFanu novel *Carmilla,* a vampire story of considerable subtle power with which Orson had fallen in love, and which had been done as a play at the Gate in 1930.

Welles spent a great deal of time and effort on the music for *Othello.* He commissioned the composing team of Francesco Lavagnino and Alberto Barberis, who were enchanted with the idea of working with him. Lavagnino recalls that the time spent with Welles was one of constant creativity; Welles gave him such force and strength that he became almost another Welles, totally at Welles's service. Many times their thoughts intermingled or ran parallel, so deep was Welles's understanding of music in a dramatic context.

A memorable example of their rapport occurred during the scoring of the steambath scene that had been so drastically improvised in North Africa. Lavagnino had composed somewhat melodramatic music for the sequence, but neither he nor Welles was satisfied with it. They sat for a time in silence. Then each said to the other that he had an idea he dared not propose. They agreed they would count to three and then blurt out the concept. They counted to three, then shouted in unison, "Mandolins!" A mandolin accompaniment would be perfect in creating the frenzy of the sequence; in the exuberance of their mutual inspiration, the two men jumped up and embraced, laughing their heads off. And Welles went beyond his inspired composer: he wanted the jangling music to reach a crescendo and then break up with the dissonant sound of the tuning of the instruments.

In recording the steambath music in Rome, Welles conducted Lavagnino as conductor, signaling him to stretch out the chaotic sound of instruments tuning. Typically of him, he needed extra music because he had decided to have a group of mandolin players appear in the scene itself, and he had not even hired them yet.

Throughout the composition of the music Welles would listen and then come up with an inspiration. When Lavagnino asked what gave him this kind of musical genius, what sparked his intuitions, he said he was "one of those whores who is indifferent to a client built like Hercules but can get turned on by a simple nobody who arrives at the brothel at the right moment."

He had an extraordinary idea for the theme that accompanied Desdemona. He heard Lavagnino's music and liked it, but he told Lavagnino that "in the finale all supporting instruments must fade out, leaving the theme to be delicately carried out only by the flute."

Welles demanded an orchestra of two hundred, which was conducted by Franco Ferrara. Impatient with the small recording rooms he had found, he had the entire score performed in the Scalera Studios. When the work was completed, Welles was still passionately involved with changes. He was unhappy with the funeral music, feeling that it sounded like "Tchaikovsky touring in Italy"; consequently it was rescored for harpsichord, and Lavagnino worked with the only harpsichord available in Rome. Lavagnino recorded the dirge with sixteen instruments and eight voices by placing three microphones to create the right music perspective.

Lavagnino was frequently on the set during the shooting. As Welles prepared to direct the funeral scene in the country near Rome, Lavagnino remembers, the composer saw an almost bare set, with scattered platforms and vertical props spaced from ten to fifty feet apart, dry stone walls, then, a little further away, a small house and, close to a basin of water, what looked to him like sheets hung out to dry. He could not understand the arrangement until Welles explained that the scene had to be shot at the precise time of day when the sun hit the water basin in such a way as to obtain the desired optical effect. Looking through the camera, Lavagnino was amazed to see a port in Cyprus in the fifteenth century: the soldiers standing on the platforms gave the perfect perspective, while the water reflection on the walls showed a sheet as a sail, the walls as a pier, and the basin as the Mediterranean. In this setting the funeral procession for Othello, Desdemona, and Emilia appeared. If proof were needed of Orson Welles's genius, surely Signor Lavagnino's description provides it.

1 4

Out of pocket again with *Othello* still in progress, Welles heard that Darryl F. Zanuck was staying at the Hôtel du Cap in Antibes and thought he might help. Instead of taking a plane, which would involve a change in Paris, Welles flagged down a cab in the streets of Rome and asked to be driven to Antibes. Since the distance was well over a thousand miles, the driver was startled. Convinced that Welles was drunk, he did not respond until Welles pulled out a bundle of lire equivalent to more than $400 and offered it for the fare. The driver consented.

Welles arrived at the hotel at 4:00 A.M., and the night manager refused to allow him to call Zanuck's suite. Zanuck learned Welles was sleeping in the lobby when he came down to breakfast. As soon as Zanuck appeared, Welles threw his arms around him and announced, "I need $75,000 to finish *Othello*." Zanuck called Hollywood, and within an hour Fox owned sixty percent of the picture. The money came from Paris by courier in a locked mail sack crammed with hundred-franc bills that had to be counted out one by one in front of Zanuck, with an auditor present. Then the money was delivered to Welles, who immediately carted it off to the casino in Monte Carlo. Zanuck was furious when he found this out. But apparently Welles did not lose much of it, and when Zanuck was misinformed later that Welles had paid his cast with it (we now know from correspondence that this was not true), he was somewhat mollified.

Once again Welles ran out of cash for *Othello*. MacLiammoir and Edwards returned to Dublin while Welles stayed on in Italy. Yet the partners remained loyal. Edwards wrote him on April 26, 1950, "We are sorry that you have had another ghastly period and you may rest assured we will do all we can to assist in the speedy finish of *Othello*." They had been appeased somewhat by the payment of 250 pounds that Welles had extracted for them from his London backers. However, there was still the question of full compensation for all the time they had put in and the sacrifices they had made. Edwards wrote on August 30, 1950.

Leaving aside your casting Micheal in [an] important part, which I assure you we appreciate, and leaving aside, too, our mutual feelings towards each other, and dealing on a purely business basis (after all we are all pros and ultimately do what we do not only for our health) I think one should remember this: Micheal has worked and waited and abandoned three lengthy seasons at the various theaters here on your advice, and in the belief that the continuance of the film after the finishing date originally suggested by you (July last) would be compensated for by the fact that he was earning his salary all the time. . . . weeks during which he has been on actual location, and is to receive no salary for the intermediate weeks when he has been waiting in Paris or St. Paul or here in Dublin.

The fact was that the partners were now desperate for money. Their household and theater expenses had accumulated; they had exhausted their savings and mortgaged their home, and they still needed 2,000 pounds at once to prevent the collapse of their organization and the seizure of their furniture by the bailiffs. They had reached the end of their tether: they had almost ruined themselves for Orson Welles.

Even their travel expenses had not been properly reimbursed. They informed Welles that they could not possibly proceed to work again unless they had some money. On September 23 Welles wrote them from Rome:

This is to officially acknowledge receipt of your request for the sum of 2,000 pounds as a minimum advance against what is owed you for your respective services in the film *Othello*. I am now in the position to assure you of payment of the equivalent of this money, or better, on or about July 20th of this year. The remainder should be forthcoming soon after this period.

But it was not. The partners would have to wait a minimum of three months before they were recompensed. Indeed, they had no assurance that they would ever be paid for the months they had sat around waiting, with their work in Dublin at a standstill.

Finally Welles simply patched together what footage he had and temporarily called it a day on *Othello*. Instead of paying the partners and undertaking *Carmilla*—a more commercial prospect because of the public's perennial interest in horror films—Welles went off on yet another tangent. He embarked on a repertory theater potpourri in Paris, *Time Runs*, with backing from the producer Jerry Laven. And he began desultorily editing *Othello* again.

Time Runs, presented in English at the Théâtre Edouard VII under the auspices of the Compagnie des Pléiades, was very strange indeed, a remarkable example of indulgence on the part of the theater's directors, Pierre Beteille and Serge Greffet. Hilton Edwards played Mephistopheles in a modernized, extremely clumsy version of Marlowe's *Doctor Faustus*, reworked from the 1937 Mercury Theater production and supplemented by passages written by Welles, who played Faustus. Eartha Kitt, an up-and-coming young actress and singer, was cast bizarrely as the beautiful Helen of Troy. The second half of the evening was a play by Welles of execrable quality, *The Unthinking Lobster*, about a female saint who appears unexpectedly in a corrupt Hollywood; Suzanne Cloutier starred. Duke Ellington's music was under the direction of Sam Matlowsky, whose wife, Janet Wolfe, worked as Welles's secretary. *Time Runs* was postponed according to Welles's wont again and again; there were last-minute delays because of problems with stagehands, lighting people and costumers, and Welles's procrastinations. The production proved to be something of a disaster all around. Few Parisians understood English, and the theater was almost empty at several performances. Suzanne Cloutier, who as a French Canadian spoke French, had to use English in the part of the saint in Hollywood.

There were plans for Welles to go to London to try to recoup the losses on the production with a British version, but they evaporated quickly. MacLiammoir did his best, but the hopelessly haphazard character of the production, together with widespread comment on Welles's misbehavior in his financial dealings with Edwards and MacLiammoir, discouraged potential backers. Grasping at straws, Welles planned a tour of Germany. He would drop *The Unthinking Lobster* and rewrite the Faustus play for German audiences, casting himself once more as Faust and MacLiammoir (instead of Edwards) as Mephistopheles. Again the music would be by Duke Ellington, and Welles would add a drastically condensed and bowdlerized version of Oscar Wilde's *The Importance of Being Earnest*. MacLiammoir would play Algernon, and Lee Zimmer, a New York actor, would play the butler; the character of Lady Bracknell, the mainstay of the play, was eliminated along with most of Wilde's brilliant lines. The result, a forty-five-minute version of the play, was the aesthetic equivalent of a

Reader's Digest condensed book. To fill out the program, Welles would follow the Wilde play with a lecture on Life, and Eartha Kitt, whom gossips linked romantically to Welles, would sing torch songs in several languages. It was even thought that scenes from *Othello* and *Julius Caesar* should be included. This mishmash, performed entirely in English, was supposed to appeal to a Germany in which the teaching of English had been largely forbidden during World War II.

The collaborators in the fiasco rehearsed all day at the Théâtre Edouard VII, then played a regular performance at night. Somehow Edwards and MacLiammoir squeezed in preparations and rehearsals for a new version of *Richard II*, to be given in Dublin the following season. By late July, Welles's health had given out completely and he lay tortured, gasping, and naked in bed in his producer's apartment in Passy, smoking cigars against doctor's orders and downing an alarming succession of gin fizzes; while the combination of gin, sugar, lemon juice, and soda might have been helpful if he had had a cold, it was virtually useless in his present state of exhaustion and nervous breakdown.

In his bedridden condition, Welles informed MacLiammoir and Hilton that he was "canceling the tent scene from *Julius Caesar* and the jealousy scenes from *Othello*" and would instead add the finale from *Henry VI*, in which the hunchback duke of Gloucester (later Richard III) murders the king in a prison. Welles would play Gloucester, MacLiammoir would be Henry. The sight of the naked Welles—like a beached white whale, a mass of quivering blubber—reciting speeches through several days' of stubble and a Havana cigar was almost too much even for his admirers. From MacLiammoir's point of view, the problem with the scene (apart from the fact that it lent itself to far different actors) was that it left him lying on the floor with a fatal wound while Welles as Gloucester delivered a seemingly interminable speech. Welles said he would also add magic tricks to the evening (MacLiammoir would introduce him), and he began conjuring up visions of handkerchief tricks, card tricks, watch tricks, money tricks, and even dog and rabbit tricks. "Orson, are you out of your mind?" MacLiammoir asked. Welles bellowed back, "Of *course* I am, didn't you *know*?" And Eartha Kitt was to moan her Ellington torch songs in the middle of the magic scene.

The muddled rehearsals continued, first without Welles until he recovered, then with him. He tottered exhaustedly around the stage and tried on a hump for Gloucester that he had made himself and that looked rather like the kind to be found on a camel. Everyone laughed, but he refused to change it. The "limited run" at the Théâtre Edouard

VII ended on August 4, when everyone had left Paris for the summer vacation season, and the company trailed off to Germany in a caravan of cars.

The tour began in Frankfurt with a disaster. The advance man had announced in garish posters all over town that Welles would be appearing in *Faust*, not the *Doctor Faustus* of Marlowe and Welles but the *Faust* of the German literary hero, Goethe. At an elaborate press conference at the American Club, Welles broke the news that "not Goethe but Welles is the author of *Faust*"—a statement that made matters worse, for the press announced that Welles was usurping the authorship of Germany's favorite play. Since some of the luggage and props were missing on arrival, members of the company were hysterical.

The production opened in Frankfurt as *Time Runs* on August 7, 1950. There were full houses, many audiences consisting of students and children, most of whom brought with them Goethe's *Faust* and turned the pages during the performance, shining their flashlights in the dark and talking loudly about what had been done to the masterwork. When Eartha Kitt sang, "Now Satan got lonely way down in the pit/So he grabbed Doctor Faustus and put him on a spit," the audience wondered whether it had wandered into an insane asylum. However, the Germans loved *The Importance of Being Earnest* even though they could have understood only a few of the words, and they cheered the final scene of *Henry VI* and Welles's magic tricks. The strange evening was rendered stranger by the fact that the theater was a converted circus building with wooden walls and every line uttered from the stage was heard in echo by players and audience. Fortunately, nobody in the crowd knew that Welles despised Goethe.

Many of the performances were very bad indeed. The show moved on to Hamburg, a city heavily bombed during the war, where it played until August 19, then proceeded to Munich. Welles found himself totally at odds with Germany and the Germans, though he continued to have receptive audiences. In a later article in the London magazine *The Fortnightly*, "Thoughts on Germany" (1951), he revived a theme from his columns in *The New York Post* and *Free World*, attacking the reconstitution of Nazism in Germany and the West's encouragement of fascism as the only possible opposition to communism. He wrote of Munich, which he had not seen since his visit in 1929:

> Considering everything, there's quite a lot of Munich left: most of the phony Gothic and some of the real baroque. . . . At eleven sharp each morning, the clock-work dancers, painted like toys,

wheel bravely in the Rat House tower and the niche above, the knights joust on schedule before their nodding iron king. You have to remind yourself that this is the city where both the Nazis and the Dadaists wrote their opening manifestos.

Welles was struck by the fact that Germans still had a superman complex and still wanted to dress up in uniforms; he was concerned that the Western powers were planning to rearm Germany against Russia. "We all know about [the German's] bloodlust, his death wish and his marvelous sentimental capacity for keeping the festival of Christmas; and let's be frank about it: we're sick to death of him." He included in the article a bitter attack on the British as well, inappropriately comparing them to the Germans.

He likened the endless discussions by Germans about Germany to "patients in a sanitorium discussing their ailments. . . . The self-loathing is a hangover." He was struck by the stale renditions of American hit tunes in the nightclubs, the drabness of the Occupation, the continuing hunger for Nazism, the "numbing sort of experience" of his journey through a country he disliked intensely. He read himself to sleep each night with the historian Tacitus, who had written about the ancient German provinces. "Germans don't seem to have changed much between Roman and allied occupations. And the solemn consternation of Signor Tacitus on such a matter as the practical chastity of German wives indicates that Mediterranian reactions have not been subject to much alteration either."

At the end of August, Welles conceived the idea of making short films of the Wilde play and the Shakespeare in a studio near Munich. The scenes were shot during the night on August 30 and 31; no trace of them seems to have survived (Welles was unhappy with the quality of the local camera crews and equipment). The company proceeded through Cologne to Dusseldorf, enduring the dreary parties the Occupation forces gave in their honor. They went to Bad Oynhausen for one performance, then on to Berlin, where they stayed at Harnack House, an American army hostelry in a handsome park outside the city. Welles was furious that he could not have coffee served in his room in the morning.

Soon after his arrival in Berlin, Welles took a walk through the ruins of the city and was horrified at the extent of the desolation. He wrote in *The Fortnightly*:

It was as if some nervous and rather vulgar god-builder had been called away suddenly from work, leaving his studio a mass of half-carved forms, the floor scattered with chips; from the echoing insides of what was once a proud commercial edifice, I heard the plaintive, piping cries of young children at play. . . . I may have imagined it, but they did really seem to be playing soldiers.

Berlin focused for Welles the lifelong horror of fascism that had animated him in his work and justified its excesses. He was edgy about fascism redivivus and the presence of communism in Berlin. He told MacLiammoir that he was still on blacklists both in America and in Europe because he had signed certain protests and manifestos. Mac-Liammoir wrote in his diary that Welles was "a disappointed capitalist who could correctly be described as feudal, if his attitude towards his employees was anything to go by." Welles sulked.

The tour ended in Berlin; Welles abandoned plans for an Italian excursion with the show and rescheduled it for Brussels. He now needed ten more days of work on *Othello* to finish the movie. He wanted to shoot in Perugia, but how was he to find the money? The tour had met its expenses, yet the profits were meager. MacLiammoir and Edwards returned to Dublin, and there was another struggle over the payments due them. On September 30 Edwards wrote to remind Welles that their bank and income tax people had been held at bay for months and that now "the bank had stopped all payments and a writ of attachment on our personal belongings was to be issued in 14 days." The couple were living from hand to mouth on the $800 paid them in Frankfurt by the producers of the Paris production; when that ran out, there would be nothing left. They were aggravated to hear that Welles had been asked to do *Othello* on the London stage, and they suggested that he at least arrange for that long-owed 2,000 pounds to be advanced from his salary to keep them from losing their furniture. Welles's response was to summon them to Rome to continue work on *Othello*.

In November the movie ground into action again, the partners having somehow fended off the bailiffs with further promises. Incredibly, everybody returned to Venice for the fourth time to shoot the pickups. A blissfully unregenerate Welles still did not pay his Irish friends, and only when they threatened a lawsuit did they receive enough money to protect their belongings.

Preparations were under way in late 1950 for the next year's Festival of Britain, an elaborate spectacle to compensate for Britain's recovery from the war. England was still in bad shape, gray, dirty, and shabby in the wake of the conflict, with rationing and long lines of people outside every store. London at the time was one of the most depressing cities on earth. But somehow the government dragged enough money from its coffers to build an ugly, airplane hangar-like Festival Hall on the south bank of the Thames, and it was in connection with this event that Welles was asked to stage *Othello* at the St. James Theater. Sir Laurence Olivier made the basic arrangements; the production would run for six weeks.

Despite his alleged disdain for the British, Welles had admirers in London. When he moved there he was surrounded day and night by fans who followed his every action. With the film of *Othello* more or less finished and his great opportunity ahead, he suddenly resumed the buoyant spirits of a few years earlier, and his health improved. The problem was that physically he was so out of shape that he lacked the breath control and the stamina needed for the sustained performance that the play demanded. Olivier, who was producing, was encouraging, and clearly Welles was grateful to him for his support. The supporting cast was strong: to MacLiammoir's disappointment, Peter Finch, the handsome Australian actor, a protégé of Olivier, was cast as Iago; Maxine Audley was Emilia, and Gudrun Ure was Desdemona. One night during the strangling scene Welles became carried away and almost knocked out Gudrun Ure by banging her head on the base of the bed.

Among those he met during the period of preparation for playing Othello was a gaunt, painfully thin, yellow-skinned youth named Kenneth Tynan, who had recently come down from Oxford and had begun to make his mark as a highly affected, sharply intelligent, and verbose young critic. He wore Edwardian suits and flowing canary-yellow ties, trying to look as much as possible like an aesthete. He fastened himself onto Welles, who generously dashed off an introduction to Tynan's first book of collected criticism, *He That Plays the King*. Now that Welles was thirty-six, he felt the need for younger acolytes, and in Tynan (whose stammer must have reminded Welles of his brother, still adrift in America) he discovered a fine-grained intelligence and liberal views that echoed his own—a perfect camp follower. Tynan was extremely tough under his effete surface; he and his wife, the actress and author Elaine Dundy, were ferocious combatants in their quarrels at their flat in Hyde Park Gardens, where Welles was a visitor.

Welles toured *Othello* in Manchester and Newcastle before opening in London on October 18, 1951. The reviews were somewhat mixed. Tynan, whom Welles now compared to Iago, wrote wickedly in *The Evening Standard* ("Citizen Coon"), "No doubt about it, Orson Welles has the courage of his restrictions." Sportingly, Welles remained friendly with Tynan; he at least had the strength of character for that.

At a midnight matinee at the London Coliseum, Welles performed his magic act before Princess Elizabeth, today Queen Elizabeth, and the duke of Edinburgh. He introduced his act by addressing the royal box. "I have just come from the St. James Theater, where I have been murdering Desdemona—or Shakespeare, according to which newspaper you read!" The princess and her consort were amused; soon after, Princess Margaret twice attended Welles's performance in *Othello*, and she went backstage to congratulate him.

Welles was always adding unpredictable bits of business to the production. On one occasion, in the scene in which Othello throws money at Emilia, the coins whizzed past her face and into the wings. On another, he threw the heavy gold coins into her face, making her cry out in agony—and her face was swollen for a week afterward. At another time, Welles staged an attack of epilepsy, a grand mal seizure, during a confrontation with Peter Finch as Iago. "Couldn't you have rehearsed it with me?" Finch asked. Orson replied, "How can you rehearse epilepsy?"

Welles embarked now on a radio series for the BBC, backed by S. A. Gorlinsky, the co-presenter with Sir Laurence Olivier of *Othello*. *The Adventures of Harry Line*, produced by Harry Alan Towers, was based on the character Welles played in *The Third Man*. He undertook the job in order to finance the completion of *Othello*, and although there is no documented proof—and MacLiammoir later denied it—it is possible that Welles finally paid his Dublin friends out of his fees for this thoroughly routine series. He went on to appear as host of *The Black Museum*, a series of radio versions of famous murder cases, based on the Scotland Yard museum. He also acted Moriarty in Harry Alan Towers's BBC production of *Sherlock Holmes*, in which Sir John Gielgud played Holmes and Sir Ralph Richardson was Dr. Watson.

The inexhaustible Welles went to Ireland in January 1952 to appear briefly in the prologue of Hilton Edwards's film *Return to Glenascaul*, a ghost story about a disappearing girl. The introduction showed Welles rehearsing *Othello* in London in shadowy images that clearly reflect his own style, then journeying by automobile into the Irish countryside. He stops to help a driver whose car's distributor is out of action. Referring to his problems with the people who handle his films in Europe, Welles tells the stranded driver, "I've also had trouble with my distributor!" Appearing in the picture free of charge was perhaps a way of repaying his friends.

He returned to London to complete the editing of the film of

Othello. He had planned to take the play to New York, but he was suffering with voice-box problems and had to cancel the trip. He took the film to Paris and began cutting it in seclusion, working night after night in order to have the film ready for the Cannes Film Festival in the spring of 1952. Disjointed, sometimes confused, drastically uneven, the movie still bore the stamp of his individual talent. In Welles's version of the tragedy, Othello is a noble human being doomed by the repressed and sexually impotent Iago, who dreads and hates his power. The movie is continually exciting; Welles's familiar theme of the destructiveness of ambition and the lust for power is persuasively conveyed in images of considerable force. The opening is remarkable: a shot of Othello's face, frozen in death, as he is laid out for an elaborate funerary procession and carried by pallbearers across the battlements of a castle against a sky full of cumulus clouds. It is clear, as Alexandre Trauner said, that the influence here is Eisenstein rather than (as in *Citizen Kane* and *The Lady from Shanghai*) the German UFA school. Othello's speech to the senate is admirably done; the duologues between Iago and Roderigo, counterpointed with Othello's making love to Desdemona, are aptly realized. Best of all is the superb sequence of the arrival of Othello's ship, its shadow cast ahead of it on the white wharf of Mogador, the gale whipping the cloaks and flags under a sky drenched in sunlight.

Throughout the picture the camera is brilliantly free; the movie is staged largely in daylight, in the glittering light of Morocco and in the subdued, shadowy, echoing canals and arches of Venice. The speech "Farewell to tranquil mind" is excitingly brought off, spoken by Othello as the rigging of the ships dissolves and dissolves again in a dazzling complex sequence of images and the sun beats down. Exciting too are the sequence in which Iago is raised in the cage to the top of the tower wall and the steambath episode, accompanied by the sound of mandolins, where the thrust of a sword through floor boards ironically echoes Othello's virility and Iago's impotence.

At Cannes the film created a sensation. The audience went mad, cheering and cheering again, and the jury awarded *Othello* the Grand Prix, shared with a British movie, *Twopenny Worth of Hope*. Welles was elated. Whatever doubts he may have had during the editing, whatever pain he may have suffered from the reviews of his stage *Othello*, all had disappeared completely.

Welles spent the next two years in almost ceaseless travel. In France he played Benjamin Franklin, friend, as we know, of his great-great-grandfather William Hill Wells, in *Royal Affairs of Versailles* for the director-actor Sacha Guitry; in Italy he appeared in *Man, Beast, and Virtue* as the beast; in England he turned up in the lifeless *Trent's Last Case* for Herbert Wilcox, who with his wife, the actress Anna Neagle, had been supportive during the period when Welles thought *Citizen Kane* would never be released. *Trent's Last Case* contains a mischievous and quite inexcusable private joke that wrecks whatever reality the film may have had. Playing the evil millionaire Sigsbee Manderson (a figure reminiscent of Ivar Krueger, the match king, whose suicide in the 1930s threw the financial world into an uproar), Welles talks of seeing the production of *Othello* at the St. James Theater: "Ah, *Othello*. . . . Didn't like the leading actor much but got a big kick out of the play. Yessir, that Shakespeare knew something abut human nature, didn't he?"

Taking a leaf from Wilcox's book, Welles considered a very different version of the Krueger story, combined with that of the armaments millionaire Sir Basil Zaharoff, whose death had also caused shock waves. And there were echoes too of the Stavisky affair in France in the novel he then wrote as *X* and later called *Mr. Arkadin*—and in the film he would spin from it, *Confidential Report*. As producer of the picture, he found a keen backer in Louis Dolivet, the publisher of *Free World*, who had moved from New York and New England to Paris. Elements of *Citizen Kane* were retreaded in the novel and the film script, which was yet another essay on the excesses of power. It contained references to Welles's own life: when the reporter, like Thompson in *Kane*, is hired to discover the truth about the dead Gregory Arkadin, he learns that Arkadin had tried to hide the truth of his past from his daughter.

Welles was as erratic as ever in those days. In July 1952, having abandoned his own plans for *Julius Caesar* as a film, he was nevertheless upset to hear of John Houseman's intent to film *Julius Caesar* at MGM. Two weeks before the official starting date of the production, Welles sent Houseman a registered letter. Assuring him that he wished him only the best, he reminded Houseman of his own efforts to film *Julius Caesar*, claiming that MGM had interfered with his plans to do a modern-dress version in Mussolini's "fairground near Rome." He suggested that MGM should postpone its production, that it should compensate him for his loss, or that he should be allowed to work with Houseman and MGM on the picture. A fourth possibility was that each would go ahead with his own version. Welles strongly hinted that Houseman should hire him to direct it in Hollywood.

Houseman replied with great dignity. He pointed out that he had begun his project without "the slightest inkling" that Welles was contemplating *Caesar*. By the time an announcement of Welles's plans had appeared in *Variety,* Joseph Mankiewicz (Herman's brother) had already cast John Gielgud and would direct the film himself. Houseman said he would love to work with Welles again. But MGM got tough with Welles and refused to do anything; they would not pay Welles off, nor would they help him to make his own film version, which would compete with theirs. Even though William Randolph Hearst's friend Louis B. Mayer had left MGM and the middle-of-the-road Dore Schary was now in charge, the feeling in Hollywood against Welles was as strong as ever. Despite its acclaim at Cannes, *Othello* was not doing well in the international market, and since Hollywood judged people by their commercial power (and, at that time, by their political respectability), Welles was in trouble and no one was interested in his returning to California. He desultorily scribbled a feeble satire on the "Coca-Colonization" of Europe, the novel *Une grosse légume (A Big Vegetable)*, published in Paris in July 1953.

Welles was no less erratic in his dealings with the British director and stage producer Peter Brook, who was preparing an elaborate avant-garde production of *Salome,* to be costumed by Salvador Dali. Brook asked Welles to play Herod, and he agreed at once; they talked about their plans on the boat train from Ostend to England, but Welles never followed through, and the opportunity slipped away. When Welles met Brook some months later, they began making other plans, but those plans too were disrupted by Welles's unreliability. Bids were made for him to appear in the movie *The Killer Is Loose* for Darryl F. Zanuck at 20th Century–Fox, the story of a policeman who accidentally kills a criminal's wife while trying to nail her husband; again, Welles's constant moving about made it impossible to go ahead with his casting in the picture.

Welles called Peter Brook and said they should do *King Lear* together. By coincidence, Brook had received an offer from the Ford *Omnibus* television program to produce a prestigious Shakespearean production, and he decided to present the play in a seventy-three-minute version with Welles as Lear. However, knowing how thoughtless Welles was about keeping appointments, and aware that Welles was now planning *Confidential Report,* temporarily called *Masquerade,* Brook insisted that Welles be on time for the first rehearsal in New York. Welles never confirmed that he would be there, and Brook was unable to reach him. Welles was then laying out locations for *Confidential Report* and casting it (for a November 1953 start) with Robert Arden, star of *Guys and Dolls* in London; Welles's new girl friend, Countess Paola Mori Di Girfalco, whom he sent to Dublin to train with MacLiammoir; Michael Redgrave; and Akim Tamiroff. The Ford organization became increasingly annoyed as it pursued Welles from London to Paris to Rome and then lost track of him. Yet Welles turned up on schedule on an icy morning in November, wearing a huge hat, a cigar stuck in his mouth. Without drawing breath, he broke free of the newspaper reporters and said to Brook, "Let's eat, and I'll tell you how I think Lear should be played!"

Welles worked around the clock, admiring of Brook and enjoying the challenge of what he felt to be Shakespeare's greatest play. The rehearsals took place at Caravan Hall on East Fifty-ninth Street, where he met with Virgil Thomson and worked with him on the score. And he resumed his professional relationship with Micheal MacLiammoir, who appeared as Edgar. Val Adams of *The New York Times* described a scene at rehearsals.

> MacLiammoir grabbed Mr. Welles's jacket and smashed a cigar in its pocket. Mr. Welles pulled the broken cigar from his pocket and waved it around. "There goes sixty-five cents," he said, turning quickly from the demented to the disconsolate. "I'm in no position to afford that." He removed the other cigars and placed them in a safe retreat on the sidelines. During the afternoon, the most trying moment for Mr. Welles seemed to occur when he was not in a scene being rehearsed. He sat on the sidelines looking a little tired, a little forlorn. Sometimes he watched the rehearsal disinterestedly, and at other moments stared into space. To relieve his idleness, he shuffled back and forth across one end of the hall, like a prison inmate serving a sentence.

Welles told the columnist Earl Wilson why he had stayed in Europe since 1948. "I wanted to come back, but it sort of stretched out. It wasn't my back taxes. You can't hide from that. I've whittled mine down, and in a year I hope to be about at the end."

He was in fact allegedly in trouble with the I.R.S., having been refused when he asked whether the losses on *Around the World* could be charged as a tax deduction. He also escaped the blacklist in Hollywood; he was appalled in absentia by how many liberals in California betrayed their fellows by naming names in order to keep their swimming pools.

He suffered from an infected throat and a vocal exhaustion that dogged him, yet he was filled with energy and vitality. He told a *New Yorker* reporter he "wanted to find out something about television here. I've never seen an American television show. Television is the one thing this country can't export to Europe. In every other way, America is so deeply involved in Europe that you don't feel cut off there."

He told the reporter that in addition to *A Big Vegetable* and *Mr. Arkadin,* he had written a book about Noah, *Two by Two.* He was now working on a nonfiction book about international organizations; it dealt with the world conspiracy of money, a consuming theme of liberals everywhere. He said he found New York little changed, unlike sad, postwar Europe; Manhattan offered an "incredible combination of friendliness and impersonality. People here like everybody, but they don't particularly like *you.*" He observed that the telephone operator at his hotel called him Honey, which meant nothing, for she had never met him. But he was amazed that telephone operators in New York were in a good humor, for no telephone operator in Europe was.

The production of *King Lear* was a great success, and it garnered Welles his best reviews in years. To celebrate, he went on a nightclub binge, eating and drinking colossally for days on end. At 275 pounds he was handicapped by dimensions that made him the butt of columnists. He returned to Europe to continue his relationship with Paola Mori, who had returned from Ireland, and to go on with *Confidential Report.* In England that August he worked on a bizarre ballet, *The Lady in the Ice.*

The Lady in the Ice was scored by Jean-Michel Demase, choreographed by Roland Petit, with decor and costumes by Welles. The ballet was presented at the Stoll Theater on September 7, 1953, and starred Colette Marchand, George Reich, and Joe Milan. Welles described the ballet as "a kind of parable, showing that two people are never in love with each other to the same degree at the same time." The setting is a fair; a group of people are standing outside a fairground booth, listening to the barker announcing the lady in the ice, who is inside the booth; the crowd enters, to see Colette Marchand in her ice block. A young man is fascinated by her and returns later to release her as the ice melts. But he in turn is bewitched into the ice.

Welles dressed a ragged collection of fairground loafers and provided a realistic booth with brown Hessian curtains decorated with prehistoric cave drawings; inside, the crimson pillar that folded up to reveal the ice block was strongly effective, and through Welles's wizardry, developed through the magic shows, Mademoiselle Marchand appeared to be actually frozen in it.

Welles lectured at the British Film Institute's summer film school, telling Denis Forman, the institute's chairman, "Let me say that I think movies are dying, dying, dying. I do not think they are going to stay dead for long. I think they are like the theater, the theater is dying all the time, but it never dies altogether. It is like the cycle of the seasons—it has its summer, autumn, and winter. Now the movies are in the autumn of the cycle." He could be forgiven this view since he was then appearing in a film that certainly bore it out, *Three Cases of Murder*, a feeble melodrama shot in Britain that fall. He attacked television despite his recent success in the medium: "The technical excellence of the images in that Punch and Judy set, television, is about as bad as a picture of a Chinese play where they bring on a chair and tell you that it is a mountain."

Welles also appeared that fall in Sacha Guitry's *Napoleon* as Napoleon's jailer, Hudson Lowe. Others in the star-studded cast were Michèle Morgan, Jean Gabin, and Patachou. It was a magnificent production, and Welles told the novelist André Maurois that it could not fail to be a triumph:

> There are very few sure-fire subjects. Napoleon is one of them. You can always write a life of Napoleon or a life of Jesus and find a hundred thousand readers. An American publisher once told me, "I only know two types of book that really sell: the life of Lincoln and the biography of a dog." He got one of his authors to write *Lincoln's Dog*. It sold a million copies.

Again Welles found Guitry fascinating; aged, suffering from a nearly total paralysis, having to be carried about the set on a sedan chair, the great French director and actor seemed to have almost superhuman creative energy. In December, Welles was present in Paris at the premiere of *Royal Affairs of Versailles*, a magnificent occasion at the Opéra, with detachments of the Republican Guard lining the great stairway and a crowd storming the foyer. The picture was a hit, as it deserved to be, and the entire profit on the film went to the reconstruction of the palace of Versailles. Welles never lost his admiration for Guitry.

Welles spent most of 1954 completing *Confidential Report*. He crossed and recrossed Europe, raising money from many disparate sources in his effort to sustain a difficult and complex work. The bulk of the shooting was done in Spain, the picture having some backing from a Spanish financial group. The cast achieved powerful vignettes: the Russian-American comedian Mischa Auer played a flea circus proprietor in a memorable grotesque scene; the Greek actress Katina Paxinou emerged as a fierce gang leader; and Suzanne Flon, a French actress of distinction, was remarkable as a world-weary aristocrat. As always, the performers gave of their best to Welles. The most interesting aspect of the picture once again reflected Welles's concern with Nazism and proved to be not only topical but prophetic, for, like *The Stranger*, it looked forward to the Klaus Barbie case of the 1980s. Patricia Medina (later Mrs. Joseph Cotten) played the part of Mily, a drunken woman who discusses Arkadin's past rather in the manner of the drunken Susan Kane; she reveals that Arkadin helped the Nazi cause during World War II by shipping a number of Nazi war criminals to South America to secure their safety in the era of anti-communism.

Individual scenes were powerful, and in many ways *Confidential Report* broke free from the restraints that the studio had clamped on *Citizen Kane*, enabling Welles to release his strong personal feelings against fascism in a freer, less schematic form. However, the cohesive force that would have bound the picture together was lacking; the shooting over eight months in all weathers with a scratch crew, often using actual interiors, and the cast arriving on random schedules from all over the map, proved to be the picture's undoing. Welles said that *Confidential Report* was ruined by the distributors, Warner Brothers, who he claimed cut it to ribbons in Europe; his producer, Louis Dolivet, thought differently and sued Welles for more than $700,000 for drunken behavior and for not delivering the picture he promised. The case dragged on ruinously for years.

Like *Othello* before it, *Confidential Report* had a bumpy passage at the box office. If Marlene Dietrich, who was still a potent attraction at the time, had played the role of the exiled baroness, it might have saved the picture. Even Welles's name as Arkadin could not rescue it. Whatever may have been done to the movie in the cutting room, it was simply too grotesque, too bizarre, too specialized, and too unpopular in its theme to attract the mass public Welles so badly needed.

He completed shooting the picture in Spain in the late summer of 1954 and started cutting it for the film festival in Venice, where the Spanish committee on selections had designated it to represent that country. The film had to be completed before midnight, September 2.

He developed the rushes in a French laboratory—a fatal mistake as it turned out, because he had to have an authorization for every foot of film arriving from Spain. Customs officials spent hours stamping the beginning and end of each roll of film or sound tape. (He had suffered similar problems with red tape during the actual shooting.) Welles did not help his relationship with Louis Dolivet when he announced in the magazine *Film Culture* in January 1955 that he had been handicapped by his producer; nor did he help matters by alleging that French officials had been responsible for his not getting the picture into the Venice Film Festival. Had he cut the picture in Madrid, where excellent facilities were available, none of these problems would have arisen.

The pathetic results of *Confidential Report*'s release put Welles in a black mood, and the movie was not shown in the United States until 1962. Nevertheless he began laying plans for *Don Quixote* to be made in Spain, and he completed an effective scene as Father Mapple in John Huston's striking version of *Moby Dick*.

For several months Huston and the writer Ray Bradbury, author of the *Moby Dick* script, had been preparing the scene of Father Mapple's famous sermon, which Huston had decided to shoot in a studio in London. Neither Bradbury nor Huston was completely satisfied with the final draft. Welles was in Paris that fall, licking his wounds over *Confidential Report*, and Huston flew there with the script and told Welles the Mapple scene was not absolutely perfect. Welles worked on it over a weekend, made it into a brilliant sequence, then flew to London for the three days of filming.

Tense and upset over *Confidential Report*, Welles was nervous about playing the scene for Huston. He took a hand in his own makeup as Father Mapple, telling Huston as he completed his face that he might fluff the difficult five-minute sermon. Climbing the ladder to the pulpit on the set of the New Bedford Church was an ordeal in his condition, and he feared that one of the ladder rungs might break under his nearly 300 pounds. Fortified with a bottle of brandy, he rehearsed the scene before the large congregation seated in the pews below. Just as he was about to begin his sermon he said, "John, I'm scared to death!" Huston assured him that he had three full days in which to be letter-perfect. Still trembling with fear, Welles retreated behind the pulpit; then he emerged, already beginning the sermon in a dry run before the other actors. Huston started the cameras rolling and asked Welles to begin the sermon again. Welles delivered it magnificently, and at the end, totally out of the context and character of the sequence, the cast stood and gave Welles an ovation. Shot in two perfect takes, it was probably the greatest acting tour de force of his career.

Welles was fired up by his triumph; returned to Paris, he planned a stage version of *Moby Dick*, to be done in the manner of a rehearsal, with little or no scenery, a presentation as spare and harsh as any he had managed at the Mercury in the 1930s. In February 1955 he found considerable support for this idea from the writer Wolf Mankowitz. Mankowitz was in France working on the screenplay of *Trapeze*, to be filmed by Sir Carol Reed, with Burt Lancaster and Tony Curtis. Mankowitz offered to help Welles set up *Moby Dick* in London and said he would make a deal for Welles to record some new programs for BBC television. Back in London, Mankowitz approached a number of major theatrical producers, who were not interested in Welles's venture; finally, he turned to Henry Margolis, a well-known entrepreneur, who was in partnership in New York with Welles's old Mercury colleague, the actor Martin Gabel.

While preparations went ahead for *Moby Dick*, Welles was in London, and there, on May 8, 1955, he married Paola Mori, countess Di Girfalco. Their relationship had deepened during the long and painful work on *Confidential Report* and its aftermath. Beautiful, intelligent, stylish, fascinating, Paola adored Orson passionately and worshiped his genius unreservedly. She understood him well; shortly before the marriage she told *The Daily Express:*

> I know what people say about him. Moody . . . erratic . . . difficult. . . . "Act with him," they said, "and you'll be sick in bed with liver trouble. He's impossible." Instead I am marrying the man. You see, I know how to cope with him. . . . It is not that Orson is abnormal—he is supernormal. The secret is finding out how normal he is underneath the super.

There was a secret, not known to the public, that bound the couple together as much as anything. Paola Mori's father had opposed Mussolini and Hitler, and the family had wound up in a concentration camp. There Paola had spent much of her childhood, suffering horribly; her hatred of Nazism and fascism in any form made her a woman after Welles's own heart. Moreover, she had a touch of the exotic: she had been born in an oasis in Tunisia, where her father was an official.

The marriage took place in Caxton Hall, the Registry Office in Westminster, just two days after Welles's fortieth birthday. Sleepless as always, he had gotten out of bed at 6:00 A.M. to rouse the municipal registrar. Despite the early hour, many reporters were present, and Welles managed to crinkle a smile at them and wave a plump hand.

Welles presented *Moby Dick°* at the Duke of York's Theater on June 16, 1955, at a cost of 1,895 pounds; his salary was a modest 200 pounds a week. He decided on a limited season without a provincial tour; he also filmed the production at the Hackney Empire and the Scala Theater in the West End. With a few packing cases and a tangle of fly ropes, Welles created theater magic. He also succeeded in acting so violently as Captain Ahab fighting the whale that he spat right in the eye of *The Daily Mirror*'s theater critic Fergus Cashin, who was seated

---

° Later renamed *Moby Dick Rehearsed.*

out front. According to the author Roy Moseley, Marlene Dietrich walked out of her box within minutes of the play's outset, exclaiming "Rubbish!" But few agreed with her. Kenneth Tynan threw out an excess of superlatives.

Among the dissenting voices was the critic for *The Times* of London, who began his review, "The theater, for Mr. Orson Welles, is an adventure; and to an adventurer so valiant our hearts go out even when he comes to wreck." Saying that "everything is against [Welles], Melville's language, which he tries in vain to versify, the symbols which lose their way amid the traffic of the stage, the absence of Melville's sea and the absence of the whale," the anonymous critic added, "Yet for a while, for something like half the performance, he succeeds against all reasonable expectation." The reviewer concluded that ultimately the "madly impossible stage representation" fell apart, that in the second half "the temperature falls and Mr. Welles's adventure is clearly making for the rocks. . . . It is like nursery heroics taken altogether too seriously." As for Welles's performance, "He has an impressive voice and an impressive face, but neither the voice nor the face is particularly expressive." That review was a far remove from Kenneth Tynan's hyperbolic claim that *Moby Dick* was "a sustained assault on the senses which dwarfs anything London has seen since, perhaps, the Great Fire." Those who saw the production still recall it as a vivid evocation, through the use of light and shadow, of Melville's world; the ropes and spars of the otherwise empty stage were converted by Welles into the very atmosphere of a Massachusetts seaport.

An unpleasant incident occurred during the three-and-a-half-week run. Welles was told one night that a group of his friends was gathered at the Caprice, a popular nightspot near Piccadilly, for a late supper after the show. He arrived close to midnight with his usual entourage and noticed that Brenda Forbes, who had been in the Mercury, was there; he also observed John Houseman, now portly, though not as heavy as Welles. Yelling, "Jacko!" Welles embraced Houseman and whirled him around the dance floor in a surprising display of affection. Houseman and his wife joined Welles at his table, and, imbibing champagne, the two men relived their epic excitements and adventures of the thirties. After 1:00 A.M. Houseman felt he had to go and Welles became extremely tense; according to Houseman, Welles hated "departures and leave-takings that were not initiated by himself." In an effort to appease his former colleague, Houseman said he was sure they would see each other soon because he was anxious to attend a performance of *Moby Dick*. And then Houseman made a gaffe: he said he was not sure which night he could come because he was waiting to hear when he could attend a performance at Stratford-on-Avon of Laurence Olivier in *Macbeth*; he would have to go to *Moby Dick* on one of the other nights.

Welles slammed his fist on the table, making glasses shatter, and spoke with deadly viciousness, "It is more difficult to get seats for *Moby Dick* than it is for *Macbeth*!" Everyone in the Caprice stared in horror as he screamed, "For twenty years, you son of a bitch, you've been trying to humiliate and destroy me! You've never stopped, have you? And you're still at it!"As Welles went on ranting—"You'd better not stick your filthy nose in my theater! If you do, I'll come down off the stage and personally throw you out!"—Houseman and his wife left the nightclub. Houseman did not see Welles again for a quarter of a century, until an awkward appearance on *The Merv Griffin Show*.

There was talk of taking *Moby Dick* to Ireland—for the Gate Theater—and to the United States in the late summer of 1955, but the plans fell through; the results were distressing to Micheal MacLiammoir, who had set aside time for the production. Once more Welles and his Irish friends discussed by mail a Shakespearean presentation, but nothing was to come of this until 1960. In November 1955 Welles moved to New York on his way to Hollywood to make the picture *Pay the Devil*; in Manhattan's Polyclinic Hospital, Paola gave birth to Welles's third daughter, Beatrice. Rebecca had visited with him briefly in Italy just a month before.

Welles agreed to do a six-week season at the New York City Center in *King Lear* and *Volpone* by Ben Jonson. Henry Margolis and Martin Gabel were to present him. However, five British actors whom Welles wanted to appear in the two productions were forbidden temporary entry applications by the Department of Immigration; American actors would have to be cast instead. A resigned Welles cast Viveca Lindfors as Cordelia, Geraldine Fitzgerald as Goneril, and the Canadian actor John Colicos as Edmund. He hired Marc Blitzstein to compose the score and Jean Dalrymple to coordinate the production. Their presence to some extent compensated for his miserable $100 a week salary and the continuing problems that dogged rehearsals. He was broke and feeling depressed as he conducted the early rehearsals in his rooms at the Sulgrave Hotel.

The plans for *Volpone* were abandoned and further plans to do *Moby Dick* in New York were also given up. The first preview of *King Lear* at the City Center was marred by technical mishaps; when the actor Roy Dean, playing Kent, met Lear on the blasted heath with "such groans of roaring wind and rain I ne'er remember to have heard," the sound effects people failed to produce the wanted tempest.

Welles whispered in Dean's ear, "Who the hell do you think you're kidding?" It was all Dean could do not to burst out laughing.

At the second preview Welles, cumbersomely robed, fell off a platform backstage and broke his left ankle. When the play opened on January 12, 1956, he performed with the ankle in a cast. Following the show, he stumbled up a stairway and sprained his right ankle. Thus he had to play the remaining performances in a wheelchair. But many members of the audience fled the theater at the sight of him, and many more canceled when they heard of his plight.

Brooks Atkinson reviewed the performance on January 13. "To judge by the *King Lear* which opened at the City Center last evening, Orson Welles has more genius than talent." As a "theatrical conception," he said, the production was "massive and resonant." He talked of Welles's making full use of the City Center stage by mountng "an enormous show." He described the bold use of space, the daring absence of an intermission in a three-hour presentation, the stirring force of the presentation as a whole. Yet he charged that Welles did not "get inside the character of Lear, nor does his production get into the heart of the poem. His reverberant style of speaking, usually at the top of his voice, has the effect of throwing the lines away; and he also breaks the lines whimsically as though he were not much interested in their meaning."

The tendency to declaim—to recite rather than interpret the lines—was a failing that would later exasperate Atkinson's successor, Walter Kerr. Atkinson's conclusion was unfavorable: "Mr. Welles has a genius for the theater. It is fine to have him back again; and it is easy to appreciate the robustness of his attack on the problems of staging a fiery, Elizabethan drama. But the attack has left Shakespeare prostrate."

Atkinson returned to the subject on Sunday, according to *New York Times* tradition. In essence, he said that Welles's interpretation of the role suffered from superficiality, capriciousness, and the wrong kind of theatricality. Something clearly had happened since the fine and penetrating interpretation of *Lear* on television for *Omnibus* in 1953; some form of incapacity or capriciousness had affected Welles.

The aftermath of his relative failure was not merely the cancellation of the other plays that were to be presented in repertoire. It meant the loss of some $50,000. As a result of his injuries, an ambulance had to be kept in readiness for Welles during the entire run of the show (at a cost of one thousand dollars), and he had to have a secretary at all times and intermittently a nurse. Although he grossed $90,000 for twenty-seven performances, there were many empty seats after he began appearing in a suit in his wheelchair. In April he wrote MacLiammoir and Edwards, "My own theater season this winter (in New York) degenerated into a miserable three weeks . . . for which I received no money, no thanks, and no professional satisfaction. I hope and pray that your year was better than mine." In fact theirs had not been much better: a reasonably successful Egyptian tour of the Gate had been followed by the news that the pair were in receivership.

Welles proceeded in February to Las Vegas, where he opened a season of magic and clairvoyance at the Riviera Hotel's Clover Room. He suspended a stooge in midair and, unable to resist it, read Antony's oration at Caesar's funeral and the dying Lear's last speech. He offered a hypnosis trick, the random selection of phone numbers from a book by members of the audience (followed by his "correct" answers), the identification of playing cards, and so forth. The audience, largely composed of tourists, was delighted, and Welles enjoyed the Nevada gambling city.

In Hollywood he appeared in *Pay the Devil* (also called *Man in the Shadow*) for the director Jack Arnold and the producer Albert Zugsmith. He rewrote a script by Paul Monash from Whit Masterson's *Badge of Evil*, which he would ultimately call *Touch of Evil.* It was a return to the familiar theme of the corruptions of power, and it reflected the long-term fascination with Mexico that had inspired his unproduced *Mexican Melodrama.* In many ways the script was reminiscent of that earlier work, for it dealt with the investigations of a Mexican-American narcotics detective in the small town of Los Robles.

The project began when Zugsmith asked Welles to play the part of Hank Quinlan, the police chief in the picture. Welles agreed. Then Charlton Heston, cast as Vargas, the Mexican-American detective, told Zugsmith he was delighted that Welles would be directing the picture. Zugsmith had not thought of Welles as director, but he was anxious to please Heston and signed Welles for both tasks and as scenarist.

Welles wrote and rewrote the screenplay in the first weeks of 1957. He met with Heston on January 14 and liked him enormously; he knew that Heston had pushed his name with Universal, and he was grateful. He showed Heston his latest rewrite, and Heston wrote in his diary for January 21 that it "now lacks only good dialogue to make it a really meritable script."

Heston made suggestions for changes, and between January 22 and 26 Welles cut twenty-five pages from the screenplay. Janet Leigh was cast as Vargas's wife, and after considerable negotiation Marlene Dietrich was pinned down to play the black-wigged, tarot-card-reading Tanya, madam of the local brothel. An impatient and restless Welles plunged with drive and energy into the first days of preparation. Meanwhile, the Universal executives were becoming restive about Welles's plans to make an experimental movie, and he had to fight for the decent budget and freedom he demanded. Heston had the power to ensure him these from the beginning, and he was a loyal friend.

Welles took a house at 1027 Chevy Chase Drive in Beverly Hills and settled in for the late winter and spring of 1957. There he rehearsed his players and arranged for Heston to have both mustache and hair dyed deep black. Despite his recurring illnesses, he whipped his excited cast rapidly into shape, and February 18 he began the final rehearsal, leading to a prolonged sequence in an apartment. At 5:45 P.M. he started shooting, and by 7:40 A.M. he had shot twelve pages in one take, using three rooms and seven speaking parts, while studio executives hovered, alarmed that he had shot nothing. He was two days ahead of schedule.

The next day he shot a scene in which two cars moved along the streets of Venice, an oceanside slum of Los Angeles that was standing in for Los Robles; he mounted cameras on the car hoods in order to avoid the unrealistic look of back projection. Some scenes involving Dennis Weaver as a stammering hotel clerk echoed the character of Welles's brother Richard, who was wandering around the northwest of America, from one job to another. Shooting Marlene Dietrich in a cast-off wig of Elizabeth Taylor and an extraordinary array of costume jewelry was tremendous fun for Welles. On March 14 he brought off the most remarkable shot in the picture: beginning with a close-up of a time bomb in a car, the camera—guided by the crusty veteran Russell Metty—swung on a crane past houses covered in peeling posters and across a busy street, taking in groups of people and the hero and heroine, and came to a halt as the car burst into flames. In his diary Heston called it "the damnedest shot I've ever seen." It took all night to do it, and at dawn everyone went to bed in a state of excitement.

On March 18 the rain began to pour, and Welles, improvising with skill, seized the opportunity to shoot an amazing traveling shot through a hotel lobby, into an elevator filled with people, up two floors, and along a hallway without a single break. On March 25 Welles was shooting all night among the odd, praying mantis–like oil derricks of the California coast. Further scenes were shot in the Venice canals with their brackish water and patches of fungus and weed. The final day of filming, April 2, saw the final scene of the script, the death of Hank Quinlan on a rubbish heap; Welles and Heston took a magnum of champagne to a bacon-and-egg joint and sat down to celebrate.

Made expertly, brought off unerringly from first scene to last,

Touch of Evil is among the best of Welles's movies. As a portrait of hell in a small Mexican town, it is hard to rival. The evocation of the Grandi gang (a dope-peddling pack of hoodlums), of the lesbian hench-woman played by Mercedes McCambridge, of the kidnaping and hu-miliation of Janet Leigh as Susan Vargas, and above all of the death of Grandi, with Quinlan and the gang leader locked in a death struggle over a brass bed, create powerful moments in the Welles canon. In no other picture did he match the feverish intensity of the action or the extremity of the black humor. (Hank Quinlan growls to a hoodlum he has trapped, "An old lady on Main Street picked up a shoe. The shoe contained a foot. We're going to make you pay for that, boy.")

Touch of Evil looked forward to a world of increased violence and corruption and the drug-oriented culture that was to emerge in the 1960s. As always, Welles was ahead of his time. And as always, he was not content to rest with so fine an achievement as this. He was busy planning a science fiction story, and he was shooting bits and piece of *Don Quixote*, begun about a year earlier. *Don Quixote* starred Akim Tamiroff along with a Mexican actor, Francisco Reiguera, who held up Welles time and time again for money, and Patty McCormack. Welles was also planning to make a telefilm of *Don Quixote* in six days in Mexico City with Charlton Heston, but this plan fell through in July when Heston could not get a passport quickly enough to do the film before he left for locations on William Wyler's ambitious western *The Big Country*.

The studio chiefs were not happy with *Touch of Evil;* the movie was far removed from the conventional melodramas they were used to. While Welles waited for the inevitable interference, the cuts and revi-sions he had suffered before and that seemed to be inevitable in Holly-wood, he shot *The Long Hot Summer*, which was cobbled together from three Faulkner stories, produced by Jerry Wald, and directed by Martin Ritt. Ritt recalls that Welles was on his best behavior through-out except that he refused to memorize his lines. He claimed they could all be satisfactorily looped—recorded and synchronized to his lip movements—and Ritt reluctantly agreed, though he was shocked that Welles would not memorize comparatively simple speeches after mas-tering entire Shakespeare plays. As Will Varner, a red-neck southern plantation owner, Welles played with memorable grotesqueness, shouting and bellowing yet at the same time suggesting vulnerability. It was an intelligent performance, acted without compromise. He en-joyed the shooting but not the presence of Anthony Franciosa, a fierce and uptight Italian-American whose methods of approach to a part were alien to his own.

As Welles had feared, the studio tampered with *Touch of Evil*, though not perhaps as excessively as he was later to claim. So nervous was the production company that it released the movie without a preview; it was clearly afraid of what the reviews might say. In fact the critical reception for the picture was not what it should have been. Part of the trouble was that, although Welles had offered to do some retakes, the studio used a contract craftsman, Harry Keller. When Heston had tried to refuse to work with another director, he had been overruled. Welles offered to help on the picture's publicity, but by December 1957 it had become clear to him that nothing was going to be done about it.*

That same month saw the marriage of Welles's daughter Christopher to Norman R. De Haan, an architectural designer with the Container Corporation in Chicago. Following two years of school in Switzerland, Christopher had gone to work for Container. The wedding took place in Chicago. After a Mexican honeymoon, the De Haans set out for two years in Seoul, South Korea, where he had been assigned to direct a State Department project for the firm.

In early 1958 Welles went to France to match up scenes shot in Africa for John Huston's *The Roots of Heaven,* a story about ivory hunters. He was cast as Cy Sedgwick, an American television commentator who rather resembles the elephants he is writing about. When at one stage he talks haughtily about a pachyderm, the director fills the entire frame with his mountainous bottom, and the big-game hunter Trevor Howard fires into it. Welles undertook the film because he was desperate for money. He had borrowed more money from Darryl F. Zanuck, and again he had taken it to the gambling tables at Monaco and lost heavily; the only way he could repay Zanuck was by acting in a series of pictures for the minimum scale established by the Screen Actors' Guild.

Welles's financial position was as parlous as ever, and he turned to anything that would earn him a few dollars. He had largely spurned television since the 1953 *King Lear* for *Omnibus,* but now he was glad to have an offer from Desi Arnaz, who owned Desilu Productions with his wife, Lucille Ball. She wanted to work with Welles, for they had been good friends when they were at RKO. Ball told me that she and Arnaz offered Welles a chance to direct a pilot for a quality television series based on famous short stories that he would narrate and some-

---

* The film has been released in the 1980s, in a longer version, but unfortunately, while more of Welles's material is in it, there is also more of Keller's.

times direct. He selected "The Fountain of Youth" by John Collier, originally published in 1952 as "Youth from Vienna" in the collection *Fancies and Good Nights.* This was the story of an endocrinologist who has discovered a secret essence that can preserve youth for two hundred years. The same theme had been used in Barré Lyndon's *The Man in Half Moon Street,* which was made into a film in the 1940s at Paramount, and in William Frye's television thriller *A Wig for Miss Devore.* The actress Caroline Coates and the tennis star Alan Brodie are determined to sustain their youth and strength through the ages, but each cheats the other by not putting the potion in the other's drink.

The Fountain of Youth is one of Welles's most creative inventions, innovative, revolutionary, as fresh and striking in its visual style as anything he had ever done. He used a device that had been given a dry run in Laszlo Benedek's *Death of a Salesman* in 1951, enhancing it and adding touches of his own. In this approach, cutting from scene to scene was eliminated; when a character was discovered in a new situation, the background dissolved into darkness, then the light came up and a new scene was disclosed. Shifts of time were indicated by changes of light, yet another extension of a device he had used on the Mercury stage. Welles also used the original device of wandering through the narrative and commenting on the characters, thereby providing a cynical and detached form of observation that illuminated the characters and situations. As in *Ambersons,* Welles was concerned with the problems of human vanity and the passage of time, of the decline of human beings into old age. In one audacious sequence the scene shifts without cut or dissolve from a gossip columnist pronouncing a change of marriage plans for the star and the tennis player to the same pair in a New York restaurant and at a party celebrating her engagement to another man, all in a swift and startling development. At times Welles as narrator speaks the dialogue himself, and it issues from the lips of the characters. The vial that contains the elixir of youth is placed on the couple's mantlepiece, with the couple seen in silhouette as the vial glows with an unearthly brightness. Welles shows the couple watching each other for wrinkles and lines with an extreme intentness, and toward the end one of the most remarkable passages in all of Welles's work occurs.

As Caroline realizes that she has not been given the youth-preserving dose, she gazes into a mirror; her profile changes into that of an ugly old woman, then into a pathologist's picture of a head threaded through with veins, then into a skull. Welles narrates: "She could feel and almost hear the remorseless erasures of time. Moment after moment particles of skin wore away, hair follicles broke, splintered, all the little tubes and lines and thread-like chains of the inner organs were silted up like doomed rivers ... the glands, the all-important glands were choking ... clogging." The moment even surpasses that in which Welles as narrator, dwelling on the crumbling face of Major Amberson, talked of the Ambersons's decline. And it crystallizes Welles's second most burning concern after that of the hopelessness and misery of power: the inevitability of physical decay, the dissolution of the flesh, and the death that, now in his forties, he had begun to think about.

The Fountain of Youth suffered a fate as grim as that of its protagonists. Welles shocked Arnaz and Ball by taking a month to do the pilot, instead of the ten days he had been allowed. She told me that he spent more money on an elaborate party at the end of shooting than he should have and that "all the money went into the party and none went into the pilot." Apart from the unforgivable sin of running over budget and over schedule in tightfisted television, Welles had created a personal and poetic work that was far beyond the usual television audience's powers of receptivity. Once again he was an artist out of place in a factory. The Arnazes dumped the pilot and abandoned the series. *The Fountain of Youth* was finally shown amid a graveyard of unused pilots on *The Colgate Theater* on September 16, 1958. Despite the fact that it won a Peabody Award, it has never been seen on television again. The failure of *The Fountain of Youth* was widely noted in Hollywood, and it set the seal of Welles's failure as a television director in America.

A depressed Welles moved to England and made a special on bullfighting for *Tempo*, with a drawn-out Kenneth Tynan dragging behind Welles's vast bulk on a tour of the arenas of Spain; a BBC documentary on the Actors Studio, *The Method;* and a documentary on the Italian actress Gina Lollobrigida that the producers dropped out of dissatisfaction with the material. An artistic triumph, followed by commercial failure and a ragpicker's search for scraps of work: the pattern was typical of Welles's career.

In Hollywood again later in 1958, Welles made an impressive acting comeback at Darryl F. Zanuck's behest in *Compulsion*, directed by Richard Fleischer and based on the novel by Meyer Levin, a treatment of the famous Leopold-Loeb case of the 1920s (which had been the basis of Alfred Hitchcock's *Rope*). More frank than Hitchcock's version, Fleischer's film unhesitatingly spelled out the homosexual character of the two murderers who were its protagonists. Welles was impressed with the honesty of the writing and was flattered and pleased to be offered the part of the great trial lawyer Clarence Darrow, whose personality, though Welles almost certainly did not know it, strongly resembled that of his great-grandfather, Orson Head. Darrow's onslaught on capital punishment in one speech reflected Welles's own political and moral position. Welles was glad to be playing a character who was the moral reverse of Arthur Bannister in *The Lady from Shanghai*. When he delivered the memorable lines, "The world has been one long slaughterhouse from the beginning until today—and the killing goes on and on and on. Why not read something? Why not think? Instead of blindly shouting for death?" Welles was uttering his own thoughts and feelings, entirely in the line of *Panic, Ten Million Ghosts*, and *Citizen Kane*.

His performance in *Compulsion* gave the lie to the judgment that if he had ever had any talent as an actor, that talent was now dead. Zanuck was delighted with his performance, and for once the critics were kind. Stimulated, Welles began planning late in 1958 to return to the stage, in Dublin with MacLiammoir and Edwards in *The Merchant of Venice* and *Chimes at Midnight*, a more compact version of *Five Kings*, in which he would again appear as Falstaff.

Meanwhile, and characteristically, his career took a temporary nose dive: in London he appeared in the absurd movie *Ferry to Hong Kong* as Captain Cecil Hart, affecting an effeminate voice and stumping around the studio decks of the ferry *Fat Annie*, which, to judge by his behavior, he regarded as a description of himself. He was scarcely more inspiring in the films *Austerlitz, Lafayette* (as Benjamin Franklin again), and *Crack in the Mirror*, directed by Richard Fleischer. In the latter his performance as a lawyer was not on the level of his performance in *Compulsion*, for the creaking plot and claustrophobic direction gave him little opportunity to emerge; nevertheless he was briefly impressive in the final scenes, when he learns that he is being deceived by his mistress, played by Juliette Greco.

The one ray of light in 1959—apart from the advancing plans for the theater in Ireland and his meeting with Hilton Edwards to discuss them—was that he was approached by the Salkind brothers, Alexander and Michael, to direct Franz Kafka's *The Trial*. Welles was vacationing in Austria when they arrived, and, he claims, they had taken a taxi from Innsbruck they had no money to pay for. They had asked him to direct, write, and appear in a version of *Taras Bulba*, and he asked them what the budget would be and how much he would be paid. They replied that they had no money, and Welles burst out laughing. He decided they were kindred spirits: he wanted to work for them.

Then he heard from the Salkinds that Yul Brynner had begun to make *Taras Bulba* in Argentina; to his great amusement, they sent him a list of eighty-two titles from which he could choose another film project. He settled on the least likely, Franz Kafka's *The Trial.*

Welles saw the book in highly individual terms: in his vision, the villain was the bureaucracy that threatens K., the protagonist. Once again a work of literature became a platform for his liberal concerns. He would attempt to make the picture a dream, a nightmare that was similar to his own dreams of a vast, gray and faceless urban world in which he was a terrified, running victim: a symbol, if ever there was one, of his own career. He changed the ending to an apocalyptic vision of the future that included a sinister mushroom cloud swallowing up the world. Kafka's visionary conception, bleak and stark, fascinated him even though its mode was the opposite of his own: he could manage almost anything except austerity, both artistically and in his private life; it was his misfortune that he had no essential feeling for the spare and the grim. Nevertheless he resolutely began preparations for the work, which he would do following the productions of Shakespeare in Ireland.

In August 1959 Welles's London agents, Christopher Mann Ltd., were in contact with Hilton Edwards, now with the Gaiety Theater of Dublin, on the matter of the production. There was talk of casting Wendy Hiller, Celia Johnson, or Diana Wynyard, but soon it became clear that there was not enough money to attract artists of their caliber. At first the production was planned for September, then it was delayed until February 1960. Welles's schedule was as complicated as ever, and his having to go to Paris to do new scenes for *Crack in the Mirror* delayed the season. Edwards and MacLiammoir put up with everything; their devotion to Welles remained impressive.

Getting Welles to Ireland was a difficult accomplishment. Since he could not drive, a car and driver were kept ready—and canceled time after time, which meant additional billings by the car-rental company for late cancellations. He went to Zagreb, Yugoslavia, to scout locations for *The Trial,* then flew to Dublin on December 20 and flew out again. His plans for the production were confused and hard to follow; he had dashed off sketch after sketch of costumes and movements, as if seeking to direct the play by correspondence. At the beginning of January, Edwards was ill with a high fever following a fall in which he injured his forehead, his hands, and an eye. He was supposed to see Welles in London, and this meeting was put off. Having to record the music in advance created other problems. Then Welles became concerned that Shakespeare's anti-Semitic portrait of a Jew in *The Merchant of Venice* might cause neo-Nazi approval in an Ireland that still contained remnants of the German sympathizers of World War II.

Thus the play was abandoned and replaced with *Twelfth Night*, which in turn was dropped when the backer, Louis Elliman, had to cut the budget.

A long letter from MacLiammoir to Welles (January 7, 1960) indicates the problems the collaborators were facing. Still unwell, Edwards was fretting about the sets and costumes, about Welles's "essential fluidity," about the constant changes of the opening date. In the days that followed, Welles rushed in cuts and emendations to the Shakespeare text, casting changed from day to day, and the time left for preparation before the opening narrowed alarmingly. It was decided to open the season in Belfast and later shift to Dublin. Edwards, working from a sickbed, mapped out the battle scenes in Welles's absence; Welles's wires and letters became more confusing by the day (and even now, after several rereadings, they remain virtually incomprehensible).

Characteristically, Welles had several things on his mind at once, and this made matters difficult for Edwards and MacLiammoir. His proposed cost accounts were a hopeless tangle of figures and facts, scribbled on pages with little rhyme or reason. Welles got into rehearsals at the beginning of February, then darted off to London for discussions of *The Trial* and other matters. He scribbled an impatient note to Edwards on Hyde Park Hotel stationery: "Sorry, but don't expect to be able to get back to rehearsals till tomorrow. . . . Do *please* rehearse Falstaff scenes without me—*concentrating on others* (and get new Pistol)—as I'm sure you'll need to." Having to replace an actor in this peremptory way was discouraging to Edwards. Meanwhile, Welles appeared before twelve hundred undergraduates at a meeting of the Debating Society of the Oxford University Union to argue against the elegant British humorist Stephen Potter on the issue, "This house holds America responsible for spreading vulgarity in European society." It was typical of Welles's career that he should be placed in the perverse position of having to defend U.S. mass culture overseas, which in his heart he deplored. "If it fails to resist [American vulgarity] Europe must look to its own weaknesses and its own form of spiritual flabbiness. Now you are catching up with us!" Welles defeated the motion, 485 to 309 votes.

The next day he returned to Dublin, dashing off complicated memoranda concerning the handling of duels, the business of dealing with Hotspur's body (he believed Falstaff should place the corpse stage center), the direction of Prince Hal's farewell speech, the use of light and shadow, and every move of each character. The memoranda, designed to stimulate and excite his partners, often left them baffled. He and Paola were firmly installed in a hotel and working on rehearsals through the middle of February. On February 9 he invited MacLiam-moir and Edwards to dinner, then hastily canceled the invitation, apologizing in a note the next morning that he felt he must concentrate on learning lines (always a problem for him) and getting in shape (a greater problem). He enclosed sketches for tables, chairs, and benches, and he even drew up a sketch for the billing in advertisements and playbills: "Orson Welles as Falstaff in *Chimes at Midnight*, being the adventures of the fat knight and the Prince of Wales from the historical plays of William Shakespeare, the play staged by Hilton Edwards."

The rehearsals at the drafty YMCA during the damp and miserable Dublin winter dragged on. Welles filmed the production at the Gaiety Theater, and it opened in both Belfast and Dublin to moderate interest. Like *Five Kings*, the production presented serious problems for the audience, and it did not run. Welles was disappointed, as were his partners, who had hoped for a commercial success based on his name. All three were drastically short of money.

Out of his despair Welles plucked another triumph. The French dramatist Eugène Ionesco had written a fashionable play, *Rhinoceros*, in which rhinoceri are heard making their way through the streets of an anonymous city in Europe and multiplying, as everybody in the city turns into a rhinoceros. The people are becoming mere animals—conformists. The playwright's parallels were firmly established with those totalitarian systems of mass brutalism that were Welles's chief concern. It was highly intelligent of Ionesco to want Welles to direct the London stage production of this work, and the producers gave Welles his head and offered him Sir Laurence Olivier as his star.

Suffering as ever from his weight, flat feet, and the digestive problems associated with overeating and drinking, Welles somehow summoned up the energy to direct *Rhinoceros* at the Strand Theater in London. In April 1960 he was deep into the work. He increasingly felt disappointed with the play, which he thought empty, but he got along well with Olivier, who took direction effortlessly. However, his pleasure in the production was hampered by yet another series of wranglings with his Irish partners in the matter of the financial backings of the ill-fated Irish Shakespearean season.

Welles directed *Rhinoceros* with all his old brilliance.* He insisted on speed, an absence of tricks, naturalistically overlapping dialogue, and all-out performances, and he pushed his players to the very edge of ham in order to overcome what he felt to be the play's intrinsic weak-

---

* According to the writer Roy Moseley, Welles left the third-act direction to Olivier.

nesses. The use of lighting was original and inspired. Kenneth Tynan was supportive, and the powerful critic of *The Times* praised not only Welles's "smooth" direction but Olivier's "weakly, amiable, shabby, and drunken" clerk. Joan Plowright, destined to be Lady Olivier, also came in for her share of praise. Once more Welles had proved himself a grand man of the theater, making one regret that he had not set up residency in New York or London in the 1940s and stayed there to devote himself to the stage.

The month of May 1960, when *Rhinoceros* was successfully running at the Strand, was consumed by unhappy correspondence with Mac-Liammoir and Edwards and their representatives on the matter of the *Chimes* accounts. Their Dublin solicitor, Terence de Vere White, charged that Welles had not "deigned" to reply to letters and that he was "indifferent to Hilton Edwards's position." Welles proved to be impatient and angry with White, writing him on May 19 that in spite of his own financial difficulties he had advanced Edwards money and would now advance him more, that Edwards's claim was very much in question, "and if you chose to press it, I shall have no alternative but to deal in the same terms. In that event, as I've warned you before, Hilton will be the loser." Welles added, even more menacingly:

> When you state that you have ruffled my feelings, you are quite mistaken. I have made full allowance for your ignorance of the real situation, and bear you no animus for your vigorous efforts to help Hilton. The truth is, he deserves all the help he can get from both of us, and I only ask you to believe that the line you persist in taking with me can do him nothing but harm. Meanwhile, unless I receive notification from him that he has changed his mind, and intends to give this matter formally into your hands, you must forgive me for considering that our correspondence is terminated.

On the same day Welles wrote Edwards from his temporary home at 10 Chelsea Park Gardens that he had received three letters from Edwards's lawyers in two weeks. This letter was perhaps the most severe he had ever written to Edwards; running to six crowded pages of single-spaced typing, it stated categorically that Welles's calculations of the accounts and Edwards's showed "considerable difference." Welles pointed out that the threats of legal action he was receiving were inappropriate; he reminded Edwards of favors done and that he had undertaken the season to help the Gate; and he charged that the producer Louis Elliman had backed down on certain offers with respect to financing, resulting in the cancellation of *Twelfth Night*. (Welles overlooked the other elements that had forced cancellation.)

He wrote, "I wonder if you have any idea what *Chimes* has cost me? I won't mention the films and TV that I had to turn down." He rudely remarked on the difference between his position and that of Edwards, who had turned down an offer to appear in a Dutch television show. "I think you'll agree that with the fullest allowance for the proportionate difference in our earning capacities, I must have lost a great deal more in this way than did you. Nobody paid me a penny."

He pointed out that he had lost some 7,600 pounds sterling through the disaster in Ireland. Was it unreasonable to ask his partner "to take on a nominal—let's say minuscule, proportionate—share in these losses?" But then, he added, the question was hypothetical; he made no such request.

Welles said that he felt he had met all his promised obligations to Edwards, that he had in no way reneged on his contractual agreements. He discussed "the awful total of my losses on *Chimes*," all of which came out of savings and really scraped the bottom of the barrel. He said he had received only 350 pounds for directing and designing *Rhinoceros.** He owed thousands more in British taxes; he owed money to Louis Elliman; he could scarcely spare hundreds of pounds to send to Edwards. In all, he said his position was as desperate as ever. The situation recalled that in the wake of *Five Kings*.

The question arises, what happened to the money he earned from acting in pictures? Probably he was squirreling it away for *The Trial*, on which he began work later that year despite the continued harrowing correspondence with Ireland. Worse trouble came with talk of staging *The Duchess of Malfi* in London, with MacLiammoir as Ferdinand, in the hope of recovering some of the losses on *Chimes*. Without warning, Welles decided he did not want MacLiammoir after all and, the latter claimed, forced him into a television job to get him out of the way. Then *Malfi* was canceled. MacLiammoir charged Welles with base treachery in a letter of great distress and bitterness on November 26, 1960.

Welles was now obsessed with *The Trial*. He flumped through parts in the films *David and Goliath* and *The Tartars* in order to fill out his budget for the Salkind film, and after a depressing and meaningless 1961 he started preparing the masterwork of which he dreamed. In Zagreb he selected a vast disused exhibition building that would sym-

---

* In fact he had received about 1,000 pounds.

bolize the horror of Kafka's totalitarianism; he cast Anthony Perkins as
the terrified clerk who was Kafka's protagonist; he began laying out
plans to shoot further sequences in Paris and at his home near Rome;
and he met and fell in love with a stunning woman who was to dominate his life, the sculptor Oja Kodar, whose father worked on the film's
design.* The picture would be shot in English and French. And Welles
added Jeanne Moreau to the cast. There was talk of casting Pierre
Fresnay and Claudia Cardinale as well, but that idea was abandoned;
money was too tight.

Welles was still picking up segments for *Don Quixote*, which meant
traveling to and from Spain; he had been shooting *Don Quixote* intermittently since August 1957. He was also fencing with Louis Dolivet in
the $750,000 breach of contract suit over *Confidential Report*. It was
charged that he "drank excessively on and off the set . . . causing him
to report late for work . . . and on occasions to absent himself entirely
for periods of time and to render himself unfit to carry out his duties
. . . in an efficient and workman-like manner when he did report for
work." It was alleged that several workers on the picture had quit after
Welles abused them. Stories of his drinking were still current as Welles
began work on *The Trial* in collaboration with the designer Jean Mandaroux.

Following a holiday with Paola and Beatrice in Kitzbühel, Austria,
Welles took his unit to Zagreb in May 1962. He furnished the exhibition building he had found with the austere and meaningless contents
that he felt appropriate to the story. He shot outside in front of low,
dilapidated houses; William Chappell described the scene in *The Sunday Times* of London on May 27: "Behind . . . towered a huge, unfinished block of new flats, gaunt, hideous, and somehow threatening.
Nearby stood a gnarled tree, dusted with a drift of blossom, a hag in a
bridal veil." This was the scene of the execution of K, Kafka's protagonist, in the finale of the story.

After three weeks in Zagreb, Welles moved to Paris. The Salkinds
had run short of money, and the scale of the film had to be drastically
reduced overnight. He decided to convert the Gare d'Orsay, the grand
old Belle Epoque railroad station of Paris that had been abandoned
some years before, into Kafka's nightmare world of, in Chappell's
words, "damp and scabrous walls, real claustrophobia in its mournful
rooms, and also intricacies of shape and perspective on a scale that
would have taken months and cost fortunes to build." Eugene Archer

---

* Paola Mori was then at his house in Rome with Beatrice.

of *The New York Times* also visited the set, and he described how "the enormous latticed ceiling emitted a dusky atmosphere entirely appropriate to Kafka's somber mood, while the acres of empty floor space gave Mr. Welles' indispensable tracks and cranes ample room for any effect he desired." Jean Mandaroux worked splendidly to convert the great depot into a microcosm of a totalitarian world.

For all its ambitions, the picture entirely fails to work. It is one of those rare movies that not only portray deadness but are dead themselves. It is muffled, dull, and unexciting on every level, and its tonelessness seeps into the audience. Moreover, in its grandiose largeness of approach, it is the stylistic antithesis of Kafka's great creation.

Having completed this least successful of his directed films, Welles returned to Italy, where he and Paola reoccupied her family house, the Villa Mori, at Frenese on the sea, where they were raising Beatrice. Welles appeared for the director Pier Paolo Pasolini, about whom he had mixed feelings, in *La Ricotta,* a sequence in the episodic movie *Rogopag.* In the fall of 1962 *La Ricotta* was filmed not far from the Villa Mon, in the countryside between two stretches of the Via Appia. It involved the staging of a crucifixion scene whose director (Welles) talks to an interviewer, quoting lines from Pasolini's verse; while he goes on talking, the crucifixion actually occurs. As a long-term resident of Italy, Welles was put in the awkward position of uttering the highly offensive statements contained in the script: "Italy has the most illiterate masses and the most ignorant bourgeoisie in Europe" and "The average man is a dangerous criminal, a monster. He is a racist, a colonialist, a defender of slavery, a mediocrity." It did not help that he also had to speak the lines, "Nail them to the crosses!" and "Unnail them!" The film's blatant Marxism, exemplified in Welles's bloated capitalist director, went far beyond Welles's own liberalism, and in March 1963 the movie was seized, accused of insulting the religion of the state. Pasolini was tried and found guilty, but the appeals court absolved him; years later the supreme court revoked the pertinent resolution. The troubled movie had only a scattered release, temporarily imperiling Pasolini's career and certainly doing nothing for Welles's.

Nor did Welles's next appearance help his career. In the idiotic British picture *The VIPs* he played a grotesque parody of Alexander Korda; he walked through the part, growling with a second-rate Hungarian accent, sporting a fur-collared coat and puffing an oversize cigar. Welles found some consolation in laying plans for a film version of *Chimes at Midnight* and raising money from various Spanish financiers. At the same time he continued to shoot bits and pieces of *Don Quixote* despite the excessive financial demands of the unknown Francisco Reiguera in the leading role. He moved from Rome to Madrid in order to proceed with *Don Quixote* as a Spanish production; he hired two Spanish art directors, and he was to begin work in 1964. In the meantime he narrated a documentary about Britain in World War II, *The Finest Hours*. His residence in Madrid gave rise to unfavorable comments by liberals that he had accepted the hospitality of Generalissimo Francisco Franco and his fascist government, but there is no evidence that Welles had anything to do with Franco beyond meeting him at a couple of receptions. It is inconceivable that he could have approved of Franco's government; it is significant that Michael O'Hara in *The Lady from Shanghai* was a supporter of the loyalists.

The shooting of *Don Quixote* continued. Paola helped Welles with it in Mexico, Spain, and Italy, acting as script girl, continuity girl, sandwich person, and administrator of business affairs. Welles would break off shooting on any other picture in order to do setups for this endlessly protracted production.

Welles acquired two editors who worked with him continuously as he shot daily footage, the father and son team Renzo and Maurizio Lucidi. They had met in 1962, during the making of Richard Thorpe's cumbersome epic *The Tartars*. Maurizio Lucidi recalls how Welles stole Victor Mature's scenes in that film by hypnotizing both director and cameraman into focusing on him exclusively—another victory over Mature, from whom he had taken Rita Hayworth.

Maurizio remembers that Welles utterly consumed him during their personal and working relationship; he regarded any sign of a private life in father or son as an intrusion into his plans. On one occasion Welles kept Maurizio up all night to discuss *Don Quixote* when he knew that the young man had a date with a girl whom he had tried for weeks to pin down. After Maurizio married, Welles was equally ruthless. Maurizio was working with Welles in the editing room on *Don Quixote* when someone announced that his wife had arrived and had to speak to him (about a problem in her pregnancy). Welles complained loudly about women interrupting serious work, disturbing the atmosphere of creativity, and adding to the costs of production. He said reprovingly, "If you leave this room now, you're not a true artist!"

A furious Maurizio stepped out anyway, followed by Welles's shouted threats. Five minutes later he returned and handed Welles 5,000 lire to cover the cost of the break. Then Welles's better side emerged: "If you went out there, you must have problems," he said, and he told his secretary to give Maurizio a check for one million lire on the spot.

Sometimes Maurizio worked on another movie to make money.

When Welles wanted him to come to Paris to shoot a fragment of *Don Quixote*, the first cable read, "Won't you come and have some fun"; the second read, "I need you"; and the third said, "Send any kind of money." Maurizio says that Welles often failed to pay his players. Akim Tamiroff, who played Sancho Panza, kept begging for cash, but Welles dismissed the issue, saying that the money was more important to him than to Tamiroff. Maurizio recalls that throughout the shooting of *Don Quixote* Welles identified himself completely with the camera: his eyes and the lenses were one. He taught Maurizio that film is like clay because it can be molded according to the creator's desires. Welles brought about a revolution in picture-making by changing the standard dubbing procedure for movies. Before *Don Quixote* was edited, he taped the entire dialogue by itself so that he could impose his own rhythm on the cutting; then he and Maurizio edited the film as if it were set to music. Maurizio once took a month and a half to reduce two hours of footage to four minutes to match the rhythm of the lines.

Along with the obsessive perfectionism there was always the restless disorder. Sometimes Welles would go over the same footage again and again, struggling with conflicts of vision even within himself. The two men worked hard on the titles of the film. Welles had engaged a Spanish musician to record an hour-long piece for solo guitar. Then he sent two cameramen to Saragossa, and they came back with 1,000 meters of film—long shots and close-ups of windmills seen from all possible angles and through all kinds of lenses. He and Maurizio chopped up the guitar music track and pasted together a four-minute tape. Then Welles had Maurizio edit the windmill footage to the four minutes of guitar. After a month of hard work, there was not one note that had not been covered by an image. Welles watched it silently, asked to see it again, and again and again; after fifty viewings, he started to say, "What if——" But, Maurizio says, "there could be no ifs about it, because whatever minor change was made would have thrown off the rhythm of the entire piece."

Welles often went back to work over old material, making corrections that only turned out like the original film. On one occasion Maurizio made a duplicate of an original negative of one scene; it showed that Welles's remake was identical with the film as it had been edited several months before.

In the opening scenes of *Don Quixote*, Welles was to tell the story of the novel in eight minutes to a girl played by Patty McCormack. Maurizio pointed out to him that this long exposition of a book that was read by every schoolchild in Europe would seem boring and presumptuous to a non-English-speaking audience. Welles was upset at this and walked out, disappearing for three days. When he turned up again, he beamed that he had a great idea for a new beginning: the picture would open with a grand masquerade ball; among the arrivals would be a guest dressed as Don Quixote, who would turn out to be the actual Don Quixote. The idea was never shot.

A relentless worker, Welles constantly challenged his own strength and that of others. One day he worked on *Don Quixote* from 8:00 A.M. until 6:00 P.M. the following day. After this marathon he dragged Maurizio off to his villa, where they had a swim in the ocean, and then he announced he was going back to the cutting. Welles was constantly impetuous. At one stage it was suggested that Maurizio Lucidi direct a version of *Treasure Island* with Welles. They met at Harry's Bar in Rome, and Maurizio said he would be happy to direct the picture. Welles then announced that he would direct his own part. Maurizio agreed—but with a proviso: he would walk out if Welles showed up on the set to direct anything else in the picture. Welles closed the subject, and it was never brought up again. On another occasion Maurizio and Welles took an apartment in Pamplona when no rooms were available. Returning late from dinner, Welles found he had forgotten his keys and he and Maurizio broke the lock with the car jack. The next morning the owner of the flat was in tears because the door had been ruined. Welles had it repaired at once.

Audrey Stainton was Welles's secretary on *Don Quixote*. She recalls that he had a unique way of tackling a scene by starting from its center and working out and around it. Often she found herself taking down the dialogue in shorthand from the Moviola. Welles never let any member of the cast know what he had in mind for the next day. Possessed by demonic energy himself, he had no consideration for other people's limited strength or capacity. While shooting *David and Goliath* in Italy, he kept Akim Tamiroff waiting in the backyard of the Safa Palatina Studios so that he could work on *Don Quixote* between his scenes as King Saul. He would even direct his own scenes in *David and Goliath;* ignoring the script, he built his part by putting together grains from the Bible—all the scenes involving Saul were essentially Orson Welles sequences. Audrey Stainton says she will never forget the Gustave Doré visions of Francisco Reiguera riding up steep slopes on his donkey. Welles used to drag the elderly gentleman into the Roman countryside, set him on his donkey, and drive donkey and rider up steep hills at all times of day or night. To Stainton this seemed cruel, but she knew that no human consideration could stem Welles's vision.

Early in 1965 Jeanne Moreau arrived in Spain to appear as Doll Tearsheet, the most English of characters, in *Chimes at Midnight;* it was typical of Welles's eccentricity that he would cast her in this part. He selected the Italian comedian Walter Chiari for the role of Silence, equipping him with a stammer identical to that of Welles's brother Richard. His daughter Beatrice appeared as a child, Welles himself was Falstaff, and John Gielgud was made to act with unnecessary effeminacy as Henry IV. The best performance in the picture was given by Keith Baxter, a virile and strikingly handsome actor who admirably achieved the character of Prince Hal.

In an interview in the French magazine *Cahiers du Cinéma* Welles described his intentions vis-à-vis the character he was playing.

> The more I studied the part, the less funny it appeared to me. This problem preoccupied me during the entire shooting. . . . I don't think very highly of those moments in which I am only amusing. It seems to me that Falstaff is a man of wit rather than a clown. . . . He is the character in whom I believe the most, the most entirely good man in all drama. His faults are trivial, and he makes the most enormous jokes from them. His goodness is like bread, like wine. That is why I lost the comic side of his character a little; the more I played him, the more I felt that he represented goodness, purity.

Welles's assistant director on *Chimes at Midnight* was Mickey Knox, whom he met while shooting *Marco Polo* in Yugoslavia in 1964. Knox recalls Welles's unbridled determination. When somebody in the producing team refused to allow a Jew to appear in the film, Welles overruled him. When the set of the inn run by Doll Tearsheet was finished, Welles said it looked fake and insisted that the wood be scraped and aged to make it look real. Knox remembers that Welles would rise at the break of dawn dressed as Falstaff and wear his full costume even to direct scenes in which Falstaff did not appear.

Chimes at Midnight is made up from the two parts of *Henry IV*, including the Battle of Shrewsbury and the renunciation of Falstaff by the young king; Falstaff's death in *Henry V* is used as a coda. The story mainly concerns Falstaff's education of Prince Hal as his tutor, surrogate father, and guardian. Falstaff insists on the pursuit of pleasure, and despite his cowardice he is good and decent. At the height of their happiest times together, Prince Hal knows that he will ultimately reject Falstaff. Falstaff knows it too, and the film's somber tone springs from the thought that England itself is already doomed. Falstaff has compulsions toward self-destruction that can also be found in Macbeth, Othello, Kane, Quinlan, and Arkadin. In the battle scene, medieval chivalry is shown dying in a horrible bloodbath of people hacking each other to death in the mud.

Originally Welles saw *Chimes at Midnight,* or *Falstaff,* as being essentially comic in tone; but as he studied the part of Falstaff further, it appeared less comic and more melancholy. He felt that Falstaff was more witty than funny, and the problem preoccupied him during the shooting of the film. The relationship between Falstaff and Prince Hal was no longer simply a comic one but a preparation for the tragic ending. Welles said, "The farewell scene is foretold four times in the scene. The death of the prince, the king and his castle, the death of Hotspur, which is that of chivalry, the poverty and illness of Falstaff, are presented throughout the entire film and must darken it." He did not believe comedy should dominate in such a film. Falstaff was waging a struggle against the disappearance of the values of goodness that he represented. The film also spoke of the terrible price the prince must pay in exchange for power. The film became a lament for Falstaff and for the vanishing of Merrie England: in *The Magnificent Ambersons* the people are destroyed by the advent of the automobile; in *Falstaff* they are destroyed by the interests of power, responsibility, and national grandeur.

At the outset Welles wanted only brief shots of the battle scene, but he decided he would have to have more sustained shots to allow the actors to develop their roles. He filmed the scene with a crane that shifted position at ground level to follow the action, and afterward he edited the fragments so that each shot would show a blow, a counter-blow, a blow received, a blow struck.

The film was to begin with the murder of Richard II, and the killing was shot, but it seemed too confusing in the larger context. Welles also began shooting the debarkation of Henry Bolingbroke, then decided it would not fit into the pattern. He also had shots of two old men walking in the snow that were cut; they would have compromised the internal rhythm of the film. It was that rhythm that dictated all his work.

Welles was always concerned that the audience might become bored. He thought the greatest virtue of cinema was speed and concentration, and he hated self-indulgence in terms of visuals. At the end of the film Henry V orders that Falstaff be set free, and here Welles cut to the bone of the scene. He would shoot a scene several times, over several days, but he seldom looked at the rushes; he liked to pass from one scene to another in the same day of shooting. In the course of a day he often changed scenes without warning because of the position of the sun or because the actors were not giving their best and he thought perhaps they would be better in another sequence. He did not work to a preplanned system, nor did he believe that a film was like a picture in which the painter painted the leaves of a tree one by one. He liked a sense of improvisation, and he liked to have music on the set in order to relax everyone. He hated everything that slowed up shooting. The sound engineer was not allowed to ask that a shot be redone, only to catch the sound correctly. Script girls were not to speak at all. He refused to allow discussion during makeup sessions. He told everyone working with him that they were second-class citizens and would never be consulted about anything.

In this third attempt at the Falstaff chronicles,* Welles emphasized again the mortality of human beings, their essential fragility, the death of chivalry, and the ruining effects of power. We see Falstaff dying in spirit when his friend Prince Hal rejects him, then we see Hal himself spiritually dying when he assumes the throne. One of the finest moments in Welles's films is the speech "Uneasy lies the head," delivered with an exhausted, agonizing pain by John Gielgud.

Despite the fact that the backgrounds of the film are inescapably Spanish, Welles achieved a universality in the wintry look of his newly adopted country. Correctly, he took the view that Shakespeare can be performed in any environment and still be totally valid—a point that several critics missed when they brutally attacked the movie. The grind of ice, the creak of wood, the thud of footsteps on hard ground, all powerfully evoke the atmosphere of the play. True, the synchronization of many of the lines was bad and there were other clumsinesses of technique; but the best of *Chimes at Midnight* echoes Welles's talent at its mellowest. There is an extraordinary poignancy in Welles's portrayal of Falstaff that goes beyond that of the ill-fated *Five Kings* of 1939 or the Belfast and Dublin production. The scenes in which Falstaff and Shallow crouch before a fire, in which Prince Hal stands like an abstract figure of medieval legend, in which Hal and Falstaff pantomime the king's might, all are ideally realized. Most remarkable is a battle scene that rivals Eisenstein in its evocation of a medieval world. Welles shows the panoply of battle and its essential weirdness, his determinations based on his wide reading of the previous twelve months. He shows knights in armor being lowered onto their horses by rope and pulley, horses trotting through the mist of a forest, armies clashing with a thud of flesh and armor, and then, in a shocking image, faces splashed with blood and feet tangled in stirrups as the soundtrack fills

---

* Interrupted for weeks in December 1965, when Welles was stricken by a gall-bladder attack.

with the screaming of the wounded. Mud founders the warriors, reducing heroes to squalid, wallowing beasts. This is Welles's ultimate pronouncement on the ugliness and futility of war.

The technical unevenness of the movie, its lack of commercial appeal, and the negative reviews led by Bosley Crowther in *The New York Times* set the seal of doom on Welles's career for the 1960s. With only a scattered release, the movie died the death of most movie versions of Shakespeare, and *The Trial* was doing no better in the international market. In the wake of this disaster, Welles struggled to finish *Don Quixote.*

Nineteen sixty-four was a year for grieving. In January, Marc Biltzston was killed by Portuguese sailors during a fight in Fort-de-France, Martinique. Two months later, Dr. Maurice Bernstein died at the age of seventy-nine after falling from a tree he was pruning outside his home in Beverly Hills. Dr. Bernstein left his estate of something over $100,000 to his wife, with the proviso that if she died within thirty days of himself, half the money was to go to Welles, the other half to Northwestern University. (Mrs. Bernstein lived for another six years.) Welles, then in Madrid, was unable to attend the funeral; he spent five days in bed in a state of severe shock. He had long since forgiven Dr. Bernstein for his money-grubbing antics in the 1940s, and, covering truth with nostalgia, he spoke with constant warmth to Paola (who had corresponded with the doctor) of his guardian's kindness to him when he was a boy.

Welles appeared briefly as the Swedish consul Raoul Nordling in *Is Paris Burning?* and made little impression. He also appeared to virtually no effect in Tony Richardson's *The Sailor from Gibraltar*, with a script by Christopher Isherwood. But he was a formidable Cardinal Wolsey in Fred Zinneman's *A Man for All Seasons*, the story of the British martyr Sir Thomas More. Welles persuaded Zinneman to allow him to use eyedrops that made his pupils look bloodshot. His presence lent force to the character of that relentless cleric.

Welles's next project for French television, based on works of the Danish novelist Karen Blixen (Isak Dinesen), was to be a two-part film starring himself and Jeanne Moreau. The first part, *The Immortal Story*, would be shot under the Spanish quota with Spanish and French financing, largely at Welles's home on the outskirts of Madrid; the second part, *The Deluge at Nordernay*, was to be produced by the Hungarian Alexandre Pal and shot in Budapest. *The Immortal Story* deals with the millionaire Mr. Clay, whose vast frame, despite its size, is as mortal as everyone's. He lives in a mansion in Macao, the Portuguese colony in China, in the nineteenth century; like Kane, he is surrounded by mirrors; he is friendless, depressed, cut off by his wealth and power from the joys of being human. He conceives the idea that he will for one brief moment vicariously enjoy the pleasures of the flesh by arranging a scene that he will watch: the daughter of the former owner of his mansion will go to bed with a sailor, chosen for his physical beauty and picked up in the street. When the boy makes love to the older woman as Clay watches, the movie gives the audience a voyeuristic experience and by implication comments on the voyeuristic nature of filmgoing. The elegiac sadness of Welles's script seems to indicate a longing for the physical beauty he never possessed. This lyrical work, based on the abiding Wellesian theme of the impotence of power, remains one of the director's finest films.

Welles began preparing *The Immortal Story* in 1967 in Paris, where he was living with Oja Kodar. On location in the Parisian suburb of Rueil-Malmaison, he got off to a false start with the cameraman Walter Wottiz, who dissatisfied him, perhaps because Wottiz was too respectful, even terrified of him. Then, through his agent Micheline Rozan, who had invested in the production, he met the diminutive and charming cameraman Willy Kurant. Wearing pink pajamas and sitting up in a huge brass bed, he interviewed Kurant at the Raphael Hotel. Welles had run Kurant's film *Anna* and expressed admiration for it; he told Kurant he would scrap the existing two days' work and start from scratch with him.

Kurant walked onto a set occupied by a hostile crew. The atmosphere at Rueil-Malmaison was tense because the operators, electricians, and gaffers, having been working for Walter Wottiz, resented Kurant's presence. However, Welles and Kurant were in rapport from the beginning; they agreed on a very rich, candlelit, sensuous visual style for the erotic scene, and a more austere, cold use of light for the sequences that suggested the millionaire's sexual impotence.

After five weeks at Rueil-Malmaison, Welles, Kurant, and the stars Jeanne Moreau and Norman Eshley (the sailor) flew to Madrid, where Paola Mori lived with him again. With great ingenuity, Welles matched up the sequences shot at his home with those done in Paris. In their first days in Spain, director and cameraman shot the erotic sequence, for which Kurant suggested the subtle light of candles reflected in mirrors, shimmering with gold light over the flesh of the boy and the middle-aged woman. Kurant recalls that Welles was totally dedicated to the work and set an outsize alarm clock for fear he would not wake up in the morning. Often starting at dawn and finishing after dark, they would shoot off the cuff if, for instance, a truck or a generator failed to arrive. Some scenes were shot at Cincón, a town near Madrid that was turned into a simulacrum of Macao, and just about every Chinese waiter in Madrid was corraled to act as an extra.

After another five weeks of dedicated shooting, Welles and Kurant flew to Budapest to start work on *The Deluge at Norderney.* In one day Welles became convinced that there was graft in the unit and that he would not have a satisfactory shooting situation, so he returned to Madrid, leaving Kurant to pick up the pieces.

Welles discovered the thriller *Dead Calm* (1965) by Charles Williams, the story of a young man who, exhausted, comes aboard a honeymoon couple's yacht in the South Pacific and leads the couple into a terrifying ordeal. Welles planned to make this into a film with Kurant, renaming it *The Deep.*

Meanwhile, he appeared in several forgettable movies: *House of Cards, The Last Roman, Start the Revolution Without Me,* and *The Southern Star.* According to the director Sidney Hayers, Welles directed the opening scenes of *The Southern Star.* Made in 1968, the film was based on a novel by Jules Verne about the discovery of the world's largest diamond, its subsequent disappearance, and the race to rediscover it in Africa. The director, Hayers, was a British craftsman of considerable intelligence and skill. The location in Senegal was probably the most harrowing Welles had ever faced; it was even hotter than Morocco during *Othello* or *The Black Rose,* with the temperature rising to 150 degrees under an equatorial sun and everybody housed in a concrete building or cement block bungalows without running water. Welles would never forget his ten days in this hell-hole. Out in the African bush, the sweat pouring off him, he felt he might collapse at any minute. Despite his discomfort, he gave an interesting performance as a somewhat effeminate, excessively mannered adventurer. It says much for Welles's basic energy that he survived this ordeal; at that time, Hayers says, he had a fifty-six-inch waist and resembled a baby elephant.

Welles started off with a fight with Sidney Hayers. Hayers recalls that the first setup had Welles playing a game of checkers with the actor Georges Jeret. Welles objected to having his character cheat at the game; Hayers was adamant that the script be followed. Finally Welles suggested that the scene be shot Hayers's way and then Welles's way, but Hayers flatly refused to consider it. Welles kept forgetting his lines, but when Hayers called his bluff and refused to bend to him, Welles learned to respect him. Thereafter he behaved perfectly, rising at 5:00 A.M. every day and politely requesting even the most minor change in the script. He had one quirk: when the French cameraman Raoul Coutard was shooting his close-ups he refused to allow another actor or actress to appear with him and would deliver his lines to an empty space. When the unit went to Dakar, the capital of Senegal, an actor who was supposed to play a mine overseer fell ill; Welles suggested that Hayers take the part, and Welles directed the sequence, which began the film.

Post-production on *The Southern Star* was done in a theater in London, where all the dialogue had to be dubbed. Welles arrived an hour late for the dubbing session, wearing a black cloak and black suit, and smoking a long cigar. Tense, sweating, and irritable, he gave a bad reading at least thirty times; finally Hayers lost his temper and told his sound technician that Welles was utterly hopeless and his aural performance would have to be built like a jigsaw puzzle, using bits and pieces from every line. When Welles heard that, he was put on his mettle and read perfectly. At one stage Hayers was so angry with Welles that he told him, "I've always respected you until now. I've worked with Carol Reed and David Lean, and I know what I'm talking about." And then, Hayers says, "Orson had the nerve to tell me he didn't think Lean was that good a director!"

In that period Welles suffered a series of grinding disappointments. *The Immortal Story* was thrown away on French television and had no theatrical release in Europe. *Don Quixote* remained unfinished. *Chimes at Midnight* made no impression at the box office, and even Welles was dissatisfied with it, believing he had removed too much of the humor of Falstaff. His plans to make *The Sacred Beasts*, a movie about bullfighting (to which he had a disagreeable addiction), had to be abandoned when *The Moment of Truth* by Francesco Rosi, another bullfighting film, proved to be a commercial failure. He hoped to add two reels to *The Magnificent Ambersons,* using the same actors many years older. One plan after another fell apart in his hands.

In August 1968 Welles embarked on *The Deep*, the delayed film version of *Dead Calm*. He hired Willy Kurant and, using money raised from an appearance in *The Battle of Neretva*, proceeded to Yugoslavia in September and rented a yacht; Jeanne Moreau and Laurence Harvey (suffering from poor health and miscast as the young, muscular, psychopathic villain) joined him. Welles played Russ Brewer, the wealthy honeymooner of the novel. In Yugoslavia Welles renewed his affair with the sculptor Oja Kodar, whom he had first met in Zagreb. Of strong and vital temperament, the gifted Kodar had exhibited her work under a pseudonym, Vladimir Zadrov, because of prejudice in her native country against women sculptors. She was cast in the picture as a victim of the psychopath. According to Kurant, Moreau was not fond of Kodar, and there was tension between the two women both at sea and in the seaport town where part of the picture was shot.

Halfway through the production Kurant had to leave to make a Marlon Brando film,* and Welles continued with Kurant's assistant. Somewhere during those final weeks the energy that animated the production ran out, and Harvey's illness did not help matters. Welles's personal capital was exhausted, and when it came to post-production and the dubbing of the dialogue, he threw up his hands and quit. Jeanne Moreau told me that she never received the air tickets he promised to send her for her travel to Rome for the looping. It is clear he had become impatient with the picture; his old unease and fear about completing a film had resurfaced, and the movie remains unseen by the public.

The best thing that came out of *The Deep* was his increasingly intense relationship with Kodar. He was delighted when she successfully exhibited her work throughout Europe, delighted too by her half-Hungarian, half-Yugoslav nature that was at once fiery and composed. And Welles was amazed that the no less remarkable Paola Mori took this new romance in stride without threatening a divorce or creating a scandal. It was wonderful to be allied physically and mentally to an artist of Kodar's merit and daring, and that alliance of artists continued until Welles's death.

The unavailability of *The Deep* makes it impossible to discuss the film's qualities. However, Willy Kurant and Jeanne Moreau, who are in a position to know, have expressed no enthusiasm for it. Nor could anyone feel enthusiasm for Welles's next few movies, including *Twelve Plus One*, a comedy; *Waterloo*, in which Welles appeared as Louis XVIII; *The Kremlin Letter*, John Huston's inept spy thriller, in which Welles played a Russian diplomat; and *Catch-22*, which Welles badly wanted to make and Mike Nichols utterly ruined.

The late 1960s, when Welles continued to move restlessly around Europe and America, were marked by the beginning of his troubled friendship with the young and talented critic and director Peter Bogdanovich, who was then not yet in orbit as a pugnacious boy wonder of the American film. Bogdanovich worshiped Welles in a manner that at once disconcerted and pleased the great director; in many ways the slight and seemingly subservient Bogdanovich, his steely ambition hidden just an inch below his coolly polite surface, occupied the same

---

* *The Night of the Following Day.*

place in Welles's life as the delicate and brilliantly affected Kenneth Tynan had some years before. Welles seemed to need familiars, yet a part of him despised them. And clearly a part of him felt uneasy about the proposal that Bogdanovich put to him: an authorized biography, *This Is Orson Welles,* to be published by Harper & Row. Like the well-known book on Hitchcock by the late François Truffaut, it would be a collection of interviews in which Welles would range over the whole of his life.

It seemed a promising project, but from the outset there were problems. The first was Welles's capricious memory and the pleasure he took in deceiving his interviewers, from the profile writers of the 1930s to Kenneth Tynan and Maurice Bessy. Bogdanovich, who was shrewder and better informed than Tynan and had a mind that was not easily fazed by false detail, knew very well that Welles was "snowing" him, feeding him false information about his childhood and other aspects of his life—information for which Bogdanovich would be held responsible if he let it pass unchallenged. The frustrated scribe flew to Guaymas, Mexico, in 1969 to tape Welles as the master trumpeted, often blowing his lines, hammily through the part of General Dreedle in *Catch-22.* It was an unpleasant, windy, dusty location, and Welles's temperament was as uneven as ever, shifting with unsettling frequency from uproarious and largely fictitious anecdotes to brooding silences and back again. The tough, single-minded, academically trained Bogdanovich made an odd contrast with his own more or less captive Dr. Johnson: he was a meticulous but frequently irritable Boswell who carried devotion far beyond the call of duty as he listened to one preposterous "fact" after another. Making *Catch-22* was a punishment, not only because Welles tried to direct his own scenes and instead had to endure the rock-hard temperament of Mike Nichols, but because, for all his admiration of Bogdanovich's scholarship, he felt privately threatened and shaken by it.

Back in Hollywood, Welles made a phonograph record, *The Begatting of the President,* that ran into a storm of controversy. Brought out by Mediarts, it was banned by Metromedia stations and broadcast mainly on FM stations. The record was a bold onslaught on Richard Nixon, delivered in a quasi-biblical mode ("A little child shall be born in a grocery store in Whittier, and he shall sit upon the throne, and his administration shall be established greatly. Now the begatting of Richard Nixon was in this wise . . ."). Welles won a Grammy for the record. Meanwhile, another of his admirers, Henry Jaglom, completed the direction of a film in which Welles appeared, *A Safe Place.* The movie featured Welles as an elderly Jew making a living from playing chess in

New York's Central Park; the references to magic in the script owed much to his influence.

Bogdanovich emerged as a fully fledged professional director with his first major movie, the evocative *The Last Picture Show*, in which his future inamorata Cybill Shepherd made her debut performance. Welles had wanted to play the part of a crusty western type, Sam the Lion, but Bogdanovich refused the master and cast instead the veteran John Ford actor Ben Johnson. Proving to be a good sport, Welles tolerated the decision and gave Bogdanovich good advice during the shooting. According to Polly Bogdanovich, whom Peter was soon to leave for Cybill Shepherd, Welles would often speak with Bogdanovich on the telephone to answer complex technical questions. This fine movie succeeded in evoking, through the skilled direction of a largely unfamiliar cast, the atmosphere of a windswept Texas backwater in the 1960s. Whether Welles deeply influenced the movie cannot be determined; but his technical advice, and the presence throughout of Polly Bogdanovich, a designer of great talent, brought out the best in the young director.

15

During the late 1960s and early 1970s, Welles planned yet another film of his own even though *The Deep* and *Don Quixote* were still uncompleted. (The production head of Paramount, Robert Evans, wanted Welles to make a picture for him, but apparently Welles never came up with a satisfactory project.)

The Other Side of the Wind was a bold and daring venture that Welles felt might restore his reputation as a major American filmmaker. When he sketched out ideas for the movie in 1963, he called it *The Sacred Beasts* and thought of it as a story of socialites following the corridas. The protagonist is the director Jake Hannaford, who has returned to Hollywood after many years of exile in Europe to find the place changed; in an effort to retrieve his banished reputation, he decides to make a purely commercial work rampant with violence and sex. The centerpiece of the narrative is an elaborate birthday party for Hannaford given by a hostess at a mansion and attended by journalists, critics, and television teams; the party would be a symbolic representation of the pretensions and the viciousness of the American press. Among the writers he would later pillory in his script was "Higgam,"* a supercilious critic and know-all journalist whom Peter Bogdanovich would play with a British accent. Several scenes were shot with Bogdanovich, who was later replaced by Howard Grossman. Pauline Kael, whose *The Citizen Kane Book* had infuriated Welles as much as my book (*The Films of Orson Welles*) had, was represented by the character of Juliette Rich, played by Susan Strasberg, who appears throughout the story to criticize Hannaford, insinuating that he is less than masculine and a cruel sadist. Kael's frequent spoken remarks about Welles's cruelty, none of which were contained in her book, had undoubtedly gotten back to Welles.

---

* A calculated mispronunciation of my name.

The character of Hannaford, cast for John Huston, whose physique was the opposite of Welles's, may have been suggested by statements made off the record (and later on the record) by Welles's former friend Maurice Bessy that implied that Welles was a repressed homosexual. Although there is no evidence to suggest this possibility, either in Welles's life or in his work, Bessy, in a critique of Welles's films, dwelled on the powerful male relationships in his oeuvre, including those between Iago and Othello and between Falstaff and Prince Hal, to draw his conclusion. An infuriated Welles made Hannaford an obsessively repressed gay character who falls desperately in love with John Dale, the leading man in his sex-and-violence movie, played by Bob Random.

Still another basis for Hannaford was Ernest Hemingway, whom Welles disliked intensely. Hemingway had written the commentary for Joris Ivens's 1937 documentary of the Spanish Civil War, *The Spanish Earth*, a left-wing, pro-loyalist tract of considerable poetic and dramatic force. Welles was to do the narration, but Hemingway decided that Welles's voice was "faggoty" and fired him, choosing to narrate the film himself. There was even a Welles story—highly unlikely in view of Orson's lack of athleticism—that the two men had had a fist fight in New York over the matter. Undoubtedly Welles shared a widespread view that Hemingway's exaggerated macho stance covered indifferent sexual performance with women and a frustrated homosexuality sometimes to be found in men of a bragging masculinity.

During the many years of work on *The Other Side of the Wind*, which was not "finished" until 1984, Welles kept adding new characters and switching locations, all with the devoted support of his cameraman, Gary Graver. He included the character of Brooks Ottarlake, a newly successful director based on Bogdanovich and played (after he stopped playing Higgam) by Bogdanovich himself. Hannaford is jealous of Ottarlake, who sports expensive cashmere sweaters, as does his real-life prototype. In the confused history of making the picture, the mimic Rich Little undertook the part of Ottarlake briefly before Bogdanovich was cast. Mercedes McCambridge described to me the episode that resulted in his dismissal. Welles was shooting a group of actors, including McCambridge and Little, on a rooftop in Phoenix, Arizona, and he instructed the performers to sway to and fro. Most of them knew better than to question Welles's random decisions, but Little demanded to know why they should sway when there was no wind. Mounted high on a crane, Welles shouted in irritation, "You are swaying because midgets have hold of your legs!" Little called back, "But there are no midgets up here, Orson!" The others groaned; Welles screamed, "I'm going to shoot the midgets in Spain!"

Oja Kodar appeared in the movie as the star of Hannaford's picture; others in the cast were Norman Foster, Edmond O'Brien, Cameron Mitchell, and John Carroll. In the party scene the directors Curtis Harrington, Paul Mazursky, Claude Chabrol, and Dennis Hopper also appeared. Marlene Dietrich was to play the hostess (modeled on herself). According to Dietrich, she gave a dinner party in honor of Welles in Paris that she prepared herself, with all her legendary skill in the kitchen; she invited the Duchess of Windsor, Paul Gallico, and other distinguished figures. Welles did not appear. To add insult to injury, his secretary called at the last minute to say he could not possibly make it from Rome. Dietrich later discovered he had been in Paris all the time. She was furious; she did not forgive him for years.* According to another version, Dietrich started work on the scene, then had to fly to Paris to attend the funeral of Coco Chanel; she lost interest in proceeding because she was unhappy with the off-the-cuff nature of the camera work and felt she would not be sufficiently protected by the lighting. She was replaced by Lilli Palmer, who had no lighting theories and worked like the trouper she is.

There were countless problems with the movie. The filming in Arizona and California was protracted, and often tempers ran short. At one stage, when company and crew had been shooting until 4:00 A.M., Welles announced that the next day's work would begin at noon. Gary Graver reported that the crew was asking for a 2:00 P.M. call in order to secure a few hours of sleep. Welles exploded. He screamed, "I can't work in this atmosphere, with everybody against me!" and fired the entire crew, announcing that he was leaving for Paris on the first plane. The next day he rehired everyone.

Another problem was that cast members grew older and fatter or thinner (or died) as the picture wore on through the 1970s, and it proved impossible to match them in shots. Joseph McBride, a critic, historian, and admirer of Welles's films, who appears in the movie, related some of his problems in an article in *American Film* (July–August 1976). He pointed out that he aged from twenty-two to twenty-eight during the shooting, gained twenty-five pounds, and lost a green trenchcoat that was needed for matching shots. On four separate occa-

---

* In the Maximilian Schell documentary about her life, *Marlene*, Dietrich said, in an unfortunate gaffe intended presumably as a compliment, "People should cross themselves when they see Orson Welles."

sions during the shooting he had to shave off a fashionable beard and cut his long hair to get back into character. With all the confusion, the results were far from satisfactory; in many ways the script was not realized by the spread-out, overedited, and muddled visual narrative style. Sequences shown at the Screen Directors' Guild some years ago gave an impression of amateurishness. Yet the originality of the vision is there, and in an intriguing sequence in a car, with Oja Kodar performing oral sex on one of the male characters, Welles's frenetic talents emerge strongly. In other scenes there are awkwardnesses and strains in the presentation.

The backing for the picture was complex. In order to support the luxury of his own vision and methods of work, Welles had to draw his finances from a variety of sources. One source was German television; I remember meeting the German television representatives in 1976, when I was writing for *The New York Times*, and I recall their shocked annoyance that all the investment had gone and there was nothing to show for it. Another backer was Avenel, a Swiss group, and a third was an Iranian group that included the Shah's brother-in-law, Mehdi Mouscheri. Apparently Welles was now prepared to sup with the devil to obtain money; in a seeming reversal of his lifelong liberalism, he narrated a one-hour color documentary of groveling admiration for the Iranian leader, produced in cooperation with the Tehran Ministry of Culture and Art. One hopes he did not mean it.

Welles shocked some of his adherents by the interest he took in the figures involved in Clifford Irving's Howard Hughes biography hoax. Himself a master of magic—and of deceit when it came to giving interviews or publishing autobiographical fragments—Welles conceived an intellectual infatuation with the art forger and crook Elmyr de Hory, who was involved with Irving and his wife in the Hughes affair. Even though *The Other Side of the Wind* called for Welles's undivided attention, he frittered away his energies on an exercise in film journalism, *F for Fake*, shot in Europe and America in four months in 1975 without incident, with the colorful Elmyr de Hory as its central figure and Oja Kodar cast in it.

Welles used Hory as a launching pad for an autobiographical meditation on the problems of financing art and dealing with charlatanry. In a critical study of Welles, Joseph McBride claims that Welles identified with Hory, his constantly precarious financial state, and his ingenious methods of putting off inevitable disaster, and that he was shocked and depressed by the forger's suicide in December 1976. It is probable that he also found identification with Clifford Irving, who was driven to fakery out of financial desperation. In the film, Welles draws a Falstaff-Hal comparison between de Hory and Irving. And Welles's familiar concern with power leads to a meditation on Hughes himself: looking up at Hughes's suite at the Desert Inn in Las Vegas, he asks the camera, "What was he doing up there? What were they doing to him? If he broke his silence, would it be—a cry for help?"

No element in Welles's pictures is ever isolated; the late François Truffaut, cited by McBride, wrote that in *F for Fake* Welles also intended to comment on Pauline Kael and her critiques of him as the thief and forger of the script of *Citizen Kane* in *The Citizen Kane Book*. Welles loved the fact that de Hory and Irving fooled the experts for a time and succeeded briefly in tricking the establishment. He hated experts, feeling that they were the greatest con men of all; and the fact that millionaires bought de Hory's painting forgeries enchanted him, with his dislike of the rich and powerful.

Yet even as a certain moral corruption was seemingly setting in, Welles found himself welcomed into the bosom of the corrupt industry he had so long derided and that had so long derided him. At the 1970 Academy Awards he was given a special statuette acknowledging his lifelong achievement in the cinema; as it was announced that he was absent from the country and unable to accept the award in person, he was watching the ceremony on a television set nearby, and his filmed acceptance speech, allegedly shot in Arizona, was done within driving distance of the Dorothy Chandler Pavilion. The insult to the Academy implied by his behavior was of course intended.

Welles behaved better when he was given the Life Achievement Award of the American Film Institute in 1975. Because of his reputation for capriciousness, the organizers, led by the Institute's president, George Stevens, Jr., had a nerve-racking time wondering whether he would in fact turn up. He did; weighing now more than 350 pounds, he shuffled painfully forward from his seat to the stage, where he delivered, with bold and familiar cunning, not the orotund or flamboyant address laced with anecdotes and baroque witticisms that everyone expected, but a fake-modest, ultimately simple, meticulously minimalist speech of sly elegance and style. The tributes to him, delivered by old friends and colleagues, were warm and sincere. Charlton Heston, Peter Bogdanovich, Janet Leigh, Joseph Cotten, and Natalie Wood spoke with affection. Cotten said that Welles was "a man of deep perception . . . who has had an awesome and profound influence on the lives and careers of all of us. . . . If it wasn't for him I could be very happy working in my uncle's in Sycamore Street in Petersburg, Virginia." George Stevens said, "We measure Orson Welles by his courage and the intensity of his personal vision. He has combined a mighty will with a child's heart to produce a legacy of enduring creation."

The evening was charged with irony. The numerous executives present (most of them fired or reassigned today) represented the opposite of Welles's own position vis-à-vis picture-making. Bent only on achieving profits, most studio executives had no patience with the artistic vision of men like Welles, and indeed more than one person in the audience had refused to work with him when Welles's agents offered his talents. Nevertheless, lip service was given, and whatever Welles's private thoughts may have been, he gave a splendid performance of seeming gratitude. Only those listening carefully could detect the touch of sly humor in his remark that he represented a friendly neighborhood store while the industry was a giant supermarket. And only those attending still more carefully would have detected the hollowness in the laughter that greeted the comparison.

In order to finance *F for Fake* and *The Other Side of the Wind,* Welles took on new projects in the 1970s. He went to France to appear in Claude Chabrol's *Ten Days' Wonder,* from a mystery novel by Ellery Queen about a Clay-like or Kane-like millionaire who lives in a house that has been deliberately preserved in the style of the 1920s in order to give him the illusion that he has never grown old. Michel Piccoli plays an outsider who invades the house to expose the millionaire's cocoonlike existence. Unfortunately, the movie was too much of a roman à clef to work independently of Welles's personality, and Chabrol's direction was pedestrian. Welles went on to appear in a gallumphing television version of the George Kaufman–Moss Hart comedy *The Man Who Came to Dinner;* apart from the irresistible presence of Mary Wickes, the nurse in the original version, the production was unsuccessful, directed with crassness by Bud Yorkin.*

In 1972 Welles turned up in a film version of *Treasure Island* as Long John Silver, seen only from the waist up because his leg was too fat to be bent double to allow for the attachment of a wooden leg. This was a continuation or a reworking of the picture he had begun in 1964, based on his own script and directed by Jesús Franco, his assistant on *Chimes at Midnight.* John Hough directed the 1972 film, with the script

---

* Welles had wanted to appear in the 1942 film version of *The Man Who Came to Dinner* as the irascible Sheridan Whiteside, and Jack Warner would have liked him to star in it and even direct it, but George Schaefer of RKO had refused to let Welles go. For years Welles denigrated Monty Woolley's brilliant performance in the movie.

largely rewritten by Wolf Mankowitz; the picture contains Welles's worst performance on screen. He stumbled into deeper mire: in Burt I. Gordon's *Necromancy* Welles was an evil voodoo-doll maker; in *Get to Know Your Rabbit,* directed by Brian de Palma, he was a magician; in *Malpertuis* he was Mr. Cassavius, whose sinister mansion is populated by captured Greek gods sewn into human skins.

Notable among the accolades of that decade was the American Film Institute's special evening "Working with Welles," at the Directors' Guild of America in November 1978. The panel assembled for the occasion included Roger Hill, his teacher at Todd, still spry and irrepressible in his eighties; Dan O'Herlihy, the Irish actor who had appeared in *Macbeth;* an ailing Kenneth Tynan, who died of emphysema not long afterward; Norman Lloyd, who was Cinna the poet in *Julius Ceasar;* and the director John Berry from the old Mercury days. Notable by their absence were John Houseman, Hiram Sherman, and the other leading figures of the Mercury Theater; much bitterness remained in that circle. Welles mischievously enjoyed putting on the crowd: if Roger Hill had been gay, he said, Welles would have been his boy. "I fell in love with him. If I am rude, it is because he is rude. If he had been gay, so would I. Talk about influence, here it is, the horse's mouth." Then, in an orgy of nostalgia, Welles sang "Gondolivia" from *Finesse the Queen,* the Todd musical with a libretto by Hill, in which Welles said he had appeared as a chorus girl. (Hill correctly denied it: "You didn't have good enough legs.")

Another reminder of the past had occurred when Richard Welles died in 1975 in San Francisco, in a depressing apartment in the worst part of town, his meager sustenance provided by Welles through Arnold Weissberger, who inexplicably failed to pay for Richard's funeral. Richard had seen Welles only once since 1938: he had turned up unexpectedly at one of Welles's wonder shows in the 1940s, volunteering his services to saw Marlene Dietrich in half. When Welles asked his name, he delivered the memorable line, "Don't you recognize your own brother?" His estate, consisting of $470.65 in cash, $504.50 in coins, and $255 in Social Security, was attached by the public administrator to pay the costs of his funeral. The estate was within $200 of the value of his mother's estate when she died in 1924.

As old friendships disintegrated and new ones—mostly with young people who admired Welles unreservedly—began, his most troubled relationship was that with the formerly devoted Peter Bogdanovich. Along with two other up-and-coming young American directors, William Friedkin and Francis Ford Coppola, Bogdanovich set up the Directors' Company, an arrangement in which each of the directors would direct two pictures and produce a third. The ceiling on the budgets would be $3 million, the movies would be of artistic merit, and the profits would be equally shared. Bogdanovich had in mind that Welles would direct the film he was to produce under the agreement.

Bogdanovich made two pictures under the contract, *Paper Moon*, a comedy with Ryan and Tatum O'Neal that was a great success, and *Daisy Miller*, based on the Henry James story, with Cybill Shepherd, which was not. (William Friedkin made no film under the contract, thereby annoying the others, and Coppola made only *The Conversation*.) When Bogdanovich asked Welles to appear in a movie outside the Directors' Company (a comedy with Ryan O'Neal and Cybill Shepherd that was never made), Welles misinterpreted the offer; he believed that Bogdanovich was blackmailing him into appearing in it in return for giving him a chance to direct. Thus the plans for the Bogdanovich-Welles film were shelved.

Another disaffection arose when Bogdanovich loaned Welles his house in Bel Air for cutting *The Other Side of the Wind*. Instead, Welles brought in his crew and filmed the picture's party scene and other sequences there, shooting through the nights and messing up the home. An irritable Bogdanovich returned from Europe and, either out of generosity or to keep Welles out of his hair, paid the rent on another house for him.

The final blow was Welles's refusal to authorize the release of *This Is Orson Welles*, Bogdanovich's book with and about him, and the advance had to be returned to Harper & Row. Despite their differences, neither Welles nor Bogdanovich would speak against the other; their loyalty remained constant.

When the Ayatollah Khomeini seized power in Iran, *The Other Side of the Wind* was locked up by the revolutionaries. The Shah's brother-in-law, Mehdi Mouscheri, claimed that he was its owner, and the negative was placed under lock and key in Paris while the French courts argued over whose film it was. The legal struggle continues to this day.

Welles's leading disciple up to the 1980s was the wealthy young director Henry Jaglom, who did his loyal best to set up Welles in a movie version of *King Lear* to be made in Paris with the support of the Mitterrand government.

In the early 1980s Welles completed—for the producers Andrew Braunsberg and Hal Ashby's North Star Productions—the screenplay *Da Capo*, based on *The Dreamers* by Isak Dinesen and intended as a starring vehicle for Oja Kodar. In a prologue he described his lifelong obsession with the author, whose work he had adapted in *The Immortal*

Story. He talked of writing to her once, a mountain of pages all of which he carefully destroyed, and of flying to Copenhagen to meet her, through friends who knew her, and spending a sleepless night before fleeing Denmark at daybreak out of fear. It is clear that she exercised so strong a fascination for him that he did not have the temerity to face her.

The screenplay begins with Welles reading from a book the story of Lincoln Forsner, an Englishman stranded at a country inn in the Alps, "with snow, storm, great clouds and a wild moon outside." He talks of having searched for a kind of ideal woman; he had once called himself a poet, and he had fallen in love with her in a brothel. He returned to the brothel and made love to her again, and they began an affair. Olalla was an image beyond any dream, and he was obsessed, jealous, and possessive of her. He determined he would marry Olalla and returned to the brothel, only to be told that she had died of a sudden fever; in fact a wealthy old man had settled her debts, and she had left for Basel. Lincoln searches for her but cannot find her; there is no trace. The search for an ideal woman and the disappointment that follows marriage are reflected in Welles's treatment with all the force of romanticism.

Nothing in the rest of the script quite matches the power of the beginning. Too many voiceovers, long speeches that strain the audience's attention, confuse the narrative. But this intensely poetic screenplay, filled with heightened prose of a quality seldom heard on the screen, written without numbered pages or camera directions, is certainly one of the most intriguing works of the master.

Jaglom made some of the younger Hollywood executives promise to read a more commercial script by Welles, who agreed under extreme pressure to put together an outline for a story that had certain resemblances to Gore Vidal's *The Best Man.* A senator about to become president is sexually involved with a politician living in Africa, and the affair imperils his political future. Once again Welles deals with a Socratic relationship between a younger and an older man, a situation that had become the obsessive theme of his work. Welles called the script *The Big Brass Ring.*

Homosexuality as a theme, like politics, has never been box office for Hollywood. When the 20th Century–Fox executive Sherry Lansing put through *Making Love,* the story of two homosexuals and their affair, the picture failed. *The Best Man* and such other important political pictures as *The Manchurian Candidate* and *Seven Days in May* did lamentably in the theaters. In a country in which barely fifty percent of those eligible even vote, and in which, despite gay lib, the vast majority are offended by the thought of homosexuality, there could be little hope for *The Big Brass Ring*, whether Orson Welles made it or not. It was as though the great man was determined to defy the fates by not doing what he promised: to put together a script that everyone would want to see on the screen.

While he was thwarting his own potential comeback as a director, Welles suddenly and unexpectedly found new fame through his appearance on television talk shows, particularly Johnny Carson's *Tonight Show*, which he hosted on occasion, and on which he established for himself the character of Grand Old Man. He confirmed his fame with a whole new generation of Americans by appearing as the centerpiece of the Paul Masson wine commercials, which arguably made him more celebrated than anything else he had done. The chief director of these commercials, with their image of a portly magnifico past his prime, was Harry Hamburg, who thoroughly approved Welles's selection by John Buckingham, account executive for Masson at the advertising firm of Doyle Dane Bernbach. The two men believed strongly that Welles, with his great size and his atmosphere of civilized relish of the best, was ideal in every way for their purposes. Wearing a red sport shirt, Welles sat on a patio of a modern house, talking with heavily overripe diction of the making of a fine wine, comparing it with the writing of a great book, assuring the vast army of viewers that Masson would "sell no wine before its time."

On his first day of work for Masson, Welles sent a memorandum to the cameraman asking that the camera be above eye level, with a special light on his left side. Harry Hamburg agreed to everything, quietly telling the cameraman to "ignore the instructions." At first Hamburg was impressed at the control with which Welles could reduce the length of a speech by as much as fifteen seconds without seemingly losing pace or understandability. But soon there were problems, many of them related by Barbara Leaming in *Playboy* (December 1983). According to Leaming, when the Masson people asked Welles to say, "Stradivarius took three years to make one of his violins," which was to lead into the time it took to mature a Masson wine, Welles was dismayed by the comparison and upset at having to deliver the line. Later, during a party scene, he complained that the people in the sequence would not be welcome in his own home; some of the extras overheard the remark and were understandably annoyed. Welles exploded over the director's idea of delivering the words "in July." He screamed, "Get me a jury and show me how [I should] say 'in July' and I'll go down on you!"

On another occasion, Welles demanded that Hamburg pique him to make him look disgruntled and brooding. Challenged, Hamburg said, "You're a fat slob," then, "You're a has-been," but neither of the jabs went home. Finally, reaching for any straw and recalling Pauline Kael's book, Hamburg asked Welles, "How come you screwed Herman Mankiewicz out of the credit on *Citizen Kane* when he actually wrote it?" Welles flushed red with extreme anger and said, "Obviously, you can't differentiate between making someone angry and making him piqued. Forget it. I'll do it myself!" Later Welles was let go when Masson introduced a range of light wines and hired the physically lighter John Gielgud to promote them.

Welles's wine-drinking image had an ironical undercurrent. He suffered so severely from kidney trouble, blood pressure problems, and his excessive weight* that he was forced to stop drinking wine entirely and could drink only Sprite, 7-Up, and other soft drinks.

Welles was now taking on increasingly marginal assignments. He became the commercial spokesman for WABC Talk Radio; he delivered promotional announcements for Man-O-War, the heavy metal band; he was heard on that band's album as a narrator; he turned up on movie trailers; and he moved back to Hollywood, where he lived in a large white house on North Stanley Avenue. Perhaps he reached his lowest point when he delivered with rounded, Shakespearean phrases in a deep midnight voice a radio commercial for Reuben's restaurants, describing with plummy scrumptiousness the dripping gravy of a juicy hamburger, the golden crispness of french fried potatoes, and the thick white splendor of an apple pie a la mode.

From Rosebud to Reuben's is quite a stretch, and along the way not least of his burdens was his isolation from two of his daughters. In the early 1970s Rebecca described in interviews her poverty in Tacoma, Washington, where she and her sculptor husband lived in a slum next door to a slaughterhouse and had to endure the stench of animals day and night. Later Welles called and asked her to Los Angeles to appear with him briefly in a commercial, but apart from scattered correspondence they were not in touch again. Rebecca has since divorced her husband and is living modestly but more happily with another man in a better part of Tacoma. She dabbles in little theater but has no real career of her own.

Christopher divorced her first husband and married Irwin Fodor and now lives in New York; she too has had little or no contact with Welles, and recently she told me that she had no idea how to get in

---

* On one occasion Welles got stuck in a small car taking him to Ma Maison, and the car had to be dismantled to free him.

touch with her father. Only Beatrice, the most attractive of the three women, a tall and Junoesque beauty with fair hair and a voluptuous figure, was close to Welles in the years before his death. Beatrice has shown talent as a magazine writer and has ambitions to be a choreographer and actress.

Many mementoes of Welles's past were wiped out when his Prescott, Arizona, home was swept away by floodwaters. Long before that, his home in Madrid, the setting of *The Immortal Story*, had burned down while the actor Robert Shaw was in residence. The fire consumed many of his maverick movies, including *Too Much Johnson* and almost certainly the films he had made of *Chimes at Midnight* in Ireland and the omnibus show he had taken through Germany with Eartha Kitt. He could not bear to see his old pictures, and he turned from the screen in despair when Johnny Carson or Merv Griffin showed excerpts from *Citizen Kane* or *The Magnificent Ambersons*. Much had been lost, and many of his memories caused him pain; he could not get over the failure of his youthful promise; and underlying all the adulation he received was the constant question, why?

In 1982 Welles was awarded the French Legion d'Honneur. With unaccustomed modesty, he said he doubted that he deserved the honor.

During the 1980s Welles was a fixture at Ma Maison in Los Angeles, which combined the structure of an Australian shearing shed with the cuisine of a two-star French restaurant. He held court in the inner room, a tiny poodle tucked in his coat, accompanied by Henry Jaglom or other admirers, while those marooned on the astroturf outside tried to hear every word he uttered. This was not always difficult, for he tended to deliver many of his best lines at stage volume.

In 1983 John Houseman received a telephone call asking him to appear on *The Merv Griffin Show*. He was told that an old friend of his would introduce and appear with him. At once, he says, he instinctively knew who that would be. He felt a great sense of apprehension but went ahead anyway. When he arrived, Orson Welles was not in the green room. Instead, as he waited in the wings, he heard Welles's voice resonantly declaring that John Houseman was one of the most brilliant, inspired, exciting, talented producers he had ever worked with. Houseman was very excited in view of the ghastly encounter in London some twenty-three years earlier, and indeed he had not spoken to Welles since. As he entered the set, Welles embraced him, and these two very large men did a kind of bear waltz around the studio floor. Although at the end of the show they left in separate limousines and were never in touch again, Houseman says that he once again regarded Welles as his friend, all previous differences forgotten and forgiven. The reconciliation was undoubtedly of major importance to both men.

Another twist of fortune promised to bring Welles back to the forefront as an American filmmaker. The Michael Fitzgeralds, the production team of husband and wife who made John Huston's *Under the Volcano*, decided in 1984 to ask Welles to direct a commercial picture. They commissioned Ring Lardner, Jr., one of the victims of the 1950s blacklist, to write *The Cradle Will Rock*, a screenplay based on the story of Welles's 1937 production and the night the audience walked the streets of New York to see the play performed in defiance of the Federal Theater Project. Lardner's script memorably evoked that occasion, and when Welles discussed the episode with the producers, they were overjoyed at his enthusiasm. Welles offered to direct the film himself. The Fitzgeralds saw that Welles must direct the film, and a production arrangement was made whereby John Landis and George Folsey would act as executive producers, with the Fitzgeralds as "line" producers, aided by Alessandro Tasca. Committing himself eagerly to the project, Welles began rewriting the script, and Rupert Everett, British star of the film *Another Country*, was cast as the young Welles. Early in 1985 financial problems were delaying production, and Welles was in Paris to discuss a new film of *King Lear*.

Unfortunately, there were differences between Welles and the French government, which had certain mandatory rules for films which were to obtain certification under the local laws applying to film financing. One of the rules was that a producer must be placed on any project, and Welles was compelled to accept this decision. He might have been more sanguine about it had not the producer allegedly advised him that he would not receive payment as director or star until every last foot of film was shot and the editing completed. The implied slur in this was, of course, that without the temptation of money at the end of the work, Welles wouldn't complete the film. There may have been some rationale in this approach, indeed in view of Welles's record one would be permitted to consider the decision sensible, but it might have been more tactful to have offered some of the money up front and the rest on completion, rather than insulting Welles by implication. Oja Kodar has publicly charged that Welles was deliberately deceived by François Mitterrand into believing that the project would take place at all. She claims that the French merely intended to use Welles as a stick to beat the United States with, pointing out that they were prepared to sponsor him while the decadent and corrupt world of Hollywood was not. This she took to be an example of Socialist thinking. However, there seems little substance to this claim, sincerely intended though it may have been.

The Cradle Will Rock also collapsed, for a variety of reasons. One of those adduced is that Barry Diller, who had recently taken over as head of 20th Century Fox Studios, allegedly refused to countenance the film's distribution on the grounds it was insufficiently commercial. Another version was that various potential distributors on the art house circuits were unable to come to satisfactory terms with Michael Fitzgerald. Still other reasons given were that potential backers did not believe Welles could be relied upon to complete the work in hand, or that his health would survive the rigors of shooting in various locations. Whatever the causes, and following a decision to shoot the picture at studios in Rome where the standing sets of Sergio Leone's *Once Upon a Time in America* could be used to simulate the New York of 1937, *The Cradle Will Rock* literally fell apart in Welles's hands. And when he learned that all was lost he is said to have broken into helpless tears.

One note of hope and triumph accompanied that last year of his life. He shot about 20 minutes of *The Dreamers*, based on the story by Isak Dinesen (Karen Blixen), starring Oja Kodar, put together with the impeccable skills of Gary Graver in the back garden of his house on North Stanley Avenue in West Hollywood, California. One sequence recently seen shows that Welles's talent was untouched by time. The force, electricity, energy and beauty of the footage could have emerged from a far younger artist, and those few feet of film, with Welles as a shadowy presence behind the camera and the magical Miss Kodar speaking the Baroness Blixen's words, constitute perhaps the only example of actual art to be found in the American film in many years.

On the night of October 9, 1985, Welles had dinner with Barbara Leaming, author of a biography to which he had contributed table talk. He returned home, driven by his chauffeur, and apparently began work on his stage directions for the next day at UCLA, where he was continuing to shoot a one-man television special featuring his expertise as a magician. According to the medical reports, he was stricken with a massive heart attack in the early hours of the morning, exactly the same fate which befell his father and, at the same age, his brother Richard. It was a swift and merciful end, and one can be grateful that, given his parlous physical condition, he had not been taken long before.

The media treated his demise with a demonstration of tastelessness. His massive body carried out in a bag was displayed on every network. The comments on his career were foolish, as one might expect. After his demise, a private funeral service was held at a mortuary chapel facing the Hollywood Cemetery on Santa Monica Boulevard. Welles, with his gallows humor and strong sense of irony, would have appreciated the indelicacy of this event. Not only did it take place in the featureless urban landscape which he deplored, in the town which had rejected him, but also the funeral itself was marked by a curious situation. His widow, the Countess Paola Mori, appeared, along with his three daughters, Christopher, Rebecca and Beatrice, who, separated as they were by birthdates, time and distance, scarcely knew each other. Oja Kodar, who had remained devoted to Welles for decades, was not invited, and her absence, while no doubt preventing potential tension in the air, was a disgrace. The alternative, a confrontation between wife and mistress, would certainly not have been desirable, but one likes to think that each of these remarkable women would have known how to behave in the confined conditions.

On the Saturday following there was a hastily but admirably arranged tribute to Welles at the Directors Guild of America on Sunset Boulevard. It was touching to note on arrival the long line of fans which ran around the block more than an hour before the afternoon was to begin. Welles's old friend and assistant, Richard Wilson, David Shepard of the Directors Guild, and Gary Graver jointly organized the occasion with the assistance of Oja Kodar. On this occasion the Countess Mori was notable by her absence; so, too, was John Houseman, whom the organizers felt would not appear due to recent differences with Welles. This seemed odd in view of Houseman's statements to me just before Welles died that they had patched up their long-term quarrels and were friends again.

The afternoon opened appropriately with Peter Bogdanovich, who moderated the occasion with subdued intelligence. Roger Hill, at the age of 90, turned up to speak of the early days in an excusably rambling but affectionate manner which could only move deeply all who heard it. Unfortunately, some of the speakers chose the occasion to give academic lectures more appropriate for a class of freshmen than for the intensely involved audience before them, while others paraded their egos to the point that Welles's own career was virtually forgotten. Among the admirable exceptions to the rule of self-flattering and self-serving mediocrity were Greg Garrison, old friend of Welles and executor of his estate, Charlton Heston, notably intelligent and dignified, and the still-beautiful Geraldine Fitzgerald.

Oja Kodar made a highly dramatic appearance on the podium. Dressed in mourning, gaunt and red-eyed from weeping, she still looked startlingly handsome in her grief. She chose the occasion to launch into a startling attack on the French government. She began by reading a telegram of condolence from Mitterrand, first in French, then in English. She denounced him and Jack Lang, French Minister of Culture, saying that it was abominable that they had tricked Welles into believing they had sincere intentions of making *King Lear*. She spoke through weeping of Welles's many disappointments in his friends, and it is understood that she very nearly committed herself to attack Henry Jaglom, who, it was alleged, had conducted a number of tape recordings of Welles without his permission or knowledge and who, it was also alleged, had failed to give him financial support, or even pay for his meals at Ma Maison, despite Jaglom's asserted net worth of $80 million. Jaglom's speech was singularly self-serving and unpleasant to listen to, especially when he announced that Welles's last thoughts had been of Jaglom and his mother. Jaglom made this curious deduction from the fact that when he woke up on the morning of Welles's death, his answering machine showed a single numeral indicating that someone had called while he was asleep. When he pressed the rewind button and played the message through, he heard Welles's voice inquiring after his mother's health; she had been in the hospital in New York. This theatrical disclosure scarcely gave one confidence in Jaglom and seemed to play into the hands of his many critics, most of whom would have preferred it if he had not spoken at all.

In the wake of the memorial tribute, some odd cross-currents emerged. Oja Kodar expressed herself as being dissatisfied with Barbara Leaming's supposedly authorized biography, and was preparing to charge her with having failed to return certain important materials. At the same time, Roger Hill was said to be disaffected with Barbara Leaming, and was making similar assertions. Countess Mori was said to have locked up the vault containing Welles's unfinished films, which Miss Kodar claimed she had the right to edit and complete. At time of writing, none of these conflicts have been resolved, and most important of all, Welles's burial had not been carried out. Hating Forest Lawn and Hollywood Cemetery, Welles did not want to be interred in either of these graveyards. Instead, he wanted his ashes carried to a small village of which he was fond in Spain. There, he would be as far removed as possible from the vulgarity of commercialized death that he detested as much as anything else. However, as I write these words, the agonizing question has not been settled of whether widow or girlfriend will have the honor of interring his remains in the place appointed.

The conventional view is that Welles was destroyed by Hollywood, which with its usual crassness drove him into exile and refused to give him the chance to make great movies that would have been a credit to America. His downfall as the most important American film director has seldom been placed at his own door except by the industry itself, which never forgot that he ran over budget and schedule on *Kane, Ambersons*, and *It's All True*. Almost every liberal intellectual in America interested in film perpetually asks himself, whenever Welles's name comes up: Why did he slide from the heights, from being the most revolutionary figure of radio, stage, and screen in the heyday of those media in this country half a century ago?

The truth is that Welles gallantly tried to do the impossible: he tried to create films as novelists create novels, as poets create poems, as composers create music, as painters create paintings. Snatching finances from any possible source, drawing from his own pocket when need be, taking all the time that seemed necessary, he went beyond any other figure of the screen, including even Kurosawa and Renoir, in seeking to convey a personal vision through celluloid, at his own pace and without restraints. Many lives were affected, not all for the better, and many pockets were emptied in this relentlessly single-minded pursuit. Yet those who understood him, who were really close to him, put up with everything in order to accommodate the genius they recognized. He displayed a manic excess and self-destructiveness that, as Leslie Fiedler disclosed in his *The Life and Death of the American Novel*, is a very American trait. And there is another consideration.

It is an axiom in the commercial cinema that the central figure of any work must be a human being with whom the mass audience can identify. He or she has to be likable, attractive, desirable, even when capable of villainy; he or she must speak the language of the people. Scriptwriters of proven commercial worth have deliberately tailored their scripts to the specific needs of stars so as not to extend their range too far, and the stars themselves more often than not make further alterations to suit their personalities. Yet so relentlessly did Welles work against the commercial grain that he even dared to make the central figures of his films unsympathetic.

In *Citizen Kane* Welles created a selfish, heartless tycoon who is destroyed spiritually by his own greed and ambition. Americans could have comfortably accepted a rogue or a pirate of this sort, but someone who was haunted by agonizing visions of lost innocence alienated and confused the mass audience for decades. In *The Magnificent Ambersons* Welles portrayed an impudent, bad-tempered puppy of a man, George Minafer, who disrupted the life of a small town; this charmless creature proved impossible to identify with in an age of heroes of the caliber of Tyrone Power and Errol Flynn. The other protagonist of the story, Aunt Fanny, was the sort of figure usually made fun of in American films: the tortured virgin spinster who hopelessly sets her cap for a man she cannot have. Contemporary audiences laughed at Aunt

Fanny, whose misery failed to touch a chord in the American heart.

Citizen Kane lost well over $100,000, and *The Magnificent Amber-sons* lost more than half a million. Following his failure to finish *It's All True*, Welles attempted a comeback with *The Stranger*, a movie in which the protagonist was a Nazi war criminal hiding in a small American town. Again it was impossible for the audience to identify with such a person; the war was only just over, and there were few families that had not been affected by it. *The Lady from Shanghai* had as its hero a liberal sailor who had supported the loyalist cause in the Spanish Civil War—and many Americans knew that people like that were Communist sympathizers. The making of Rita Hayworth, reigning sex goddess of the American screen, into a murderess further alienated the public.

Shakespeare has never been box office in America, so Welles's Shakespearean trilogy sank without a trace. Ironically, while the films he directed were failing, Welles himself was highly bankable as an actor and public personality. In Europe, Welles's discipline disintegrated, and he lost control of his career. As his waistline grew, his career shriveled; it was almost as though eating and drinking were substitutes for creativity.

Today we mourn Welles's passing at a time when his proposed return to the director's chair was a matter for rejoicing. He was a national treasure. But to pretend that he was maliciously rubbed out by Holly-wood is of no help to history. Some perverse streak of anticommercialism drove him; he was the brilliant architect of his own downfall, and it is impossible to avoid that truth today.

APPENDIX 1

Radio,

Television,

Film, and

Theater

RADIO

1934 *Panic*, NBC (actor).

1935–1936 *The March of Time* series, NBC (actor).

1936 *The Great McCoy: The Relief of Lucknow*, WGB Chicago (co-producer and actor).

1936 *Musical Reveries* series, CBS (narrator). *Hamlet*, CBS (actor). *The Edgar Bergen and Charlie McCarthy Show*, NBC (guest star). *The Columbia Workshop*, CBS (actor).

1937 *The Shadow* series, Mutual (actor). *Les Misérables*, Mutual (adaptor, director, actor). *Cavalcade of Ameica* series, CBS (actor and narrator). *Streamlined Shakespeare* (actor).

1938 *America's Hour* series, CBS (actor and narrator). *First Person Singular* series, CBS (producer, director, actor, narrator). *Mercury Theater of the Air* series, CBS (producer, director, actor, narrator);

"The War of the Worlds," October 30, 1938. *A Christmas Carol,* CBS (actor).

1938–1940 *The Campbell Playhouse with Orson Welles* series, CBS (producer, director, actor, narrator).

1940 *KTSA Texas News Show,* KTSA (guest). *The Rudy Vallee Show,* CBS (guest).

1941 *The Free Company,* "His Honor the Mayor," CBS (writer, producer, narrator). *The Lady Esther Show* series, CBS (producer, director, actor, narrator).

1942 Occasional broadcasts on Brazilian radio. *Ceiling Unlimited* series CBS (writer, producer, director, actor, narrator).

1942–1943 *Hello, Americans* series, CBS. *The Orson Welles Show* series, CBS (producer and host). *Suspense* series, CBS (director and actor).

1943 *The Socony Vacuum Hour* series, CBS.

1944 *Orson Welles's Almanack* series, CBS (producer and host). *Columbia Presents Corwin,* CBS (director and actor). *American Eloquence,* CBS (director and reciter). *The Texarkana Program,* CBS (reciter).

1944–1945 *This Is My Best* series, CBS (director, narrator, actor). *Lux Radio Theater,* "Jane Eyre," CBS (actor).

1945–1946 *Exploring the Unknown* series, Mutual (actor).

1946 *Schlitz Summer Mercury Playhouse* series, CBS (producer, actor, narrator, host).

1951 *The Adventures of Harry Lime* series, BBC (actor).

1952 *The Black Museum* series, BBC (host). *Sherlock Holmes,* BBC (actor).

1953 *Song of Myself,* BBC (actor and narrator). *Queen of Spades,* BBC (actor).

1955 *Sherlock Holmes* series, BBC/NBC (actor).

TELEVISION

1953 *Omnibus: King Lear,* CBS (actor).

1955 *The Orson Welles Sketchbook* series, BBC (producer and host). *Around the World with Orson Welles* series, BBC (producer and host).

1956 *I Love Lucy,* CBS (guest star). *Four-Star Jubilee: Twentieth Century,* CBS (actor).

1957 *The Merchant of Venice; Macbeth; Othello,* CBS (actor). *The Fall of the City,* CBS (narrator).

1958 *Colgate Theater: The Fountain of Youth,* NBC (director). *The Method,* ABC London (director).

1961 *Tempo* series, ABC London (narrator and host). *Around the World* series, CBS (narrator and host).

1962 *Continental Classroom: Out of Darkness,* WCBS New York (narrator).

1971 *The Silent Years*, PBS (narrator). *Future Shock*, Metromedia (narrator and host).

1972 *The Marty Feldman Comedy Machine* series, ABC (guest).

1973 *Orson Welles's Great Mysteries* series, Syndicated (producer and host).

1974 *The Man Who Came to Dinner*, NBC (actor).

1976 *The First Fifty Years: The Big Event*, NBC (narrator). *Survival: Magnificent Monsters of the Deep*, NBC (narrator).

1979 *The Orson Welles Show* pilot film, Syndicated (narrator and star).

1980 *Shogun*, NBC (narrator).

1984 *Scene of the Crime*, NBC (narrator).

Welles has also appeared frequently on *The Tonight Show* (as guest and occasional host), *The Merv Griffin Show*, *CBS News*, *Dean Martin's Celebrity Roast*, *The Dom De Luise Show*, and in numerous commercials, notably for Paul Masson wines.

FILMS

Welles as Director

1933 Scenes from a stage production of *Twelfth Night*

1934 *Hearts of Age*

1938 Sequences to accompany a stage production of *Too Much Johnson*

1941 *Citizen Kane*

1942 *The Magnificent Ambersons*

1946 *The Stranger*

1947 *The Lady from Shanghai*

1948 *Macbeth*

1950 Scenes from a stage production of *Time Runs* (in Munich)

1952 *Othello*

1955 *Confidential Report/Mr. Arkadin*

1955 A stage production of *Moby Dick* (in London)

1957 *Touch of Evil*

1962 *The Trial*

1966 *Chimes at Midnight*

1968 *The Immortal Story*

1973 *F for Fake*

1980 *The Making of Othello*
It's All True (unfinished)
Don Quixote (unfinished)
The Deep (unfinished)
The Other Side of the Wind (unfinished)

1985 *King Lear* (in preparation)
The Cradle Will Rock (in preparation)

Welles as Actor

1941 *Citizen Kane*
1943 *Journey into Fear*
1944 *Jane Eyre; Follow the Boys*
1946 *The Stranger; Tomorrow Is Forever*
1947 *The Lady from Shanghai*
1948 *Macbeth*
1949 *Black Magic; Prince of Foxes; The Third Man*
1950 *The Black Rose*
1951 *Return to Glenascaul*
1952 *Othello*
1953 *Trent's Last Case; Royal Affairs of Versailles; Man, Beast, and Virtue*
1954 *Napoleon; Three Cases of Murder*
1955 *Trouble in the Glen; Confidential Report/Mr. Arkadin*
1956 *Moby Dick*
1957 *Pay the Devil; The Long Hot Summer; Touch of Evil*
1958 *The Roots of Heaven*
1959 *Compulsion; David and Goliath; Ferry to Hong Kong*
1960 *Austerlitz; Crack in the Mirror*
1961 *Lafayette; Désordre*
1962 *The Tartars; The Trial*
1963 *Rogopag; The VIPs*
1964 *Marco the Magnificent*
1965 *Casino Royale*
1966 *Is Paris Burning?; A Man for All Seasons; Chimes at Midnight*
1967 *The Sailor from Gibraltar; I'll Never Forget What's 'Is Name*
1968 *Oedipus the King; House of Cards; The Last Roman*
1969 *Start the Revolution Without Me; The Southern Star; Twelve Plus One; The Battle of Neretva; The Merchant of Venice[?]* [*]
1970 *The Kremlin Letter; Catch-22; Waterloo*
1971 *A Safe Place; The Canterbury Tales*
1972 *Ten Days' Wonder; Get to Know Your Rabbit; Necromancy; Treasure Island; Malpertuis; Sutjeska*
1976 *Voyage of the Damned*
1978 *The Filming of Othello* (as participant)
1979 *The Muppet Movie; The Secret of Nicolai Tesla; Never Trust an Honest Thief*
1982 *The Muppets Take Manhattan*
1983 *Butterfly*
1984 *Where Is Parsifal?*

Welles provided the narration for the films *The Swiss Family Robinson, The Magnificent Ambersons, Duel in the Sun, Cinerama South Sea Adventure, The*

---

[*]Welles allegedly made this film, partly in Yugoslavia.

Vikings, Les Seigneurs de la Forêt, High Journey, King of Kings, Der Grosse Atlantik, The Finest Hours, A King's Story, Barbed Water, Bugs Bunny Super-star, Challenge of Greatness/The Challenge, The Late, Great Planet Earth, and *Genocide* (with Elizabeth Taylor).

Welles's unproduced film scripts include *The Smiler with a Knife, Heart of Darkness, The Way to Santiago* (as *Mexican Melodrama*), *Don't Catch Me, War and Peace, Salome* (with Fletcher Markle), *Crime and Punishment, Henry IV* (Pirandello), *Cyrano de Bergerac, Moby Dick, Around the World in Eighty Days, Ulysses, Julius Caesar, Operation Cendrillon, Paris by Night, Carmilla, The Naked Lady and the Musketeers, The Merchant of Venice, Portrait of an Assassin, The Odyssey, The Iliad, The Autobiography of Cellini, Masquerade, The Pickwick Papers, The Sacred Beasts*, and *Da Capo, King Lear* and *The Cradle Will Rock*. He provided the script for the Abraham episode in *The Bible* and co-wrote *Treasure Island* (1972).

THEATER

1931   Gate Theater, Dublin: *Jew Süss* by Ashley Dukes, *The Dead Ride Fast* by David Sears, *The Archdupe* by Percy Robinson, *Mogu of the Desert* by Padraic Colum (actor in all).

1932   Gate Theater, Dublin: *Death Takes a Holiday* by Alberto Cassella, *Hamlet* by Shakespeare (actor in both); *The Circle* by Somerset Maugham (director); *The Chinese Bungalow* by Matheson Lang, an Abbey midnight benefit (director and actor).

1933   Todd School, Woodstock, Illinois: *Twelfth Night* by Shakespeare (co-director, designer, actor).

1933–1934   Katharine Cornell company, on tour: *Romeo and Juliet* by Shake-speare, *The Barretts of Wimpole Street* by Rudolph Besier, *Candida* by Bernard Shaw (actor in all).
Todd School, Woodstock, Illinois: *Trilby* by George du Maurier, *Hamlet* by Shakespeare, *Tsar Paul* by Dmitry Merezhkovsky (associate producer and actor in all).

1935   Imperial Theater, New York: *Panic* by Archibald MacLeish (actor).

1936   Lafayette and Adelphi Theaters, New York: *Macbeth* by Shake-speare (co-producer and director).
Maxine Elliott Theater, New York: *Horse Eats Hat* by Eugène Labiche (co-producer, director, actor).
St. James Theater, New York: *Ten Million Ghosts* by Sidney Kingsley (actor).

1937   Maxine Elliott Theater, New York: *The Tragical History of Doctor Faustus* by Christopher Marlowe (co-producer, director, actor).
Playhouse Theater, New York: *The Second Hurricane* by Aaron Copland (director).

Venice Theater, New York: *The Cradle Will Rock* by Marc Blitzstein (co-producer and director).

Mercury (Comedy) Theater, New York: *Julius Caesar* by Shakespeare (co-producer, director, actor).

1938 Mercury (Comedy) Theater, New York: *The Shoemaker's Holiday* by Thomas Dekker (co-producer and director).

National Theater, New York: *Heartbreak House* by George Bernard Shaw (co-producer, director, actor).

Stony Creek summer theater: *Too Much Johnson* by William Gillette (co-producer and director).

Mercury (Comedy) Theater, New York: *Danton's Death* by Georg Buechner (co-producer and director).

1939 Theater Guild/Mercury Theater, on tour: *Five Kings* from Shakespeare (co-producer, director, actor).

RKO vaudeville circuit, Chicago: *The Green Goddess* by William Archer (actor).

1941 St. James Theater, New York: *Native Son* by Paul Green and Richard Wright (director).

1942 Various locations: *The Mercury Wonder Show* by Welles.

1946 Adelphi Theater, New York: *Around the World* by Cole Porter and Welles (director).

1947 Utah Centennial Festival, Salt Lake City: *Macbeth* by Shakespeare (director and actor).

1950 Théâtre Edouard VII, Paris: *Time Runs* by Christopher Marlowe (*Doctor Faustus*), Welles (*The Unthinking Lobster*), Duke Ellington, others.

1950–1951 On tour in Germany: *Time Runs* by Christopher Marlowe (*Doctor Faustus*), Oscar Wilde (*The Importance of Being Earnest*), Welles, Duke Ellington, Shakespeare, others.

1951 St. James Theater, London: *Othello* by Shakespeare (director and actor).

1953 Stoll Theater, London: *The Lady in the Ice* (ballet with decor and costumes by Welles).

1955 Duke of York's Theater, London: *Moby Dick* by Orson Welles, from the novel by Herman Melville (director and actor).

1956 City Center, New York: *King Lear* by Shakespeare (director and actor).

1960 Theater Royal, Belfast, and Gaiety Theater, Dublin: *Chimes at Midnight* adapted by Welles from Shakespeare (associate producer and actor).

Royal Court Theater, London: *Rhinoceros* by Eugène Ionesco (director).

Other appearances at the Gate and Abbey theaters of Dublin are wrongly attributed to Welles. Welles is the co-author of *Marching Song* with Roger Hill and author of *Bright Lucifer*, unpublished and unproduced plays for the stage.

APPENDIX 2

Discography

ORSON WELLES ON RECORDS

Like every other aspect of his career, Orson Welles' work in recording defies the conventional. With his first great success on Broadway in *Julius Caesar*, Welles was invited by Columbia Records (then newly acquired by CBS) to document ten scenes from his revival with members of his theatrical company.

The album sold well enough to convince Columbia to allow Welles to adapt four other Shakespeare plays to the medium of records, with narration to help bring the scenes to life. Even the packaging was unusual, for all four sets of 78's were issued in opulent, wine-colored cloth bindings, with a hardbound booklet pouched inside each front cover. In addition to the play's text, each booklet contained fascinating drawings and historical background on each of the plays. Although catalogues cite the actors only as Orson Welles and Members of the Mercury Theater, several prominent players, including Fay Bainter, appear on these sets. The albums were later reissued in conventional packaging.

From 1944 through 1946, Welles recorded a wide variety of historical, literary, and political speeches for Decca. These were gathered into several collections, although quite a few remain unissued till this day.

From the 1950s on, Welles has recorded only sporadically, although his voice has been heard on several soundtrack albums from his movies. However, he is generously represented on record shelves for albums that he neither recorded for commercial release, nor from which he gains any financial remuneration.

For more than two decades, a vast number of tiny, independent labels has made a practice of issuing early radio appearances by Welles, particularly from *The Shadow*, *Mercury Theater on the Air*, and the *Campbell Playhouse*. Though often unauthorized, these albums offer a fascinating insight into the intense, hypnotic quality that Welles brought to the medium of radio during the 1930s and 1940s.

Only sketchy information is available on many of Welles' albums. For example, Columbia has no personnel information on *12th Night*, and many of the original broadcast dates seem uncertain. While every attempt has been made to provide a complete listing of Welles' commercial recordings in the order of their release, it would be folly to assume that such a list could ever be compiled with certainty.

For their contribution in time, effort, and often actual recordings, this writer wishes to thank Tina McCarthy (Columbia), Joan Manners (MCA), George Garabedian (Mark 56), Bernard C. Solomon (Everest), David Hall, Don McCormick, Tom Owen, Ramon Latorre (Rodgers and Hammerstein Archives of Recorded Sound), and Martin Halperin.

Miles Kreuger
Los Angeles, California

May 29, 1985

1. *Julius Caesar*
   Ten scenes featuring original cast members of the Mercury Theater revival, Mercury Theater, November 11, 1937. Orson Welles (Brutus), Joseph Holland (Caesar), George Coulouris (Marcus Antonius), Martin Gabel (Cassius), Hiram Sherman (Casca), John Hoystradt (Decius Brutus), John A. Willard (Trebonius). Incidental music by Marc Blitzstein.
   Recorded March 1, 11, 21, 25, 1938.
   Five 12" 78's   Columbia M–325 (manual), AM–325 (slide automatic), MM–325 (drop automatic)

2. *12th Night*
   Recorded June 14, 16, 17, 1938.
   Ten 12" 78's   Columbia C–7 (manual), MM–790 (drop automatic)

3. *The Merchant of Venice*
   Orson Welles (Narrator, Shylock, Prince of Morocco), Joseph Holland (Antonio), Eric Mansfield (Salarino), Norman Lloyd (Salanio, Launcelot Gobbo), Edgar Barrier (Bassanio, Prince of Arragon), Guy Kingsley (Lorenzo), Sidney Smith (Gratiano), Brenda Forbes (Portia), Sarah Burton (Nerissa), Erskine Sanford (Old Gobbo, The Duke), Anna Stafford (Jessica), George Duthie (Tubal), Richard Wilson (Salerio, Stephano), William Alland (Balthazar), singing by Adelyn Colla-Negri, guitar by Julius Wexler. Incidental music by Eliot Carter.
   Recorded July 27, 28, 29, August 23, 25, September 7, 14, 1938.
   Twelve 12" 78's   Columbia C–6 (manual), MM–789 (drop automatic)

4. *Julius Caesar*
   Orson Welles (Narrator, Marcus Antonius, Caius Cassius), Edgar Barrier (Julius Caesar, Octavius Caesar), George Coulouris (Marcus Brutus), Walter Ash (M. AEmil. Lepidus), Jack Berry (Publius, Popilius Lena, Volumnius), Everett Sloane (Casca, Artemidorus), Guy Kingsley (Cinna the Conspirator, Lucius), J. Arthur Kennedy (Trebonius, Metellus Cimber, Titinius, Clitus), William Alland (Marullus, Young Cato), Anna Stafford (Calpurnia), Erskine Sanford (Ligarius, Pindarus), Richard Baer (Decius Brutus, Cinna the Poet), Margaret Curtis (Portia), Stephen Roberts (Lucilius).
   Recorded June 28, 29, 30, 1939.
   Eleven 12" 78's   Columbia C–10 (manual), MM–791 (drop automatic)

5. *The Tragedy of Macbeth*
   Orson Welles (Macbeth), William Alland (Narrator, Donalbain), Fay
   Bainter (Lady Macbeth), Robert Warrick (Banquo), Erskine Sanford
   (Duncan, The Porter, Siward, Seyton), George Coulouris (Macduff, Angus,
   The Doctor), Edith Barrett (Lady Macduff, Gentlewoman), Edgar Barrier
   (Malcolm), Sam Edwards (Fleance, Macduff's son), Richard Wilson (Len-
   nox), Richard Baer (Ross, Young Siward).
   Incidental music by Bernard Herrmann.
   Recorded April 17, 18, 19, 20, 23, 25, 26, 1940.
   Nine 12″ 78's   Columbia C–33 (manual), MM–792 (drop automatic)

6. *The Liberation of Paris* 1944
   Documentary with commentary by Welles and Emlen Etting, speeches
   by General Dwight Eisenhower and General Charles De Gaulle.
   Three 12″ 78's   Asch 50

7. *The Song of Songs* (*Which Is Solomon's*) 1945
   A fragmentary wedding idyll from the Bible
   Recorded August 23, 1944.
   One 12″ 78   Decca 29157, DU 90018, DU 10

8. *In the American Tradition* 1945
   Speeches by Thomas Jefferson, Abraham Lincoln, Woodrow Wilson,
   Franklin Delano Roosevelt, with descriptive notes by Howard Fast.
   Recorded August 31, September 9, 1944, August 20, 1945.
   Three 12″ 78's   Decca A–394
   Note: Lincoln's second inaugural address also issued on DL 9065.

9. *The Happy Prince* 1946
   An Oscar Wilde Fairy Tale with Bing Crosby, Lurene Tuttle. Music by
   Bernard Herrmann. Conducted by Victor Young.
   Recorded August 21, 1945.   Decca   1–10″ 78 CU–115, 2–10″ DA 420
                                        1–45   2–110, ED 2525
                                        12″ LP DL 6000, DL 4283, 15017

10. *No Man Is an Island* 1946
    A collection of immortal speeches on the independence of man, by Peri-
    cles, John Donne, Thomas Paine, Lazare Carnot, Patrick Henry, Daniel
    Webster, John Brown, Abraham Lincoln, Emile Zola.
    Recorded August 30, 31, September 8, 9, 11, 13, 1944, September 19,
    1945.   Decca   5–12″ 78 A–439
                    12″ LP DL 9060

11. *This Is the U.N.* 1950
    Speeches with Franchot Tone and members of the United Nations.
    Tribune KI–2807

12. *The War of the Worlds* c.1950
    Mercury (10–30–38)
    Audio Rarities 12″ LP LPA 2355

13. *Abraham Lincoln* 1951
eches and poems with Carl Sandburg, Walter Huston, Agnes Moorehead.
Decca DL 8515

14. *Julius Caesar* 1953
Reissue of #4.
Entree EL 52 2–LP's

15. *Compulsion* (20th Century-Fox, 1959) 1959
Soundtrack of court room scene.
20th Fox FEP 101 1–45

16. *A Lincoln Treasury* 1959
Poetry and prose with Carl Sandburg, Walter Huston.
Decca DL 9065

17. *The Finest Hours* (Columbia, 1964) 1964
Soundtrack with Patrick Wymark.
Mercury SRP 2–604 2–LP's

18. *Julius Caesar* 1967
Reissue of #4, 14.
Lexington LE 7570/7575 2–LP's

19. *A Man for All Seasons* (Columbia, 1966) 1967
Soundtrack.
RCA Victor VDM–116 2–LP's

20. *Song Of Myself* 1968
From Walt Whitman's *Leaves of Grass*.
Westminster WBBC–8004

21. *The Begetting of the President* 1969
Mediarts 41–2

22. *The War of the Worlds* 1969
Mercury (10–30–38)
Evolution 4001 2–LP's

23. *Song of Myself* 1972
Reissue of #20.
CMS 636

24. *The Begetting of the President* 1972
Reissue of #21.
United Artists UAS–5521

25. *The War of the Worlds* 1972
Mercury (10–30–38)
Longines Symphonette Society SY 5251

26. *Suspense: The Hitchhiker* (9–2–42)/*The Master of Ballantree* 1973
Pelican LP 107

27. *The Shadow: Volume Two* 1973
Murder on Approval/The Giant of Madras
Mark 56 608

28. *Huckleberry Finn:* Campbell Playhouse (3–17–40) 1974
    Mark 56 634
29. *The Shadow: Volume Three* 1974
    The Poison Death/The Society of the Living Dead
    Mark 56 657
30. *The Golden Days of Radio* 1975
    Introduction to *Huckleberry Finn* (see #28).
    Mark 56 713 2–LP's
31. *The Great Radio Horror Shows* 1975
    Mercury: *Dracula* (7–11–38)
    Murray Hill 933977 3–LP's
32. *Dracula* 1976
    Mercury (7–11–38)
    Mark 56 720
33. *The Shadow* 1976
    The White God/Murder on Approval
    Aboard the Steamship Amazon/The Creeper
    The Power of the Mind/The Hypnotized Audience
    Murray Hill 894599 3–LP's
34. Blitzstein: *The Airborne Symphony* 1976
    Columbia M34136
35. *Great American Documents* 1976
    With Henry Fonda, Helen Hayes, James Earl Jones.
    Columbia USA 1976
36. *The Shadow* 1977
    The Tomb of Terror/The Tenor with the Broken Voice
    Everest 5001
37. *The Shadow: Volume Two* 1978
    Death from the Deep/The Firebug
    Everest 5029
38. *Citizen Kane* (RKO Radio, 1941) 1978
    Soundtrack.
    Mark 56 810 2–LP's
39. *Orson Welles Interviews H.G. Wells* 1979
    KTSA, San Antonio, Texas (11–7–40)
    Radiola MR–1101
40. *Orson Welles and Helen Hayes at Their Best:* 1979
    Campbell: *Victoria Regina* (6–2–39)
    I Will Not Go Back (4–45)/*Deep to the World*
    Mark 56 829 2–LP's
41. *More of the Shadow* 1979
    Temple Bells/The League of Terror/Poison Death/Three Ghosts/Sabotage/Society of the Living Dead/The Phantom Voice/Bride of Death/Silent Avenger
    Murray Hill M 51212 3–LP's

42. *Obediently Yours Orson Welles* 1980
    14 August (8–14–45)/*Mercury Summer: King Lear* (9–13–46)
    Mark 56 833
43. *A King's Story* (Columbia, 1967) 1980
    Soundtrack.
    DRG SL 5185
44. *The Shadow: An Anthology* 1980
    Death under the Chapel/Blind Beggar Dies/Murder in Wax/Caverns of Death/The Message from the Hill
    Murray Hill S 55111 7–LP's
45. *Bette   Orson   Ingrid* 1982
    Mercury: *A Tale of Two Cities* (7–25–38) ; Opening scene
    Mark 56 848
46. *The Count of Monte Cristo* 1983
    Mercury (8–29–38)
    Radiola MR-1145
47. *I Know What It Is To Be Young* 1984
    GBNP Crescendo GNPS 1206
48. *The Liberation of Paris* 1985
    Reissue of #6.
    Folkways FH 5260

DATES UNKNOWN

49. *The Citadel*
    Campbell (1–21–40)
    Sandy Hook 15293
50. *Calling All Stars*
    Welles sings "You Made Me Love You."
    Star-Tone 203
51. *The Feminine Touch*
    Star-Tone 205
52. *The Shadow*
    The Message from the Hill/Murder in Wax
    Command Performance LP–3
53. *Imagination: The World of Inner Space*
    Scholastic 12008
54. *The Immortal Sherlock Holmes*
    Radiola 1036
55. *The Count of Monte Cristo*
    Campbell (10–1–39)
    E. O. H. 99603
56. *World War Two*
    History in Sound 1941
57. *The War of the Worlds*
    Mercury (10–30–38)
    Murray Hill S 44217 2–LP's

Bibliography

PUBLISHED WORKS BY ORSON WELLES

Everybody's Shakespeare: Three Plays Edited for Reading and Arranged for Staging by Roger Hill and Orson Welles. Woodstock, Illinois: Todd Press, 1934.

The Lives of Harry Lime by Orson Welles and others. London: News of the World, 1952.

Mercury Shakespeare: Edited for Reading and Arranged for Staging by Orson Welles and Roger Hill. New York: Harper & Row, 1939.

Miracle à Hollywood: à bon entendeur (The Unthinking Lobster). Translated from the English by Serge Greffet. Paris: La Table Ronde, 1952. Play.

Moby Dick Rehearsed. New York: Samuel French, 1965. Play.

Mr. Arkadin. New York: Crowell, 1956; London: W. H. Allen, 1956. Novel. Also, translated and adapted into French by Maurice Bessy. Paris: Gallimard, 1955.

Une grosse légume (A Big Vegetable). Translated from the English by Maurice Bessy. Paris: Gallimard, 1953. Novel.

BOOKS WITH AN INTRODUCTION
BY ORSON WELLES

Anonymous. *The Sleepy Lagoon Case*. Los Angeles: Mercury Press, 1942.

Davies, Marion. *The Times We Had*. New York: Bobbs-Merrill, 1975.

Elliott, Bruce. *Précis de prestidigitation*. Translated by Pierre Lanoé. Paris: Gallimard, 1952.

MacLiammoir, Micheal. *Put Money in Thy Purse: The Diary of the Film of "Othello."* London: Methuen, 1952.

O'Brady, Frédéric. *Extérieurs en Venise*. Paris: Gallimard, 1950.

Tynan, Kenneth. *He That Plays the King*. London and Toronto: Longmans, 1950.

BOOKS ABOUT ORSON WELLES

Bazin, André. *Orson Welles: A Critical View*. Translated by Jonathan Rosenbaum. Foreword by François Truffaut, preface by Jean Cocteau. New York: Harper & Row, 1978.

Bessy, Maurice. *Orson Welles.* Translated by Ciba Vaughan. New York: Crown, 1971.

Bogdanovich, Peter. *The Cinema of Orson Welles.* New York: Museum of Modern Art, 1961.

Cantril, Hadley. *The Invasion from Mars: A Study in the Psychology of Panic.* With the complete script of "The War of the Worlds." Princeton: Princeton University Press, 1940.

Cowie, Peter. *The Cinema of Orson Welles.* London: Zwemmer, 1965. Revised as *A Ribbon of Dreams: The Cinema of Orson Welles.* South Brunswick, New Jersey: Barnes, 1973.

Fowler, Roy. *Orson Welles.* London: Pendulum, 1946.

France, Richard. *The Theater of Orson Welles.* Lewisburg, Pennsylvania: Bucknell University Press, 1977.

Gottesman, Ronald (editor). *Focus on Orson Welles.* Englewood Cliffs, New Jersey: Prentice-Hall, 1976.

Higham, Charles. *The Films of Orson Welles.* Berkeley: University of California Press, 1970.

Kael, Pauline. *The Citizen Kane Book.* New York: Bantam Books, 1971. Reissued by Limelight Editions in 1984.

Koch, Howard. *The Panic Broadcast: Portrait of an Event.* With an introductory review by Arthur C. Clarke. Boston: Little, Brown, 1970.

Leaming, Barbara. *Orson Welles.* London: Weidenfeld & Nicolson, 1985.

McBride, Joseph. *Orson Welles.* New York: Viking, 1972.

McBride, Joseph. *Orson Welles, Actor and Director.* New York: Harvest Books, 1977.

Naremore, James. *The Magic World of Orson Welles.* New York: Oxford University Press, 1978.

Noble, Peter. *The Fabulous Orson Welles.* London: Hutchinson, 1956.

Valentinetti, Claudio M. *Orson Welles.* Florence: La Nuova Italia, 1980.

A number of related works are also useful. John Houseman's admirable trilogy, *Run-Through* (1972), *Front and Center* (1979), and *Final Dress* (1983), was published by Simon and Schuster. Robert L. Carringer's *The Making of Citizen Kane* (University of California Press) (1985) is excellent. Micheal MacLiammoir's interesting trilogy, *All for Hecuba* (1947), *Put Money in Thy Purse* (1952), and *Each Actor on His Ass* (1955), was published in London by Methuen. Hallie Flanagan's *Arena: The History of the Federal Theatre* (1940) was published by Little, Brown. Marvin L. Sieger's unpublished thesis *The Mercury Theater on Broadway, 1937–1939* (1950) is very useful; it is in the John Houseman collection at UCLA. A large collection of Welles's original radio scripts, and works by his ancestors Richard Wells and William Hill Wells, are available at the Library of Congress. Privately printed works on the Well(e)s genealogy, including Albert Wells's, can also be found at the Library of Congress. C. H. Browning's *Americans of Royal Descent,* published by the author at Pleasant Lake, Indiana, in 1909, contains an exhaustive account of Welles's ancestry back to the Plantagenets.

MANUSCRIPT COLLECTIONS

The Orson Welles collection of the Lilly Library of Indiana University at Bloomington consists of some 5,750 items. The Chicago Historical Society collection of Richard Wells (the first Wells settler) includes letters to his family in England and letters by his mother, father, and brothers. Other important sources of documents include the John Houseman collection at UCLA; the Paul Green Foundation of Chapel Hill, North Carolina; the Federal Theater Project collection of George Mason University; the Gate Theater Collection at Northwestern University; the Inter-American Affairs Committee files at the National Archives, Washington; the Orson Welles State Department file; the Library of Congress; the Museum of the City of New York; the Lincoln Center Library of the Performing Arts (of the New York Public Library); the Los Angeles Public Library; the Bibliothèque Nationale in Paris; and the British Film Institute.

INDEX